KU-353-578

The Uncommon Child

Genesis of Behavior

Series Editors: **MICHAEL LEWIS**
Institute for the Study of Exceptional Children
Educational Testing Service Princeton, New Jersey

and **LEONARD A. ROSENBLUM**
Downstate Medical Center
Brooklyn, New York

136.76

WITHDRAWN

W 5108985 8

The Uncommon Child

Edited by
MICHAEL LEWIS
Institute for the Study of Exceptional Children
Educational Testing Service
Princeton, New Jersey

and

LEONARD A. ROSENBLUM
Downstate Medical Center
Brooklyn, New York

PLENUM PRESS · NEW YORK AND LONDON

Library of Congress Cataloging in Publication Data

Main entry under title:

The Uncommon child.

   (Genesis of behavior; v. 3)
   Includes index.
   1. Exceptional children. I. Lewis, Michael, 1937 (Jan. 10)-   II. Rosenblum,
Leonard A. III. Series.
RJ499.U46   305.2'3   80-20601
ISBN 0-306-40499-0

305.23
LEW

©1981 Plenum Press, New York
A Division of Plenum Publishing Corporation
227 West 17th Street, New York, N.Y. 10011

All rights reserved

No part of this book may be reproduced, stored in a retrieval system, or transmitted,
in any form or by any means, electronic, mechanical, photocopying, microfilming,
recording, or otherwise, without written permission from the Publisher

Printed in the United States of America

60544

Contributors

GERSHON BERKSON, Department of Psychology, University of Illinois, Chicago Circle, Chicago, IL 60680

WILLIAM B. CAREY, Pediatric Practice, Media, PA 19063; Department of Pediatrics, University of Pennsylvania Medical School, Philadelphia, PA 19104

BERNICE T. EIDUSON, UCLA, Department of Psychiatry, School of Medicine, The Center for the Health Services, Los Angeles, CA 90024

JOEL GRINKER, Rockefeller University, 66th Street and York Avenue, New York, NY 10021

MARCI HANSON, San Francisco State University, Department of Special Education, 1600 Holloway Avenue, San Francisco, CA 94132

MICHAEL LEWIS, Institute for the Study of Exceptional Children, Educational Testing Service, Rosedale Road, Princeton, NJ 08541

HANUŠ PAPOUŠEK, Max Planck Institut für Psychiatrie, Kraepelinstrasse 10, D-8000 Munich, Federal Republic of Germany

EDWARD H. PLIMPTON, State University of New York, Downstate Medical Center, 450 Clarkson Avenue, Brooklyn, NY 11203

HENRY RICCIUTI, Department of Human Development and Family Studies, Cornell University, Ithaca, NY 14850

HALBERT B. ROBINSON, Child Development Research Group, Department of Psychology, University of Washington, Seattle, WA 98195

LEONARD ROSENBLUM, State University of New York, Downstate Medical Center, 450 Clarkson Avenue, Brooklyn, NY 11203

ARNOLD SAMEROFF, Illinois Institute for Developmental Disabilities, 1640 West Roosevelt Road, Chicago, IL 60608

STEPHANIE SCHAEFFER, 140 Cadman Plaza West, Brooklyn, NY 11201

RONALD SEIFER, Institute for the Study of Developmental Disabilities, University of Illinois, Chicago Circle, Chicago, IL 60680

URSULA THUNBERG, Child Adolescent Service, Bedford/Stuyvesant Community Mental Health Center, 1360 Fulton Street, Brooklyn, NY 11216

Preface

How are we to understand the complex forces that shape human behavior? A variety of diverse perspectives, drawing upon studies of human behavioral ontogeny, as well as humanity's evolutionary heritage, seem to provide the best likelihood of success. It is in the attempt to synthesize such potentially disparate approaches to human development into an integrated whole that we undertake this series on the Genesis of Behavior.

In many respects, the incredible burgeoning of research in child development over the last decade or two seems like a thousand lines of inquiry spreading outward in an incoherent starburst of effort. The need exists to provide, on an ongoing basis, an arena of discourse within which the threads of continuity between those diverse lines of research on human development can be woven into a fabric of meaning and understanding. Scientists, scholars, and those who attempt to translate their efforts into the practical realities of the care and guidance of infants and children are the audience that we seek to reach. Each requires the opportunity to see—to the degree that our knowledge in given areas permits—various aspects of development in a coherent, integrated fashion. It is hoped that this series, which will bring together research on infant biology, developing infant capacities, animal models, the impact of social, cultural, and familial forces on development, and the distorted products of such forces under certain circumstances, will serve these important social and scientific needs.

Each volume in this series will deal with a single topic that has broad significance for our understanding of human development. Into its focus on a specific area, each volume will bring both empirical and theoretical perspectives and analysis at the many levels of investigation necessary to a balanced appreciation of the complexity of the problem at hand. Thus, each volume will consider the confluence of the genetic,

vii

psychological, and neurophysiological factors that influence the individual infant and the dyadic, familial, and societal contexts within which development occurs. Moreover, each volume will bring together the vantage points provided by studies of human infants and pertinent aspects of animal behavior, with particular emphasis on nonhuman primates.

Just as this series will draw upon the special expertise and viewpoints of workers in many disciplines, it is our hope that the product of these labors will speak to the needs and interests of a diverse audience, including physiologists, ethologists, sociologists, psychologists, pediatricians, obstetricians, and clinicians and scientists in many related fields. As in years past, we hold to our original objectives in this series of volumes to provide both stimulation and guidance to all among us who are concerned with humans, their past, their present, and their future.

The present volume deviates from our traditional approach of presenting chapters which center around a particular theme in the social development of the young child. We have instead chosen to consider the more general topic of uncommonness and have collected a group of scholars who have spent some time focusing on this problem from their particular perspective. Each paper, operating from a particular view, deals with the notion of uncommonness by considering both the subjects' characteristics as well as the contextual cues provided by the social environment. Although we have chosen to title this volume *The Uncommon Child*, we recognize that by giving this label to the child it is implied that the uncommonness is inherent to it; that is, it is a characteristic of the child. The chapters recognize that uncommonness is the function of both child characteristics and environmental conditions. Uncommonness has been defined as (1) possession of certain subject characteristics, such as Down's syndrome; (2) a circumstance of rearing or the nature of the environment such as having a schizophrenic parent; and (3) the characteristics of these subjects as they interact and function within a particular social and physical milieu. Although some of the chapters have chosen to enter the dialogue from the subject-characteristics or the environmental-features point of view, each reflects the definition of uncommonness as the interaction of subject characteristics and environmental-demand qualities.

Following a chapter which describes the ecological perspective in viewing uncommonness in children, the first set of chapters, dealing with temperament differences, intellectual giftedness, Down's syndrome, obesity, and the sick and dying infant, focuses on specific characteristics of the child as they interact with the environment to the benefit or detriment of the child and family. The subsequent chapters view interactive process from an alternative perspective, namely, the impact of uncommon encounters on the infants' developing capacities. These latter chapters, then, deal with such topics as malnourishment and maltreatment of infants, and the effects of otherwise disordered socializing experiences as may occur with mentally ill or absent parents or peers, or within nontraditional family and social structures.

The chapters in this volume derive from papers presented and discussed at a conference on The Uncommon Child held under the auspices and with the support of the Educational Testing Service in Princeton, New Jersey. The participants in the conference were Gershon Berkson, Jeanne Brooks-Gunn, William B. Carey, Anke Ehrhardt, Bernice T. Eiduson, Nathan Fox, Joel A. Grinker, Marci J. Hanson, Michael Lewis, Hanuš Papoušek, Edward H. Plimpton, Henry N. Ricciutti, Halbert B. Robinson, Leonard A. Rosenblum, Stephanie Schaeffer, Arnold J. Sameroff, and Ursula Thunberg.

MICHAEL LEWIS
LEONARD A. ROSENBLUM

Contents

The Uncommon as the Common
A Relative View

MICHAEL LEWIS AND LEONARD A. ROSENBLUM

WHAT DO WE MEAN BY UNCOMMON?

Webster's Dictionary defines "uncommon" as "not ordinarily encountered." This definition suggests that uncommonness is neither positive nor negative but does imply that uncommonness is to be judged against some type of normative value. The feature of such a definition is that it is relative rather than absolute. In one culture or setting, a particular behavior may be common, whereas it may be uncommon in another. Nonstandard English, for example, may be common in a poor inner-city community but uncommon in the suburbs. While some might hold to an absolute standard, say, for example, in mental health, against which deviation in any culture or setting could be viewed as uncommon, we prefer the more relative view as implied in the definition as given. We shall hold uncommon to mean: (1) that there exists a norm, (2) that this norm is relative, and (3) that all deviance is to be viewed in terms of that relative norm.

MICHAEL LEWIS • Institute for the Study of Exceptional Children, Educationl Testing Service, Rosedale Road, Princeton, New Jersey 08541   LEONARD A. ROSENBLUM • State University of New York, Downstate Medical Center, 450 Clarkson Avenue, Brooklyn, New York 11203.

SOURCES OF UNCOMMONNESS

In discussing the sources of uncommonness, we need first to focus on the various potential forces, which because of their distinction, may affect developmental outcome. With some exceptions, it can be argued that the single-culprit-variable approach to deviation is incorrect. That is, uncommon development cannot be caused solely by any one of the potential sources of distinction.

The two primary potential sources of uncommonness, like the sources of development in genral, can be identified to include both the biological and social environmental factors. In the case of chiefly biological potential sources of uncommonness, the uncommonness is located in the organism. The deviation we study pertains most to the unusualness of the child itself. These potential sources are highlighted in the chapters on Down's, obese, sick and dying, temperamentally difficult, and, perhaps, the gifted child. The second potential source of deviance in the child pertains to the external environment or social setting in which each child develops. We have identified some of these sources in the chapters on malnourished, maltreated, neglected, and unusual family styles as well as schizophrenic environments as potential sources of uncommonness. As most of the chapters, especially Chapter 2 on the ecology of normal and pathological variability, make clear, neither the biological nor environmental forces working alone can be used to predict uncommonness as an end product. Rather, the interplay of various sources is necessary to produce any particular developmental effect, either common or deviant.

THE DEVELOPMENT OF UNCOMMONNESS

Having defined the primary potential sources of uncommonness, we need to focus attention on how the development of distinction may occur. Explicit in the biological notion of uncommonness, either in terms of some positive outcome such as superior IQ performance or in terms of a negative outcome like Down's syndrome, is the view that the deviant characteristics of the individual are an intrinsic property of the individual. This conception likens the uncommonness to a trait or attribute of the individual which acts on the developmental process to effect distinction. Certainly such explanations appear reasonable in terms of some forms of uncommonness. The Down's child is a good example of such a view. It would be difficult to argue that the behavior or even physical appearance of these children is not solely a function of their particular chromosomal makeup. Nevertheless, even here the simple notion of a trait explanation for the developmental end product appears somewhat less than adequate. One developmental outcome associated with Down's syndrome is fairly profound retardation as measured by standard IQ tests. As has been repeatedly pointed out, the IQ score of Down's children is generally below 50. Thus, poor mental scores are associated with a potential biological source of deviation. Even with such a biological source, this simple model of development fails. Removing Down's children from institutions and returning them to family care in their own homes has substantially increased their IQ scores. Moreover, educational intervention programs (see Hanson, this volume) have had similar success. If the uncommonness, i.e., mental retardation, of the Down's child is caused by the biological source alone, then the environmental intervention would have little effect. That mental retardation itself can be affected by social intervention suggests that even biologically based uncommonness has to interact with an environmental setting in some measure and can have a positive effect on development when altered in some productive fashion. For those cases of deviation which have even less of a known biological source this may be even more the case.

Uncommonness also can be produced by distinctive environmental and social settings. Such individuals are made less common not because of a particular attribute associated with themselves but because of the nature of the setting in which they find themselves. The children of parents who are schizophernic may be uncommon because the environment in which they develop is deviant from the norm. The same can be said for children being raised in unusual or distinctive family structures. However, as we know from other studies, as well as the chapters in this volume, children raised in uncommon environments do not necessarily have unusual developmental outcomes.

It should come as no surprise that the developmental process of uncommonness should mirror that of norml development in that both child and environment characteristics interact in some complex fashion to determine developmental outcomes.

THE BIOLOGICAL AND SOCIAL SIGNIFICANCE OF DIVERSITY

As we come to understand the degree to which "uncommonness" must be defined in terms of the environmental context in which the child or other organism develops, we gain an additional perspective regarding the importance of individual diversity. In the broadest sense, it may be considered true that the one essential outcome of the evolutionary emergence of sexual as opposed to asexual reproduction was to ensure a range of genotypic and phenotypic diversity in each generation. If it were the case that the essential ingredients of the environment were unchanging over long periods of time, such general diversity would be energetically wasteful to say the least. In a sense, in an unchanging world, only alterations in a single direction, i.e., toward increasing success in the current environment would be favored. In the short term that is of course the case. Yet, divergence in form, structure, and function from that most characteristic of the population at a given time continues to emerge; most often in a state of nature such divergent forms contribute little if anything to the genetic pool of subsequent generations. Nonetheless, the strategy of evolution, i.e., the continuity of forms over broad expanses of time, requires exactly this repetitive divergence. Why is this so? Stated quite simply, the uncommon individuals of a group are the "insurance" against future environmental change or the movement of existing populations into previously unneeded and unused existing environments. Consider, for example, children who appear within a stable familial and societal context as uncommonly precocious in their development of independent function; such children in this setting may appear unusually emotionally detached from others and lack the commitment to social integration generally deemed "appropriate" in such "normal" settings. As such, these children, whose lack of normal attachments may reflect the interplay of constitutional and rearing effects, may function outside the common ground of interaction within their society. But, as recent human history unfortunately attests, when families, and indeed whole societal units are disrupted and displaced, as in wartime, when virtually all familial and societal support systems may be destroyed, which children can best survive these losses? In the aftermath of such disruption who will be common and who uncommon? Indeed, as one examines the roster of designated uncommonnes for modern Western societies, it is not difficult to imagine all but the most severely handicapped as representing potentially adaptive forms under other, less commonplace circumstances.

But this brings us to a related and most significant issue. It is clear that many societies expend considerable effort toward aiding many types of uncommon individuals without any overt expectation of their value for future success of the species under unforeseen circumstances. Why then do we maintain individuals that do in fact deviate significantly from group norms? In terms of modern sociobiological theory, organisms, whether parents or more distantly related members of the group, should only invest themselves in the sustenance of others to the degree that such investment enhances the likelihood that genetic material held in common with the other will continue to survive into the future. From this biological perspective the group should act altruistically in direct proportion to the degree of shared genetic inheritance with the other, that is, in keeping with their degree of genetic kinship and with the likelihood of their reproductive potential in the future. But is this an adequate description of the range of human response to uncommon children or adults? Is total reproductive potential (i.e., inclusive fitness) the only basis upon which such care and acceptance depends? We would suggest that, in humans, the presence of complex social–cognitive capacities allows for the development of forms of altruism that transcend genetic relatedness. When adequate resources are available, modern man creates economic structures and societal mores directed toward sustenance of a variety of (albeit not all) forms of biologically and biosocially unusual group members. The handicapped infant, the dysfunctional adult, the aged and otherwise infirm, not because they directly share our genotypic constituents nor because of their potential reproductive success, but rather because they are members of our own political, religious, or ideological group, all come to evoke our care and concern. For those uncommon individuals who as children or adults manifest assimilable forms of deviance, rejection or exclusion from the genetic pool does not occur. We suggest that the prosocial quality of behavior embodied in the expression of "acceptance" and care of the unusual, supports the sense of group cohesion and belonging among those that express it and aids thereby in counterbalancing the disruptive forces potentially engendered by the competitive and aggressive patterns which can emerge when societies are under stress. Such a social perspective of the indirect positive effects of inclusion of deviance is not incompatible with, but rather supplements the biological imperatives which place a value on the maintenance of uncommon characteristics as a hedge against the unknowable and possibly altered circumstances of the future.

ASSESSING THE UNCOMMON

Given the multidimensional relativity of uncommonness as discussed above, how then shall the psychological study of the uncommon child proceed? The most commonly used normothetic approaches seem, in this context, self-contradictory. We would join those who contend that we make a basic error in attempting to understand the development of all individuals in terms of their distribution around some central tendency. Uncommonness in this traditional scheme is seen as deviance from a normal set of characteristics toward which all members of the designated population are drawn. It would be more appropriate to organize our groupings among the cluster of attributes within smaller units viewed as separate populations, subject to more immediately similar forces and relatively distant from those that may more generally characterize the larger population. In practical terms, then, we must forego the use of means and standard deviations as our organizing principles and consider instead, for example, various forms of cluster and multivariate analyses as the basis for description and classification.

This approach views those within the less common clusters as different from rather than as deviant from the larger group. As one proceeds to refine the boundaries of each cluster, one approaches the idiographic method in which each individual is distinguished from any other and not viewed as a "variation on a theme." These latter steps of increasing appreciation of individual diversity rather than deviance from a norm are crucial lest we simply spread the normothetic cloak around our initially disparate, i.e., uncommon, clusters. Shall we attempt, in other words, to describe and study the common aspect of the uncommon, the norms of those that deviate from another norm? Will we ultimatly attempt to define the uncommon common? In our view, diversity must become our ally in the study of development. Embodied in the path of development of the uncommon child are all the forces at work in all children. What we seek are methods which have as their goal not the central tendencies of a number of uncommon children designated as members of a labeled group, but rather the ways in which the separate forces of biological, physical, and social environmental factors interact in shaping the individual child. In each uncommon child is the expression of factors shared to varying degrees by most children but suffused with the effects of one or more distinctive features to create a unique constellation. Generalities must be sought in terms of the ways in which diverse beginnings can result in common endings and the processes through which commonalities of intial constellations result in broad divergence during development.

THE REPRESENTATION OF UNCOMMONNESS

We have been discussing the potential sources of uncommonness in terms of the influence of biological and environmental factors. In terms of the child's own psychological processes, its internal sense of uncommonness also derives from several sources. Certainly, as indicated above, the social world, depending upon environmetal circumstances, may label the child of any cluster of characteristics as uncommon; whether the terms used imply a positive valence (e.g., "gifted" or "precocious") or a negative one (e.g., "different," "handicapped," or "strange") the communication of the way in which the child is perceived within its own social nexus will affect the infant's developing sense of self. At the same time, there are direct effects of the developing child's interaction with its environment and its perceived comparisons of the relative performance of others; thus, even in the absence of any attribution by others of uncommonness, such a self-percept may emerge in the child. Not surprisingly, we may except the social-attributive and self-evaluative factors to interact in shaping the child's perception of this fundamental facet of self—the feelings of either identification with and belonging to or difference and apartness from those that surround us. This point of view suggests, however, that the internal sense of uncommonness may not always reflect a veridical perception of the child's world and its place within it, either on its own part or on the part of others that play a role in influencing its developing sense of self. Moreover, the same child placed in different environments, which require different characteristics for achievement or failure, in which salient features may be mastered with ease or difficulty, can emerge with different feelings of uncommonness. Thus, for example, the spastic child that performs poorly when confronted with a world of staircases may function without handicap in a world of elevators and ramps.

The general principle represented in this example reverts us back to our initial definition of uncommonness. Not only does the physical and social environment exert forces which may shape uncommon-ness, the same domains provide the very basis upon which uncom-monness may be defined. Change the norms and you redefine uncom-monness; change the environment and that which was previously uncommon now fits the norm.

2

Traits, Environments, and Adaptation

GERSHON BERKSON

Individuals with chronic handicapping defects exist in societies of people and of animals. Estimates of the prevalence of handicapping conditions among humans vary broadly around 10%. Prevalence rates among animals have not been estimated but are significant at least in some populations. Conventional wisdom, derived from the theory of evolution, holds that defects are selected against. However, under certain circumstances, selection against defects is minimal and individuals with defects function normally in society. This is most true in human societies but also occurs in animal populations (Berkson, 1977).

Of course, survival of disabled individuals is more probable when disease and predation are minimal and when food and other resources are at least adequate for maintenance of the population. However, perhaps more important for our considerations here, disabled individuals in certain animal species are more likely to survive than those in others because their group cares for them. In general, animal species that live in stable groups, having few infants in the litter, and with infants going through an extended growth period, tend to provide compensatory care for defects, thus promoting adaptation of the animal with the defect. Societies of higher primates have these characteristics and do tend to provide compensatory care for disabled individuals in

GERSHON BERKSON • Department of Psychology, University of Illinois, Chicago Circle, Chicago, Illinois 60680.
The studies reported here were supported in part by a grant from the National Institute of Child Health and Human Development (HD-10321). I am indebted to Daniel Romer for his contributions to the research.

their group (Berkson, 1977). Human societies have, of course, developed elaborate institutions for preventing defects, and when that is not possible, for ameliorating them. In short, factors influencing survival of disabled individuals include not only the defect and its relationship to the physical environment, but also are defined by their social ecology.

ECOLOGY

The basic assumption of any ecological analysis is that adaptation is a joint function of individual charcteristics and of the environment. Working out such an analysis also assumes that adaptation, traits of individuals, and environments can be defined independent of one another. As will be shown below, this process is not always unambiguous, but the logic of the approach is straightforward and has been used fruitfully for a century. Ecology assumes that adaptation can be measured in the same way across environments and traits. Mortality, fertility, academic success, and income level have all been used as measures of adaptation. It is also assumed that an individual possesses certain traits across envrionments. For instance, an animal is the same size no matter what environment it is in. Or intelligence and social competence are general attributes which characterize a person in any environment. A final assumption is that it is possible to define the characteristics of environments independent of the traits of the individual whose adaptation is being measured. There are more fruiting trees in one forest than another; institutions in rural areas are different from urban community facilities.

Once these components of the equation have been defined, it is a relatively simple matter to show that adaptation is not completely predictable from knowledge of an individual's traits. This can be seen clearly in some studies of the consequences of a visual defect in macaque monkeys. In these studies (Berkson, 1977) the trait studied was blindness. Ordinarily, such a defect present from birth would be expected to be devastating because the interactions of macaque monkeys with their physical and social environments is mediated to a large extent by vision. Three environments were used: a natural habitat which was arid and which contained potential predators of infant monkeys; an island where there were no predators and where food and water were provided; and a large laboratory cage where food and water were easily available and where blind monkeys would have no problem staying with their group. The measures of adaptation used in the studies were mortality and degree of participation in normal group interactions.

In the natural habitat, partially-sighted animals disappeared from their group at seven months of age, even though the group provided them with special care and protection. On the island where there were no predators and food was easily available, monkeys with a similar defect survived and remained with their groups until they were three years old, when the study was terminated. In this relatively nonselecting environment, they were also given more care than a normal animal when they were infants, but became socially isolated within their groups as they approached maturity. In the laboratory environment, where there was no dificulty keeping up with the group and obtaining food and water, partially-sighted and even totally blind animals survived well into adulthood and were essentially normal members of their groups.

These studies demonstrate nicely that a defect has different consequences for adaptation depending on the environment. Blindness, a severe defect for monkeys, is a trait consistent across environments, but whether it affects adaptation (i.e., whether it is handicapping) depends on the environment. The studies also demonstrate that the degree to which a defect is seen as handicapping also depends on the measure of adaptation used. Mortality and social affiliation had different functions in the defect–environment interaction.

A further example, from studies of the prevalence of human mental retardation, also makes these same points. Gruenberg (1964) has summarized several studies of the prevalence of mental retardation. Figure 1 is taken from his review-article. The graph shows that prevalence of mental retardation (the measure of adaptation) is a function at least of age and of the particular prevalence survey. This curve of changing prevalence is not at all what one expects from a psychometric (trait) concept of mental deficiency. That is, if one believes that the prevalence of mental retardation is predictable only on the basis of the trait of measured intelligence (i.e., two standard deviations below the mean), then one would expect prevalence level to be invariant across age and across study.

The difference between the various surveys has generally been interpreted as the result of their using different criteria for counting a person as mentally retarded. The more interesting change in prevalence is the age curve. Note that the pattern of change across age is about the same for all of the surveys. Prevalance increases from a very low level in infancy to its peak at twelve to fifteen years of age and then declines thereafter. The most generally accepted explanation for this variation is that the high school environment requires more of the intellectual skills of children. Those who have dificulty learning will obviously have more troubles when more complex learning is required. If these difficulties are very great the teacher refers the child for

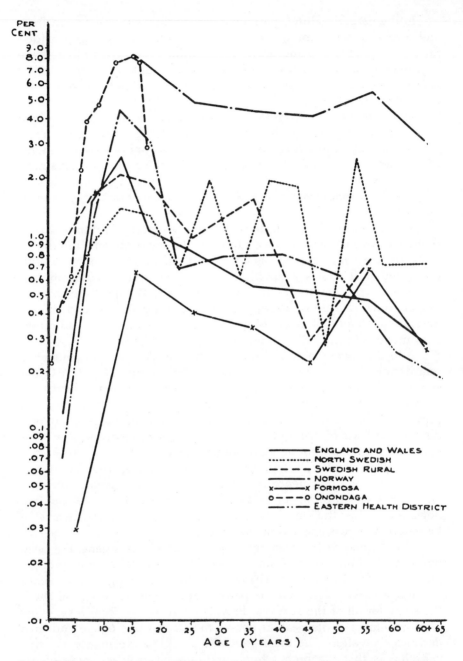

FIG. 1. Prevalence of mental retardation as a function of age and prevalence survey. This graph was taken from an article by Gruenberg (1964). Reprinted from *Mental Retardation*, H.A. Stevens and R. Heber (Eds.), by permission of The University of Chicago Press.

psychological testing. Then, if the child is referred for special-education services, he is counted as mentally retarded. However, when he graduates from school, he may get a job and can live independently without need of social supports. If that happens, he is no longer regarded as being mentally retarded.

The major point is that defects such as blindness or low intelligence do not themselves predict adaptation. It is necessary also to specify what criterion of adaptation one wishes to use and, at least as important, the environment one is predicting to. Adaptation is a function not only of the individual's traits (defects) but of the definitions of adaptation and of the environment.

Some Complexities in Defining Adaptation, Traits, and Environments

Although the variability of adaptation of individuals with disabilities is well established, there are sometimes difficulties in going further and describing this variability. These difficulties come partly from the complexity of defining the three components of the equation predicting adaptation.

Adaptation

The ultimate criterion of adaptation in evolutionary theory is fertility. Animals having a greater number of offspring who are themselves fertile are regarded as having adapted successfully to the environments in which they live. The business of ecology is to define the traits of individuals and the characteristics of environments which predict fertility. In the ideal case, one would follow a number of individuals in several unchanging habitats and determine which individuals reproduce successfully and what are the trait–environment interactions which determine their success. In practice this is not done very often. Most frequently, the investigator samples the members of a particular species in a number of habitats at a single time and correlates frequency of some of their traits with certain characteristics of the environment. The assumption in doing this is that frequency of a trait is a good indirect measure of fertility and that the overall method is a good model of the actual evolutionary process. However, note that studying distributions of a trait at a single time is not actually the same as looking at differential fertility over time.

Sometimes, in the study of animal behavior, the method becomes more extended; the trait itself becomes the only measure of adaptive success and the independent criterion of adaptation disappears. Take for example the study of dominance. In general, it has been assumed that the dominant animals in a group tend to be more fertile than the others. To the extent that this were perfectly true, one might use dominance as an indirect measure of fertility, i.e., dominant animals would be regarded as better adapted to their environments. The difficulties with making this assumption are many. Apparently dominance is not a well-defined trait characteristic of an animal over all situations and times. Instead, it is defined by a number of measures which do not correlate very well with one another. Dominance status of an animal can also change markedly across times and situations. Perhaps, most basic, there is even a question now whether dominance is usually correlated with frequency or time of breeding, let alone fertility (Bernstein, 1976).

A somewhat similar situation has occurred in the study of intelligence in general and mental retardation in particular. Man's intellectual traits no doubt account for his evolutionary success in competition with other closely related animals. However, it is also clear now that intelligence does not predict differential fertility within the species very well. When the extremes of intelligence are excluded, fertitlity is uncorrelated with general intelligence (Higgins, Reed, & Reed, 1962).

There are two important consequences of the tendency to shift from direct to indirect measures of adaptation. In the context of evolutionary theory, the substitution of trait for fertility criteria can make the logic of the basic ecology equation tautological. This is not necessarily a bad thing since relating environments to traits can be a descriptive heuristic. On the other hand, if the trait is regarded as a major *determinant* of fertility rather than merely as a measure of it, then such a causal relationship should be demonstrated before the trait is substituted. Some recent theorists in animal behavior (Dawkins, 1976; Trivers, 1974; Wilson, 1975) have failed to do this.

For our purposes, the shift from measures of fertility to behavioral measures of adaptation has reflected an even more important issue. The lack of any important relationship between intellectual level and fertility has moved studies of the adaptation of mentally retarded people away from where they were in an earlier period, when it was feared that higher fertility among people with genetically determined mental retardation would reduce the general quality of human populations (Goddard, 1914/1972). Instead, the focus has shifted to an effort to maximize participation of mentally retarded people in society and (perhaps related) to minimize the cost of disabilities to society. Thus, while studies of adaptation of the mentally retarded continue to be guided by the same general logic as any study of adaptation, the ultimate criterion of adaptation in such studies is not fertility, but degree of participation in society.

Traits

Defining adaptation is thus complex, but how it is done is critical for any ecological analysis. The same is true of the definition of individual traits. Influenced strongly by early concepts of variability of physical and behavioral characteristics, psychologists have generally defined traits as varying continuously and being normally distributed. This approach has worked reasonably well for normal variation, but the situation becomes more complex when abnormalities become part of the picture.

Variability is a central concept in evolutionary theory. Normal genetic variation is the source of evolution. Pathological mutations are generally deleterious. However, sometimes a pathological trait (e.g., sickle cell anemia) can be adaptive and is maintained in the population. In some environments, pathological conditions resulting from mutations or from some environmental insult become frequent. To the extent that pathological features are present in a population, the statistical distributions of traits depart from the normal distribution we ordinarily use to describe behavioral traits.

Perhaps the best-known example is the excess of population at the lower end of the IQ distribution (Dingman & Tarjan, 1960). The people represented in the bump at the lower end of the IQ curve are usually the victims of some abnormal condition in the prenatal or perinatal period. As a result, they are usually not only retarded in their mental development, but their mental retardation is associated with a large number of sensory and motor disorders and even bizarre behaviors not characteristic of normal development. Because of the complexity of this picture, there has been some question whether traditional orientations toward normal child development or simple concepts of variability of general intelligence can adequately deal with some of the pathological characteristics of the mentally retarded population (Berkson, 1966). Certainly, simple descriptions of traits will provide only limited precision in the ecology of defects.

Environments

The situation is also complex when one attempts to describe environments. A social ecology of defects requires some categorization of social environments. It would be nice if there were simple dimensions which one could use to describe environments. Social ecologists have used a number of approaches with some success. Organizational structures (Schoggen, 1978), social norms (Richardson, 1975), and estimates of the psychological characteristics of environments (Moos, 1974) have all been used. But these approaches are mainly descriptive and do not adequately deal with the complexities of trait–environment interactions. Environments vary almost infinitely in ways in which they can be defined. A successful assessment of the contribution of the environment to adaptation requires some kind of theory of the relationship between environmental characteristics and adaptation. To the extent that such a theory is explicit, it is possible to hope for an efficient and successful test of its validity. Sometimes environments and adaptation are defined globally, and the meaning of adaptation is not made clear. In such a case, only very general predictions can be expected.

TRAIT VERSUS ENVIRONMENT APPROACHES IN TREATMENT PHILOSOPHY

One way of assessing the contributions of both traits and environments is to attempt to vary traits or environments in order to maximize adaptation. Psychologists have traditionally been concerned with the description of the disabled individual, first in order to predict his adaptation, and then to educate him in order to make his adaptation more like that of nondisabled people. By describing characteristics of mentally retarded people in standard situations (IQ tests, tests of social competence), and by analyzing how they became the way they are, psychologists and educators have been able to describe adaptation with some degree of accuracy at least in the short run. They have also modified early rearing conditions and trained and educated disabled people in order to alter their traits (Simeonsson, 1978). These early-intervention and training programs have been oriented toward making the adaptation of people with defects more like that of people without defects.

To say the least, these efforts have met with only limited success. Behavior modification, early intervention, special education, and vocational rehabilitation tend to be most successful when the defect is minor, transitory, or limited. With chronic generalized disorders such as moderate or severe mental deficiency, childhood psychosis, severe auditory disorders, or generalized cerebral palsy, psychologists and educators have had less success in increasing adaptation through training.

Another way of increasing adaptation is to alter the environment.

Adaptation clearly has been increased suddenly and dramatically by altering the enviroments in which people with disabilities live. One of the obvious examples with which all of us are familiar is the architectural changes which have allowed physically handicapped people to move more freely in public places. Another instance is presentation of television news programs which communicate to hearing-handicapped people through signs. An even more dramatic example has been the shift of mentally ill and mentally retarded people from institutions in rural areas to a variety of environments closer to their home communities.

The development of these programs has involved a radical reorientation in society's conception of the ecology of defects. Rather than depending only on training to adapt people with defects to a narrow range of environments, there has been an effort to broaden the range of environments in which people with defects can live reasonably normal lives. Some psychologists and educators, who have been caught in a static conception of society, have assumed that the *only* way to increase a person's adaptation is to change him so that he can be part of normal society. The alternative view, that society is pluralistic, changeable, and adaptable to the people in it, has not motivated them as strongly. The development of a more open concept of society has come instead from the civil rights movement, from parents of the handicapped, and from handicapped people themselves.

MENTALLY DISABLED ADULTS IN COMMUNITY SETTINGS

The deinstitutionalization movement has been the most dramatic manifestation of a reorganization of society to foster integration of mentally disabled people into it. Although the ideal of this movement has been independent living of all mentally disabled people, in fact a range of environments has been created which constitutes a compromise between completely normal living and isolated institutions. These intermediate environments include large sheltered-care residential facilities, small-group homes, foster-care living arrangements, and sheltered work-environments. The description of how these various social forms function is very much in its infancy.

A simple comparison of various types of environments is probably going to have limited value. Differences within type of facility are often as great as differences between types. Moreover, there is evidence (Zigler & Balla, 1977) that traits and history of the individual interact with the environment to produce the specific behaviors seen.

Our research with mentally retarded and mentally ill adults has assumed that a complex approach is necessary. We have recognized that most places where moderately and severely disabled people live are environments where they are supervised and where they live and work together. Instead of comparing general types of facilities, we have been more concerned with analyzing how adaptation in these environments can best be predicted and improved. We have been studying the correlates of social behavior of people who work in large sheltered workshops.

We began with the general notion that there are two major characteristics that many people regard as measures of adaptation. The first of these is participation in productive work activity which is rewarded in some way; the second is participation in freely chosen informal groups of two or more people. This second criterion of adaptation, informal social relationships, has been the main focus of our research. We have been interested in discovering those character-istics of individuals and environments which predict affiliations. Our main criterion of adaptation is frequency of association in informal groups. We measure this in a number of ways which will be made clear below.

We have worked with a "not-for-profit" service agency which manages four large sheltered workshops for mentally ill and mentally retarded adults. We chose to study these workshops because they provide services that are typical: neither exemplary nor abominable. The many problems that this agency faces are typical of those of many community facilities. These problems include high staff turnover rates, inconsistent management practices, lack of consistent contract work, morale problems, strikes, etc. On the other hand, the agency provides a place for the clients to spend their days in productive activity; the clients receive a certain amount of training; and they experience acceptance by others. Many of the people we have studied also reside in a single sheltered-care home, and we have studied people there also. The data I will talk about include information on 315 separate individuals. In the sample there are more males than females, more younger adults than older people, and more mentally retarded than mentally ill people. The racial distribution is typical of the areas in which the workshops are located (Table 1).

The data I will describe come from four sources: client records, interviews with staff, interviews with clients, and direct observations. In all cases, we study and report data only on clients who have agreed to participate in the study. Data-collection and analysis procedures carefully maintain confidentiality of information on individuals. From client records, we obtain historical and demographic information and information related to diagnosis. When records were inconsistent, we

TABLE 1.   CHARACTERISTICS OF SUBJECTS IN THE SAMPLE ($N = 315$)

Characteristic		Frequency	Characteristic		Frequency
Sex	M	202	Race	White	250
	F	113		Black	39
				Latin	9
Age	18–20	6		Oriental	2
	21–45	174		Missing	15
	46–60	99			
	61–99	30	Residence	Supervised	223
	Missing	6		Independent	40
				With family	52
IQ	0–30	27			
	31–50	66	Years in	Less than 1	29
	51–75	128	institution	1–5	25
	76–90	46		5–10	21
	91–110	22		10–20	30
	Over 110	8		20–30	50
	Missing	18		30–40	24
				Over 40	8
Diagnosis	MR	212		Numerous stays	15
	MR–MI	43		None	113
	MI	47			
	Other	11			
	Missing	2			

determined the accuracy of the statements through consultation with staff. All IQ scores were corroborated with a Peabody Picture Vocabulary Test administered by an experienced tester.

Interviews with staff were conducted by questionnaire. The first of these questionnaires included items intended to determine who the staff thought the clients' friends were. The second questionnaire concerned the rated physical attractiveness of each client. Each questionnaire was administered to at least two staff members. Client interviews were conducted privately and also included an assessment of who their friends were. In addition, a "social self-concept" scale was administered to each client. This scale determined the kinds of activities that clients prefer to engage in and provided an index of sociability from the clients' perspective.

The fourth source of information was a series of about 100 behavioral observations done on each client in the workshop. An additional 100 observations were done on 116 clients in the sheltered-care residence where they lived. These observations were made only when the clients were free to associate with whom they wished. That is, they were not observed in situations to which they had been assigned by staff (at work stations or in classes). In the workshops they were observed at break periods or lunch. In the residence their behavior was recorded in many free situations in and around the home, including a recreation room, halls, bedrooms (when doors were open), the dining room, and television rooms, as well as in stores and on the street near the facility.

The basic procedure for each observation was a five-second look at the client followed by a recording of the observation. Observations were carried out on different clients in a predetermined random order and individual observations on the same client were separated by at least five minutes to minimize redundancy. Following each observation the behavior in which the individual was engaged was recorded (see Table 2). If the behavior was social, the people with whom he was interacting were also noted, and whether the subject initiated or received the behavior was recorded. If the behavior was nonsocial, a judgment was made whether he was solitary or in a group of people. If he was in a group, the identity of its members was recorded. Finally, the identity and distance of the person closest to the subject at the time of the observation were recorded.

The main measure of social behavior which will be discussed here is "percent affiliation," the percent of time a person was seen interacting with others. Some of the data also include components of percent affiliation: number of groups seen in and intensity of affiliation, i.e., the proportion of time seen with others per other individual. The results which will be presented show that the social behavior of mentally disabled adults is predictable from some individual traits, but that exact predictions require a consideration of environmental variables.

Table 3 portrays scores of various traits and of some social behaviors in different settings. As may be seen in the table, the differences between the facilities are multidimensional. Even within one classification (i.e., sheltered workshops), differences between facilities cannot be described simply. This complexity is apparent not only when one looks at average scores for various measures, but also when predictors of adaptation in the different settings are considered. Table 4 portrays the overall predictions of our main measure, percent affiliation. It is clear that the degree to which any trait variable predicts social behavior varies with the environment.

With many trait variables confounded with one another, it seems difficult at first to go beyond a simple statement that there are differences between facilities. That is, showing that different places typically have different levels of social behavior (e.g., Butler & Bjaanes, 1978) only begins the process of determining which variables predict

TABLE 2. BEHAVIOR CATEGORY DEFINITIONS

COMFORT	(CO)	Show genuine effort to ease the sadness, disappointment, failure of another person
HELP	(HE)	Aid another to accomplish a given task or to more effectively deal with a given situation, verbal included
APPEASEMENT	(FR)	Use friendly restraint on person acting violently
AFFECTION	(AF)	Any flirtatious or courting behaviors including affectionate touching such as stroking, pat on back—examples: asking someone for a date; holding hands and talking, smiling and dancing closely with another
SEXUAL ACTIVITY	(SX)	Specific sexually-related activities, alone or with others, involving direct physical contact in an intimate manner
SUPERVISION	(SU)	Assume a leader–instructor role related to routine or household tasks, including evaluation and planning of such activities
OFFERING	(OF)	Altruistic behaviors related to distributing resources in a generous or equitable manner
VOCALIZATION	(VO)	$\underline{S}$ utters sound not recognizable as language
VERBALIZATION	(VE)	Speak in a recognizable language, or use a formal symbolic substitute such as finger spelling or American sign language
UNCLEAR VERBALIZATION	(UV)	Same as verbalize but observer cannot understand or hear; excludes symbolic substitute
AMBIGUOUS SOUND	(AS)	Observer cannot determine whether subject's sound is interactive or not
GESTURE	(GE)	Primitive movements of the body, hands, face, etc., to express a meaning (like hand waving, hand out, palm up to receive handout)
TELEPHONE	(OT)	$\underline{S}$ is talking on telephone
LETTER WRITING	(LW)	$\underline{S}$ has writing implement and paper and is expressing himself to another on the paper, or $\underline{S}$ is dictating a thought to a staff member who is writing it down for him or $\underline{S}$ is dictating a tape to be sent to an acquaintance
ANNOYANCE	(AN)	Pester, irritate, persistently follow, whine; tease in nasty way
AGGRESSION	(AG)	Angry disagreement with or without physical violence
APPROVAL	(AP)	Social behavior involving bestowing sanction or "positive" reinforcement on others for identified action
TEACHING	(TE)	Inform another person about specific facts, usually in an educating manner either verbally or physically—examples: showing how to make change, teaching about moral issues, explaining how to fix something broken, or how to say a new word
DISAPPROVAL	(DA)	Indicate clearly that actions of another are not acceptable, liked, etc., by reprimanding, scolding, depriving of privileges, etc.—clearly educational reprimands should be scored under teaching

TABLE 2.   (CONT.)

ROUGH PLAY	(RP)	Push or shove another person in a playful manner
INFORMAL PLAY	(IP)	Joke or tease in a cheerful, pleasant way; casual play in which no rules are used, such as ball tossing
INTERACTIVE GAME PLAY	(IG)	S plays game with other people
ISOLATED OBSERVATION	(IO)	Attends to the activity of a group but is not a participant in it; or S watches another person with great interest
OTHER SOCIAL	(OS)	A specific social behavior for which we have no code
OTHER NONSOCIAL	(ON)	A specific nonsocial behavior for which we have no code, will be recorded if nothing else can be recorded
DISRUPTIVE BEHAVIOR	(DB)	S acts out alone (cries, speaks in loud violent tone to no one, bangs or throws, etc.)
STEREOTYPE	(ST)	S engages in repetitive behavior which has no apparent function (eye-poking, rocking, hand and finger movements)
ABNORMALITY	(AB)	Very atypical, unacceptable, or asocial, maladaptive behaviors (pica, exposure)
ODDITY	(OD)	Less deviant abnormal behavior
MUSIC LISTENING	(ML)	S is actively involved with equipment or singing along or tapping foot
TV VIEWING	(TV)	S's attention is focused directly on the monitor and he appears to be watching the action on the screen
BODY CARE	(BC)	Bathing, grooming, dressing, toileting, health-related activities
SLEEP	(SL)	Eyes are shut, breathing regular, and subject does not respond to the others around him
EAT AND DRINK	(ED)	Ingesting or preparing to ingest food and/or beverages
WORK	(WO)	Staff-assigned task which produces income
SELF MANIPULATION	(SM)	S manipulates part of his body (picks nose, rubs genitals, scratches)
PURCHASE	(PU)	Buy goods either from the machines or from an attendant who is dispensing merchandise
INDEFINITE SOCIAL	(IS)	S judged to be a member of a group and is not doing anything else interactive
UNABLE TO OBSERVE	(UO)	S was not observed during an observation period—this designation is only given after observers have consulted following an observation period
ABSENCE	(AT)	S has been determined not to be in attendance at the facility being studied—this designation is given only once during a day's observations
SIGN LANGUAGE	(VS)	S uses a nonverbal language substitute, e.g., ASL

TABLE 3. MEANS AND TESTS OF VARIOUS MEASURES IN THE DIFFERENT FACILITIES

Measure	Facility					F ratio
	WA$_1$	WI	WH	WE	H	
Age (yrs)	46	40	45	33	44	14.91
IQ	50	60	51	72	47	21.06
Percent female	36	31	37	43	26	1.85
Percent affiliation	38	32	45	54	29	21.20
Number of groups	2.6	3.0	2.7	3.4	1.7	8.80
Strongest relationship (%)	8	9	10	14	7	7.64
Average distance (ft)	4.6	2.3	3.1	2.1	3.6	44.00
Self-concept	−.43	−.27	−.21	.55		4.69
Pay (dollars/hour)	.31	.41	.40	.49		5.83
Hours worked	19.0	29.8	28.8	29.0		36.11

the difference. One approach to going further is to control trait differences by observing the same people in different contexts. Figure 2 shows the level of three measures of social affiliation in the living and work environment of individuals who both worked in the sheltered workshops and lived in the sheltered-care home. The contribution of environment is evident from the clear difference in levels of social behavior in the two situations. In the intensity measure the difference in the direction of the means depends on the workshop studied. On the other hand, it should also be noted that the correlations of scores in the two situations were positive and significant for both social measures ($r = .80$ for percent affiliation and $r = .42$ for intensity).

TABLE 4. PREDICTIONS OF PERCENT AFFILIATION FROM SEVERAL MEASURES OVERALL AND FOR EACH FACILITY

Predictor	All		F ratio	Facility				
				WE	WI	WH	WA$_1$	H
	r	Beta		Significant beta				
All	.64		12.69					
Age	−.40	−.19	7.75			−.40		−.31
Diagnosis	−.37	−.37	27.06	−.38		−.46	−.66	−.25
IQ	.24	.16	4.29				.55	.23
Sex	.17	.08	1.66					
Attract	.12	.04	0.35					
Hours worked	.27	.04	0.14		.48			
Pay	.34	.20	3.13	.27				
Self-concept	.35	.16	5.05		.53			

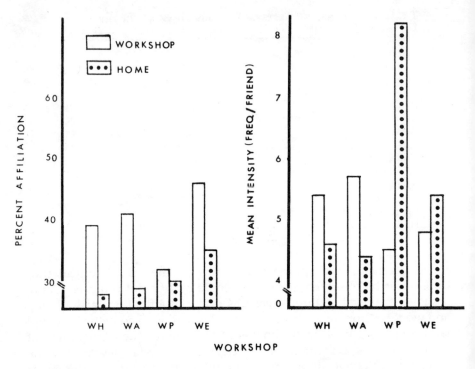

FIG. 2. Three measures of social affiliation of individuals in their sheltered care facility and their sheltered workshop by workshop.

These correlations indicate that even when environments can affect average level of social behavior markedly, sociability as an individual trait transcending situations can also be evident.

This point is made even more dramatically from a study of percent affiliation of people during the first ten weeks after they had entered the programs of the agency we worked with (Figure 3).The percent affiliation scores are plotted for the first eight weeks, in which the clients were all together in a single screening program, and then for two weeks after they had been transferred to one of two of the sheltered workshops of the agency. Data from subjects who were ultimately sent to different workshops are plotted separately for the evaluation phase, even though both groups are together in evaluation. As may be seen from the figure, there was an initial difference in social affiliation between those people who ultimately were assigned to different workshops. However, with time, the average levels of social behavior converged, only to separate again when the clients were transferred.

Correlations between initial and later social affiliation, however, remained quite high ($r = .51–.67$). In these data, then, trait differences were evident from the correlations over time and situation. However, average scores revealed that exact determination of level of social behavior depended on an environmental factor, time in the facility.

A further approach to identifying environmental variables associ-

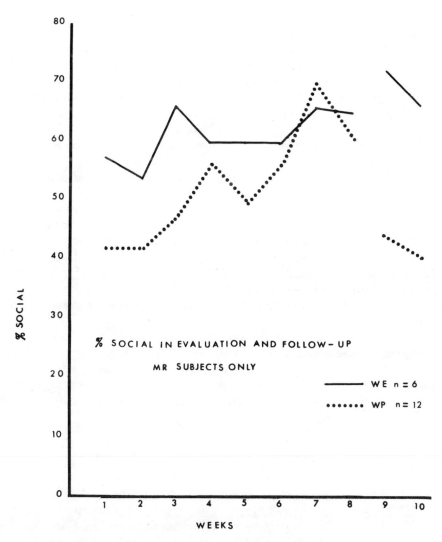

FIG. 3. Percent affiliation during evaluation and follow-up of mentally retarded people who were then transferred to one of two workshops.

ated with social affiliation of mentally disabled people is to consider variables which are generally thought to determine social behavior of man and of animals. One of these variables is the extent to which the individual has had an opportunity to interact with certain other people (Harrison, 1977; Hill, 1978). In our studies, it was possible to ask whether mentally disabled people were seen to affiliate more with others in one situation, given that they were exposed to each other in another situation. We asked whether, in the sheltered workshops, clients preferred to associate with others with whom they lived. We also asked whether, in their homes, they tended to be seen with others with whom they worked. Table 5 presents the ratio of affiliation with people they were exposed to more relative to those they were exposed to less. Staff, client, and observational assessments of choice indicated that people associated with others to the extent that they had opportunity to interact with them. In other words, propinquity or exposure facilitates affiliation of mentally disabled people.

A somewhat more complex approach to the analysis of trait and environment contributions to affiliation is to separate the traits of individuals from the traits of groups to which they belong. In a previous study (Landesman-Dwyer, Berkson, & Romer, 1979), we had shown that sex and intelligence predicted various measures of social behavior. Being more intelligent and being female were correlated with more social behavior (see Table 6). However, in that study, these results were completely determined by the mean sex and IQ of the home in which the study occurred. That is, IQ and sex of *individuals* did not predict social behavior at all. Apparently, it was the fact of a number of people of the same sex or IQ being together that promoted affiliation.

The same distinction between individual and group predictors may also be seen from the study of sheltered work and care facilities (Table 6). In this case, individual age and diagnosis did predict social behavior, irrespective of location, age, and diagnosis. However, intellectual level of individuals again did not significantly predict social

TABLE 5.   EXPOSURE RATIOS FOR STAFF, CLIENT AND
OBSERVATION MEASURES OF SOCIAL CHOICE

	WE	WI	WH	WA$_1$	WA$_2$	H
Staff	5.70*	4.72*	2.15	2.02*	2.03*	2.19*
Client	4.57*	3.82*	2.05*	1.38*	1.86*	1.95*
Observation	5.17*	2.38*	1.64	1.36*	1.80*	1.95*

*$p < .05$

TABLE 6.   F VALUES FROM REGRESSION ANALYSES OF SOCIAL BEHAVIORS

Variables	Group home study			Sheltered care and living		
	Av int.	Hi int.	% social	Av int.	Hi int.	% affiliation
Individual						
Intelligence	.24	.52	1.04	.84	–	5.63
Age	(.46	.62	11.46*)	2.00	9.50*	17.84*
Sex	.01	1.25	2.26	2.09	6.35	6.56
Diagnosis				4.06	17.08*	70.55*
Attractiveness				5.02	5.45	5.13
Social self-concept				8.67*	6.58	5.13
Location						
Intelligence	3.25	4.62*	1.50	6.63	17.66*	36.64*
Age	(.46	.62	11.46*)	–	–	6.30
Sex	3.60	4.27*	.38	–	–	–
Diagnosis				–	–	–
Attractiveness				.67	5.16	6.06
Social self-concept				–	–	–

– Variable did not enter equation because its effect was too small.
( ) Individual and location age were completely confounded so that their relative contribution could not be assessed in the group home data.
* $p < .01$

behavior, while average level of the people in a program did. One way of summarizing these results is to say that younger and mentally retarded people tended to be more sociable irrespective of the age and diagnosis of the people around them, but that more intelligent people were more sociable only when there were other relatively intelligent people available to interact with.

CONCLUSION

The results have shown that traits and environments are both important determinants of social behavior and that, statistically speaking, traits and environments can have either additive or interactive effects. Moreover, it is possible not only to recognize that environments vary in a complex way to influence adaptation, but also to analyze the sources of variation. When that is done, it becomes clear that a person's affiliation with others depends on the degree to which he is exposed to them. Less obviously, it is possible to define which individual traits predict adaptation and, alternatively, when the characteristics of others around the individual are the primary determinants of his adaptation. Apparently the relationship between intelligence and amount of social behavior is not an individual trait characteristic.

On a more general level, the research makes clear that treatment approaches which depend exclusively on describing characteristics of the individual and attempting to modify them can have only limited validity. Describing in detail the nature of the environment to which the individual is expected to adapt and changing environments to respond to human needs constitutes a complementary orientation which undoubtedly increases adaptation. When this approach has been taken in the past, it has depended primarily on pragmatic intuition. More formal theory and research are needed.

REFERENCES

Berkson, G. When exceptions obscure the rule. *Mental Retardation*, 1966, *4*, 24–27.

Berkson, G. The social ecology of defects. In S. Chevalier-Skolnikoff & F. E. Poirier (Eds.), *Primate bio-social development.*New York: Garland Publishing Co., 1977, pp. 189–204.

Bernstein, I. E. Dominance, aggression and reproduction in primate societies. *Journal of Theoretical Biology*, 1976, *60*, 459–472.

Butler, E. W., & Bjaanes, A. T. Activities and the use of time by retarded persons in community care facilities. In G. P. Sackett (Ed.), *Observing behavior* (Vol. 1). Baltimore: University Park Press, 1978, pp. 379–399.

Dawkins, R. *The selfish gene.* Oxford: Oxford University Press, 1976.

Dingman, H. F., & Tarjan, G. Mental retardation and the normal distribution curve. *American Journal of Mental Deficiency*, 1960, *64*, 991–994.

Goddard, H. H. *Feeblemindedness.* Freeport: Books for Libraries, 1972 (first published, 1914).

Gruenberg, E. M. Epidemiology. In H. A. Stevens & R. Heber (Eds.), *Mental retardation.* Chicago: University of Chicago Press, 1964, pp. 259–306.

Harrison, A. A. Mere exposure. In L. Berkowitz (Ed.), *Advances in experimental social psychology* (Vol. 10). New York: Academic Press, 1977, pp. 39–83.

Higgins, J. V., Reed, E. W., & Reed, S. C. Intelligence and family size: A paradox resolved *Eugenics Quarterly*, 1962, *9*, 84–90.

Hill, W. F. Effects of mere exposure on preferences in nonhuman mammals. *Psychological Bulletin*, 1978, *85*, 1177–1198.

Landesman-Dwyer, S., Berkson, G., & Romer, D. Affiliation and friendship of mentally retarded residents in group homes. *American Journal of Mental Deficiency*, 1979, *83*, 571–580.

Moos, R. H. *Evaluating treatment environments.* New York: Wiley, 1974.

Richardson, S. Reaction to mental subnormality. In M. J. Begab & S. A. Richardson (Eds.), *The mentally retarded and society.* Baltimore: University Park Press, 1975, pp. 77–97.

Schoggen, P. Ecological psychology and mental retardation. In G. P. Sackett (Ed.), *Observing behavior* (Vol. 1). Baltimore: University Park Press, 1978, pp. 33–62.

Simeonsson, R. J. Social competence. In J. Wortis (Ed.), *Mental retardation and developmental disabilities* (Vol. 10). New York: Brunner/Mazel, 1978.

Trivers, R. Parent–offspring conflict. *Amer. Zool.,* 1974, *14,* 249–264.

Wilson, E. O. *Sociobiology: The new synthesis.* Boston: Harvard University Press, 1975.

Zigler, E., & Balla, D. A. Impact of institutional experience on the behavior and development of retarded persons. *American Journal of Mental Deficiency,* 1977, *82,* 1–11.

3

The Importance of Temperament –Environment Interaction for Child Health and Development

WILLIAM B. CAREY

Children's temperaments contribute significantly to their interactions with their environments. Sometimes this happens in stressful ways that result in problems in their health or development. Although the quality of the interaction is generally more important than either the temperament or the environment alone, some temperament patterns seem more likely than others to lead to these problems in the child. For example, the "difficult child" syndrome appears to predispose to a variety of behavioral dysfunctions in diverse caretaking settings, while the characteristics of high activity or low sensory threshold seem to do so only under certain circumstances.

This chapter reviews what has been reported recently about children's temperament: its definition, measurement, origins, stability, and clinical importance. These few pages cannot possibly be as comprehensive as the recent book, *Temperament and Development*, by Thomas and Chess (1977). This presentation, besides being briefer and more recent, places a greater emphasis on the practical significance of children's temperament.

WILLIAM B. CAREY • 319 West Front Street, Media, Pennsylvania 19063.

DEFINITION

The term "temperament" is best defined as the individual's emotional reactivity or behavioral style in interacting with the environment. In other words, it describes *how* the child behaves, rather than *what* he can do, which is his abilities, or *why* he does it, which is a matter of internal psychological organization or motivation (Thomas & Chess, 1977). For example, an intense, negative child may bellow for five or ten minutes when punched by an older sibling, this response being based on a loud voice, an inability to strike back with equal force, and a desire to attract as much parental sympathy as possible. A milder, more positive child with the same bruise and the same capacities and purposes might simply go quietly to his mother to plead his case.

Various conceptualizations of temperament have been popular during the course of Western civilization. The Hippocratic humoral theory has undoubtedly had the longest history, lasting from ancient Greece into the nineteenth century. The varying proportions of blood, phlegm, black bile, and yellow bile in the individual were thought to determine his health and emotional reactivity. The word "temperament" is derived from the Latin verb *temperare*, which means to mix, blend, or regulate.

While the first half of the twentieth century was largely a period of environmentalism in the social sciences, the modern scientific study of temperament differences was beginning. These early investigations have been reviewed by Korner (1971), Buss and Plomin (1975), and Thomas and Chess (1977). Among the more recent definitions of temperament is that of Buss and Plomin (1975), consisting of emotionality, activity, sociability, and impulsivity. Unlike the ancient humoral theory, which attributed behavior directly to physical causes, the modern theories generally describe behaviors without clear implication of origins.

Probably the most widely known and applied view of temperament today is the one introduced by Thomas, Chess, Birch, Hertzig, and Korn (1963; Thomas, Chess & Birch, 1968, 1970) in their New York Longitudinal Study (NYLS), which began over twenty years ago. Their investigation is the most comprehensive and extends over the longest period of observation. On theoretical and clinical grounds they decided upon nine variables for study: activity, rhythmicity of biological functions, initial approach–withdrawal, adaptability, intensity, mood, persistence, distractibility, and sensory threshold. From these nine characteristics they derived three clinically significant clusters of traits: (1) the difficult child (arrhythmic, low in approach and adaptability, intense and predominantly negative in mood), (2) the easy child (opposite characteristics: rhythmic, approaching, adaptable, mild, and positive), and (3) the slow-to-warm-up child (low in activity, approach, and adaptability, and negative but variable in rythmicity, and mild in intensity). The approximately 40% of individuals not falling into one of these groups have been designated intermediate high (difficult) and intermediate low (easy) (Carey, 1970). Other investigators using the NYLS scheme have suggested additional variables such as fastidiousness (Graham, Rutter, & George, 1973) and predictability (Hegvik, McDevitt, & Carey, 1980).

As a pediatrician who laments the slow pace at which his colleagues are accepting and using the concept of temperament, I must add that it is defined in the leading pediatric textbooks as the blank space in the index between tantrums and temperature.

MEASUREMENT

The process of measuring temperament remains intrinsically difficult, although there has been progress recently. Such behavioral qualities as mood or adaptability do not lend themselves readily to precise quantifications as do physical measurements like blood pressure or serum calcium or capacities like reading speed or comprehension. It is more like describing an oriental rug than sorting apples and oranges. The ideal method for measuring temperament has yet to be evolved. Currently available techniques are parent interviews, parent questionnaires, and observations of the child.

The NYLS group used parent interviews, which obtained from the mother detailed descriptions of how the child was currently reacting in a variety of daily situations, avoiding general impressions and interpretations. The interview, dictation, and rating took at least two hours, making it not readily applicable by other researchers, although some have used it (Graham *et al.*, 1973; Garside, Birch, Scott, Chambers, Kolvin, Tweddle, & Barber, 1975), and not at all practical for clinicians. The authors themselves described the process as "rather elaborate" (Thomas & Chess, 1977).

A parent questionnaire seemed like a reasonable solution to the problem if it could obtain comparable data and be psychometrically sound. The Infant Temperament Questionnaire (Carey, 1970) was the first published attempt to convert the NYLS research interview into a practical clinical instrument. After eight years' experience with the original version, Carey revised it with the help of McDevitt (Carey & McDevitt, 1978a) to improve its psychometric properties, in particular the internal consistency.

Parent questionnaires of similar construction for older children have followed. The period of 1–3 years is now covered by the Toddler

Temperament Scale (Fullard, McDevitt, & Carey, 1978), the span of 3–7 years by the Behavioral Style Questionnaire (McDevitt & Carey, 1978), and work has just been completed on a Middle Childhood Temperament Questionnaire for 8- to 12-year-old children (Hegvik *et al.*, 1980). Thomas and Chess (1977) have also developed both parent and teacher questionnaires for the 3–7 group. Several other researchers, such as Mary Rothbart, Frank Pedersen, John Bates (Bates, Freeland, & Lounsbury, 1979), Persson-Blennow and McNeil (1979a), and Buss and Plomin (1975) have been working on other questionnaires primarily for the infancy period, but only the last three have been published and none of them has been used clinically.

In Eastern Europe, where the theoretical orientation of Pavlov continues to prevail, the questionnaire of Jan Strelau (1980) is used for self-rating of adults as to the Pavlovian dimensions of strength of excitation, strength of inhibition, and mobility of nervous process.

Some data are available on the psychometric characteristics of our three completed instruments: the ITQ, TTS, and BSQ. The internal consistency and one-month retest reliability for the nine categories are at an acceptable level for all three. For the revised ITQ, internal consistency was: range 0.49–0.71, median 0.57, total 0.83; for the TTS: range 0.53–0.86, median 0.70 for one-year-olds and 0.72 for two-year-olds, total 0.85; and for the BSQ: range 0.47–0.80, median 0.70, total 0.84. For the revised ITQ, retest reliability figures were: range 0.66–0.81, median 0.75, total 0.86 ($n = 41$); for the TTS: range 0.69–0.89, median 0.81, total 0.88 ($n = 47$); for the BSQ: range 0.67–0.94, median 0.82, total 0.89 ($n = 53$).

Sound external validity data are necessary to convince critics and users that possible maternal distortions are being kept to a minimum. However, one must utilize a technique appropriate for the situation. Researchers, in particular psychologists, tend to disbelieve reports by parents and deprecate them as "maternal perceptions." They assume that parents are too emotionally involved to be capable of accurate observations. They seem to believe that the hour or two the outsider spends observing the child in his laboratory or elsewhere produces scientific data of an order much superior to any parental reports, even though the latter are based on thousands of hours of experience. They seem rather little concerned about adequacy of sampling, observer effects, and the absence of standard techniques for such observations.

On the other hand, those of us trained in clinical medicine have a different point of view. We do not have the luxury of evaluating our patients by extended examinations of any sort. Pressures of time and cost compel us to rely on information obtained from parents. While not believing all of everything we are told, we know from experience that the right questions asked in the right way usually produce data sufficiently valid for responsible, effective clinical management. Questionnaire data are, of course, supplemented by office interviewing and observations to round out the picture of the parent–child interaction.

A reasonable compromise between these two attitudes toward parental reports is possible. Both parent reports and observations are needed for a valid composite picture of the child. However, nobody knows more about a young child than the mother or other full-time caretaker. Our job as scientists and clinicians is to provide mothers with objective means of describing their children's behavior, in addition to asking for their general impressions and for the stresses they are feeling in the interaction. We then score the reported data and form our own diagnostic impressions, which may or may not agree with those of the mothers. (Some researchers have been confused on this point.) When direct observations of outsiders are to be compared with data received from parents, the former must be for long enough to insure an adequate sample and must consider exactly the same behaviors that are dealt with in the parental reports. When disrepancies are found, observers must acknowledge that the reason is just as likely to be a failure in their technique as poor reporting by parents.

For the BSQ this has been done well by Billman & McDevitt (1980). With 78 nursery school children they found significant correlations for six out of seven categories attempted (range 0.18–0.46, median 0.38) between mothers' ratings on the BSQ and independent observers' evaluations using the Teacher Temperament Questionnaire of Thomas and Chess (1977) after watching these children intermittently over a span of several weeks. Since the two determinations were an average of 5 months apart, one would expect even higher correlations with contemporaneous ratings.

Comparable opportunities with young infants are scarce. Nevertheless, some evidence is presently available that mothers report somewhat accurately on the ITQ, and no competent study to date has shown mothers to be unreliable observers. Two studies using the original version verified that difficult babies do cry more (Campbell, 1977; Sarret, 1976). Searls, employing the revised ITQ, rated 20 babies on selected items suitable for her 90-minute observations and obtained significant correlations with mothers' ITQ category ratings in four out of eight categories. Using this appropriate technique with longer observations would undoubtedly have raised the correlations (Searls, Fullard, & McDevitt, in press).

Further evidence of the external validity of parent rating on the ITQ has been reported by Berberian (1979) and by Bates et al. (1979).

In my pediatric practice I have recently been comparing independent ratings of 6-month-old infants by their mothers and fathers. Fathers are theoretically ideal for a validation study since they are probably the second best informed persons about specific babies. The principal disadvantages of using fathers are (1) that they may inadvertently use information obtained from the mothers, or (2) that they may not be well enough informed about their babies to complete the questionnaire sufficiently. In fact, 5 mother–father pairs out of this series of 46 had to be dropped from the study because the fathers were unable to answer 32 or more of the 95 items.

Of the remaining 41, several comparisons showed that the two parents were definitely describing the same behavior. Agreement as to above or below the mean occurred in 261 out of 369 category scores (χ^2 = 63.4, $p < 0.001$). Category scores fell into the same quartiles (determined by the means and standard deviations) in 165 out of 369 cases, about twice as often as would be expected by chance ($\chi^2 = 76.5$, $p < 0.001$). Correlation coefficients ranged from 0.37 to 0.72 with a median of 0.54. The greatest parental agreement as to category ratings was in approach, mood and adaptability and the least in intensity, distractibility, and activity. The highest general agreement included the two families in which the engineer fathers were just back from family vacation trips. The most meager agreement occurred when the fathers were seldom home, as was the case with a golf pro in the summertime and a man just starting his own restaurant 20 miles away from home.

Although these data do not qualify well for external validation, they contrast favorably with Plomin and Rowe's (1977) experience of little resemblance between mothers' and fathers' reports on temperament questionnaires. The explanation may lie in the global nature of their questions, which are likely to permit a greater degree of subjectivity and departure from the child's actual behavior, as compared with the ITQ's more specific item descriptions. For my 41 pairs of parents, category general impression correlations were much lower than category questionnaire ratings based on about twelve items each (range −0.07–0.48, median 0.35).

Various factor analyses of the nine categories have been performed. The reader is referred elsewhere for these data (McDevitt, 1976; Thomas & Chess, 1977).

Clinicians of a generation or two hence will probably still be using a combination of interview, questionnaire, and observation, since all contribute to an understanding of the child and his relationships. Since temperament is not fixed at birth or at any later point, serial determinations must be made if the clinician wishes to keep in touch with changes in this aspect of his patient.

ORIGINS

One may briefly summarize what is presently known about the origins of temperamental characteristics by stating that they appear to be largely constitutional, observable at least in part in the first few days of life, somewhat more elaborated and stable by three or four months, and constantly interacting with the environment with mutual modification. Therefore, to investigate these origins one must consider several factors: (1) genetic, (2) intrauterine, (3) perinatal, (4) postnatal, and (5) central nervous system status.

Genetic Factors

The strongest case for the congenital nature of temperament comes from genetic studies. As early as 1909, Garrod, in discovering Mendelian inheritance of certain diseases, suggested that all differences in people might be genetically determined biochemical variations (Childs, 1970). Genetics has developed greatly since then. Evidence today for a genetic basis of temperament comes from twin studies, sex and racial differences, and from genetic defects.

Twin studies are considered to demonstrate a genetic component to a characteristic or illness when identical twins manifest it significantly more often than like-sexed fraternal twins. Some object that in behavioral studies this method is unsuitable because parents are thought to treat identical twins more alike. However, there is good evidence that parents are as likely to be responding to, as creating, differences and similarities between their twins (Lytton, 1977). Furthermore, environmental influences within families appear to make both kinds of twins less alike, at least in social responsiveness (Plomin & Rowe, 1979).

Using the eight pairs of twins in the original NYLS sample, Rutter, Korn, and Birch (1963) reported the strongest evidence for a genetic component in the characteristics of activity, approach, and adaptability. More recently Torgersen and Kringlen (1978), in an analysis of 53 twin pairs in Norway, showed monozygotic twins were more alike than dizygotic ones for only three of the NYLS traits at 2 months but for all nine at 9 months. The dizygotic twins became more different from each other during that period; the monozygotic ones grew slightly but not significantly more alike.

Supportive of these findings but using slightly different variables are the reports of Scarr (1966, 1969), Wilson, Brown, and Matheny (1971), and Plomin and Rowe (1977).

Since males and females are genetically different, any clearly established temperament differences between the sexes may be a reflection of that fact. Efforts to separate genetic effects from environmental modifications have perplexed researchers. Nevertheless, two recent comprehensive reviews are instructive. Maccoby and Jacklin (1974) concluded that, in addition to girls' greater verbal ability and boys' greater visual–spatial and mathematical ability, boys are more aggressive. Hutt (1978) goes further to say that "boys were more active and energetic, more exploratory, more 'thing oriented,' and more interested in the inanimate; girls were more affiliative and 'person oriented,' and more easily inhibited by novelty or uncertainty; they tend to construe personal relationships and social situations in a more complex manner and differentiate more subtly along social and emotional dimensions." Of course, not all of these behaviors are temperament traits either in these studies or the others to be mentioned in the next few pages.

The revision of the Infant Temperament Questionnaire of Carey and McDevitt (1978a) is in agreement with the above insofar as it shows that the only significant sex differences at 4–8 months is less approaching in females. This difference endures into the second year, as demonstrated by the standardization sample for the TTS. Also, some other low sex correlations were found with the TTS and BSQ.

Racial differences in temperament are mentioned more as a theoretical possibility of genetic variation than as an established fact. Sparseness of scientific data and the sensitivity of the subject require us to avoid careless statements. Freedman and Freedman (1969) found that "Chinese-American newborns tended to be less changeable, less perturbable, tended to habituate more readily when upset and tended to calm themselves or to be consoled more readily when upset" than European-American newborns. Further studies of larger populations with more attention to effects of social class, risk factors, and questionnaire-answering techniques are called for before racial differences in temperament can be accepted as proven.

Finally, if genetic differences within the range of normal can be shown to be responsible for variations in behavioral style, then one might expect to find some consistent characteristics in children with certain genetic abnormalities. Investigations to date have only been preliminary. Baron (1972) evaluated temperament patterns in 18 infants with Down's syndrome and found them no more difficult or easy than the normal standardization population. However, 13 children with the XXY chromosomal defect (Klinefelter's syndrome) were more inactive, irregular, withdrawing, socially adaptable, and mild than controls (Walzer, Wolff, Bowen, Silbert, Bashir, Gerald, & Richmond, 1978). Further investigations of these and similar conditions are awaited in the years to come.

Intrauterine Effects

Intrauterine effects on the temperament development of the fetus remain uncertain. There is no clear evidence so far that physical complications of pregnancy, such as hyperemesis or toxemia, exert any consistent influence. However, it appears that full-term, small-for-gestational-age babies behave differently from their full-weight peers as newborns and continue to be more difficult during the first year (Als, Tronick, Adamson, & Brazelton, 1976). Waldrop, Pedersen, and Bell (1968) reported behavioral differences in children with multiple minor congenital anomalies and they believe that the anomalies result from noxious influences early in the intrauterine period, but there is no certainty of this. Chess, Korn, and Fernandez (1971) found 227 children with congenital rubella were not significantly more difficult than controls.

The emotional status of the pregnant woman has long been popularly thought to leave a lasting imprint on the child, but existing studies purporting to prove or disprove this point suffer from a variety of important methodological problems, such as failure to allow for postnatal effects (Sameroff & Kelly, 1977), use of retrospective data (Cadoret, Cunningham, Loftus, & Edwards, 1975), too small a sample (Carey, Lipton, & Myers, 1974), or employing indirect evidence (Huttunen & Niskanen, 1978).

A variety of other possible intrauterine factors deserve further consideration. Maternal diet in particular warrants attention. Chavez, Martinez, and Yaschine (1974) demonstrated that rural Mexican mothers on marginal diets produced more active and intense infants when given a diet supplement during pregnancy. (This was confounded by the newborn infants also having an augmented diet.) The possibility that a variety of drugs, such as hormones, taken during pregnancy may induce enduring alterations in behavior has been increasingly investigated (Kolata, 1978). The potential long-range behavioral consequences of pregnant women drinking alcohol (Streissguth, 1977), smoking tobacco, and taking narcotics have only recently been appreciated.

Perinatal Effects

Perinatal effects on temperament are those attributable to events around birth: early, late, or complicated. Despite the impression given by the largely retrospective studies by Passamanick and Knobloch (1966) that perinatal complications lead to a variety of developmental disabilities, more recent work by Littman and Parmelee (1978) concludes that with modern technology these complications are mostly "insults not injuries. In that regard, therefore, the impact on the infant is more likely to be a transient one." They did not, however, evaluate temperament. Hertzig's group of sixty-eight premature infants had temperament patterns similar to the normal range (1977). A number of studies claiming to demonstrate a relationship between perinatal events and later temperament, such as ones by Ucko (1965) on neonatal asphyxia and by Field, Dabiri, Hallock, and Shuman (1977) on postmaturity, are too clouded by methodological problems to settle matters.

Postnatal Influences

Postnatal influences are undoubtedly important in shaping the congenital temperament patterns of children. Perhaps the most obvious illustration is the apathy caused by deprivation of nutrition (Rossetti Ferreira, (1978) or environmental stimulation (Rutter, 1972).

Less dramatic psychosocial influences probably account for most of the changes seen in children's congenital temperament patterns, but these phenomena are poorly understood at present. Social class made no difference in a stratified sample of 160 Swedish infants (Persson-Blennow & McNeil, 1979b). Birth order does not affect the frequency of difficult temperament (Carey, 1970), although mothers globally judged their firstborn "average" or "more difficult than average" significantly more often than did mothers of later-born infants (Carey in Wilson & Matheny, 1980). However, "parental intolerance, inconsistency and conflict were associated with negative temperament changes" according to Cameron in his analysis of the trends in temperament ratings in the original NYLS population (1977). This is certainly one of the most imortant areas for further research.

Effects of excretion of certain maternal drugs in breast milk (Ananth, 1978) and the presence of food additives in the child's diet (Feingold, 1975) are under active consideration with little support so far for the latter (Wender, 1977). It now appears that lead exposure at doses below those producing symptoms severe enough to be recognized clinically is associated with neuropsychologic deficits including disturbances of attentional function (Needleman, Gunnoe, Leviton, Reed, Peresie, Maher, & Barrett, 1979).

Physical handicaps such as congenital deafness due to maternal rubella (Chess et al., 1971) or remediable deafness due to chronic serous otitis (Zincus, Gottlieb, & Schapiro, 1978) have not been shown to affect the child's temperament but may render him more vulnerable to behavior problems due to the handicap itself.

Central Nervous System Status

There is probably no more confused area in pediatric medical and psychological diagnosis today than that of the impact of altered brain structure or function on children's behavior. The wisest conclusions for the present seem to be that abnormality of the central nervous system does not impose any specific behavioral pattern on the child (Rutter, 1977), and that difficult children are no more likely than others to have objective evidence of brain malfunction (Thomas & Chess, 1977).

Chess and Korn (1970) determined that retarded children had temperament patterns similar to normal ones, although the retardation itself might make them more vulnerable to behavior problems. Of the three children with confirmed brain damage in the NYLS only one was rather difficult (Thomas & Chess, 1977).

The popular syndrome of "minimal brain dysfunction" (MBD) is supposedly derived from malfunction of the central nervous system and is thought to include behavioral variables like activity, distractibility, and short attention span (Clements, 1966). However, at present the pheomenon is very loosely conceptualized and applied and is poorly differentiated from normal temperament variables. No proponent of this syndrome has yet explained how we should distinguish between these behaviors when they are normal temperament variables and the same ones when they are thought to be evidence of brain dysfunction. What, for example, is the difference between high activity and hyperactivity? This attribution of behavioral characteristics to unproven body changes reminds one of the ancient humoral theory of temperament. Let us leave for fuller discussion elsewhere the problems created by this syndrome and some suggestions for a way out of the confusion (Carey & McDevitt, in press; Carey, McDevitt, & Baker, 1979). Suffice it to say for now that evidence is slender that such a behavioral syndrome, if it exists, is derived from malfunction of the brain (Rutter, 1977).

STABILITY

While clinicians have been impressed with the importance of temperamental characteristics as they affect contemporary problems of the child, theorists are more interested in exploring the degree to which they remain stable over time. No temperament researcher has maintained that behavioral style is fixed at any point, but we should expect to find some degree of continuity in such basic characteristics that appear to be determined in part by genetic factors. We also look for evidence of modification by experience. One can hold up for comparison the fact that IQ scores in children have been shown to vary by 10 points or more in 50% and by 22 points or more in 25% between the ages of 3 and 17 years (Hindley & Owen, 1978).

A variety of normal phenomena confound our efforts to demonstrate stability of temperament: (1) transient intrauterine effects wearing off in the early weeks or months of life; (2) the great postnatal growth and development of the human brain with the resulting trend toward organization of behavior (Parmelee, 1977); (3) the changing expression of characteristics as the child matures, such as activity before and after locomotion; (4) varying rates of maturation, which frustrate comparisons of individuals since changes in capacities may obscure similarities of style; and (5) differing experience varying the expression of temperament characteristics without altering the basic style (Rutter, 1970; Thomas & Chess, 1977).

Nevertheless, comparisons between reaction characteristics in the newborn period and later times have shown some evidence of consistency, as did the measures of irritability, sensitivity, tension, and soothability between birth and 4 months when studied by Birns, Barten, and Bridger (1969). On the other hand, the meager correlations of some other studies (Bell, Weller, & Waldrop, 1971; Sostek & Anders, 1977) are attributable to the use of different variables at the two points of comparison.

When the same variables have been evaluated over later time spans, evidence of stability has increased (Bronson, 1966). The NYLS group, using parent interviews, reported significant correlations from one year to the next for six of the nine categories during the first 5 years. For intervals longer than 1 year fewer significant correlations were found. Similarities and changes as these children moved into adolescence have also been reported (Chess & Thomas, 1977).

Using their three temperament questionnaires based on the NYLS conceptualization, McDevitt and Carey have demonstrated greater degrees of stability:

1. Category scores. McDevitt (1976), using the original ITQ and the BSQ, found stability of seven of the nine characteristics between 6 months and 3–5 years but only for activity for both sexes between 6 months and 5–7 years. However, employing the revised ITQ and the TTS, McDevitt and Carey (in press) have shown stability of all nine characteristics for 115 children from 6 months to 1–3 years (range of correlations 0.24–0.58, median 0.38).

2. Factor invariance. Using the nine NYLS categories, McDevitt (1976) found continuity of factor structure for sociability ($r_{iv} = 0.83$

and 0.75) and emotionality dimensions (r_{iv} = 0.77 and 0.55) from infancy to 3–5 and to 5–7 years. Stability of individual differences on factor scores was obtained from infancy to 3–5 and to 5–7 years for emotionality (r = 0.34 and 0.25) and from infancy to 3–5 years for sociability (r = 0.30).

3. Individual diagnostic clusters. While difficult 6-month-old infants generally became easier by 3–7 years, there was a significant tendency (χ^2 = 10.93, $p < 0.001$) for these infants to continue being difficult during that later period (Carey & McDevitt, 1978b).

The reasons for these continuities and discontinuities are not clear at this time but probably include, in addition to the factors mentioned above, a variable modifiability of the several temperament traits and the diverse demand characteristics of the environment. As will be mentioned later, some components of the difficult-infant syndrome predicted which infants were likely to remain difficult (Carey & McDevitt, 1978b).

As techniques for measuring temperament continue to improve and greater care is taken to measure the same behavioral phenomena throughout studies, it seems likely that further evidence of stability will be forthcoming. Whatever future research may tell us about the origins and stability of temperament traits, the ultimate social value of such knowledge is its clinical applications.

Clinical Importance

Knowledge of temperament differences enhances the clinician's effectiveness in three principal ways. First, it is valuable simply for him to be aware that these differences exist and to discuss this fact with parents. For example, one can point out to parents that some normal children are highly active; this trait does not have to mean the child is brain-injured or overstimulated.

Second, it is sometimes(but not always)helpful for the clinician to be able to define in detail the temperament characteristics of a particular child. Experience has taught us that general impressions offered us by parents are often distorted by such influences as social desirability. On the other hand, clinicians' diagnoses based on extensive behavioral descriptions from interviews or questionnaires are less likely to be so affected. With such detailed information the clinician is in a much better position to facilitate the adjustment between the child's individual pattern and his handling, and to alleviate misplaced parental guilt and anxiety about the child. Labels should, of course, be avoided. In particular, parents need help in recognizing and understanding difficult temperament. Parents frequently blame difficult temperament in infants on food sensitivity or mistakes in their handling and are greatly relieved to know that the infant's behavior is not due to inadequate parenting. At later ages parents often confuse behavioral style with motivations and environmental effects, such as blaming low activity on laziness or vitamin deficiency.

Third, significant relationships have been demonstrated between temperament and a number of areas of clinical concern. Several conditions, once thought to be entirely due to organic or environmental factors, now appear to have important temperamental components. Several other areas are under investigation as likely possibilities for finding further involvement of temperament. The final section of this chapter reviews what recent research has told us about the importance of temperament–environment interactions for child health and development. Clinical areas to be considered are: (1) behavior problems, (2) colic and night waking, (3) accidents and illnesses, (4) developmental delay, and (5) school problems.

1. *Behavior problems.* The important work of Thomas *et al.* (1968) has convinced most researchers in the field that certain temperamental patterns, particularly that of the difficult child, predispose children to behavior problems, often requiring professional intervention. While McNeil (unpublished) has prepared an analysis of the methodological problems in the NYLS, the study stands undiminished as a major milestone in child psychiatry. Two later projects by Graham *et al.* (1973) and McInerny and Chamberlin (1978), while smaller and less elegant in execution, are supportive in their conclusions. Broussard (1976) found that firstborn infants rated by their mothers as not better than average at 1 month were more likely to develop "mental disorder" up till 10–11 years later. She attributed this difference to maternal expectations and mentioned only in passing "the unique personality characteristics of the neonate."

From this work the clinician in primary care may conclude that certain children can be identified as having temperamental patterns putting them at risk, and that, when problems in behavior occur, the child's temperament should be considered among the contributing factors. However, it must be stressed that it is the quality of the parent–child interaction, rather than the characteristics of either alone, that determines the child's behavioral outcome.

As we gain additional experience with children of varying ages, we are discovering that what parents regard as difficult temperament may change at a different developmental stage. In the period of 1–3 years mothers who judged their children overall to be more difficult than average at the end of the questionnaire also rated them on the questionnaire itself with four of the five component characteristics of the difficult-child syndrome. However, at 4–8 months mothers' estimates of difficulty in their babies were correlated with negative mood, high activity, and low distractibility (soothability) (Carey & McDevitt, 1978a). By 3–7 years certainly rhythmicity has become unimportant as a component of difficulty but low persistence and high activity have assumed greater significance, at least with teachers (Carey *et al.*, 1979).

Recent disclosures from other caretaking settings should caution us to remember that what is difficult for middle-class American parents may not be of such consequence in other cultural groups. Korn with Puerto Ricans in New York and Super in rural Kenya (Wilson & Matheny, 1980) found difficult infants less likely to develop problems in behavior, apparently due to the greater flexibility of those environments.

Nevertheless, for clinicians in the mainstream of American culture several management questions remain.

(a) What does one do when an infant or child is identified by a questionnaire as difficult? If there is stress in the interaction, then some sort of intervention is called for. If, however, as often happens, the parents are not complaining about an infant whom they have rated as difficult, the course is less clear. Certainly the clinician must be especially attentive to subsequent signals of distress in this latter sort of relationship, but it would seem unwise to burden parents with an unflattering label and gloomy predictions. For this reason one must doubt the value of programs screening for temperamental characteristics if the objective is the early labeling of difficult infants. A more useful strategy at this time would be to investigate why these parents are not reporting discomfort in the interaction. Is it inexperience, denial, or successful coping?

In considering the parents' response to the child's temperament, we should bear in mind the experience of Thomas and Chess (1977) that it is "determined not so much by the degree of congruence with their own personality characteristics as by the consonance with their goals, standards and values."

(b) How does one decide when a child with difficult temperament has developed a behavior problem? In the extreme case this is not a complex task, but how should one deal with a child who, for example, is rather domineering with his playmates? Is this low adaptability or a behavior problem? Perhaps the line as been crossed when the child is experiencing chronic isolation from peers because the low adaptability has led to the expression of an excess of aggressive or withdrawing behavior.

(c) Is the continuation of difficult temperament from infancy to childhood a sign of unsuccessful handling by the parents or of especially unmodifiable characteristics in the child? We really do not know, although there is evidence that the very active and negative difficult infants are more likely to remain difficult into early childhood (Carey & McDevitt, 1978b).

(d) If difficult temperament leads to the development of a true behavior problem, how does this affect the forms and goals of psychotherapy? Even with successful psychiatric intervention one might expect that the child would still be difficult. Should not the objective be not only to alter the parent–child relationship so that the child's reactive symptoms disappear, but also to help parents and teachers become more tolerant and flexible with the less modifiable temperamental characteristics?

2. *Colic and night waking.* Two disturbances of physiological function in the first year of life have been shown (among other factors) to be related to the child's temperament. Both colic in the first 4 months (Carey, 1972) and night waking between 6 and 12 months (Carey, 1974) occurred more often in infants with a low sensory threshold. Colic was also seen more in difficult infants (Carey, 1972). Although these two problems in interaction have a major environmental stimulation component (Carey, 1968, 1974; Pruett & Leonard, 1978) and effective management lies mainly in decreasing the inappropriate sensory input, knowledge of the temperamental predisposition provides a valuable perspective that shifts part of the responsibility off the parents. Also, the use of sedation for a week or so becomes theoretically sound in that it can be thought of as raising the sensory threshold temporarily while the parents learn better interaction patterns.

If these predisposing characteristics were clearly detectable in the newborn infant, extra effort might be invested in the prevention of these problems. Primary health care personnel should understand that infants are not uniformly excitable or soothable.

3. *Accidents and illness.* Blame for childhood accidents has traditionally fallen on inattentive parents or social stress in the family and child (Padilla, Rohsenow, & Bergman, 1976). However, two reports have offered a different view that the behavioral style of the child may be equally important. Difficult infants in a pediatric practice population sustained lacerations requiring sutures in their first two years significantly more often than easy ones (Carey, 1972). The Louisville Twin Study had similar conclusions about accidents (Matheny, Brown, & Wilson, 1971). A recent analysis of 105 children under age 5 with accidental poisoning revealed them to be "more anxious, harder and more active than controls" (Sibert and Newcombe, 1977). Also, difficult infants in the same pediatric practice had more physician visits for any sort of illness or injury in the first two years, although this does not necessarily mean that they had more illnesses or injuries (Carey in Wilson & Matheny, 1980).

These findings may help toward an understanding of how the accidents occurred. One is puzzled, however, as to how to derive from these data a new plan for accident prevention. We might give extra instructions to the parents of difficult infants but with care to avoid dangerous labeling that might lead to self-fulfilling prophecies. If high activity should emerge as a predisposing factor in accidents, there are available behavioral methods for coping with that (Schmitt, 1977).

Acute minor illness management may be clarified by physicians and parents realizing that certain children tend to be rather disagreeable when ill and cause their parents to worry more and consult doctors excessively. For example, one wonders whether a difficult child with acute abdominal pain is not more likely to have his appendix removed than a more quiet, agreeable child with the same illness. Such fussy children should properly receive more patient home care and fewer concerned trips to the doctor. On the other hand, it may turn out that difficult infants and children actually do have more nontraumatic illnesses.

An important area awaiting study is the possible effect of temperament on the outcome of various illnesses, especially major and chronic ones. For example, do more adaptable and persistent children master rehabilitative measures more rapidly?

4. *Developmental delay.* The age of achievement of developmental milestones appears to reflect not only inborn potential and environmental stimulation but also to a minor degree some temperament variables, that is, differences in the style of utilization of experience. Escalona (1968) demonstrated how high activity tends to accelerate development presumably because the active infant stimulates himself. Active infants in a pediatric practice study were walking more often at one year and persistent infants talking more (Carey, 1972). Matheny and Brown (1971) also observed earlier walking in the more active of twins. Lewis (1977) reported that activity and approach enhanced social interaction in preschool children and low sensory threshold made them more isolated and restrained. Certainly there must be other correlations one could discover rather easily, such as adaptability with age of toilet training.

This information, while far from conclusive or complete, is of value to the clinician in that it demonstrates that temperament sometimes may provide an explanation other than organic or environmental factors as to why a child may be late in achieving certain milestones.

5. *School performance.* A child's performance at school is presently explained in terms of his past experience, neurological status, intelligence, and emotional adjustment, but a growing body of evidence is substantiating the view that the child's temperament must also be considered. Gordon and Thomas (1967) demonstrated that the charac-

teristics of approach and adaptability in children affect their teachers' judgments of their intelligence. Chess, Thomas, and Cameron (1976) established that the same two traits correlated significantly with higher academic achievement scores regardless of ratings on intelligence tests. Teacher judgments of school adjustment were related to the pupils' adaptability in a recent study by Carey, Fox, and McDevitt (1977). Finally, in a group of 30 children referred to a pediatric neurologist by schools and given by him a diagnosis of "minimal brain dysfunction" by present standards, the most common characteristic was low adaptability (Carey et al., 1979). Twenty-six out of 30 were low and 16 out of 30 were very low.

Low persistence (or attention span) emerged in the school adjustment study as related to errors in the Matching Familiar Figures Test (along with low adaptability) and as the second most common characteristic in the "MBD" group. One should take special notice of the fact that distractibility failed to achieve significance in all of these investigations and activity only in the "MBD" group.

An illustrative example may be useful at this point. Two years ago the mother of an 8-year-old boy reported to me that he was intelligent enough and doing well in school but that the teacher had just upset her by expressing concern that he was a "loner" and would not follow instructions. Reference to his office records reminded me that both at 6 months and 7 years the mother had rated him with a slow-to-warm-up profile on temperament questionnaires. Further discussion revealed that the real problem was his balking only at new tasks. It became clear that this was a matter of behavioral style rather than a behavior problem. We agreed that both parents and teacher should be sympathetic in these new situations, but should encourage him to take over increasingly for himself the job of meeting novelty without negative withdrawal. A year later, in the course of a visit for strep throat, I learned that he was still similar in his behavioral style but was regarded as more mature and happier.

Therefore, when children are having problems in school adjustment and academic achievement, behavioral style must be taken into consideration along with the usual factors. If preschool testing of children is undertaken, perhaps it should include an evaluation of temperamental characteristics, particularly adaptability and persistence (or attention span), but such an innovation should be carefully weighed before inauguration.

There are several additional clinical problems in which it seems likely that a temperament–environment interaction will become evident with further scrutiny:

1. *Child abuse* is usually attributed to various personality problems in the parents and to social pressures impinging upon them. Only a

few reviews have recognized that sometimes the child may have characteristics that attract or provoke parental wrath and no published study has yet investigated this possibility prospectively (Friedrich & Boriskin, 1976). It seems that a difficult child would be more likely than an easy one to become the victim of potentially abusing parents.

2. Nonorganic *failure-to-thrive* is presently viewed as the result of a deficit in mothering (Rutter, 1972), yet there may be some infants who are more vulnerable than others. Schaffer (1966) thought it might be the less active infants, but perhaps it is rather the less demanding, easy ones who are least likely to get attention and nourishment in a setting of deprivation and most likely, therefore, to grow and develop poorly. Korner (1971) suggested also the possible importance of a high sensory threshold.

3. *Obesity* is generally agreed upon as resulting from an imbalance of caloric intake over energy expenditure. There is evidence both of genetic and psychosocial factors in its etiology (Weil, 1977). Since the genetic factor has not been shown to be a difference in metabolism in most cases, it seems plausible that predisposing behavioral characteristics may be responsible. It is frequently observed that obese children are less active than others, but we need to know whether they were also less active before they became overweight.

4. *Psychosomatic disorders,* such as functional abdominal pain, are thought to occur in children with some sort of physiological weakness who become involved in parental conflict or stress. Minuchin, Baker, Rosman, Liebman, Milman, & Todd (1975) spoke of "psychosomatic families," in which such problems are likely to occur.

The possible physiological weaknesses are poorly understood, but not likely to be as general a phenomenon as the "neurovegetative dystonia" mentioned in the European pediatric textbooks (Peltonen & Hirvonen, 1971). More plausible is the example of the theory of a specific underlying altered respiratory physiology in children who become asthmatics (Leffert, 1978).

We should consider the possibility of temperamental predispositions as well, not in terms of a "psychosomatic child" but as a variety of patterns that tend toward a variety of symptoms. Apley (1975) described children with functional abdominal pain as "highly strung, fussy, excitable, anxious, timid or apprehensive. Most gave an impression of over-conscientiousness, as did many of their parents." Kaffman and Elizur (1977) depicted the behavior of children who later became enuretic as being active and aggressive, and also as showing a "low level of adjustment to new situations and routines . . . and lack of aversion to urine contact and to wetness." Further studies of these problems and others involving children with functional constipation, peptic ulcer, bronchial asthma, high blood pressure, etc., are awaited.

Thus, much needs to be done to clarify the additional clinical issues just mentioned. The more established relationships described earlier must be studied further to consolidate them and elaborate our understanding of them. With the recent development of more competent instruments for clinical and research study of temperament, we can look forward to an accelerated pace in the expansion of our knowledge of the clinical importance of temperament–environment interactions.

SUMMARY

This chapter has reviewed current evidence as to the origins, stability, and clinical importance of temperament differences in children. Temperament is defined as behavioral style. The possible means of measurement are by parent interviews or questionnaires or by observations of the child. A recently devised set of questionnaires offers the best combination of simplicity and psychometric sophistication.

Temperament characteristics seem to be derived from genetic, intrauterine, and postnatal environmental factors but at present show little consistent effects from perinatal complications or confirmed brain dysfunction. These traits are not completely fixed at any point, but their stability has been established to a greater degree as better instruments have been used and the same variables measured.

Temperament–environment interactions appear to play a contributing role in behavior problems, the physiological disturbances of colic and night waking, the incidence of accidents and illness visits, minor developmental delay, and school performance. They seem likely to be involved also in child abuse, failure-to-thrive, obesity, and other psychosomatic problems.

ACKNOWLEDGMENT

I wish to thank my associate, Sean C. McDevitt, Ph.D., for his assistance in reviewing this chapter.

NOTE: The four temperament questionnaires may be obtained from the following sources:

Infant Temperament Questionnaire (for 4–8 months) from William B. Carey, M.D., 319 West Front Street, Media, Pa. 19063.
Toddler Temperament Scale (for 1–3 years)—see Fullard et al., 1978.

Behavioral Style Questionnaire (for 3–7 years) from Sean C. McDevitt, Ph.D., Devereux Center, 6436 E. Sweetwater, Scottsdale, AZ 85254.

Middle Childhood Temperament Questionnaire (for 8–12 years)—see Hegvik *et al.*, 1980.

Since these instruments were developed without any grant support, please send a contribution of $5 for each instrument to cover expenses.

REFERENCES

Als, H., Tronick, E., Adamson, L., & Brazelton, T. B. The behavior of the full-term but underweight newborn infant. *Developmental Medicine and Child Neurology,* 1976, *18,* 590–602.

Ananth, J. Side effects in the neonate from psychotropic agents excreted through breast feedings. *American Journal of Psychiatry,* 1978, *135,* 801–805.

Apley, J. *The child with abdominal pains* (2nd ed.). Oxford: Blackwell Scientific Publications, 1975.

Baron, J. Temperament profile of children with Down's Syndrome. *Developmental Medicine and Child Neurology,* 1972, *14,* 640–643.

Bates, J.E., Freeland, C.A.B., & Lounsbury, M.L. Measurement of infant difficultness. *Child Development,* 1979, *50,* 794–803.

Bell, R.Q., Weller, G.M., & Waldrop, M.F. Newborn and pre-schooler: Organization of behavior and relations between periods. *Monographs of the Society for Research in Child Development,* 1971, *36* (Nos. 1–2, Serial No. 142).

Berberian, K.E. *Infants' reactions to strangers. The effects of memory development and temperament.* Unpublished doctoral dissertation, Bryn Mawr College, 1979.

Billman, J., & McDevitt, S.C. Convergence of parent and observer ratings of temperament with observations of peer interaction in nursery school. *Child Development,* 1980, *51,* 395–400.

Birns, B., Barten, S., & Bridger, W.H. Individual differences in temperamental characteristics of infants. *Transactions of the New York Academy of Sciences,* 1969, *31,* 1071–1082.

Bronson, W.C. Central orientations: A study of behavior organization from childhood to adolescence. *Child Development,* 1966, *37,* 125–155.

Broussard, E.R. Neonatal predictions and outcome at 10–11 years. *Child Psychiatry and Human Development,* 1976, *7,* 85–93.

Buss, A.H., & Plomin, R. *A temperament theory of personality development.* New York: Wiley, 1975.

Cadoret, R.J., Cunningham, L., Loftus, R., & Edwards, J. Studies of adoptees from psychiatrically disturbed biologic parents. *Journal of Pediatrics,* 1975, *87,* 301–306.

Cameron, J.R. Parental treatment, children's temperament, and the risk of childhood behavioral problems. *American Journal of Orthopsychiatry,* 1977, *47,* 568–576.

Campbell, S.D. Maternal and infant behavior in normal, high risk, and "difficult" infants. Paper presented at biennial meeting of the Society for Research in Child Development, New Orleans, March, 1977.

Carey, W.B. Maternal anxiety and infantile colic. *Clinical Pediatrics,* 1968, *7,* 590–595.

Carey, W.B. A simplified method for measuring infant temperament. *Journal of Pediatrics,* 1970, *77,* 188–194.

Carey, W.B. Clinical applications of infant temperament measurements. *Journal of Pediatrics,* 1972, *81,* 823–828.

Carey, W.B. Night waking and temperament in infancy. *Journal of Pediatrics,* 1974, *84,* 756–758.

Carey, W.B., & McDevitt, S.C. Revision of the Infant Temperament Questionnaire. *Pediatrics*, 1978a, *61*, 735–739.

Carey, W.B., & McDevitt, S.C. Stability and change in individual temperament diagnoses from infancy to early childhood. *Journal of the American Academy of Child Psychiatry*, 1978b, *17*, 331–337.

Carey, W.B., & McDevitt, S.C. M.B.D. and hyperkinesis. A clinical viewpoint. *American Journal of Diseases in Children*, 1980, *134*, in press.

Carey, W.B., Lipton, W.L., & Myers, R.A. Temperament in adopted and foster babies. *Child Welfare*, 1974, *53*, 352–359.

Carey, W.B., Fox, M., & McDevitt, S.C. Temperament as a factor in early school adjustment. *Pediatrics*, 1977, *60* (suppl.), 621–624.

Carey, W.B., McDevitt, S.C., & Baker, D. Differentiating minimal brain dysfunction and temperament. *Developmental Medicine and Child Neurology*, 1979, *21*, 765–772.

Chavez, A., Martinez, C., & Yaschine, T. The importance of nutrition and stimuli in child mental and social development. In J. Cravioto, L. Hambraeus, & B. Valquist (Eds.), *Early malnutrition and mental development*. Uppsala: Almquist & Wiksell, 1974.

Chess, S., & Korn, S. Temperament and behavior disorders in mentally retarded children. *Archives of General Psychiatry*, 1970, *23*, 122–130.

Chess, S., & Thomas, A. Temperamental individuality from childhood to adolescence. *Journal of the American Academy of Child Psychiatry*, 1977, *16*, 218–226.

Chess, S., Korn, S., & Fernandez, P. *Psychiatric disorders in children with congenital rubella*. New York: Brunner/Mazel, 1971.

Chess, S., Thomas, A., & Cameron, M. Temperament: Its significance for school adjustment and academic achievement. *New York University Educational Review*, 1976, *7*, 24–29.

Childs, B. Sir Archibald Garrod's conception of chemical individuality. A modern appreciation. *The New England Journal of Medicine*, 1970, *282*, 71–77.

Clements, S.D. *Minimal brain dysfunction in children* (NINDS Monograph No. 3, U.S. Public Health Service Publication No. 1415). Washington, D.C.: U.S. Government Printing Office, 1966.

Escalona, S. *The roots of individuality*. Chicago: Aldine Publishing Co., 1968.

Feingold, B.F. *Why your child is hyperactive*. New York: Random House, 1975.

Field, T., Dabiri, C., Hallock, N., & Shuman, H.H. Developmental effects of prolonged pregnancy and postmaturity syndrome. *Journal of Pediatrics*, 177, *90*, 836–839.

Freedman, D.G., & Freedman, N.C. Behavioral differences between Chinese-American and European-American newborns. *Nature*, 1969, *224*, 1227.

Friedrich, W.N., & Boriskin, J.A. The role of the child in abuse: A review of the literature. *American Journal of Orthopsychiatry*, 1976, *46*, 580–590.

Fullard, W., McDevitt, S.C., & Carey, W.B. *Toddler Temperament Scale*, 1978. (Unpublished test form, available from William Fullard, Ph.D., Dept. of Educational Psychology, Temple University, Philadelphia, PA 19122. Please send $5 to cover costs.)

Garside, R.F., Birch, H.G., Scott, D.M., Chambers, S., Kolvin, I., Tweedle, E.G., & Barber, L.M. Dimensions of temperament in infant school children. *Journal of Child Psychology and Psychiatry*, 1975, *16*, 219–231.

Gordon, E.M., & Thomas, A. Children's behavioral style and the teacher's appraisal of their intelligence. *Journal of School Psychology*, 1967, *5*, 292–300.

Graham, P., Rutter, M., & George, S. Temperamental characteristics as predictors of behavior disorders of children. *American Journal of Orthopsychiatry*, 1973, *43*, 328–339.

Hegvik, R., McDevitt, S.C., & Carey, W.B. *Middle Childhood Temperament Questionnaire*,

1980. (Unpublished test form, available from Ms. Robin L. Hegvik, 307 North Wayne Avenue, Wayne, PA 19087. Please send $5 to cover costs.)

Hertzig, M. Personal communication, in Thomas, A., & Chess, S., *Temperament and Development*. New York: Brunner/Mazel, 1977.

Hindley, C.B., & Owen, C.F. The extent of individual changes in I.Q. for ages between 6 months and 17 years, in a British longitudinal sample. *Journal of Child Psychology and Psychiatry*, 1978, *19*, 329–350.

Hutt, C. Biological bases of psychological sex differences. *American Journal of Diseases in Children*, 1978, *132*, 170–177.

Huttunen, M.O., & Niskanen, P. Prenatal loss of father and psychiatric disorders. *Archives of General Psychiatry*, 1978, *35*, 429–431.

Kaffman, M., & Elizur, E. Infants who become enuretics: A longitudinal study of 161 kibbutz children. *Monographs of the Society for Research in Child Development*, 1977, *42* (No. 2., Serial No. 170).

Kolata, G.B. Behavioral teratology: Birth defects of the mind. *Science*, 1978, *202*, 732–734.

Korner, A.F. Individual differences at birth: Implications for early experience and later development. *American Journal of Orthopsychiatry*, 1971, *41*, 608–619.

Leffert, F. Asthma: A modern perspective. *Pediatrics*, 1978, *62*, 1061–1069.

Lewis, J.L. The relation of individual temperament to initial social behavior. In R.C. Smart & M.S. Smart (Eds.), *Readings in child development and relationships*. New York: Macmillan, 1977.

Littman, B., & Parmelee, A.H., Jr. Medical correlates of infant development. *Pediatrics*, 1978, *61*, 470–474.

Lytton, H. Do parents create, or respond to, differences in twins? *Developmental Psychology*, 1977, *5*, 456–459.

Maccoby, E.E., & Jacklin, C.N. *The psychology of sex differences*. Stanford, Ca.: Stanford University Press, 1974.

Matheny, A.P., Jr., & Brown, A.M. Activity, motor coordination and attention: Individual differences in twins. *Perceptual and Motor Skills*, 1971, *32*, 151–158.

Matheny, A.P., Jr., Brown, A.M., & Wilson, R.S. Behavioral antecedents of accidental injuries in early childhood: A study of twins. *Journal of Pediatrics*, 1971, *79*, 122–124.

McDevitt, S.C. *A longitudinal assessment of continuity and stability in temperamental characteristics from infancy to early childhood*. Unpublished doctoral dissertation, Temple University, 1976.

McDevitt, S.C., & Carey, W.B. The measurement of temperament in 3–7 year old children. *Journal of Child Psychology and Psychiatry*, 1978, *19*, 245–253.

McDevitt, S.C., & Carey, W.B. Stability of ratings vs. perceptions of temperament from early infancy to 1–3 years. *American Journal of Orthopsychiatry*, in press.

McInerny, T.K., & Chamberlin, R.W. Is it feasible to identify infants who are at risk for later behavior problems? *Clinical Pediatrics*, 1978, *17*, 233–238.

McNeil, T.F. Temperament revisited: A research-oriented critique of the New York Longitudinal Study of Temperament. Unpublished manscript.

Minuchin, S., Baker, L., Rosman, B.L., Liebman, R., Milman, L., & Todd, T.C. A conceptual model of psychosomatic illness in children. *Archives of General Psychiatry*, 1975, *32*, 1031–1038.

Needleman, H.L., Gunnoe, C., Leviton, A., Reed, R., Peresie, H., Maher, C., & Barrett, P. Deficits in psychologic and classroom performance of children with elevated dentine lead levels. *The New England Journal of Medicine*, 1979, *300*, 689–695.

Padilla, E.R., Rohsenow, D.J., & Bergman, A.B. Predicting accident frequency in children. *Pediatrics*, 1976, *58*, 223–226.

Parmelee, A.H., Jr. Remarks on receiving the C. Anderson Aldrich Award. *Pediatrics*, 1977, *59*, 389–395.

Passamanick, B., & Knobloch, H. Retrospective studies in the epidemiology of reproductive casualty: Old and new. *Merrill-Palmer Quarterly of Behavioral Development*, 1966, *12*, 7–26.

Peltonen, T., & Hirvonen, L. Why close our eyes to neurovegetative dystonia? *Clinical Pediatrics*, 1971, *10*, 299–302.

Persson-Blennow, I., & McNeil, T.F. A questionnaire for measurement of temperament in six-month-old infants: Development and standardization. *Journal of Child Psychology and Psychiatry*, 1979a, *20*, 1–13.

Persson-Blennow, I., & McNeil, T.F. Personal communication, 1979b.

Plomin, R., & Rowe, D.C. A twin study of temperament in young children. *The Journal of Psychology*, 1977, *97*, 107–113.

Plomin, R., & Rowe, D.C. Genetic and environmental etiology of social behavior in infancy. *Developmental Psychology*, 1979, *15*, 62–72.

Pruett, K.D., & Leonard, M.F. The screaming baby. Treatment of psychophysiological disorder of infancy. *Journal of the American Academy of Child Psychiatry*, 1978, *17*, 289–298.

Rossetti Ferreira, M.C. Malnutrition and mother–infant asynchrony: Slow mental development. *International Journal of Behavioral Development*, 1978, *1*, 207–219.

Rutter, M. Psychological development: Predictions from infancy. *Journal of Child Psychology and Psychiatry*, 1970, *11*, 49–62.

Rutter, M. *Maternal deprivation reassessed*. Middlesex, England: Penguin Books 1972.

Rutter, M. Brain damage syndromes in childhood: Concepts and findings. *Journal of Child Psychology and Psychiatry*, 1977, *18*, 1–21.

Rutter, M., Korn, S., & Birch, H.G. Genetic and environmental factors in the development of "primary reaction patterns." *British Journal of Social and Clinical Psychology* 1963, *2*, 161–173.

Sameroff, A., & Kelly, P. Socio-economic status, racial and mental health factors in infant temperament. Unpublished manuscript, quoted in Thomas A., & Chess, S., *Temperament and Development*. New York: Brunner/Mazel, 1977.

Sarett, P.T. *A study of the interaction effects of infant temperament on maternal attachment*. Unpublished doctoral dissertation. Rutgers, The State University of New Jersey, 1976.

Scarr, S. Genetic factors in activity motivaton. *Child Development*, 1966, *37*, 663–673.

Scarr, S. Social introversion-extroversion as a heritable reponse. *Child Development*, 1969, *40*, 823–832.

Schaffer, H.R. Activity level as a constitutional determinant of infantile reaction to deprivation. *Child Development*, 1966, *37*, 595–602.

Schmitt, B. Guidelines for living with a hyperactive child. *Pediatrics*, 1977, *60*, 387.

Searls, E., Fullard, W., & McDevitt, S.C. Relationship between Infant Temperament Questionnaire ratings and observations during a short home visit. *Infant Behavior and Development*, in press.

Sibert, J.R., & Newcombe, R.G. Accidental ingestion of poisons and child personality. *Postgraduate Medical Journal*, 1977, *53*, 254–256.

Sostek, A.M., & Anders, T.F. Relationships among Brazelton Neonatal Scale, Bayley Infant Scales, and early temperament. *Child Development*, 1977, *48*, 320–323.

Streissguth, A.P. Maternal drinking and the outcome of pregnancy: Implications for child mental health. *American Journal of Orthopsychiatry*, 1977, *47*, 422–431.

Strelau, J. The temperament inventory: A Pavlovian typology approach. Unpublished manuscript, Institute of Psychology, University of Warsaw, Poland, 1980.

Thomas, A., & Chess, S. *Temperament and Development*, New York: Brunner/Mazel, 1977.

Thomas, A., Chess, S., Birch, H.G., Hertzig, M.E., & Korn, S. *Behavioral individuality in early childhood*. New York: New York University Press, 1963.

Thomas, A., Chess, S., & Birch, H.G. *Temperament and behavior disorders in children*. New York: New York University Press, 1968.

Thomas, A., Chess, S. & Birch, H.G. The origin of personality. *Scientific American*, 1970, *223*, 102–109.

Torgersen, A.M., & Kringlen, E. Genetic aspects of temperamental differences in infants. *Journal of the American Academy of Child Psychiatry*, 1978, *17*, 433–444.

Ucko, L.E. A comparative study of asphyxiated and non-asphyxiated boys from birth to five years.*Developmental Medicine and Child Neurology*, 1965, *7*, 643–657.

Waldrop, M.F., Pedersen, F.A., & Bell, R.Q. Minor physical anomalies and behavior in preschool children. *Child Development*, 1968, *39*, 391–400.

Walzer, S., Wolff, P.H., Bowen, S., Silbert, A.R., Bashir, A.S., Gerald, P.S., & Richmond, J.B. A method for the longitudinal study of behavioral development in infants and children: The early development of XXY children. *Journal of Child Psychology and Psychiatry*, 1978, *19*, 213–229.

Weil, W.B., Jr. Current controversies in childhood obesity. *Journal of Pediatrics*, 1977, *91*, 175–187.

Wender, E.H. Food additives and hyperkinesis. *American Journal of Diseases in Children*, 1977, *131*, 1204–1206.

Wilson, G.S., McCreary, R., Kean, J., & Baxter, J.C. The development of preschool children of heroin-addicted mothers: A controlled study. *Pediatrics*, 1979, *63*, 135–141.

Wilson, R.S., Brown, A.M., & Matheny, A.P., Jr. Emergence and persistence of behavioral difference in twins. *Child Development*, 1971, *42*, 1381–1398.

Wilson, R.S., & Matheny, A.P., Jr. Conference on Temperance Research. Abstracts of presentations. *JSAS Catalog of Selected Documents in Psychology*, 1980, *10* (10) (Ms. No. 1978).

Zinkus, P.W., Gottlieb, M.I., & Schapiro, M. Developmental and psychoeducational sequelae of chronic otitis media. *American Journal of Diseases in Children*, 1978, *132*, 1100–1104.

4

The Uncommonly Bright Child

HALBERT B. ROBINSON

Most of the attention of professionals who deal with children has been directed toward those with problems, ranging from mild to severe. When we speak of children who deviate significantly from the average and are thus uncommon in some way or another, we almost always refer to those whose behaviors we want to "normalize," to change for the better. Having been involved in programs of remediation, I have some familiarity with the values and rewards as well as the discouraging aspects of such efforts.

However, I would like to turn now to questions concerning children who are "uncommon" because they are extraordinarily adept or talented in some respect, or have exceptional potential to produce something of great value. These are the children who are "at risk for greatness." The ways in which they differ from others is, in general, something we want to nurture rather than minimize. As clinicians and educators, we are concerned with identifying such children and promoting their healthy development. As researchers, we are presented with a virtually untapped realm of inquiry that may produce findings with important implications for our theories of cognitive growth and our understanding of the relationships among physical, social–emotional, and cognitive aspects of development.

HALBERT B. ROBINSON • Child Development Research Group, Department of Psychology, University of Washington, Seattle, Washington 98195. Research supported in part by grants from the Spencer Foundation and the Ford Foundation. Many of the analyses upon which this paper is based were done by my colleagues in the Child Development Research Group, notably Nancy Jackson, Wendy Roedell, and Charles Stillman.

THE RESEARCH BASE

In contrast with other areas of psychology, knowledge about the development of intellectually gifted individuals is based on work accomplished in the first half of this century. Little new information has accrued since the findings of studies begun more than 50 years ago. Existing knowledge about the characteristics of children with superior intellectual abilities is, in fact, based to a very large extent on the work of Lewis Terman, in particular his monumental *Genetic Studies of Genius* initiated in 1921 (Burks, Jensen, & Terman, 1930; Cox, 1926; Oden, 1968; Terman, 1925; Terman & Oden, 1947, 1959). This longitudinal study of approximately 1500 individuals, most of whom were identified when they were school children, continues to the present day (P.S. Sears & Barbee, 1977; R.R. Sears, 1977). Terman and his colleagues demonstrated that superior intelligence, indicated by superior performance on a standardized test, is associated with a high degree of academic and vocational–professional success, and with a degree of personal and social adjustment which equals or exceeds that of the population at large. These conclusions have been confirmed by a large number of more recent, smaller-scale studies (Gallagher, 1975; U.S. Office of Education, 1972). Indeed, Getzels and Dillon have noted that "research into intellectual giftedness continues to identify and describe high IQ children, confirming Terman's findings with a regularity bordering on redundancy" (1973, p. 34).

Terman began his investigations at a time when gifted individuals were thought to suffer from an affliction of mysterious origin. He was rightly convinced that the prevailing notions about intellectual precocity were largely myths—that such individuals were *not*, as a group, physically inadequate, social misfits, or prone to insanity, and that the early ripening of their talents did not lead to the early rotting of their psyches. His findings had a very salutary effect in laying to rest these strongly entrenched folk beliefs.

There were, however, a number of shortcomings in the Terman studies (see, e.g., Hughes & Converse, 1962). The sample was a biased one; schools in economically poorer neighborhoods were inadequately canvassed, and most of the children accepted for individual testing were nominated by teachers. Furthermore, Terman tended to treat the sample as a homogeneous group, ignoring the wide range of individual differences on all dimensions, including the cognitive. He also probably tended to exaggerate his major conclusion that high-IQ children are superior in almost all respects and to gloss over the fact that intellectually advanced children do not develop equally well under all circumstances. Even so, the directions proposed by Terman were very much needed in his day, were generally sound, and continue to dominate the field more than half a century after he initiated them. Indeed, most of his findings have held up remarkably well through numerous replications.

It can be said, then, that we possess a fair amount of descriptive longitudinal data about the development of brighter individuals who were doing relatively well when identified in middle childhood. There is much, however, that we do not know. We still know practically nothing, for example, about the development of such individuals during infancy and early childhood. We have little insight into the emergence of various "gifts," or into the fate of those children who seem remarkable when very young but are not so identified later on. Furthermore, our grasp of the intellectual, personal, and social differences within and between groups of gifted persons is completely insufficient.

We have undergone a period of rapid expansion of knowledge in many areas of psychology during a time of virtual standstill in the scientific study of intellectually gifted individuals. We know a great deal more now about basic cognitive processes, for example, and we are possessed of much more sophisticated theories of learning and cognitive development. In many respects, though, most psychological researchers have for the past thirty years or more turned away from an interest in individual differences while they have centered upon specialized theories and specific psychological phenomena.

The single major group which has been approached from a point of view which has emphasized individual differences is that diverse population of individuals who are mentally handicapped in one way or another. For the most part, the descriptive–normative approach to cognitive, motivational, and interpersonal processes, yielding not only means but standard deviations, has otherwise fallen out of favor. It is a perplexing commentary on the state of the art in psychology and education that during the past two or three decades of unprecedented scientific inquiry we have been content to remain with the cognitive measures developed by our old mentors, Alfred Binet, Lewis Terman, and David Wechsler, while we have proceeded to pioneer new frontiers in many areas of lesser importance.

The time appears ripe, as we enter the 1980s, for a new wave of research concerned with individual differences in a variety of functions, particularly intelligence. It would be highly advantageous, I suspect, to apply the insights of the past several decades to that group of individuals who are in one way or another superior in mental functioning. We are now in a much better position than were Terman and his followers to investigate the precise ways in which gifted children and adults deviate from the average and differ among themselves. We can, for example, look for possible qualitative differences in the organization of their mental abilities; examine the strategies they use to process, store, and retrieve information; investigate the processes and formulations they employ in solving problems of various kinds; and so on. Such research could, of course, yield insights into the nature of normal as well as unusual development. We might, moreover, discover better ways to identify, nurture, and support important gifts and thus benefit the individuals who possess them as well as the society as a whole.

THE UNIVERSITY OF WASHINGTON CHILD DEVELOPMENT RESEARCH GROUP

A research and service project focused upon gifted children was initiated at the University of Washington in 1974. Our interest was in the identification and nurturance of very young, highly precocious infants and preschool children. It soon became obvious that the needs of this population were great, much greater indeed than we had anticipated. Within days of the first inconspicuous announcement of the study in a local newspaper, more than 300 families had contacted us. Approximately one-half of these returned a lengthy questionnaire concerned with their children's intellectual development. Almost 100 of these families had children in the age range from 2 to 5 years, and approximately 1 in 10 of their children performed at an extraordinarily advanced level in some cognitive domain and/or achieved a Stanford-Binet IQ at least 4 standard deviations above the mean (IQ 164+).

During subsequent years we have refined our criteria and have added to our sample. By the spring of 1979, we had tested a total of 509 children who were thought by their parents to be very intelligent. Approximately one-half of these were identified as very intelligent, i.e., they scored among the top 1% of their age mates when they were 2, 3, 4, or 5 years old. Of this group, a total of 84 were assessed as "highly gifted"; i.e., they exhibited at least one cognitive skill (e.g., verbal reasoning, spatial reasoning, short-term memory, reading, or mathematics) at a level expected of children twice their age, and/or they attained a Stanford–Binet IQ of 164 or above.

Some characteristics of the sample are listed in Table 1. The families come from many segments of the population, though there is a strong overrepresentation of middle-class parents. About one-fifth of the families are from racial minorities. Most of the children in our

TABLE 1. CHARACTERISTICS OF THE LONGITUDINAL SAMPLE OF PRECOCIOUS YOUNG CHILDREN—1979

	Percentage of cases in	
	Entire sample[a] (N = 509)	Highly precocious group (N = 84)
Male	51.3	61.9
Female	48.7	38.1
Ethnic minority	20.5[b]	20.7
Firstborn	69.7	75.0
Mothers—college graduates or above	67.6	76.8
Fathers—college graduates or above	78.5	86.6

[a]This summary includes an estimated 25 cases that are no longer active. None of these are in the highly precocious group.
[b]This figure is estimated from data available for 91.9% of the total sample. All of the data are available for the highly precocious group.

sample are firstborn. The educational levels of parents of both the overall sample and the highly gifted subsample tend to be very high. Indeed, of the latter group, 25 fathers and 11 mothers hold a doctor's degree, whereas only one of these children comes from a family in which the father has only a high school diploma. Most of the children come from intact families.

We recognize, of course, the inherent biases of sample acquisition in studies such as ours. We rely on family initiative in contacting us. Simple logistics prohibit our trying to obtain a "representative" sample of gifted children. Perhaps as a reflection of this fact, the families with whom we interact are highly invested in the welfare of their children.

Almost all of the families have told us that they were surprised by their children's abilities. Most of the parents of the highly gifted group, in addition, admit to some ambivalence about the situation in which they find themselves. On the one hand, they are pleased with their children and proud of their extraordinary progress. On the other hand, they recognize and at times are concerned about the extra burdens they encounter as parents. They are, for example, frustrated by the dismal lack of resources which might provide appropriate learning experiences for their children. Public-school personnel typically indicate that they cannot handle their children but few appropriate private schools are available and all are expensive. Finally, many parents have been accused of bragging about their children, of pushing them and thus robbing them of their childhood. It is as though something has gone wrong for which some fault has to be assigned. Most parents tell us that they experienced a significant sense of relief when we objectively assessed their children's development, documented their special abilities and needs, and provided support for their efforts to cope with the challenge of providing for a child who does not fit the system.

In response to the intriguing research questions which developed as we began to work with these precocious children, as well as to the needs which their families expressed, our program has evolved and expanded. It was soon obvious that we could not simply identify extraordinarily gifted young people and then abandon them. We had somehow to try to support their development through the difficult formative years. The urgent requests of families with older gifted children with unmet needs also made an impact on our plans. As a result of complex forces, then, a comprehensive research and service program has emerged at the University of Washington. The activities of the Child Development Research Group now include:

1. The longitudinal study, which, as I have indicated, is concerned with the development of approximately 500 children identified when they were 2 to 5 years of age as being "at risk" for intellectual and/or academic precocity. This study, which began in 1974, is supported by the Spencer Foundation.

2. A preschool for 36 intellectually gifted preschool children, all of whom are included in the longitudinal study. This program, begun in 1976, has been supported in part by the Spencer Foundation and the U.S. Office of Education, as well as by parent fees.

3. A kindergarten-through-high-school program for children and young people exhibiting extraordinary advancement in academic skills. This Individual Progress Program (IPP) is run by the Seattle Public Schools in collaboration with the Child Development Research Group. It is designed for students who are achieving at least four grade levels beyond the grade appropriate for their age. Some of these children are included in the longitudinal study. Begun in 1978, the IPP currently serves 75 children, balanced for sex and reflecting the racial makeup of the Seattle population. Developmental funds have been supplied by an ESEA, Title 4-C award, but the program will function with a nonsupplemented allotment from the Seattle Public School District.

4. A program of early entrance to the University of Washington for youngsters below the age of 14 who are demonstrably ready for University work. Currently, 17 young people, ranging in age from 10 to 16 years, are enrolled, 9 of them as full-time and 8 as part-time students. It is expected that the Early Entrance Program (EEP) will expand to 40 full-time students during the next two years. This program, begun in 1977, is supported by the Ford Foundation; families are responsible for the usual tuition charges, fees, books, etc.

5. A diagnostic and counseling program for families who are

concerned about the personal, social, and academic progress of their intellectually advanced children. Approximately 60 families have been seen each year since 1977. The program is supported, in part, by the Ford Foundation.

Four Exceptional Children

The children with whom we have worked are an extremely diverse group who exhibit a variety of extraordinary talents. Some of them show startling skills in specific areas while others seem capable across-the-board. There is, then, no typical gifted child in our group. In an attempt, however, to impart a feel for our young subjects, we present thumbnail sketches of four of them. Michael and Susan were identified for the longitudinal study. Steven was first seen as a diagnostic and counseling case and is now a part of the EEP. Barbara was the first child identified for the EEP.

Michael is one of the most astonishing children we are following. We were contacted by his parents, both of whom have advanced professional degrees, when he was not quite 2 years old. They were distressed at not knowing how to respond to the very rapid development of their only child. When Michael was 2 years and 3 months old, the family visited our laboratory. At that time, they described a youngster who had begun speaking at age 5 months and by 6 months had exhibited a vocabulary of more than 50 words. He started to read English when he was 13 months old.

In our laboratory he spoke five languages and could read in three of them. He understood addition, subtraction, multiplication, division, and square root, and he was fascinated by a broad range of scientific constructs. He loved to make puns, frequently bilingual ones. He exhibited an uncanny directional sense and was able to use maps without difficulty. He located on a city map the block in which he lived, for example, and he easily found Seattle, New York, and other cities on a map of the U.S., in a regional atlas, and on a world globe. He had an intensely experimental attitude; he dropped a raisin and then climbed onto a stool to drop it again, for example, to see "if gravity works high up, too." Michael was a very active youngster in our laboratory, not especially interested in our tests, but he was eventually persuaded to try some items. On the Stanford–Binet at age 2 years, 3 months, the minimum estimate of his mental age was 4 years, 9 months. We listed him at that time as having an IQ in excess of 180.

Michael was again tested at age 4 years, 6 months. On the Stanford–Binet, he attained a mental age of 12 years, 1 month; the resulting IQ is in excess of 220. He attained a Basal at Year X, and earned credit even at the Average Adult level by correctly defining 20 vocabulary words. He was restless and playful, especially during verbal tasks which did not call for action responses, and it was the feeling of the examiner that he might well have succeeded at additional items. He repeated 9 digits forward and 5 backwards, and performed the Block Design subtest of the WISC-R on a par with children 10 years and 6 months old. On the Peabody Individual Achievement Test, Reading Recognition was at the 18-year-level, his Reading Comprehension at the 11-year level, his general information at the 12-year level, and his mathematical reasoning at the 10½-year level.

Michael is, indeed, a remarkable youngster with very special educational needs and a devoted but frustrated family. His parents have provided for his education as best they can. He has had tutors in foreign languages, mathematics, and some sciences. His father has worked with him on a broad range of subjects, always following Michael's lead and trying to maintain a comfortable pace. He has not been, as yet, in any formal educational program.

Susan's parents contacted the project in response to the initial newspaper announcement. They reported outstanding language skills, memory, and reading ability. When tested at age 2 years, 11 months, she attained a Mental Age of 6 years, 4 months on the Stanford–Binet, and an IQ in excess of 180. Susan's parents reported that she had spoken five-word sentences by the age of 20 months, and had begun reading at 2 years, 10 months. When we tested her academic skills at age 3 years, 11 months, she was reading at the third-grade level and demonstrated a knowledge of mathematical concepts at the first-grade level.

Susan attended the project's preschool for two years, and began kindergarten in our program. The staff was hard pressed to keep up with her extremely advanced skills and her incredible enthusiasm for learning. She was an active, vivacious, highly verbal child. By age 5, she was reading for pleasure advanced children's books such as *The Little House on the Prairie* series. Her parents reported that she had become good friends with the local librarian, whom she would visit on her own, riding the bicycle she had mastered at age 4. She enjoys creative writing; one of her poems won honorable mention in *Cricket* magazine.

When the family moved out of the state in the middle of her kindergarten year, they were understandably concerned about finding the right school for Susan. She was eventually placed in a first-grade classroom of a program for gifted children. When last tested at age 6 years, 5 months, Susan was reading at the sixth-grade level and her mathematics skills were at the seventh-grade level. She charmed the tester by dramatizing her definitions to the vocabulary items of the Stanford-Binet, which she passed at the Average Adult level by correctly defining 22 words. She attained a mental age of 12 years, 10 months, and an estimated IQ again in excess of 180.

Steven was recognized early as an obvious misfit in age-graded classes. He attended kindergarten at age 5 in a suburban school, followed by first grade in a private school for gifted children, and second grade back in his suburban neighborhood school. When he was 8 years old, school authorities advanced him to fifth grade and at 9 he began junior high school. At age 10 he entered the EEP, taking university courses in mathematics while simultaneously taking English and physical education courses at a junior high school and mathematics and science classes at a senior high school. He became a full-time university student during Summer, 1979, at which time he was 11 years old.

Steven was first seen as a Diagnostic and Counseling Center case at age 9 years, 0 months. His performance on the WISC-R was off scale; his mental age on the Stanford–Binet was 20 years, 6 months, yielding an IQ in excess of 200. When he was 9 years, 6 months old he was administered the Washington Pre-College Test and scored at the 85th percentile on verbal scales and at the 65th percentile on quantitative scales compared to high school juniors who subsequently attended four-year colleges. His SAT scores at age 9 years, 11 months were 630 on the M (mathematics) scale and 550 on the V (verbal) scale.

Steven is an extraordinarily well-adjusted and articulate, but rather quiet youngster, who is well liked by his classmates at all levels. His extracurricular interests tend to center around cars, engines, and electronic gadgets. He is poised and self-confident, able to hold his own in conversations with chronological-age peers as well as adults. He has had no difficulty in adjusting to college, either academically or socially. He has had several vexing problems, however; he still writes in block letters and finds it difficult to take notes, and his mother won't let him take the chemistry laboratory course because she feels it is too dangerous.

Barbara was always an exceptional student, but during elementary school there was little to challenge her. On the advice of her fifth-grade teacher, her parents enrolled her in a private school for gifted children, but even that school was soon outgrown. Barbara was seen when she was 12 years, 5 months old. On the Stanford–Binet and the WISC-R she exceeded the ceiling. On the Washington Pre-College Test she scored at the 90th percentile in the quantitative areas and at the 75th percentile in verbal areas when compared with high school juniors who subsequently entered four-year colleges in the State of Washington. On the SAT she scored 750 M and 630 V.

Every index indicated that Barbara was academically prepared for college. In Spring Quarter, 1977, she became one of the first two students admitted to the EEP, taking calculus and astronomy at the University while continuing full-time in the junior high school for gifted children. During the following year she attended a private high school, skipping one grade. She entered the University full-time in Summer, 1978. Currently a junior, she is taking honors courses in mathematics, physics, and literature and has earned a cumulative grade point average of 3.87. (Course grades are awarded in decimal gradations from 0.0 to 4.0.)

Barbara appears pleased with her life as a university student. She reports that she has never been so happy. She had few friends before, most of them friends of her older brother and sisters. She says that she now has a broad circle of her own friends. In addition to her course work she maintains an active extracurricular schedule of sports and entertainment with friends, most of whom are other girls in the EEP and college men. To observers, she appears to be a poised, intelligent, articulate, and warm young woman who is in a challenging situation but is very positive in her outlook.

QUESTIONS AND TENTATIVE ANSWERS

In the process of working with our subjects and their families and in initiating and developing research and service activities on their behalf, the investigators of the Child Development Research Group have been forced to consider a number of important issues concerning intellectually gifted individuals. Precisely how, for example, should we define "giftedness"? What is its etiology? What characteristics are displayed by individuals who are "gifted"? To what extent and with respect to what dimensions can they be considered a homogeneous group? How many highly gifted individuals exist in our population? Are there meaningful long-term differences between those who are highly gifted and those who are moderately gifted? What is the nature of current educational programs for gifted children? How appropriately do they address the special needs of those they serve?

In subsequent sections of this paper, I will consider in a summary fashion our working hypotheses and tentative conclusions with respect to each of these questions. What follows is based on our understanding of the research literature, our day-to-day experience with gifted children and their families, and our initial research findings.

Definition of Giftedness

Prior to this century "giftedness" or "genius" was identified as exceptional performance in a valued area, a performance exceeding ordinary adult standards by some sort of quantum jump. The notion of genius as a function of age was not given prominence, and young children were rarely, if ever, considered geniuses. Individuals such as Karl Gauss, John Locke, and Wolfgang Mozart were certaintly recognized as child prodigies because of their extraordinary abilities, but it was not until they became young adults and produced truly remarkable new and substantive achievements that they were thought of as geniuses.

With the development of intelligence tests, the definition of giftedness has come increasingly to refer to performance on these standardized instruments rather than to extraordinary achievement in a socially valued area of the real world. Particularly for children, the characteristics of genius has been specified as attainment of the top of the distribution of intelligence test scores. Tests have achieved enormous prestige for the identification of individuals with unusual intellectual abilities. Many children have been identified as "geniuses" whose actual achievements in life tasks have been merely average or even lower.

Today we maintain a two-faceted definition, one for adults and one for children. When we refer to an adult as a "genius," we are likely to mean that he or she actually demonstrates remarkable skills and is making an unusual and welcome contribution to human endeavors, perhaps as a scientist, mathematician, pianist, painter, or statesman. On the other hand, when we refer to a child as a "genius," we are likely to mean that his or her development has progressed at a remarkable rate in a more general sense, i.e., that the child behaves like individuals who are considerably older. Rate of development is the important component of this definition. Our switch to deviation IQs rather than ratio IQs notwithstanding, the determination of intelligence levels of children is predicated on the operation of a developmental age-gradient.

Using rate as our criterion, we tend to evaluate the progress of gifted children in any of three ways. Sometimes we refer to children who attain high IQs, i.e., who score exceptionally high on tests of general intelligence such as the Stanford–Binet or one of the Wechsler scales. For other children, giftedness is identified through tests of mental functioning which tap reasonably specific intellectual abilities; we may, for example, identify children who excel at memory, at spatial reasoning, or at verbal tasks. Finally, we may identify children whose giftedness is seen in a talent that is valued, such as the ability to solve scientific problems, to perform with a musical instrument, to write with skill, or to play a masterful game of chess. With any such children, whether one uses general ability (IQ), a specific component of cognitive functioning (e.g., short-term memory), or a specific talent (e.g., chess), it is the rate model that determines the children to be singled out.

Terman's research, and that which has followed, has demonstrated that, at least for school-age children who attain high scores on intelligence tests, the rate model tends to allow for reasonably accurate predictions of adult status. There appears to be a finite maturational period during which most development occurs; children who grow intellectually at the most rapid rate progress further during the developmental era and maintain their superiority into adulthood. A few of these high-IQ individuals subsequently earn the rubric "genius" by our adult standards; that is, by their unusual contributions and achievements. Just how to predict which of them will attain this exalted status remains a mystery.

We also use rate concepts at the other end of the scale, to define deficiency in intelligence as retardation in mental development. A broad range of studies (see Robinson & Robinson, 1976) have demonstrated the validity of this approach. The value of low scores on intelligence tests for the prediction of such performance variables as success in school is even greater than is the value of high scores; indeed, very low scores, even within the first two years of life, tend to be surprisingly stable.

The evidence for a rate model is, then, well established. It is also clear, however, that differences exist among gifted, average, and retarded persons which are difficult to ascribe altogether to differences in speed or rate of development. Many people have talked of qualitative differences in cognitive functioning which might help to explain these differences, but, to my knowledge, no single phenomenon has been unmistakably described in such terms. In our work, we have not yet been able to come up with any useful descriptions of qualitative differences which hold across even a subgroup of gifted children. For the most part, indeed, rate descriptions do rather well. We are pursuing this issue on a number of fronts and are not at all willing to admit defeat, but it remains clear to us that rate-related developmental descriptions have great utility and generality in describing the unusual abilities of highly intelligent children.

We are aware that some progress is being made by researchers who have been interested in possible qualitative features of the cognitive functioning of retarded persons. The group working with Herman Spitz (1978) at the Johnstone Center in New Jersey, for example, has been investigating cognitive tasks on which mentally retarded persons do significantly worse than expected on the basis of the level of their performance on general intelligence tests. Similarly, the failure of retarded persons to activate and select memorial strategies or to be aware of their own behavior in this regard in comparison with nonretarded persons of similar mental age is a potential area of investigation (Ellis, 1979).

Another group of investigators who have suggested the role of qualitative features in the cognitive functioning of gifted individuals are some Piagetian developmentalists. Webb (1974), for example, minimized the notion of individual differences in rate of stage-attainment, but maintained that once gifted children attained a stage, their mastery of the mental operations associated with that stage was highly efficient and broadly generalized. He suggested that intellectually superior children, identified as such by standard intelligence tests, are less precocious in logical reasoning ability, or "true intelligence," than they are in superficial verbal knowledge and verbal fluency. Others, however, have pointed to the high correlations between the more traditional psychometric measures and tests of Piagetian attainment (e.g., Humphreys, 1979; Jordan & Jordan, 1975). Our gifted preschool children tend to achieve mental functions, such as conservation of quantity and the understanding of the constancy of gender across situations and over time, many months before children of average ability. Moreover, attainment on such measures appears more highly correlated with mental age than chronological age (Krinsky, 1978; Miller, Roedell, Slaby, & Robinson, 1978).

Etiology of Intellectual Precocity

Although one must surely wonder about the origins of precocity, and especially about the differential contribution of genetic and environmental factors to this unusual status, our study is not likely to shed much light on this question. On the face of it, our children seem to have had the best of everything—a very positive kind of genetic endowment and physical integrity, nurtured in stimulating and appreciative families.

On the basis of our experience, we are able to comment on the degree to which parents report having consciously tried to produce a "gifted," or at least a developmentally accelerated child, through direct teaching. We have in fact very few cases in which the parents admit to having pushed their children to excel. As far as we know, no one instituted a plan to "raise a genius." Almost all of our parents have provided environments that are rich in cognitive inputs and social and emotional supports, but we have no evidence that the homes of our children are any richer or more supportive than countless other middle-class homes.

One obvious fact about our sample is its diversity. Most of our parents are obviously very intelligent, but not all are well educated. Most of them are interested in recognizing their children's potentials and nourishing them, but not all. While we are completely dependent in the longitudinal study on the initiative of parents, this is not the case with nominations for the IPP or the EEP. There are, in all our groups, exceptions to the overall trend for the children to come from very favorable backgrounds. It is worth noting, however, that the proportion of children from unremarkable or even apparently detrimental backgrounds is low in all the groups.

The 84 highly gifted children come from families with even more education than the families in the larger sample. Yet, in almost every case, the children in the highest group have amazed their parents with their precocious development. There are instances in which parents have actually tried to slow down their children. A few parents of early readers have, for example, removed from their homes all the children's books which might prove tempting. Most parents, however, have taken their lead from their children and have tried to supply what they seemed to need and to enjoy.

We have come to think of the children's intellectual abilities in trait terms—"highly verbal," "highly spatial"—or at least as defining precocious states—"early readers," "precocious mathematicians." We are aware, however, that such trait-state descriptors yield no etiological information. An important aspect of our longitudinal study will be to examine the reliability and stability of these descriptors over time. Will children of age 2 or 3 years who are extraordinary performers on verbal tasks, such as defining vocabulary words, still be "gifted" at age 8 or 9? Will they grow up to produce verbal products of exceptional worth? What is to be the fate of a 2-year-old who can repeat seven digits forward and five digits in reverse order? What about a 3-year-old who can solve most of the block-design and maze problems on the WISC-R? Do identifiable patterns emerge with some regularity? Are the precursors of extraordinary ability in adulthood the obvious ones, or are there complex interactions of abilities that permit children to develop exceptional talents? To what extent can education and interpersonal experiences be devised to exert positive influence on the rate of development, the richness, pleasure, and productivity of an adult life?

Variability with Groups of Gifted Children

If any of us should be asked to write a paper describing the average child, we would probably refuse, arguing that the concept of "the average child" is a useless abstraction. The same argument is certainly appropriate with respect to gifted children. Many writers have attempted to specify the characteristics of intellectually gifted children, but it is impossible to do so. If one defines giftedness in terms of unusually rapid development in at least one area of cognitive functioning, one is left with at least as much diversity in this group on the traits *not* selected for as in any other group of children. By the spring of 1979, for example, we had identified a group of 22 children who, when they were 2 to 5 years old, were reading at or above levels expected for children twice their age. Although homogeneous in their extraordinary reading achievements, these children are extremely diverse in other ways. Their Stanford–Binet IQs, for example, range from slightly above average to "off scale."

Granted that there is a great diversity in traits other than those by which the children have been identified, what about diversity within the dimensions used to identify homogeneous groups—scores on intelligence tests and on tests of academic skills, motivational descriptors, scientific interests, and so on? No index has been used more often in the identification of gifted children than has the IQ. A Stanford–Binet IQ range of 67–133 is expected to encompass 98% of the population, though the actual proportion is probably slightly smaller than this. In our sample, the range of scores above 133 is, however, greater than 66 points, for we have several children with IQs exceeding 200. Within the top 1% of the IQ distribution, then, there is at least as much spread of talent as there is in the entire range from the 1st to the 99th percentile. Moreover, those we might call the "supergifted," (those with IQs 4 or more standard deviations above the mean) tend to be as unlike the "garden-variety gifted" (with IQs 2 or 3 deviations above the mean) as the "garden-variety gifted" are unlike children with scores clustered within 1 standard deviation of the mean of the population.

Patterns of Variability

One of the most interesting preliminary findings to come from our longitudinal study of gifted young children is the fact that many of them show highly differentiated abilities in important cognitive areas. Contrary to popular folklore and to cognitive theories which hold development to be a process of increasing differentiation of specific, independent characteristics from an initial unitary system or organismic whole (Thompson & Grusec, 1970), we are discovering distinct subgroups of very young children who show highly developed spatial reasoning abilities, highly developed vocabularies and other indices of verbal development, exceptional ability at memory tasks, unusual mathematical skills, or very early reading, as well as a group who score very high across-the-board on tests of general intelligence.

As has been indicated, our criteria for designating extraordinary ability are very strict. For the groups designated as extraordinary in specific abilities the criterion is a score on tests such as the Wechsler Block Design and Mazes (to assess spatial abilities) or the Peabody Individual Achievement Test (to assess reading and mathematics skills) equal to the average score for children at least twice the gifted child's chronological age. For the group designated as high in general intellectual skills, the criterion is a score on the Stanford–Binet Intelligence Scale which is at least four standard deviations above the mean, i.e., 164+ (Robinson, Jackson, & Roedell, 1977, 1978).

An important point with respect to specific abilities is that young children who are exceptionally adept in one area are not necessarily very unusual in other areas. Intraindividual differences among abilities are the rule, not the exception. Extraordinary spatial reasoning is often accompanied by only moderately advanced verbal skills. Children who performed remarkable feats of memory may exhibit more ordinary abilities in other respects. We have not, however, found individuals who are extraordinary in one area of mental functioning and average or below average on all others. We certainly have not identified any idiot savants.

Of the 84 children who were 5 years old or younger when they met at least one of our criteria for extraordinary giftedness, there are 29 children with extraordinarily high IQs, 22 early readers, 22 spatial reasoners, 37 memory experts, and 4 mathematicians. (Some children are, of course, in more than one subgroup). Almost all are from the greater Seattle area, which has a population of approximately one million. We know that we have by no means located all such children in the area. We have approximately once each year placed an appeal in the Seattle newspapers, and have waited for the parents to call. In fact, we have had all we could handle responding to the parents who contact us. Initial evaluation takes place through a questionnaire sent to all the parents and intensive testing of their children. All children whose parents completed the identification process have become part of our longitudinal study sample.

In the process of evaluating children, we have been forced to recognize that there are many more truly exceptional young children in the population than would be predicted on the basis of the normal curve alone. Simply on IQ grounds, one would expect no more than three children in 100,000 to score 164 or above. In a population of approximately 150,000 children in the age range 2 to 5 years during the period 1974–1979, we have already located 27 children[1] with Stanford–Binet IQs of 164 or higher, thus exceeding our theoretical allowance six times over, even with a sample restricted to those whose parents were alerted to our program, aware of their child's unusual abilities, and interested enough to contact us. We cannot estimate in the same statistical fashion how many early readers, spatial whizzes, or verbally skilled children we should discover, but our criteria are strict and the numbers found have certainly exceeded our expectations.

Stability of Advanced Status

As I have mentioned, the literature is almost completely devoid of studies which have attempted to shed light on the stability of precocity identified at a very early age. None of the longitudinal studies of gifted children has begun with infants or preschoolers. The single exception is a report by Willerman and Fiedler (1974, 1977) concerned with the development of infants who were part of the National Collaborative Study. Approximately 100 of these children achieved an IQ of 140 or above when they were 4 years old. These children were not generally advanced on the Bayley Scales at 8 months, nor were they as advanced on the Wechsler Intelligence Scale for children at 7 years of age. At 8 months their mean mental and motor scores corresponded with a developmental quotient of about 95, their mean IQ at 4 years was 148, and their mean IQ at 7 years was 123.

Our study is designed to yield longitudinal data of several kinds. We have as yet only preliminary data, but preliminary inspection of the longitudinal patterns in the test performance of our initial sample suggests that stability of test scores themselves is not very high. Among the first 65 children tested initially at age 2 or 3 years, and again at age 4 or 5 years, the correlation is only about .50. About as many children gained in IQ as lost, although extreme changes were more likely to be positive than negative in direction. The modal phenomenon was a loss of up to 1 standard deviation, but 19 children gained more than 16 points from first to later testing while 5 lost more than 16 points. One child, a girl, gained 65 points from one session to

---

[1] Two children were not living within a fifty-mile radius of the University when they were identified.

the next. There was no relationship between sex and IQ change. As might be expected, the direction of change was significantly related to the child's initial IQ level. The pattern suggests that, within this sample, the children's scores regress on retest, but to a population mean close to the sample mean (IQ approximately 130) rather than to the mean of 100 for the standardization population (Jackson, 1978).

Predictive Validity of Parental Report

We have been surprised and pleased with the predictive validity of parental reports. We do not ask parents to estimate their child's maturity level, which they often cannot do, but we do request of them straightforward descriptions of their child's capabilities which we can match to developmental norms. Parents are also asked to tell us of unusual specific incidents that might suggest outstanding abilities.

In a study of 36 of our children it was determined that the parent-questionnaire score, awarded at the time the child was 2 or 3 years old, predicted the Stanford–Binet IQ at 4 or 5 years as well ($r = .53$) as did Stanford–Binet IQ at 2 or 3 years ($r = .51$). The parent-information score, the Stanford–Binet IQ, and mother's education accounted for 53% of the variance in IQ at 4 or 5 years (multiple $R = .73$). The addition of the parent-questionnaire scores significantly improved the prediction made on the basis of first IQ alone (R^2 change $= .18$), as did the subsequent addition of mother's educational level (R^2 change $= .09$) (Jackson, 1978).

The Highly Gifted

It is important to note that most previous research has, in fact, dealt with "garden-variety gifted" children. We know that these moderately gifted children (roughly those in the IQ range 120–150, if IQ is taken as the index) tend as a group to be socially adept, popular with age mates, and well adjusted (Dolbear, 1912; Terman, 1922, 1925, 1954; Witty, 1940). In comparison with average children, they are more socially involved with peers and the community at large (Hollingworth, 1930; Martinson, 1961; Miles, 1964). On the average, they are even better athletes (Terman, 1925). In other words, these children as a group seem to achieve a rather positive quality of life with respect not only to intellectual and achievement skills, but also in their relationships with others.

None of these studies reveals the whole truth about gifted children, however. Very few have touched upon the truly exceptional group whose developmental rate approaches and occasionally exceeds twice the average. The evidence about such children is extremely scanty, due to their relative rarity and the episodic way in which they have come to the attention of professionals. The data which are available tend to be anecdotal. Generally speaking the literature concerning the highly gifted consists of case reports (e.g., McCurdy, 1957, 1966; Mill, 1924; Weiner, 1956), an examination of the few children with IQs above 170 in the Terman sample, and a small group of children examined and described by Hollingworth (1942) in New York City.

The weight of this largely clinical evidence suggests that members of the highly advanced group may not fare as well in many respects as those with more moderate gifts. Terman himself did not pay much attention to this group, and it is, therefore, difficult to extract specific evidence about them from his reports. There is some indication, however, that the subjects in his study with IQs exceeding 170 did less well during childhood with respect to a number of personal and social variables (Burks et al., 1930). On subsequent follow-up during the middle years they were not, however, significantly different on a variety of personal-social adjustment indices from the group as a whole (Terman & Oden, 1947). Hollingworth's (1942) famous study of school-age children with IQs over 180 yielded some tragic findings of under-achievement, alienation, and suicide. As Terman admitted, "The child of 180 IQ has one of the most difficult problems of social adjustment that any human being is ever called upon to meet" (Burks et al., 1930, p. 265). Similarly, Hollingworth concluded that the majority of children testing above 180 IQ "have great difficulty in finding playmates in the ordinary course of events who are congenial both in size and mental ability. Thus they are thrown back upon themselves to work out forms of solitary, intellectual play" (1942, p. 78).

These authors were not saying that extraordinary talent carries with it the seeds of maladjustment. Rather, they recognized the discrepancy between the expectations of family members, peers, and teachers, on the one hand, which tend to be based on the child's age and size, and the child's own abilities, interests, and desires, on the other hand, which tend to reflect quite a different maturity level. Extraordinarily gifted children are often not seen as merely bright and competent; they are perceived as different and strange, and are often unsettling to those with whom they interact.

In light of the paucity of knowledge about this group, and simultaneously in light of their extraordinary potential for contribution to the common good, and perhaps for serious maladjustment and under-achievement, the Child Development Research Group has focused in particular on extraordinarily gifted children and young people. As I have said, we have thus far with the longitudinal study accumulated a target group of 84 highly gifted youngsters identified by age 5; the Individual Progress Program in the Seattle Public Schools admits highly gifted children; and the Early Entrance Program, by selecting only children below age 14 who are ready for university entrance, is also targeted on highly gifted youngsters. It is our hope and expectation that as we follow their development over the next few years we will learn a good deal about the adjustment patterns of highly gifted children.

Acceleration versus Enrichment of Education

Educators have the task of dealing with the discrepancy between gifted children's intellectual advancement and their chronological age. Their responses have tended to vary considerably over time. The proponents of special approaches to education for intellectually gifted children can be divided into two distinct camps: one group favors enrichment (i.e., keeping children for the most part with their own age mates but extending their horizons through special projects, challenging special classes, or individualized instruction), and the other group, a much smaller number today, favors acceleration (i.e., exposing younger children to educational programs intended for those one to several years older). Both these approaches are intended to provide a challenge or growth experience for the children.

Acceleration practices were at one time the common mode, both in one-room schoolhouses and in urban schools where passing, failing, and skipping grades were options exercised deliberately by educators to match children and learning tasks (Kett, 1974). Indeed, even today we see acceleration as the *usual* pattern for children with unusual gifts in art, music, foreign language, and athletic skills. In classes for students learning to paint, to swim, to ski, to play the violin, to read a foreign language, and to accomplish in myriad other skill areas, teachers are much less interested in chronological age than in the individual's ability to execute the tasks involved and his or her maturity of understanding and judgment in the specific area.

The research literature tends to favor the various acceleration models of education as better supporting academic progress *and* more effectively facilitating personal social development. Appropriately selected individuals who enter kindergarten or first grade at a younger-than-average age tend to do very well (Birch, 1954; Hobson, 1963; Worcester, 1956) as do those who skip grades (Burks et al., 1930; Engle, 1935; Morgan, 1959; Terman & Oden, 1947) and those who leave high school a year or two early to enter college (Fund for the Advancement of Education, 1953; George, Cohn, & Stanley, in press). The results of numerous studies indicate that acceleration is frequently beneficial from an academic point of view and also as concerns personal, social, and emotional development. Indeed, following an exhaustive review of the available research, Daurio (1977) was forced to conclude that acceleration, when accomplished in a sensible manner, seems to produce beneficial results when viewed from almost any perspective.

Enrichment programs are, in fact, seldom able to meet the needs of the very highly gifted. Such children are usually grouped with others who are only modestly advanced, so that the discrepancy with their own level is insufficiently reduced and they are very nearly as bored in classes for the gifted as in their regular school classes. It is also true that enrichment classes tend to promote a certain degree of acceleration, at least in basic skills. Unfortunately, school systems have seldom formulated consistent programs for children of advanced abilities which provide continuity of experience over the span of the school years. A child subjected to an "enrichment" program one year and none the next may be more exquisitely disappointed in school, and more discrepant with age mates because of the acceleration provided in the gifted class, than the child who has been undiscovered or given no special attention. Although children while enrolled tend to do well in enrichment programs (Daurio, 1977) over the long run, the results are likely to be disheartening and perhaps even detrimental to the child who is extraordinarily gifted (Meeker, 1968; Stanley, 1977).

It is important to note again that almost all of the enrichment versus acceleration research has concerned the moderately gifted. Evidence concerning highly gifted individuals is much less extensive and systematic. However, retrospective case studies of eminent men and women, persons with extraordinary abilities and outstanding achievements, indicate that their talents were generally recognized when they were very young (Pressey, 1955) and that their childhoods were spent in relative isolation from their peers (Cox, 1926). They were nurtured throughout their developing years by their gifted families and were tutored individually rather than enrolled in schools with their age mates (McCurdy, 1957).

Under these circumstances it is discouraging that the current consensus among educators and the general public strongly favors the enrichment model, even for highly exceptional children (Birch, Tisdall, Barney, & Marks, 1965; Braga, 1971; Famiglietti, Jackson, & Robinson, 1977; Haier, & Solano, 1976; Pyryt, 1976). This stance seems to stem from a commitment to the cherished proposition that "all men are created equal," and the corollary assumption that it is undemocratic or at least nonegalitarian and elitist to move bright children ahead of their slower age mates. There is also an assumption, which is totally at odds with the evidence, that children denied the opportunity to grow up with chronological peers may be impeded in social and emotional development (Hollingworth, 1936; Meister & Odell, 1951). Only recently has the assumption been questioned that "peer" status is conferred by anything other than equal chronological age (Lewis, Young, Brooks, & Michelson, 1975; Lougee, Grueneich, & Hartup, 1977).

A FINAL WORD

The purpose of this paper has been to demonstrate that the field of intellectual excellence, much neglected after a promising start in the 1920s and 1930s, is an area in which good research is possible, and that the potential value of such research is incalculable. The definition of giftedness should, though, be expanded beyond the concept of general intelligence or "high IQ" to include unusual competence in specific cognitive functions and skills areas.

More descriptive research is needed. The course of development from infancy and early childhood to the middle school years is almost completely uncharted for bright children, especially for those who are highly gifted. Experimental research which seeks to determine the nature of cognitive functioning among and between groups of gifted individuals is even more necessary. For example, although there may well be qualitative differences in the intellectual processes by which gifted and nongifted children learn and solve problems, the research findings in this area demonstrate conclusively only that there are rate differences. Is it the case that gifted children simply develop more rapidly and attain a quantitatively higher level of functioning as adults, or are they also in some ways qualitatively different?

Those doing research with gifted children should be aware of the probability that they will find more of them than the normal-curve table would lead them to predict. This may be particularly the case for those in the extraordinarily gifted group. Prospective researchers should also recognize that parents may be better at identifying gifted children than are teachers or even psychometric instruments. Above all, those who propose to do research with gifted young people should be prepared for a challenge. They are an enormously exciting and charming, if sometimes perplexing, group with which to work.

REFERENCES

Birch, J. W. Early school admissions for mentally advanced children. *Exceptional Children*, 1954, *21*, 84–87.

Birch, J. W., Tisdall, W. J., Barney, W. D., & Marks, C. H. *A field demonstration of the effectiveness and feasibility of early admission to school for mentally advanced children.* Pittsburgh: University of Pittsburgh School of Education, 1965.

Braga, J. L. Early admission: Opinion versus evidence. *The Elementary School Journal,* 1971, *72,* 35–46.

Burks, B. S., Jensen, D. W., & Terman, L. M. The promise of youth, *Genetic Studies of genius* (Vol. 3). Stanford Ca.: Stanford University Press, 1930.

Cox, C. M. The early mental traits of three hundred geniuses. *Genetic Studies of genius* (Vol. 2). Stanford, Ca.: Stanford University Press, 1926.

Daurio, S. P. *Educational enrichment versus acceleration.* Report from the Study of Mathematically Precocious Youth (SMPY). Baltimore: Johns Hopkins University Press, 1977.

Dolbear, K. E. Precocious children. *Pedagogical Seminary,* 1912, *19,* 461–491.

Ellis, N. R. (Ed.) *Handbook of Mental Deficiency* (2nd Ed.). Baltimore: University Park Press, 1979.

Engle, T.L. Achievements of pupils who have had double promotions in elementary school. *The Elementary School Journal,* 1935, *36,* 158–159.

Famiglietti, J., Jackson, N. E., & Robinson, H. B. Kindergarten and first grade teachers' attitudes toward early entrance of intellectually advanced students. *Technical Report: Child Development Research Group,* University of Washington, 1977.

Fund for the Advancement of Education of the Ford Foundation. *Bridging the gap between school and college.* New York: Research Division of the Fund, 1953.

Gallagher, J. J. *Teaching the gifted child.* Boston: Allyn & Bacon, 1975.

George, W., Cohn, S. J., & Stanley, J. C. *Acceleration and enrichment: Strategies for educational change.* Baltimore: Johns Hopkins University Press, in press.

Getzels, J. W., & Dillon, J. T. The nature of giftedness and the education of the gifted child. In R. W. M. Travers (Ed.), *Second handbook of research on teaching.* Chicago: Rand McNally, 1973.

Haier, R. J. & Solano, C. H. Educators' stereotypes of mathematically gifted boys. In D. P. Keating (Ed.), *Intellectual talent: Research and development.* Baltimore: Johns Hopkins University Press, 1976.

Hobson, J. R. High school performance of underage pupils initially admitted to kindergarten on the basis of physical and psychological examinations. *Educational and Psychological Measurement,* 1963, *1,* 159–170.

Hollingworth, L. S. Do intellectually gifted children grow toward mediocrity in stature? *Journal of Genetic Psychology,* 1930, *37,* 345–358.

Hollingworth, L. S. The founding of Public School 55: Speyer School. *Teachers College Record,* 1936, *38,* 119–128.

Hollingworth, L. S. *Children above 180 IQ Stanford–Binet origin and development.* Yonkers-on-Hudson, N.Y.: World Book Co., 1942.

Hughes, H. F., & Converse, H. D. Characteristics of the gifted: A case for a sequel to Terman's study. *Exceptional Children,* 1962, *29,* 179–183.

Humphreys, L. G. The construct of general intelligence. *Intelligence,* 1979, *3* (2), 105–120.

Jackson, N. E. Identification and description of intellectual precocity in young children. In H. B. Robinson (Chair), *Intellectually advanced children: Preliminary findings of a longitudinal study.* Symposium presented at the Annual Convention of the American Psychological Association, Toronto, August, 1978.

Jordan, V. B., & Jordan, L. A. Relative strength of IQ, mental age and chronological age for predicting performance on Piagetian tests. Paper presented at meeting of the Society for Research in Child Development, Denver, Colorado, 1975. ERIC ED 111 510.

Kett, J. History of age grouping in America. In J. S. Coleman *et al.* (Eds.), *Youth: Transition to adulthood.* A report to the panel on youth of the President's Science Advisory Committee. Chicago: University of Chicago Press, 1974.

Krinsky, S. Conservation in intellectually advanced preschool children: Levels of performance and relation to other academic abilities. *Technical Report: Child Development Research Group*. University of Washington, 1978.

Lewis, M., Young, G., Brooks, J., & Michelson, L. The beginning of friendship. In M. Lewis & L. A. Rosenblum (Eds.), *Friendship and peer relations*. New York: Wiley, 1975.

Lougee, M. D., Grueneich, R., & Hartup, W. W. Social interaction in same- and mixed-aged dyads of preschool children. *Child Development*, 1977, *48*, 1353–1361.

Martinson, R. *Educational programs for gifted pupils*. Sacramento: California State Department of Education, 1961.

McCurdy, H. G. The childhood patterns of genius. *Journal of the Elisha Mitchell Scientific Society*, 1957.

McCurdy, H. G. *Barbara*. Chapel Hill: University of North Carolina Press, 1966.

Meeker, M. Differential syndrome of giftedness and cirriculum planning: A four-year follow-up. *Journal of Special Education*, 1968, *2*, 185–196.

Meister, M., & Odell, H. A. What provisions for the education of gifted students? *NASSP (National Association of Secondary School Principals) Bulletin*, 1951, *35*, 30–46.

Miles, M.B. *Innovation in Education*. New York: Bureau of Publications, Teachers College, Columbia University, 1964.

Mill, J. S. *Autobiography of John Stuart Mill*. New York: Columbia University Press, 1924. Originally published, 1873.

Miller, J. K., Roedell, W. C., Slaby, R. G., & Robinson, H. B. Sex-role development among intellectually precocious preschoolers. Paper presented at the Annual Meeting of the Western Psychological Association, San Francisco, April, 1978.

Morgan, A. B. Critical factors in the academic acceleration of gifted children: Hypotheses based on clinical data. *Psychological Reports*, 1959, *3*, 71–77.

Oden, M. H. The fulfillment of promise: Forty-year follow-up of the Terman gifted group. *Genetic Psychology Monographs*, 1968, *77*, 3–93.

Pressey, S. L. Concerning the nature and nurture of genius. *Science*, 1955, *68*, 123–129.

Pyryt, M. Attitudes toward teaching the gifted child. *Intellectually Talented Youth Bulletin*, 1976, *2*, 1–2.

Robinson, H. B., Jackson, N. E., & Roedell, W. C. *Annual Report to the Spencer Foundation: Identification and nurturance of extraordinarily precocious young children*. Seattle: Child Development Research Group, University of Washington, 1977 (ERIC Document Reproduction Service No. ED. 151095).

Robinson, H. B., Jackson, N. E., & Roedell, W. C. *Annual Report to the Spencer Foundation: Identification and nurturance of extraordinarily precocious young children*. Seattle: Child Development Research Group, University of Washington, 1978 (ERIC Document Reproduction Service No. ED, 162756).

Robinson, N. M., & Robinson, H.B. *The mentally retarded child: A psychological approach* (2nd Ed.). New York: McGraw-Hill, 1976.

Sears, P. S., & Barbee, A. H. Career and life satisfactions among Terman's gifted women. In J. C. Stanley *et al.* (Eds.), *The gifted and the creative: A fifty-year perspective*. Baltimore: Johns Hopkins University Press, 1977.

Sears, R. R. Sources of life satisfaction of the Terman gifted men. *American Psychologist*, 1977, *32*, 119–138.

Spitz, H. H. The universal nature of human intelligence: Evidence from games. *Intelligence*, 1978, *2*, 371–379.

Stanley, J. C. Rationale of the study of mathematically precocious youth (SMPY) during its first five years of promoting educational acceleration. In J. C. Stanley, W. L. George, & C. H. Solano (Eds.), *The gifted and the creative: A fifty-year perspective*. Baltimore: Johns Hopkins University Press, 1977.

Terman, L. M. A new approach to the study of genius. *Psychological Review*, 1922, *39*, 310–318.

Terman, L. M. Mental and physical traits of a thousand gifted children. *Genetic studies of genius* (Vol. 1). Stanford, Ca.: Stanford University Press, 1925.

Terman, L. M. The discovery and encouragement of exceptional talent. *American Psychologist*, 1954, *9*, 221–230.

Terman, L. M., & Oden, M. H. The gifted child grows up: Twenty-five years' follow-up of a superior group. *Genetic studies of genius* (Vol. 4). Stanford, Ca.: Stanford University Press, 1947.

Terman, L. M., & Oden, M. H. The gifted group at midlife. *Genetic studies of genius* (Vol. 5). Stanford, Ca.: Stanford University Press, 1959.

Thompson, W. R., & Grusec, J. Studies of early experience. In P. H. Mussen (Ed.), *Carmichael's Manual of Child Psychology* (Vol. 1). New York: Wiley, 1970.

U.S. Office of Education. *Education of the gifted and talented.* A report to the Congress of the United States by the U.S. Commissioner of Education. Washington, D.C.: U.S. Government Printing Office, 1972.

Webb, R. A. Concrete and formal operations in very bright six to eleven year olds. *Human Development*, 1974, *17*, 292–300.

Weiner, N. *I am a mathematician: The later life of a prodigy.* Cambridge, Mass.: Massachusetts Institute of Technology Press, 1956.

Willerman, L., & Fiedler, M. F. Infant performance and intellectual precocity. *Child Development*, 1974, *45*, 483–486.

Willerman, L., & Fiedler, M. F. Intellectually precocious preschool children: Early development and later intellectual accomplishments. *Journal of Genetic Psychology*, 1977, *131*, 13–20.

Witty, P. A. A genetic study of fifty gifted children. In *Intelligence: Its nature and nurture.* Thirty-ninth Yearbook of National Society for the Study of Education, Part 2. Bloomington, Ill.: Public School Publishing Co., 1940.

Worcester, D. A. *The education of children of above average mentality.* Lincoln: University of Nebraska Press, 1956.

5

DOWN'S SYNDROME CHILDREN
CHARACTERISTICS AND INTERVENTION RESEARCH

Marci J. Hanson

Down's syndrome is generally believed to be the most common specific form of mental retardation. For a number of years, this syndrome has evoked great interest from researchers in a variety of fields—education, psychological, medical. Given that the physical stigmata typically associated with this syndrome are recognizable from birth, that medical complications often are present, and the finding that individuals with Down's syndrome have benefited greatly from educational intervention, it is not surprising that this syndrome has been the target of many research efforts.

The pattern of development associated with Down's syndrome results from a chromosomal anomaly—the presence of extra chromosomal material. This chromosome aberration expresses itself in a cluster of physical characteristics and some degree of mental retardation in the affected individual. Thus, there is a biological or constitutional basis for this condition. As such, Down's syndrome is irreversible—no drugs or chemicals can "cure" it.

The medical model of development assumes that the status of the individual at time 1 predicts the status of the individual at time 2.

Marci J. Hanson • Department of Special Education, San Francisco State University, 1600 Holloway Avenue, San Francisco, California 94132.

Given the constitutional or genetic basis for Down's syndrome, it follows from this model that the Down's syndrome infant at birth will exhibit abnormal development throughout the infancy period and beyond. In other words, given the genetic disorder of the infant at birth (time 1), the infant's later development at any given time period (time 2) could be predicted. In fact, there is some evidence to support this view. The descriptive literature (Benda, 1949, 1960, 1969; Dameron, 1963; Dicks-Mireaux, 1966, 1972; Share, Koch, Webb, & Graliker, 1964) shows that the development of Down's syndrome children and adults does lag behind that of their normal peers. However, the descriptive literature is based for the most part on individuals who were not provided with any "enrichment" or intervention activities. Thus, the effects of environmental variables could not be measured except in those studies that compared Down's syndrome infants reared at home with those reared in institutions (Centerwall & Centerwall, 1960; Kugel & Reque, 1961; Shipe & Shotwell, 1965; Stedman & Eichorn, 1964). Indeed, those studies did find differences, favoring the home-reared group and, thus, calling into question the medical model of development. As in studies with nonhandicapped populations (to be reviewed), these studies suggested the power of environmental influences in developmental processes. Insofar as many intervention programs now exist for Down's syndrome children, the medical model must be questioned as a means of predicting future status. Rather, a more interactive model as articulated by Sameroff & Chandler (1975) and Lewis (1972; 1979b) appears more appropriate for use by medical, educational, and psychological personnel involved in designing treatment programs for infants and advising parents of Down's syndrome infants.

The purpose of this chapter, therefore, is to review the vast amount of information available on Down's syndrome and discuss this information in light of intervention or environmental change efforts. Particular attention will be given to describing the early development of these children and to reviewing the educational-intervention data. These data will be examined as they pertain to predicting the developmental status of the Down's syndrome child.

This chapter is organized according to the following format. A description of the types of Down's syndrome will be presented as well as prevalence and incidence information. This will be followed by a discussion of the characteristics of Down's syndrome, including physical and medical characteristics and developmental characteristics in the areas of motor, mental, and social development. A third section will review early-intervention research with emphasis on intervention efforts with Down's syndrome infants. Finally, data from a longitudinal investigation of Down's syndrome infants at the University of Oregon will be presented and conclusions drawn.

Overview of Research on Down's Syndrome

Description and Types of Down's Syndrome

The term "Down's syndrome" was chosen because the condition was first described and differentiated from other conditions by a British physician, Dr. Langdon Down (1866). This term is preferred over the more common label "mongoloid" because there is no relationship between persons with this condition and inhabitants of Mongolia and because of the misconceptions often associated with "mongolism." Though this syndrome was described over a century ago, it was not until 1959 (Lejeune, Gautier, & Turpin, 1959) that Down's syndrome was found to be associated with the presence of an extra chromosome, typically an extra twenty-first chromosome (trisomy 21).

Types of Down's Syndrome

Trisomy 21. Trisomy 21 results from a chromosome nondisjunction during meiosis. Thus, instead of the normal 46 chromosomes (23 pairs), the individual with Down's syndrome has 47 chromosomes. The extra chromosomal material appears with the number 21 chromosome pair forming 3 sets of genes (trisomy).

Translocation. While over 90% of Down's syndrome individuals have a trisomy 21 chromosomal karyotype, approximately 4% have the translocation form. This condition results when chromosomes (usually from the number 14 pair) are broken or rearranged and become attached to another chromosome (number 21). This also produces a trisomy condition. Unlike the trisomy 21 type of Down's syndrome, the translocation chromosomal error may be inherited. The translocation carrier has a translocation chromosome but the normal amount of genes and as such is physically and mentally normal.

Mosaic Trisomy. The condition known as mosaic trisomy or mosaicism results from a mitotic chromosome nondisjunction. Thus, this chromosome division error takes place after a number of normal cell divisions have occurred. Further development produces a mix of normal and abnormal trisomy cells. The person, therefore, has two different cell types. Research reports present a controversy as to whether persons with the mosaic trisomy are higher functioning or not than those with other types of Down's syndrome (Fishler, Koch, & Donnell, 1976; Johnson & Abelson, 1969; Rosencrans, 1968).

Frequency of Down's Syndrome—Incidence/Prevalence

Stein and Susser's (1977) recent review of frequency trends in Down's syndrome reports divergent trends in incidence and prevalence rates. While the incidence of Down's syndrome has gone down, the prevalence of this disorder has increased.

Incidence

Incidence of Down's syndrome has decreased from the often-quoted estimate of 1 in every 600–650 to approximately 1 in 900 births (Stein & Susser, 1977). The data (reviewed by Stein & Susser, 1977) indicate that the risk factor for giving birth to a Down's syndrome infant is still highest for an older maternal age group. However, the overall incidence for older mothers has declined.

A number of theories have been proposed to account for the increased risk of bearing a Down's syndrome child with advanced maternal age. These theories include a deterioration theory (changes in female ova take place over the maturation process) and a production-line theory (the last oocytes in the ovaries are last to "ripen' and are inferior) (Stein & Susser, 1977). Other factors postulated include increased risk due to environmental factors, such as irradiation, and an association of age-related disorders of the mother, such as thyroid disorders or diabetes, with Down's syndrome occurrence. However, paternal origins of the extra chromosome also have been noted (Magenis, Overton, Chamberlin, Brody, & Lourien, 1977; Sasaki, 1973; Uchida, 1973). To date, though a higher incidence of Down's syndrome births is found in older-group maternities, no known etiology has been proved to account for this syndrome.

While incidence rates are higher for older mothers, a decline has been noted. The factors which influence the decline are undoubtedly related to changes in proportions of overall older-age-group maternities. These may include factors such as availability of amniocentesis and legalization of abortions, changes in family-size patterns, and shifts in age of marriage and female career choices and opportunities.

Prevalence

Though incidence figures have generally dropped, prevalence of Down's syndrome has increased. This is not surprising in light of medical advances in controlling respiratory infections and in surgery techniques for congenital defects (e.g., cardiac defects). Readers are again referred to Stein and Susser's (1977) review for specific figures on prevalence, as well as incidence, rates.

Characteristics Associated with Down's Syndrome

Characteristics which set Down's syndrome persons apart from other individuals have been noted across behavioral and developmental domains. A review of these characteristics, divided by domains, follows.

Physical and Medical Characteristics

Over fifty clinical signs or stigmata are associated with Down's syndrome. All are rarely present in a given individual. However, the characteristics are evident at birth and can be used to identify these babies. Some of the more common characteristics are:

Small head, flat face
Dysplastic ear—small ear
Palpebral fissures (eye openings slanted)
Epicanthal eye folds
White spots in iris of eyes (Brushfield spots)
Protruding tongue, small oral cavity
Abundant neck skin
Clinodactyly (incurving) of the fifth finger
Fifth finger short with single flexion crease
Transverse palmar crease (simian line)
Wide space between first and second toes

Coleman (1978) provides a further reyiew of clinical signs often present which may be used by the physician to diagnose Down's syndrome in the neonate. While the presence of these signs or characteristics is generally sufficient for initial diagnosis, chromosomal analysis is typically performed to verify the diagnosis. Early diagnosis, thus, is possible and parents are usually informed of the diagnosis shortly after the child's birth.

In addition to the clinical signs described, several medical complications are associated with Down's syndrome. Approximately 40% of Down's syndrome infants have congenital heart defects. The cardiac lesions present are most commonly atrioventricular-canal and ventricular septal defects (Coleman, 1978). Another congenital defect, duodenal stenosis (duodenal obstruction), occurs with a higher frequency in these infants, though only a small percentage of the infants are afflicted. This condition is fatal unless early surgery is undertaken.

Coleman's (1978) review of medical complications lists several other conditions found with a greater frequency in Down's syndrome children. Congenital hematologic abnormalities are seen in these infants and leukemia is more prevalent in children with Down's syndrome than in normal children. Ocular signs, such as the Brushfield spots, may also be present. Eye abnormalities (strabismus, lens opacities, nystagmus, and cataracts) often develop as the Down's syndrome person grows older. Additionally, these children have a tendency toward dry skin and chapping. Finally, Down's syndrome children are more prone to upper respiratory infections and conductive hearing losses. In fact, the speech and language problems characteristic of these children may be linked to hearing disorders.

Mortality rates during the first years of life are higher for Down's syndrome than normal infants. This is most likely due to the presence of cardiac defects and proneness to respiratory disorders. However, the use of antibiotics and advances in cardiac surgery are increasing survival rates. After the age of five to around forty years of age, mortality rates for Down's syndrome persons are similar to those of the population in general but increase at about fifty.

In summary, the Down's syndrome child can typically be identified at birth due to the presence of a cluster of physical signs. These infants show certain physical differences from normal infants. In addition, they are more likely than normal infants to have medical complications and suffer from certain illnesses.

Mental and Motor Development Characteristics

Delays in both the mental and motor development of Down's syndrome children have been noted in a number of research studies. A longitudinal investigation by researchers at Los Angeles Children's Hospital on Down's syndrome children from birth to seven years showed that Down's syndrome children experienced steady developmental progress. However, a progressive deceleration in rate of growth was noted as computed by developmental quotient (DQ) [DQ = mental age (MA)/chronological age (CA) × 100] measured by the Gesell Developmental Scales (Koch, Share, Webb, & Graliker, 1963; Share et al., 1964; Share, Webb, & Koch, 1961).

Share and colleagues also provided specific descriptive information on the ages at which behaviors of the Down's syndrome children were acquired. Fishler, Share, and Koch (1964) examined 71 Down's syndrome children in the areas of motor, language, and personal-social development. They suggested that in motor development, Down's syndrome infants typically followed a relatively normal motor pattern in the first 6 months of life, but by 1 year fell as much as 6 months behind chronological age norms and that the lag nearly doubled by 2 years of age. Further, they targeted the area of language development as that area of slowest progress for the Down's syndrome infant and suggested that it takes a Down's syndrome child nearly 2 years to perform what a "normal" child can do at 10 months. In the area of personal-social development, these investigators indicated a lag for Down's syndrome children of 10 to 24 months behind normal peers with the least discrepancy in the area of self-care habits such as toilet training.

Share and French (1974a,b) presented and discussed motor-developmental landmarks of Down's syndrome children under 5 years. Data were on 211 New Zealand children ranging from 1 to 67 months (48 institutionalized, 163 lived at home). Data showed Down's syndrome infants performing slightly below the pattern of normal development (behaviors: holds head erect, rolls over, transfers object, etc.) during the first 6 months. From that point on, a growing discrepancy from normal development was noted. Behaviors studied included crawling, walking with and without support, seating selves in chairs, and walking up and down stairs. Share (1975) presented these data and those on language, personal-social, and adaptive landmarks and compared the New Zealand sample to the UCLA sample. The Los Angeles Children's Hospital longitudinal sample matched the New Zealand home-reared sample closely. These data generally indicated a 4- to 5-month lag from normal at 1 year for Down's syndrome children in motor development, significant delays in language, and similar delays in other areas. For example, while Gesell norms indicated that children usually walked with support by 13 months, the New Zealand Down's syndrome sample reported a median age of 21 months and the Los Angeles sample 22 months. Likewise, for "obeys commands" the Gesell (norms) median age was 18 months; the New Zealand home-sample age was 29 months, and the Los Angeles home-sample median age was 41 months. Finally, Share and Veale (1974) tabulated the ages at which the 211 children in the New Zealand sample first exhibited specific developmental landmarks as reported by their parents. These data are useful as a guideline of the current developmental status of Down's syndrome children as a group across all areas of development.

Carr (1970), a British researcher, also performed extensive observations on Down's syndrome children from 1.5 to 24 months. The children were tested at approximately 6 weeks, 6, 10, 15, and 24 months using the Bayley Infant Scales of Mental and Motor Development (Bayley, 1964). Both home-reared and boarded-out children ($N = 54$) were observed. Normal control children matched for sex, age, and social class with the home-reared Down's syndrome sample ($N = 45$) were examined also. Carr's data showed that both Down's syndrome groups scored significantly ($p < .01$) below the controls as early as 6 weeks of age. Carr (1975) reported additional data for Down's syndrome children (both home-reared and boarded-out) aged up to 48 months. Mean mental ages for the home-reared group were 1.05 at 1.5 months, 4.76 at 6 months, 6.67 at 10 months, 9.26 at 15 months, 13.44 at 24 months, 17.25 at 36 months, and 21.94 at 48 months. Mean mental ages for the boarded-out group were lower than those for the home-reared children at all age levels beyond 6 months. Carr (1970, 1975) also indicated larger score variations in the Down's syndrome children than the normal controls and concluded that the pattern of development of Down's syndrome children may not only be slower but that it also may be different from that of normal children.

While the studies previously reviewed present the most comprehensive and detailed data on the development of specific behaviors in young Down's syndrome children, notable other descriptive studies are those by Dameron (1963) and Dicks-Mireaux (1966, 1972). Dameron (1963) tested institutionalized Down's syndrome infants and found the developmental quotient for 3-month-olds to be average (around 94) but reported that by 6 months of age, "retardation" was evident and the trend of increasing deviation from normal continued thereafter. Findings by Dicks-Mireaux (1966) contradict both the Dameron results for 3-month-olds and the Fishler et al. (1964) suggestion that Down's syndrome infants' motor patterns were relatively normal for the first 6 months. The 12 Dicks-Mireaux infants (all Trisomy-21 and home-reared) as a group were observed to have a developmental quotient (DQ) below average at age three months: DQ = 73 for motor behavior, 64 for adaptive behavior, and 68 for social behavior. Expanding on the preliminary study (1966), Dicks-Mireaux (1972) administered the Gesell Developmental Scales five times to 21 Down's syndrome infants between the ages of 16 weeks and 18 months. The Down's syndrome infants had developmental quotients significantly lower than the normals at all ages. Further analyses which examined linear relationships between chronological age (CA) and mental age (MA) indicated that Down's syndrome infants showed both a slower rate of development than normal infants and one which deteriorated with age. Similar trends in the development of Down's syndrome children were noted also in studies by Benda (1949, 1960, 1969), Clements, Bates, and Hafer (1976): Cornwell and Birch (1969), and Melyn and White (1973).

Another "cognitive" dimension, recognition memory, was investigated with Down's syndrome infants. Miranda and Fantz (1974) compared the novelty preference of Down's syndrome infants and normal infants at three age levels: 8–16 weeks, 17–29 weeks, and 30–40 weeks. Sixteen infants in each age group were observed. Results indicated that Down's syndrome infants followed the same course of stimulus-preference development as normals but exhibited developmental lags in recognition memory. In every problem, the control normals showed a preference for novel stimuli several weeks before the Down's syndrome infants. The investigators suggested this finding was indicative of normal superiority in the development of recognition memory.

Research on the mental and motor development in young Down's syndrome children thus consistently shows developmental lags in these domains. The data also suggest a deceleration in rate of growth over time on mental and motor skills.

Temperament Characteristics and Social Development in Young Down's Syndrome Children

Down's syndrome persons represent one group of developmentally delayed individuals for whom extensive anecdotal descriptions of temperamental or personality characteristics exist. These individuals are typically described as affectionate and lovable, imitative, humorous, stubborn, and cheerful (Benda, 1969; Brousseau & Brainend, 1928; Smith & Wilson, 1973; Tredgold, 1922) and more pleasant as a group than other institutionalized groups (Domino, Goldschmid, & Kaplan, 1964). Other work, however, has refuted the universality of predominantly favorable characteristics in persons with Down's syndrome (Blacketer-Simmonds, 1953). It appears that no firm conclusions can be drawn from these inquiries regarding the uniformity of personality–temperamental characteristics of Down's syndrome persons. This is due to the lack of empirical investigation in this area and the fact that most research cited has been primarily concerned with institutionalized populations and older children.

Several studies have examined some temperament variables in young Down's syndrome children. Baron (1972) compared 18 home-reared Down's syndrome infants (ages 6 to 18 months) to normal infants (ages 4 to 8 months) in a previous study (Carey, 1970). Parents in both studies completed a questionnaire designed to measure temperament categories. Although no differences between the Down's syndrome and normal infant groups were found, the results are difficult to interpret given the author's reported "matching" of subjects by mental age. Mental ages for Down's syndrome infants were determined by purported IQ scores for older Down's syndrome children from previous studies.

Cicchetti and Sroufe (1976) conducted a longitudinal investigation on affective development with 14 Down's syndrome infants from the age of 4 months until the age of 24 months. Results indicated that Down's syndrome infants laughed at stimulus items in the same developmental order as normal infants previously sampled. However, onset of laughter was delayed for the Down's syndrome babies and they were reported to smile more on occasions when normal subjects were more likely to laugh. A positive relationship between cognitive development as measured by the Bayley and Uzgiris–Hunt scales and affective development also was demonstrated in this study for the Down's syndrome group.

Serafica and Cicchetti (1976) studied the attachment and exploration behavior of 12 Down's syndrome children (median age 33.5 months) and 12 normal children (median age 32.8 months) in the Ainsworth strange situation. The Down's syndrome infants differed from their normal peers primarily in the use of one signaling behavior, crying. Normal children cried significantly more than the Down's syndrome children during episodes with mothers absent. Normal children also vocalized more than the Down's syndrome group during certain structured episodes, particularly when the children's mothers were out of the room. Serafica and Cicchetti interpreted these findings as indicating that the absence of the mothers evoked more attachment behavior for the normal than for the Down's syndrome subjects. They suggested this may result from Down's syndrome children being less threatened by strange situations than normal children.

Variability

Though the research previously reviewed suggests that Down's syndrome children are a relatively homogeneous group in that marked developmental delay is usually evident across all areas of development, a number of investigations point to the variability among persons with Down's syndrome. Carr (1970, 1975) reported larger variations in DQ among Down's syndrome children than among the normal children in her sample as measured by the Bayley Scales. Levinson, Friedman, and Stamps (1955) also emphasized the great variability among the 50 Down's syndrome patients in terms of developmental history (ages at which developmental landmarks were observed) and number and types of physical stigmata or features present. Further, Melyn and White (1973) and Cornwell and Birch (1969) indicated that although the IQs of Down's syndrome children tended to decrease with age, great variability was noted with respect to each aspect of development. Recent studies also underscored the wide range of development and great variability found in Down's syndrome children. Golden and Pashayan (1976) reported data on 34 patients seen at the Child Development Center of the Boston Floating Hospital for Infants and Children. The mean IQ for the 34 children was 46.9 with a range of 0 (untestably low) to 78. Thus, as was noted in the temperament literature, it is apparent that although Down's syndrome individuals share many characteristics as a group, great variability among individuals is present.

Home-Reared versus Institutionalized Populations

One factor which has been identified as a contributing factor to different developmental growth patterns in Down's syndrome children is the environment in which they were reared. The negative effects of early institutionalization have been well documented (Dennis & Sayegh, 1965; Skeels, 1966; Skeels & Dye, 1939; Spitz, 1945, 1946). Similar conclusions for the effect of institutionalization on Down's syndome children appear to be warranted. Centerwall and Centerwall (1960), in what apparently was the first study comparing Down's syndrome children reared at home with those reared away from home (foster homes or institutions), concluded that home environment was more conducive to better growth. The home-reared group was closer to normal levels in weight, had higher IQs, and walked at earlier ages than did the comparison "reared away from home" group. Results indicated statistically significant differences between the two groups both in IQ and SQ (Social Quotient) scores (Shipe & Shotwell, 1965; Stedman & Eichorn, 1964).

Summary

The descriptive literature reviewed suggests that though young Down's syndrome children continue to progress developmentally with age, their rate of development, in general, becomes slower. While marked developmental delay is characteristic of these children, a great deal of variability among individuals and intraindividual variability across behaviors has been documented and the effects of different environments noted.

Intervention Research

The studies described in this review universally report delayed mental and motor development for the young Down's syndrome child, as well as some delays in social development. Though these characteristics are expressed to variable degrees across individuals, Down's syndrome persons are nevertheless a homogeneous group with respect to the chromosomal anomaly and a particular pattern of development. For these reasons, this group has been the target of a variety of interventions, both medical and educational.

Medical Interventions

With regard to medical efforts, obvious medical interventions for Down's syndrome children are surgical corrections of cardiac and duodenal defects and drug treatment (antibiotics) for infections. However, a number of biochemical interventions and drug treatments have also been tried in an attempt to modify physical and intellectual development of Down's syndrome persons. These treatments include siccacell therapy, thyroid extracts, pituitary extracts, glutamic acid and its salt, vitamins, aslavital (procaine hydrochloride), dimethylsulfide (DMSO), and Turkel's "M" series (a mixture of about 48 vitamins, minerals, enzymes, and common drugs). In addition, because of low levels of serotonin in the blood, 5-hydroxytryptophan (5-HTP) was administered in studies by Coleman and colleagues (Coleman, 1973). Coleman (1979) is currently studying the effects of large doses of vitamin B_6 on the development of Down's syndrome infants using double-blind procedures.

Though many claims have been made for improved development resulting from biochemical and drug treatments, to date, studies exercising proper methodological controls have failed to produce evidence of significant changes resulting from the use of these substances. Extensive reviews of this literature are provided by de la Cruz (1977) and Share (1976).

Educational Intervention—Overview

In terms of educational intervention, the prognosis for improving the development of Down's syndrome children is more hopeful. It is generally accepted that some degree of mental retardation is associated with Down's syndrome. As the literature previously reviewed suggested, Down's syndrome individuals typically were labeled as severely retarded (Benda, 1949, 1960, 1969). This label is rarely attached to these individuals anymore. Rather, Down's syndrome persons are more often thought to be in the moderately retarded range (Robinson & Robinson, 1976), though many probably should be more appropriately classified as educable or mildly retarded (Rynders, Spiker, & Horrobin, 1978). These shifts in performance and expectation levels are probably due to several factors. First, Rynders et al. (1978) suggest there are many problems with earlier studies. Additionally, environmental factors such as home-rearing versus institutional placement and early training are contributing to the higher functioning levels of these persons.

The degree to which environmental change or intervention can modify the development of an individual with a biological, constitutional impairment, such as that found in Down's syndrome, remains a question. It is implicit in the acceptance of an interactional model of development that exogenous or environmental factors make major contributions to the individual's status. The nature–nurture controversy has long involved heated debates over the proportion of variance explained by hereditary and environmental factors. Obviously, no "absolutes" exist; this issue has not been solved. However, a number of early-enrichment or -intervention studies are worthy of review at this point in that they give some indication of the degree to which environmental stimulation can alter child behavior and performance.

Several of these studies are "classics" in the environmental-intervention literature. Among them is the Skeels and Dye (1939) investigation. These researchers reported dramatic improvement as tested on IQ measures for a group of orphanage children who were transferred to an institution for the mentally retarded where they received an "enriched" environment. The average IQ gain for the "experimental" group was 28.5 points as compared to an average loss of 26.2 IQ points for the contrast group, a group which remained in the orphanage. A follow-up 20 years later showed similar and dramatic differences between groups (Skeels, 1966).

Another intensive intervention program, the Milwaukee project, was conducted at the University of Wisconsin Infant Education Center in Milwaukee by Heber and colleagues (Heber & Garber, 1975). This program placed infants of mothers whose IQs were below 70 in a daily early-enrichment program which included cognitive, social, and communication and language activities. The infant's mothers received a program in homemaking and vocational training. Although this study has been criticized on methodological grounds, it nevertheless serves as a test of the environmental model. Results indicated striking differences between the experimental and control children at ages 3–4 with the treatment group scoring an average of 33 IQ points above the control group.

A wide range of additional early-enrichment programs have reported improved performance of experimental group children over controls, though the gains reported are not as dramatic as in the Heber (Heber & Garber, 1975) and Skeels and Dye (1939) investigations.

These programs have typically focused on "culturally disadvantaged" infants and include the research studies by Gordon (1969), Painter (1969), and Schaefer (1969).

Few would dispute, in the face of the enrichment evidence, that environmental factors contribute to improving the performance of young children. These enrichment efforts have improved performance as much as two standard deviations as assessed by standard IQ measures. However, most of these studies have focused on "at risk" or "culturally disdvantaged" children. The programs are worthy of review in light of the improvements they produced and also for implications they may carry for working with handicapped populations.

How malleable is the development of children with identified biological impairments? Children with Down's syndrome are an obvious group for testing the effects of such early enrichment or intervention. The remainder of this paper, therefore, will be devoted to exploring these effects by reviewing data from the primary investigations done with Down's syndrome infants and their families. A major focus will be placed on my longitudinal investigation at the University of Oregon of the development of Down's syndrome infants in an intensive, early-intervention program.

A Review of Early-Intervention Programs with Down's Syndrome Children

Involving Down's syndrome children in systematic early-intervention programs is a relatively new phenomenon, having begun only in the last five to ten years. It is likely that many programs throughout the nation now include these youngsters in their educational-treatment programs. However, several programs deserve special mention because of their intensive involvement with this population. One of these is the Down's Syndrome Program in the Model Preschool Center for Handicapped Children, University of Washington (Hayden & Dmitriev, 1975; Hayden & Haring, 1976). The objectives of that program are to develop and apply sequential teaching to increase the child's rate of development in motor, communication, social, cognitive, and self-help skills (Hayden & Haring, 1977). Emphasis is placed on involving parents as their child's teacher, as liaison agents with classroom teachers, in parent-to-parent programs, and as participants in clinic activities such as conducting site-visitor interviews (Hayden, 1976). Classes for Down's syndrome children include an infant learning class, an early preschool, and a kindergarten class. As Hayden and Dmitriev (1975) reported, training goals for the infant class were based primarily on norms from the Denver Developmental Screening Test (Frankenburg & Dodds, 1969) and Gesell scales (Gesell & Amatruda, 1969). The author's data showed that infants were meeting developmental objectives as tested by the Gesell Preliminary Behavior Inventory. Results of the early and advanced preschool programs (Hayden & Dmitriev, 1975) indicated that all children in the early preschool met self-help objectives to the 85–100% competency level and other skills in gross-motor, language, and concept development ranged from 39 to 100% competency levels. In a later report, Hayden and Haring (1977) stated that children in the Model Preschool Center increased in developental level and progress rates as they grew older and had longer exposure to the preschool program. The Model Preschool children leveled off at approximately 95% of normal development (measured by Model Preschool Down's Syndrome Inventory) while a contrast group which did not attend the Model Preschool leveled off at about 61% of normal development. Hayden and Dmitriev (1975) concluded that data from the University of Washington program confirmed their belief that impressive gains could be made by children typically considered severely retarded or "trainable" when systematic educational programming was provided.

A second major program directed at intervention for Down's syndrome children was project EDGE, the University of Minnesota's Communication Stimulation Program for Down's syndrome infants (Rynders & Horrobin, 1975). In that study, Down's syndrome children (20 experimentals and 20 controls) were enrolled between 3 and 9 months of age. Experimental infant group mothers were given 6 weeks of training on instructional methods and materials, followed by semi-weekly home visits and monthly group meetings. Parents provided 1-hour instruction daily to their children. The primary focus of the Minnesota Program, thus, was the use of maternal tutoring to develop receptive- and expressive-language skills in Down's syndrome children. Rynders (1973) reported that at age 3, after approximately 2½ years in the program, the children receiving the stimulation scored higher than controls on measures of intellectual and receptive-language development. Additional reports of successful intervention attempts with Down's syndrome children include the work by De Coriat, Theslenco, and Waksman (1968), Bidder, Bryant, and Gray (1975), Connolly and Bussell (1976), and Zausmer, Pueschel, and Shea (1972).

It is evident from the investigations reviewed that Down's syndrome children can benefit from early-intervention programs. However, longitudinal descriptive research is needed to more thoroughly document specific gains attributable to intervention and further determine if the developmental delay trends typical of these children can be modified. Thus, the remainder of this chapter will present data from such a longitudinal, descriptive investigation.

UNIVERSITY OF OREGON INVESTIGATION

The University of Oregon longitudinal investigation of Down's syndrome infants (Hanson, 1978, 1979) was undertaken: (1) to provide a descriptive account of the behavioral changes of the Down's syndrome infants from birth to two years, and (2) to provide comparative data on the development of Down's syndrome infants with two sets of comparisons or referent groups which included normal infants and, for one measure, Down's syndrome infants who were reared at home but not involved in early-intervention programs. This investigation assumes importance by its contribution of descriptive data on the very young Down's syndrome child, the infant, and by its use of multiple measures of the behaviors of a small sample of infants in an intensive intervention program over a two-year time period.

Subjects

Down's Syndrome Subjects

Fifteen Down's syndrome infants and their parents who were participants in an early-intervention program were the subjects for this investigation. Eight infants were girls and seven were boys; eight infants were firstborns and seven had older siblings. All but two children (Mosaic) were Trisomy-21. Data are available on all measures for these infants with several exceptions. Two of the infants were born during the last year of the intervention program and, therefore, were included only in the early measures of the Infant Behavior Questionnaire (IBQ).

Infants were identified as being Down's syndrome at birth and intervention was begun as soon as possible after they were referred by medical and social-service personnel. The only selection criterion for participation was that the child had to be positively identified as Down's syndrome by a geneticist. Every Down's syndrome infant who was born and referred during an identified time period (one year) in a given geographical area (western Oregon) was included in the study.

Medically, subjects appeared to be representative of the Down's syndrome infant population. Of the fifteen children in the study, five had serious heart problems, three with severe, inoperable conditions.

All families were residents of western Oregon. They lived in both rural and urban areas and represented a typical range of occupational and educational backgrounds for persons from that region of Oregon. The infant subjects were all Caucasian and all but one (an adopted child) lived with their natural parents. The average ages of the mothers and fathers at the time of the child's birth were 27 (range 21–41) and 28 (range 23–37) respectively.

Description of Intervention Program in Which Down's Syndrome Infants Participated

All infants were participants in the Down's Syndrome Infant–Parent Program, a home-based early-intervention program implemented by the child's parents. The program was conducted at the Center on Human Development, University of Oregon, with support from the Bureau of Education for the Handicapped/HEW, and was established to provide continuous infant skill training soon after birth to Down's syndrome infants in an effort to keep their development within the normal range. Active educational programming was begun with infants between 4 weeks and 6 months of age (mean = 14 weeks). Those admitted as late as 4 to 6 months were unable to begin earlier due to health problems or late referral. The duration of participation in the program ranged from 15 to 30 months (mean = 24.4 months) depending on when the children were born and referred.

Parents were visited weekly or biweekly by a staff member, a Parent Advisor. During these home visits, the infant's development was evaluated and goals were established based upon the assessed needs of infants and the parents' input. The Parent Advisor then wrote behavioral, step-by-step educational programs for the parents to follow on a daily basis. Parents performed four to five programs per week (10 trials per day for each program). The Parent Advisor also made recommendations as to play and caregiving activities and changes in the child's physical environment which could be facilitative to the child's development. Parents collected data on each training trial and moved through the teaching programs at rates appropriate to their children by utilizing the data they collected to determine when to modify or advance through the program. By the end of the research program, parents were independently assessing their children, establishing goals, writing teaching programs, and modifying and/or advancing through programs based on the data they gathered. The Parent Advisor's role at that time was shifted to the role of a consultant.

Teaching programs were established by task-analyzing target behavior. From the task analyses, sequential teaching steps were derived.

Most behaviors were taught with shaping procedures usually incorporating physical prompts which were gradually withdrawn.

Goals for infant skill training were primarily normal developmental milestones. Since Down's syndrome children typically acquire these behaviors in the same order as a normal child but at a slower rate, training was aimed at accelerating their acquisition of these developmental landmarks. Descriptions of training procedures are also provided in Hanson (1976), Hanson and Bellamy (1977), and Hanson (1977a). In addition, a complete account of specific teaching programs and procedures utilized is available in a book, *Teaching your Down's syndrome infant: A guide for parents* (Hanson, 1977b).

Normative Comparison Samples

Sample 1—Referent Group for Infant Activity Checklist (IAC) and Caregiver–Infant Behavior Code. Forty-seven normal infants ranging in age from 4 to 18 months were recruited from the local community. An advertisement was placed in a local newspaper and the first children whose parents responded and who were of the appropriate age were included for observation. Data are available on two to five "normal" infants (at least one male and one female) at each month age level from 3 to 18 months.

Infants were all Caucasians and lived with their natural parents. Twenty-six were firstborns and 21 had older siblings; 21 were female and 26 were male. The average ages of the parents at the time of the child's birth were 27 years (mothers) and 29 years (fathers).

Sample 2—Normative Group for Infant Behavior Questionnaire (IBQ). During item-refinement for development of the Infant Behavior Questionnaire (Rothbart, Furby, Kelly, & Hamilton, 1977), parents of 6-month-old (116 infants), 9-month-old (157 infants), and 12-month-old (107 infants) normal infants, half girls and half boys, filled out Infant Behavior Questionnaires. Subjects represented a wide range of socioeconomic status groups and educational levels and were included in the study by the parents' responses to questionnaires mailed to all parents listed in the birth announcements in the local newspaper.

Instrumentation and Data-Collection Procedures

Multiple measures of infant and caregiver behavior were taken to provide an empirical description of the development of the Down's syndrome infants. Measures included: (1) a standardized instrument, the Bayley Scales of Infant Development (Bayley, 1969); (2) a parent advisor (trainer) report on infant behavior attainment, the Parent

Advisor Infant Development Checklist; (3) a parent report on infant temperament, the Infant Behavior Questionnaire (Rothbart, Furby, Kelly, & Hamilton, 1977); (4) a parent direct-observation measure of infant behavior, the Infant Activity Checklist; and (5) a direct-observation measure of infant and caregiver behaviors coded by independent observers, the Caregiver–Infant Behavior Code.

Results

Bayley Scales of Infant Development

Findings from the Bayley Scales indicated the average Mental Development Index (MDI) scores for Down's syndrome infants in this program were in the 70s (range of averages 75.8 to 69.2). Results were similar for the Psychomotor Development Index (PDI) with average scores for the Down's syndrome infants ranging from 88.1 to 63.8. A gradual decline in scores was noted over the two-year time period on both Mental and Motor scales. These scores indicate that on the average the Down's syndrome infants in this program scored below the normative range. However, they tended to score approximately 20 points (averages) above Down's syndrome infants not in an intervention program as described in a British study (Carr, 1970) (see Figure 1).

Parent Advisor Infant Development Checklist

A behavior checklist (criterion-based) was compiled from the behaviors sampled in a variety of infant development scales. Group data on the attainment of major developmental milestones were calculated for the Down's syndrome infants in this program. Results indicated some developmental lags across all areas of development (gross motor, fine motor–cognitive, social–self-help, and speech and language) when Down's syndrome infant mean ages of attainment were compared with normative data. Delays were evident particularly in the areas of gross motor development and speech and language development (for the older infants).

Data on the attainment of several critical skills by the Down's syndrome infants in this study, however, were compared to norms and to data from Down's syndrome infants not involved in an intervention program (Share, 1975; Share & French, 1974a; Share & Veale, 1974). As can be seen in Figure 2, the Down's syndrome children from this program, though delayed, performed at near normal levels, consistently attaining developmental milestones at earlier ages than the comparison group of Down's syndrome infants.

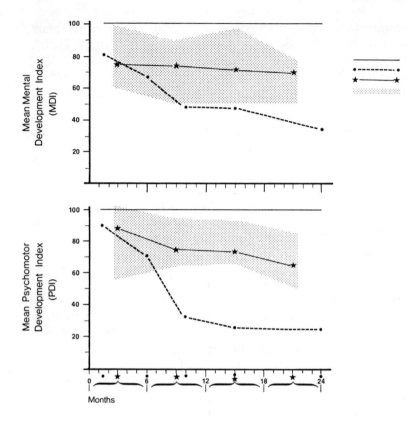

FIG. 1. Bayley Scale scores.

Infant Behavior Questionnaire (IBQ)

The Infant Behavior Questionnaire was constructed at the University of Oregon by Dr. Mary K. Rothbart as part of a research effort to investigate the interactions between infant temperament and caregiver behavior using both a caregiver report (the IBQ) and observational measures of infant temperament (Rothbart, 1977). Items on the Infant Behavior Questionnaire were developed to refer to specific concrete behaviors and caregivers were asked to respond on the basis of the infant's behavior during the previous week. Variables measured included motor activity, smiling and laughter, distress and latency to approach sudden or novel stimuli, distress to limitations, soothability, duration of orientation, vocal activity, and motor development.

The temperament scale scores on the IBQ of the Down's syndrome infants were compared to scores from a normative sample at 6, 9, and

12 months of age. Differences were found between groups on vocal activity and motor development (at all ages) and smiling and laughter (at 6 and 12 months) with normal infants scoring higher on these scales than the Down's syndrome infants. Down's syndrome infants, however, scored higher on motor activity at 12 months, and higher on distress and latency to approach sudden or novel stimuli and duration of orienting at 6 and 9 months. No differences between groups were noted on other scales. Results are summarized in Rothbart and Hanson (unpublished).

Infant Activity Checklist (IAC)

The Infant Activity Checklist is a caregiver report on infant activities observed at prespecified periods of time during the child's daily routine. Parents were asked to record the frequency with which their child engaged in a listed behavior. A proportion measure was then calculated to indicate the observed frequency of the behavior divided by the total number of observations.

Differences between groups (Down's syndrome and normal) were minimal on this parent-observation measure with respect to trunk-and-head-control development in that both groups displayed similar trends. Additionally, an important finding using this measure was that groups did not differ markedly with respect to activity level (arm and leg movements) and when differences did occur typically the Down's infants scored higher (i.e., exhibited more such movement). Likewise, no differences were evident across groups on state variables. Some differences, though, were found with regard to the activities in which the infants engaged. Normal infants scored higher on standing, vocalizing, and smiling–laughing behavior than did the Down's syndrome infants.

Caregiver–Infant Behavior Code

The Caregiver–Infant Behavior Code was designed to record the frequency of specific caregiver–infant behaviors as they occurred in selected standard situations. The three standard situations for recording were: (1) caregiver playing with infant using a toy provided by experimenter (a squeak toy in all cases); (2) caregiver playing with infant alone (without additional objects); and (3) caregiver performing a routine caregiving activity with infant (diapering).

Findings from the Caregiver–Infant Behavior Code showed the greatest differences between groups (Down's syndrome vs. normal) to occur in the Infant Physical (motor) domain. When analyzed (propor-

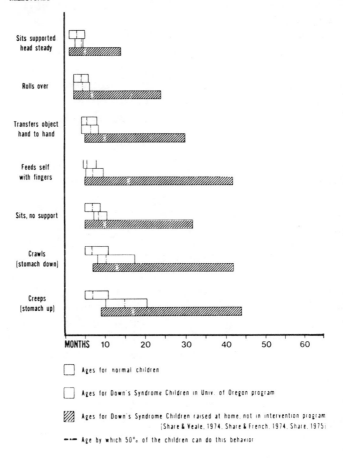

SUBJECTS KEY: Infants on which information is reported
Sits supported, head steady --12 infants
Rolls over --12 infants
Transfers objects hand to hand--12 infants
Feeds self with fingers ---12 infants
Sits, no support ---12 infants
Crawls--12 infants
Creeps--12 infants
Pulls to stand ---11 infants
   Infants not completing program:
     1 28-month-old (heart disorder–restricted activity)
Cruises ---11 infants
   Infants not completing program:
     1 28-month-old (heart disorder–restricted activity)

FIG. 2. Comparison of Down's syndrome infants in the University of Oregon program with norms and with Down's syndrome infants who were home-reared but not involved in an intervention program.

DEVELOPMENTAL
MILESTONES

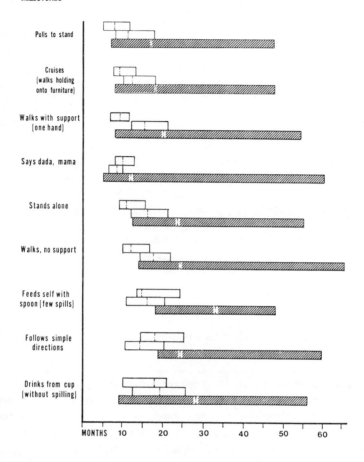

Pulls to stand

Cruises
(walks holding
onto furniture)

Walks with support
(one hand)

Says dada, mama

Stands alone

Walks, no support

Feeds self with
spoon (few spills)

Follows simple
directions

Drinks from cup
(without spilling)

MONTHS   10   20   30   40   50   60

Walks with support (one hand) --11 infants
    Infants not completing program:
        1 28-month-old (heart disorder–restricted activity)
Says Dada, Mama--12 infants
Stands alone --11 infants
    Infants not completing program:
        1 28-month-old (heart disorder–restricted activity)
Walks, no support--- 9 infants
    Infants not completing program:
        28-month-old (heart disorder–restricted activity)
        1 23-month-old
        1 16-month-old
Feeds self with spoon (few spills) --11 infants
    Infants not completing program:
        1 16-month-old
Follows simple directions ---12 infants
Drinks from cup unassisted (without spilling)---10 infants
    Infants not completing program:
        1 24-month-old
        1 16-month-old

tion of time spent in the activity) by individual physical behavior variables, normal infants showed more vigorous movement and touching behaviors than did the Down's syndrome infants. Down's syndrome infants, though, showed slightly more general motor activity than the normal infants.

On Infant Verbal behavior, the only major differences detected were those for the variables of saying words and smiles. On both these variables, normal infants scored higher than Down's syndrome infants. No major differences on Infant Attention variables (i.e., what infants looked at) were noted.

In the caregiver-behavior realm, no differences between groups on the Verbal or Attention domains were evident. Only differences in a few physical behavior variables were found. Mothers of normal infants, for instance, tended to restrain more; the mothers of Down's syndrome infants tended to physically prime more than the other mothers. When variables were clustered into a composite score, one group difference was noted with mothers of normal infants exhibiting more physical behaviors with respect to their infants than mothers of Down's syndrome infants.

Convergence of Measures

One of the purposes of this study was to determine if the measures converged or diverged as to the occurrence of various infant behaviors. Results indicated no divergence but rather convergence across measures with respect to a variety of infant behaviors (see Table 1).

The area where all measures converged as to the occurrence of specific infant behaviors was the physical motor behavior domain. Results from each measure indicated some delayed motor development in terms of Down's syndrome infants' attainment of developmental milestones though the "delays" were less than would have been predicted from previous literature reviewed. However, results from the IBQ, IAC, and the Code (to a lesser extent) showed that the general activity level (arm and leg movements) of the Down's syndrome infants was comparable to or higher than the activity level of the normal infants.

Though the results are less marked in the vocal–verbal behavior domain, the same trends in development were found across all measures in this area. The Parent-Advisor Infant Development Checklist and the IBQ results both showed some delays in infant vocal–verbal behavior as compared to norms. On the IAC, findings indicated that normal infants tended to vocalize to others more than the Down's syndrome infants. In addition, the MDI scores on the Bayley were

Table 1.   Measurement Convergence—Infant Behaviors

Measure	Physical behavior domain		Verbal behavior domain	Social behavior domain
	development	activity level		
Balyey	+		+(mental score)	
Development checklist	+		+	
IBQ	+	+	+	+
IAC	+	+	+	+
Code	+	+	+(trend)	+

"+" indicates that measures reported the occurrence of the same infant behaviors.

typically below normal levels for the Down's syndrome babies. This test of mental abilities is composed of a large number of verbal items. While these items cannot be sorted out for scoring purposes, the trend does provide supportive data with which to compare to the other instruments. Finally, though major differences were not found between groups on the Behavior Code, the trend was for the normal infants to score higher (i.e., exhibit more vocal–verbal behaviors) than the Down's syndrome infants in the verbal domain. They also scored consistently higher on "saying words" than did the Down's syndrome infants.

Smiling and laughter behaviors were the major social behaviors which were examined across measures. The IBQ, IAC, and Code results all indicated at some level that the normal infants scored higher (i.e., did more smiling and laughter) than the Down's syndrome infants. Specific and accurate age measures of smiling–laughter were not available from the Bayley measures or for the Development Checklist as several infants entered the program after they had begun demonstrating this behavior.

Both the IAC and Code reported no differences between infants with respect to state and attention to objects and people in the environment. The attention measures merely reflected what the infant's eyes were on at a given time rather than measures of visual fixation, duration, or preference.

In summary, findings from the measures of infant behavior in this study tended to converge across a variety of behaviors. Principally, convergence was found with respect to physical, verbal, and social (smiling) infant behavior. Developmental delays were noted across measures on these behaviors for the Down's syndrome subjects. However, levels or degrees of delay were minor as compared to the "normative" data.

CONCLUSIONS

The Down's syndrome infants in this early-intervention program as a group showed a stable developmental pattern and/or steady progress over time across skill areas as measured by multiple procedures. However, as evidenced by the Mental and Psychomotor Development Index scores from the administration of the Bayley Scales, infants' overall "rate" of development decreased slightly over the two-year period. This was particularly apparent in the area of motor development. While other measures showed developmental progess for the Down's syndrome babies, indications as to rate of growth could not be obtained from them.

Though steady progress was noted, differences were found in the development of this group as compared to normative samples for the various measures. Those areas in which differences were apparent tended to be in areas or domains in which some evidence of similar phenomena was reported in the educational and psychological literature (previously reviewed). These areas included delays in physical, verbal, and social behavior domains.

The magnitude, however, of the delays or differences between Down's syndrome infants and normative comparison groups in this study was not great. Considerable variability among individual Down's syndrome children was noted also with some children performing within the normal range. In addition, on measures where descriptive data on Down's syndrome children not involved in intervention programs were available, it appears that infants in this program acquired behaviors earlier than would have been expected on the basis of this descriptive information.

Were one to predict the status of Down's syndrome infants from information in the descriptive literature reviewed and on the basis of biological constraints, a different picture of their development would arise than that presented by this investigation. Data from this investigation suggests that a structured early-intervention effort can alter the development of these children who have a biological handicap resulting from a chromosomal aberration. As such, these results are consistent with an interactional (Lewis, 1972), or transactional model (Sameroff & Chandler, 1975) of development.

Briefly, the interactional model of development described by Lewis (1972) states that the status of the individual at a given point is a product of the individual's previous status and environmental variables $(S_{t_2} = fS_{t_1} \times E_{t_1})$. As Lewis (1979a) suggested, the interaction of time, status, and environment can be seen as also interacting with present environment factors to produce the individual's present status at time 2 $[S_{t_2} = f(S_{t_1} \times E_{t_1}) \times E_{t_2}]$. This model is essentially the same as that articulated by Sameroff and Chandler (1975) as the transactional model. They described the transactional model as one in which a "continual and progressive interplay between the organism and its environment" occurs (p. 234). Data from the Lewis and Coates (1979) investigation provide support for the interactional—transactional model of development. They reported in their study of normal infants at 3 and 12 months of age a correlation of .36 between infant Bayley MDI scores at 3 and 12 months and a correlation of .36 between mother responsivity to infant distress (at 3 months) and the infant 12-month MDI; each factor accounted for approximately 13% of the variance. However, when both the infant-status variable (MDI at 3 months) and environmental variable (mother responsivity) were combined, these factors accounted for twice the variance of either the status or environmental variable alone. Again, the developmental status of the individual can be seen as a consequence of both constitutional-status and environmental factors interacting.

The interactional or transactional model suggests that we cannot predict the child's development from pure status or environmental factors. This refutes the constitutional–medical and environmental models of development (reviewed by Lewis & Fox, 1980).

The practice among professional and laypersons alike has been reliance on a medical model of development when determining prognoses for obviously handicapped children, such as Down's syndrome children. However, data from the educational interventions reviewed clearly indicate that such a model is inappropriate. Intervention attempts by definition are aimed at altering the behavior of the child and the child's environment. The Oregon investigation, for instance, focused on systematic teaching through structured caregiver interactions with the child.

The intervention data do, however, lend support to the interactional model of development. Interaction implies that the child is continually changing and as such alters the environment and is altered by the "new" environment. This appears to be the case with the Down's syndrome child given the apparent malleability in the condition as indicated by the data presented. The great variability among these children also can be accounted for in the interactional model.

The group is homogeneous in that by definition all have extra chromosomal material which produces a cluster of characteristics and behavior associated with Down's syndrome. However, constitutional differences among children and environmental differences and their interactions result in the variable expression of the condition both interindividually and intraindividually.

It is unlikely at present that the informed observer would make reference to the Down's syndrome child as severely retarded. The data do not support the use of that label in most cases. Thus, we can either conclude that the syndrome or the manifestation of the condition has changed over time or that environmental variables are interacting with the constitutional status of these individuals such that the developmental status of Down's syndrome children is higher than assumed from previous predictions.

REFERENCES

Baron, J. Temperament profile of children with Down's syndrome. *Developmental Medicine and Child Neurology*, 1972, *14*, 620–643.

Bayley, N. *Manual of direction for infant scales of development*. Washington, D. C.: National Institute of Mental Health, 1964.

Bayley, N. *Bayley Scales of Infant Development*. New York: The Psychological Corporation, 1969.

Bellamy, G. T., Dickson, A. S., Chamberlain, P., & Steinbock, E. Evaluation of parent training as a method of increasing skill acquisition by a Down's syndrome infant. *Mental Retardation*, 1975, *13*, 43.

Benda, C. E. *Mongolism and cretinism* (3rd ed.). New York: Grune & Stratton, 1949.

Benda, C. E. *The child with mongolism*. New York: Grune & Stratton 1960.

Benda, C. E. *Down's syndrome: Mongolism and its management*. New York: Grune & Stratton, 1969.

Bidder, R. T., Bryant, G., & Gray, O. P. Benefits to Down's syndrome children through training their mothers. *Archives of Diseases in Childhood*, 1975, *50*, 383–386.

Blacketer-Simmonds, D. A. An investigation into the supposed differences existing between mongols and other mentally defective subjects with regard to certain psychological traits. *Journal of Mental Science*, 1953, *99*, 702–719.

Brousseau, K. & Brainend, M. *Mongolism: A study of the psychical and mental characteristics of mongoloid imbeciles*. Baltimore: Williams & Wilkins, 1928.

Carey, W. B. A simplified method for measuring infant temperament. *Journal of Pediatrics*, 1970, *77*, 188.

Carr, J. Mental and motor development in young mongol children. *Journal of Mental Deficiency Research*, 1970, *14*, 205–220.

Carr, J. *Young children with Down's syndrome: Their development, upbringing, and effect on their families*. London: Butterworths, 1975.

Centerwall, S. A., & Centerwall, W. R. A study of children with mongolism reared in the home compared to those reared away from the home. *Pediatrics*, 1960, *25*, 678–685.

Cicchetti, D., & Sroufe, L. A. The relationship between affective and cognitive development in Down's syndrome infants. *Child Development*, 1976, 47, 920–929.

Clements, P. R., Bates, M. V. & Hafer, M. Variability within Down's syndrome (Trisomy-21): Empirically observed sex differences in IQs. *Mental Retardation*, 1976, 14, 30–31.

Coleman, M. (Ed.) *Serotonin in Down's syndrome*. Amsterdam: North Holland, 1973.

Coleman, M. Down's syndrome. *Pediatric Annals*, 1978, 7(2).

Coleman, M. Personal communication, 1979.

Connolly, B., & Bussell, F. Interdisciplinary early intervention program. *Physical Therapy*, 1976, 56(2), 155–158.

Cornwell, A. C., & Birch, H. G. Psychological and social development in home-reared children with Down's syndrome (mongolism). *American Journal of Mental Deficiency*, 1969, 74, 341–350.

Dameron, L. E. Development of intelligence of infants with mongolism. *Child Development*, 1963, 34, 733–738.

De Coriat, L.F., Theslenco, L. & Waksman, J. The effects of psycho-motor stimulation on the I.Q. of young children with Trisomy 21. In *Proceedings: First Congress of the International Association for the Scientific Study of Mental Deficiency*, Montpelier, 1967. Surrey, England: M. Jackson Publishing Company, 1968.

de la Cruz, F. Genetic disorders in mental retardation. In P. Mittler (Ed.), *Research to practice in mental retardation: Biomedical aspects* (Vol. 3). Baltimore: University Park Press, 1977.

Dennis, W., & Sayegh, Y. The effect of supplementary experiences upon the behavioral development of infants in institutions. *Child Development*, 1965, 36, 81–90.

Dicks-Mireaux, M. J. Development of intelligence of children with Down's syndrome: Preliminary report. *Journal of Mental Deficiency Research*, 1966, 10, 89–93.

Dicks-Mireaux, M. J. Mental development of infants with Down's syndrome. *American Journal of Mental Deficiency*, 1972, 77(1), 26–32.

Dodd, B. J. Comparison of babbling patterns in normal and Down's syndrome infants. *Journal of Mental Deficiency Research*, 1972, 16, 35–40.

Domino, G., Goldschmid, M., & Kaplan, M. Personality traits of institutionalized mongoloid girls. *American Journal of Mental Deficiency*, 1964, 68, 498–502.

Down, J. L. Observations on ethnic classifications. *London Hospital Reports*, 1866, 3, 259–262.

Fishler, K., Share, J., & Koch, R. Adaptation of Gesell Developmental Scales for evaluation of development in children with Down's syndrome (mongolism). *American Journal of Mental Deficiency*, 1964, 68, 642–646.

Fishler, K., Koch, R., & Donnell, G. N. Comparison of mental development in individuals with Mosaic and Trisomy 21 Down's syndrome. *Pediatrics*, 1976, 58(5), 744–748.

Frankenburg, W. K., & Dodds, J. D. *Denver Developmental Screening Test*. Denver: University of Colorado Medical Center, 1969.

Gesell, A. L., & Amatruda, C. S. *Developmental diagnosis* (2nd ed.). New York: Harper & Row, 1969.

Golden, W., & Pashayan, H. M. The effect of parental education on the eventual mental development of noninstitutionalized children with Down's syndrome. *Journal of Pediatrics*, 1976, 4, 603–605.

Gordon, I. J. Stimulation via parent education. *Children*, 1969, 16, 57–59.

Hanson, M. J. Evaluation of training procedures used in a parent implemented intervention program for Down's syndrome infants. *American Association for the Education of the Severely/Profoundly Handicapped (AAESPH) Review*, 1976, 1(7), 36–52.

Hanson, M. J. Parent-professional coordination: An approach and an example. Working paper, Center on Human Development, University of Oregon, 1977a.

Hanson, M. J. *Teaching your Down's syndrome infant: A guide for parents.* Baltimore: University Park Press, 1977b.

Hanson, M. J. A longitudinal, descriptive study of the behaviors of Down's syndrome infants in an early intervention program. *Center on Human Development Monograph.* Eugene: Oregon University Press, 1979.

Hanson, M. J. & Bellamy, G. T. Continuous measurement of progress in infant intervention programs. *Education and Training of the Mentally Retarded,* 1977, *12*, 52–58.

Hayden, A. H. A center-based parent-training model. In D. L. Lillie & P. L. Trohanis (Eds.), *Teaching parents to teach.* New York: Walker and Company, 1976.

Hayden, A. H., & Dmitriev, V. The multidisciplinary preschool program for Down's syndrome children at the University of Washington Model Preschool Center. In B. Z. Friedlander, G. M. Sterritt, & G. E. Kirk (Eds.), *Exceptional infant: Assessment and intervention* (Vol. 3). New York: Brunner/Mazel, 1975.

Hayden, A. H., & Haring, N. G. Programs for Down's syndrome children at the University of Washington. In T. D. Tjossem (Ed.), *Intervention strategies for high risk infants and young children.* Baltimore: University Park Press, 1976.

Hayden, A. H., & Haring, N. G. The acceleration and maintenance of developmental gains in Down's syndrome school-age children. In P. Mittler (Ed.), *Research to practice in mental retardation: Care and intervention* (Vol. 1), Baltimore: University Park Press, 1977.

Heber, R. & Garber, H. The Milwaukee Project: A study of the use of family intervention to prevent cultural–familial mental retardation. In B. Z. Friedlander, G. M. Sterritt, & G. E. Kirk (Eds.), *Exceptional infant: Assessment and intervention* (Vol. 3). New York: Brunner/Mazel, 1975.

Johnson, R. C. & Abelson, R. B. Intellectual, behavioral and physical characteristics associated with Trisomy, Translocation and Mosaic types of Down's syndrome. *American Journal of Mental Deficiency,* 1969, *73*, 852–856.

Koch, R., Share, J., Webb, A., & Graliker, B. V. The predictability of Gesell Developmental Scales in mongolism. *The Journal of Pediatrics,* 1963, *62*, 93–97.

Kugel, R. B. & Reque, D. A comparison of mongoloid children. *Journal of the American Medical Association,* 1961, *175*, 959–961.

Lejeune, J., Gautier, M., & Turpin, R. Etudes des chromosomes somatiques de neuf enfants mongoliens. *C. R. Acad. Sci.,* 1959, *248*, 1721.

Levinson, A., Friedman, A., & Stamps, F. Variability of mongolism. *Pediatrics,* 1955, *16*, 43–54.

Lewis, M. State as an infant–environment interaction: An analysis of mother–infant interaction as a function of sex. *Merrill–Palmer Quarterly,* 1972, *18*, 95–121.

Lewis, M. Personal communication, 1979a.

Lewis, M. The social nexus: Toward a theory of social development. Invited address, Eastern Psychological Association meetings, Philadelphia, 1979b.

Lewis, M., & Coates, D. L. Mother-infant interaction and cognitive development in twelve-week-old infants. 1979, Unpublished.

Lewis, M., & Fox, N. Assessment and detection of handicap in early life: Current theory and research. In B. Camp (Ed.), *Advances in Behavioral Pediatrics* (Vol. 1). Greenwich, Connecticut: JAI Press, 1980.

Magenis, R. E., Overton, K. M., Chamberlin, J., Brody, T., & Lourien, E. Parental origin of the extra chromosome in Down's syndrome. *Human Genetics,* 1977, *37*, 7–16.

Melyn, M. A., & White, D. T. Mental and developmental milestones of noninstitutionalized Down's syndrome children. *Pediatrics,* 1973, *52*(4), 542–545.

Menolascino, F. J. Psychiatric aspects of mongolism. *American Journal of Mental Deficiency*, 1965, *69*, 653–660.

Miranda, S. B., & Fantz, R. L. Recognition memory in Down's syndrome and normal infants. *Child Development*, 1974, *45*, 651–660.

Painter, G. The effect of a structured tutorial program on cognitive and language development of a culturally disadvantaged group. *Merrill–Palmer Quarterly*, 1969, *15*, 385–391.

Robinson, H. B., & Robinson, N. M. *The mentally retarded child: A psychological approach* (2nd ed.). New York: McGraw-Hill, 1976.

Rollin, H. R. Personality in mongolism with special reference to the incidence of catatonic psychosis. *American Journal of Mental Deficiency*, 1946, *51*, 219–237.

Rosencrans, C. J. The relationship of normal/21 Trisomy Mosaicism and intellectual development. *American Journal of Mental Deficiency*, 1968, *72*, 562–566.

Ross, R. T. The mental growth of mongoloid defectives. *American Journal of Mental Deficiency*, 1962, *66*, 736–738.

Rothbart, M.K. Research with "normal" infants: Its application to work with severely/profoundly handicapped babies. Paper presented at the Fourth Annual Conference of the American Association for the Education of the Severely/Profoundly Handicapped (AAESPH) San Francisco: October 1977.

Rothbart, M.K., & Hanson, M.J. A comparison of temperamental characteristics of Down's syndrome and normal infants. Unpublished manuscript.

Rothbart, M.K., Furby, L., Kelly, S.K., & Hamilton, J.S. Development of a caretaker report temperament scale for use with 3, 6, 9, and 12 month old infants. Paper presented at the meeting of the Society for Research in Child Development, New Orleans, March 1977.

Rynders, J. *Two basic considerations in utilizing mothers as tutors of their very young retarded or potentially retarded children.* Washington, D. C.: Department of Health, Education and Welfare, U. S. Office of Education, Bureau of Education for the Handicapped (ERIC Document Reproduction #ED 079908), 1973.

Rynders, J. E., & Horrobin, J. M. Project EDGE: The University of Minnesota's Communication Stimulation Program for Down's Syndrome Infants. In B. Z. Friedlander, G. M. Sterritt, & G. E. Kirk (Eds.), *Exceptional infant: Assessment and intervention* (Vol. 3). New York: Brunner/Mazel, 1975.

Rynders, J. E., Spiker, D., & Horrobin, J. M. Underestimating the educability of Down's syndrome children: Examination of methodological problems in recent literature. *American Journal of Mental Deficiency*, 1978, *82*(5), 440–448.

Sameroff, A. J. & Chandler, M. J. Reproductive risk and the continuum of caretaking causality. In F. Horowitz (Ed.), *Review of child development research* (Vol. 4). Chicago: University of Chicago Press, 1975.

Sasaki, M. Paternal origin of the extra chromosome in Down's syndrome. *Lancet*, 1973, *2*, 1257.

Schaefer, E. S. A home tutoring program. *Children*, 1969, *16*, 59–61.

Serafica, F. C. & Cicchetti, D. Down's syndrome children in a strange situation: Attachment and exploration behaviors. *Merrill–Palmer Quarterly*, 1976, *22*, 137–150.

Sewell Early Education Development Program (SEED) (Prepared by J. Herst, S. Wolfe, G. Jorgensen, & S. Pallan). *SEED Developmental Profiles* (Rev.). Denver: Sewell Rehabilitation Center, 1976.

Share, J. B. Developmental progress in Down's syndrome. In R. Koch & F. F. de la Cruz (Eds.), *Down's syndrome (mongolism): Research, prevention, and management.* New York: Brunner/Mazel, 1975.

Share, J., Webb, A., & Koch, R. A preliminary investigation of the early developmental status of mongoloid infants. *American Journal of Mental Deficiency*, 1961, 66, 238–241.

Share, J. B, & French, R. W. Early motor development in Down's syndrome children. *Mental Retardation*, 1974a, 12(6), 23.

Share, J. B., & French, R. W. Guidelines of early motor development in Down's syndrome children for parents and teachers. *Special Children Journal*, 1974b, 1(2), 61–65.

Share, J. B., & Veale, A. M. *Developmental landmarks for children with Down's syndrome (mongolism)*. Dunedin, New Zealand: The University of Otago Press, 1974.

Share, J., Webb, A., & Koch, R. A preliminary investigation of the early developmental status of mongoloid infants. *American Journal of Mental Deficiency*, 1961, 66, 238–241.

Share, J., Koch, R., Webb, A., & Graliker, B. The longitudinal development of infants and young children with Down's syndrome (mongolism). *Americal Journal of Mental Deficiency*, 1964, 68, 685-692.

Shipe, D., & Shotwell, A. M. Effect of out-of-home care on mongoloid children: A continuation study. *American Journal of Mental Deficiency*, 1965, 69, 649–652.

Shotwell, A. M., & Shipe, D. Effect of out-of-home care on the intellectual and social development of mongoloid children. *American Journal of Mental Deficiency*, 1964, 68, 693–699.

Skeels, H. M. Adult status of children with contrasting early life experiences. *Monographs of the Society for Research in Child Development*, 1966, 31(3, Serial No. 105), 1–65.

Skeels, H. M., & Dye, H. B. A study of the effects of differential stimulation of mentally retarded children. *Proceedings of the American Association on Mental Deficiency*, 1939, 44, 114–136.

Smith, D. W., & Wilson, A. A. *The child with Down's syndrome (mongolism): Causes, characteristics, and acceptance*. Philadelphia: W. B. Saunders Company, 1973.

Spitz, R. A. Hospitalism: An inquiry into the genesis of psychiatric conditions in early childhood. *Psychoanalytic Study of the Child*, 1945, 1, 53–74.

Spitz, R. A. Hospitalism: A follow-up report. *Psychoanalytic Study of the Child*, 1946, 1, 113–117.

Stedman, D. J., & Eichorn, D. H. A comparison of the growth and development of institutionalized and home-reared mongoloids during infancy and early childhood. *American Journal of Mental Deficiency*, 1964, 69, 391–401.

Stein, Z. A., & Susser, M. Recent trends in Down's syndrome. In P. Mittler (Ed.), *Research to practice in mental retardation: Biomedical aspects* (Vol. 3). Baltimore: University Park Press, 1977.

Tredgold, A. F. *Mental deficiency (amentia)*. New York: William Wood & Company, 1922.

Uchida, I. A. Paternal origin of the extra chromosome. *Lancet*, 1973, 2, 1258.

Zausmer, E., Pueschel, S., & Shea, A. A sensory–motor stimulation program for the young child with Down's syndrome: Preliminary report. *MCH Exchange*, 1972, 2(4), 1–4.

6

Behavioral and Metabolic Factors in Childhood Obesity

Joël A. Grinker

Obesity is one of the most prevalent nutritional disorders in America today. Epidemiological studies report that from 25 to 45% of adult American men and women suffer from overweight or obesity (Ten State Nutrition Survey, 1972).[1] In spite of the number and variety of approaches to weight reduction, including special diets, exercise, behavior modification, and pharmacological intervention, obesity remains intractable (Bray, 1978; Stunkard & McLaren-Hume, 1959). The major failures of treatment lie not in the ineffectiveness of various procedures to produce weight reduction but in the inability to sustain the weight loss. For example, hospitalization accompanied by severe or total caloric restriction leads to dramatic but short-lasting weight loss. Within three years following hospitalization, over 90% of the patients have regained the lost weight (Drenick, 1973).

It has been suggested (Grinker and Hirsch, 1972; Bjorntorp, Carlgren, Isaksson, Krotkiewski, Larrson, & Sjostrom, 1975; Knittle, 1977) that the failure of obese adults to maintain a permanent reduction in

---

[1] Obesity can be loosely defined as a greater than 20% increment over ideal body weight (body weight norms are standardized for age, sex, and stature). (See for example, Metropolitan Life Insurance Company, 1959.)

Joël A. Grinker • Associate Professor, Rockefeller University, 1230 York Avenue, New York, New York 10021   This work has been supported by grants RR-102 (Clinical Research Center) and AM-18325 from the National Institutes of Health and BNS 76-09957 from the National Science Foundation.

body weight is not simply a failure of dietary restriction but a failure to correct those morphological, metabolic, or behavioral factors which are responsible for obesity. Early identification of prospectively obese children and the development of methods to prevent obesity, rather than treatment after obesity is well established, is clearly desirable. Estimates of the prevalence of childhood obesity suggest that 10 to 13% of American children are overweight. Many of these overweight children may go on to become overweight adults. Thus, increasing attention has been focused on the genesis of obesity and in particular on the development of obesity in early infancy and in childhood. Furthermore, while obesity in adult years may increase the risk or complicate a variety of other diseases including hypertension, diabetes, and coronary heart disease, childhood obesity can also have serious social and psychological consequences.

This paper will consider several issues in childhood obesity:

1. Can potentially obese children be identified and what is the association between childhood obesity and adult obesity? Are the adult obese likely to have been obese in childhood and are obese children likely to become obese adults? Prospective and retrospective data will be reviewed.

2. What are the current theories of the ontogeny of obesity? In particular, what are the contributions of genetic, familial, and environmental factors to the development of obesity? Animal data will be reviewed and research on behavioral and nutritional factors in the early development of obesity will be assessed. The possible contribution of maternal behaviors to the development of infant obesity will be discussed.

3. Finally, what are the social and mental health consequences of early obesity? Stereotyping of the obese child as deviant or irresponsible may have consequences for adult self-perception, peer relations, or responses to treatment.

Correlation between Childhood and Adult Obesity

Does childhood obesity lead to adult obesity? The answer to this question is intimately related to the decision to attempt prevention or treatment in infancy or wait for the child to "grow out" of the obesity. Two types of data exist, prospective or longitudinal data on obese and nonobese children and infants, and retrospective data from obese adults. Of the two, the retrospective data more convincingly relate adult obesity to childhood obesity.

Prospective

Studies of severe obesity in late childhood rather than studies of moderate obesity in infancy or early childhood suggest that childhood obesity is significantly associated with adult obesity. One study (Abraham, Collins, & Nordsieck, 1971) has demonstrated that for a large percent of the population, relative body-weight levels established in childhood are maintained in adult years. The weights 35 to 40 years later of 1000 white male schoolchildren were compared. The results show stability in all body-weight groups. Only 4% of those who had been below average weight in childhood became markedly overweight as adults and only 17% attained above average weight. In contrast, none of the markedly overweight children was below average weight as adults, and only 16% maintained an average weight. Fifty percent of the below-average weight group remained in this group as adults while 63% of the markedly overweight group remained overweight as adults. Clinical studies confirm a definite relationship between severe childhood obesity and adult obesity. The long-term prognosis for severe obesity in children is reported to be uniformly poor, with 80% remaining obese in adult life (Knittle, 1977; Lloyd, Wolff, & Whalen, 1961; Hammer, Campbell, & Wooley, 1971).

Moderate overweight in childhood shows little or no relationship to weight or fatness in infancy. Moderate overweight (110% of standard) in Turkish 10-year-olds was not significantly related to the occurrence of overweight before age 6 (Neyzi, Saner, Binyildiz, Yazicioglu, Emre, & Gurson, 1976). A prospective study of fatness (skinfold thickness) in normal children in Switzerland showed no strong relationship between skinfolds at 1 year and at puberty (Hernesniemi, Zachmann, & Prader, 1974; Prader, Hernesniemi, & Zachmann, 1976).

Other studies have attempted to identify early predisposing factors to obesity. Factors such as parental weight, birth weight, and rate of weight gain in the first six months of life have been examined in an effort to ascertain the development of obesity and choose appropriate predictors. However, the identification of separate high- and low-risk categories, such as the presence or absence of familial obesity prior to longitudinal observation, has not frequently been reported. The majority of studies report data on normal infants from unspecified familial backgrounds. An additional problem is the inclusion of moderately fat as well as severely obese infants or children in the overweight category and the use of a variety of criteria for making such determinations.

Several studies have related birth weight itself to subsequent fatness. It is difficult to make predictions from birth weight alone since it is greatly affected by length of gestation and parity (see Tanner, 1974;

Ounsted & Sleigh, 1975). In spite of these limitations, some investigators (Mossberg, 1948; Illingworth, Harvey, & Gin, 1949) have reported a positive relationship between birth weight and later obesity. Illingworth classified subjects into four birth-weight groups and compared their heights and weights at age 5. Sixty percent of the highest birth-weight group was at least 10% overweight, compared to only 9% of the lowest birth-weight group. In contrast, other investigators (Bruch, 1939; Wolff, 1955; Heald & Hollander, 1965; Dorner, Grychtolik, & Julitz, 1977) reported no differences in birth weights between obese and nonobese children.

Attempts to predict obesity based on weight at 6 months of age or weight/height ratios have had mixed success. Weight achieved in the first few months of life was reported to be poorly correlated with weight in adulthood (Tanner, 1962b). Huenemann (1974) has presented data on infants at 6 months of age and at 3 years. None of the children with high weight-for-height ratios at age 3 years had been in that group at 6 months. Another study, however, reported significant correlations between weight/height ratios at 4 months and 12- and 48-month weight/height ratios (Mellbin & Vuille, 1968).

The rate of change in weight in the first few months has also been used as a predictor of later obesity. Weight gain from birth to 1 year has been studied in relationship to weight/height ratios at age 7 (Mellbin & Vuille, 1968) in normal children in Sweden. Only 10% of the overweight school children had been obese as infants and the relationship was less strong in girls than boys. In a subsequent study, rate of weight gain was again only moderately related to subsequent obesity in boys (Mellbin & Vuille, 1976). Several English studies have also utilized rate of change as a predictor of subsequent obesity. Rapid weight gain over the first 6 weeks to 6 months of life was predictive of excessive weight at school age (Eid, 1970; Taitz, 1971; Asher, 1966). However, the average birth weight of the slow-weight-gain group was significantly higher than that of the rapid-weight-gain group, suggesting that those children who weighed less at birth gained more rapidly following birth. The number of obese children (defined as weighing 20% more than expected for height) was highest in the rapid-weight-gain group. A German study has also reported that infants gaining more than 3 kg during the first 3 months of life were significantly obese at age 5 and at 15 years (Dorner et al., 1977).

A Swedish study (Svenger, Lindberg, Weibull, & Olsson, 1975) related the early development and persistence of obesity to nutritional levels in the first year of life. Compared with British samples, a relatively small percentage of infants were found to be obese or overweight. On the average, nutritional levels were close to recommended standards. The mean caloric intake during the months before and after overweight and obesity were diagnosed exceeded the normal by only 10%. Follow-up at age 2½ years revealed that 50% of those children who had become obese by age 1 remained so while several moderately overweight children became more overweight and no normal-weight children became obese. Twenty-five percent of the obese children had one obese parent, compared with 5% of the normal and overweight children. The authors suggest that the low incidence of overnutrition in the Swedish population and the low incidence of obese and overweight infants support the idea that high caloric intake is important for the development of obesity in infancy.

The failure to find consistent results among the various prospective studies illustrates several problems in predicting adult obesity from obesity in early infancy or childhood (Weil, 1977). The large degree of variability in measures and indices of obesity makes comparison difficult. But a more critical problem lies in the variability in obesity over time. While it is clear that obesity in adulthood can be reliably and significantly correlated with obesity in childhood, not all obese infants or children become obese adults. An obvious question is what differentiates those obese children who "grow out" of their obesity from those who do not. A related question is whether those adults who have been obese during childhood are at a significantly greater risk for subsequent obesity. These questions have received little research attention.

Retrospective

Adult obesity can, of course, exist without childhood antecedents. Nevertheless, retrospective data suggest that the severely obese adult is likely to have been an obese child (Hirsch & Batchelor, 1976). A study of obese adolescent girls in the United States showed that these girls had gained weight more rapidly during the first year of life and were heavier at one year than nonobese adolescents Heald & Hollander, 1965). Mossberg (1948) has reported that of 493 cases of childhood obesity (6–15 years of age) at least half had become obese by age 2.

The results of another retrospective study suggest that a least one-third of obese adults treated in a clinic had been obese in childhood (Mullins, 1958), a finding which is supported by a recent similar study of obese adults in the Rocheser, New York area. A strong relationship between childhood or infant obesity and adult obesity was reported (Charney, Goodman, McBride, Barbro, & Pratt, 1976). Thirty-six percent of those exceeding the 90th percentile of weight as infants were overweight adults, compared to 14% for average and lightweight infants. Those who had attained the 90th percentile in the first 6 months were 2.6 times more likely to be overweight as adults. A significant increase in adult obesity was evident when the infant exceeded the 75th percentile at 6 months, independent of height. Moreover, a cumulative or interactive effect between infant weight and parental overweight was found. When at least one parent was overweight, and the infant's weight was above the 75th percentile, 51% of the children became overweight as adults.

These data add support to the hypothesis that the first few months or year of life can be critical in establishing lifelong patterns of body composition, and that detection of significant obesity can be achieved in the child by 2 years of age. These studies further suggest that predictions of which children will become obese later in life may be improved by including significant risk factors (e.g., presence of familial obesity and birth weight). They also suggest that important determinants of subsequent obesity include nutritional status, infant feeding practices, and maternal–infant interactions.

ANTECEDENTS OF CHILDHOOD OBESITY

Genetic predisposition, excessive feeding in infancy and childhood, susceptibility to dietary manipulations, and underactivity or low caloric expenditure have all been suggested as causal factors in severe early-onset obesity. The next section will summarize the importance of these various factors in producing obesity in early childhood or infancy.

Genetic versus Environmental Factors

Evidence for a genetic component in human obesity is based on epidemiological studies. While obesity occurs in only 7% of children of normal-weight parents, 40% of the children from families with one obese parent and 80% of the children from two obese parents are overweight (Mayer, 1965). There is also a higher correlation between the weights of parents and natural offspring than between the weights of parents and adopted children (Withers, 1964; Biron, Mongeau, & Bertrand, 1977). Garn and Clark (1976) report data from the Ten State Nutrition Survey (1972) of fatfold thicknesses (triceps and subscapular) for more than 40,000 infants, children, and adults. Significant family correlations exist. Parent–child fatness correlations approximate .25 and increase with the age of the child. Husband–wife fatness correlations, however, approximate .30, suggesting that propinquity may also contribute to familial fatness trends.

Garn (Garn, Bailey, Cole, & Higgins, 1977) has presented persuasive evidence for both biological and learned or environmental influences on childhood fatness. A comparison of fatfold measurements in seriologically verified biological parents and children and seriologically verified unrelated adopted children and parents results in significant correlations in both. Furthermore, the fatness level of the biological child increases according to the parental fatness combination, from lean–lean to obese–obese. The fatness level of adopted children also increased in stepwise fashion according to the fatness levels of the parents. These data suggest that fatness follows family lines. Learned attitudes toward food or eating, energy expenditure, and possible early overfeeding by parents, could all contribute to this resemblance. However, these data are inconclusive since the definition of parental obesity used in this study was the 85th percentile or higher for skinfold measures. While this criterion includes the recognizably obese individual it also includes those who are only 20% above normal weight/ height ratios. The severely obese (50–100% overweight) may constitute a distinct category.

Significant mother–neonate fatness correlations have also been noted. Whitelaw (1976) reports that obese mothers have fatter babies than normal-weight mothers who in turn have fatter babies than thin mothers. It should also be noted that infants with obese foster mothers are reported to be significantly heavier during the first year than infants with nonobese foster mothers (Shenker, Fisichelli, & Long, 1974). Borjeson (1976) studied the incidence of obesity in twins. By age 7, monozygotic twins strongly resemble each other in fatfold size while the resemblance of dizygotic twins is significantly less. He concludes that nutritional and environmental influences modify the basic genetic factors in obesity, but the genetic factors remain the strongest influence.

The high correlation in parent–child obesity no doubt reflects both genetic and environmental components since it is well documented that different environments can alter the risk for obesity in man. One extreme class of environmental factors includes socioeconomic status and ethnic background. A consistent relationship between socioeconomic factors and the incidence of obesity has been demonstrated (Goldblatt, Moore, & Stunkard, 1964; Silverstone, Gordon, & Stunkard, 1969; Stunkard, d'Aquili, & Filion, 1972; Stunkard, 1975). These authors report a strong negative correlation between obesity and social class in both males and females and in both adults and children. These relationships were obtained in both British and American urban populations and in a variety of ethnic groups. Huenemann, Hampton, Shapiro, and Behnke (1966) have reported similar findings in adolescents. Garn (1971), however, has reported a low incidence of obesity in low-socioeconomic-class girls but a higher incidence of obesity in low-socioeconomic-class women, and the reverse for high-socioeconomic-class girls and women. However, British data suggest that from 1955 to 1970 the incidence of obesity in children in the lowest socioeconomic classes has increased and the incidence of obesity in the highest socioeconomic classes has decreased (Hammond, 1955; Lawrence, 1970; Whitelaw, 1971). These data suggest a nonlinear relationship between obesity and socioeconomic class.

At present, the data on genetic influences, derived mostly from epidemiological studies or from twin studies, are inconclusive. Equally inconclusive are the studies of family-line resemblances (Garn *et al.*, 1977). The usefulness of an interactive model is clearly apparent. An extremely persuasive documentation of the combined effects of genetic and environmental influences appears in data obtained from a set of identical twins in our laboratory. Both twins have had a lifelong problem with obesity, yet one has always been fatter than the other. This greater fatness is reflected in a different adipose cellularity profile; while both twins show an increase in the number of adipose cells, the fatter twin has a greater number.

Interactive Model

If the antecedents of severe obesity exist in early infancy, they may be a consequence of one or the other of two extreme conditions. One, similar to that seen in genetically obese rodents, involves a genetic predisposition which can be manifested even in the face of caloric restriction or moderation (Cox & Powley, 1977; Cleary, Vasselli, Jen, & Greenwood, 1978). The other involves overnutrition or overstimulation by the familial environment. This latter condition is well represented by dietary-induced obesity in the rat (Sclafani & Springer, 1976; Faust, Johnson, Stern, & Hirsch, 1978). A combination of the two conditions (i.e., some mixture of genetic predisposition combined with responses to environmental factors) may produce varying degrees, or a continuum, of obesity. A transactional model suggests that both influences continue to be critical (see Sameroff & Seifer, this volume).

Any comprehensive investigation of the origins of obesity must examine not only the infant, but also the influence of the mother or the caregiver on the infant. In the case of pure genetic obesity (if it exists in man), the influence of the mother or caregiver is minimal and may be seen as a purely passive response to the infant's genetically determined need to accumulate large amounts of fat. In the case of pure environmental obesity, the caregiver can forcefully or conclusively shape events, and determine a differential trajectory of weight gain and ultimate adult fatness in the preobese child. Experimental studies are necessary to examine (1) whether in fact maternal influences do occur, (2) whether they are different in obese and nonobese mothers, (3) whether infants of obese mothers are different at birth, and (4) whether early and sustained overfeeding or exposure to highly concentrated fat or carbohydrate diets has consequences for later taste preferences and food selection. Further investigations of activity levels and feeding responses in neonates with familial obesity may provide important information on genetic predisposition and susceptibility to environmental factors.

The expression of genetic and environmental influences can be directly examined in animal studies. Animal experiments also allow examination of the controls of food intake and the development of adipose cellularity in both normal-weight and obese animals. Animal models have typically included the experimentally-produced obese rat or mouse (electrolytic or chemical lesions of the region of the ventromedial hypothalamus—VMH), the genetic obesity of the Zucker rat (Zucker & Zucker, 1961) and the obese mouse (ob/ob and A^{vy}), and the dietary-produced obese rat.

Adipose Tissue Cellularity

Normal Development in Rodents

There is evidence from animal studies that adipose-tissue cellularity and quantity of body fat are in large part determined early in normal development. The pattern of adipose cellularity has been extensively studied in rodents and humans in this laboratory by the methods of electronic counting of osmium-fixed cells (Hirsch & Gallian, 1968). As in other counting procedures, only lipid-filled cells are counted. Techniques for detecting either "preadipocytes" or adipocytes that are as yet unfilled are only now being developed.

In experimentally produced obesity following lesions of the ventromedial hypothalamus (VMH) the obesity of rats fed standard laboratory chow is primarily associated with hypertrophy of the adipose depots (Hirsch & Han, 1969). In normal rats, adipose-cell proliferation is generally complete by the time of weaning (Knittle & Hirsch, 1968; Greenwood & Hirsch, 1974). Using the technique of *in vivo* labeling with tritiated thymidine into precursor adipocyte DNA, Greenwood and Hirsch established that adipocyte proliferation in the epididymal fat pad of the standard laboratory, chow-fed rat occurs at a rapid rate from birth to approximately 20 days but by 40 days ceases completely.

Further growth of the epididymal fat pad normally occurs only by increases in the lipid stores of already formed adipocytes.

Earlier observations of the effects of nutrition on growth and development had suggested that early over- or undernutrition might be a major factor determining the adiposity of the adult. Nutritional manipulations (e.g., rearing in artificially large litters) prior to weaning produced permanent stunting of rats with a concomitant reduction in adipose-cell number even when the rats were subsequently placed on a normal *ad libitum* diet (Knittle & Hirsch, 1968). In contrast, adult rats starved to reduce weight (McCance & Widdowson, 1962) or force-fed for short periods to gain weight (Cohn & Joseph, 1962) regained their normal weights after *ad libitum* feeding was restored. Hirsch and Han (1969) also found that adult rats do not lose adipocytes when starved. Instead weight loss involves only a reduction in fat-cell size.

The above studies were instrumental in promoting the concept of a critical period for adipocyte-number determination. A basic tenet of this concept was that alterations in adipocyte number are only possible during the critical period. However, more recent data have forced a reformulation. We now know that even mature animals can increase the measurable number of adipose cells when stimulated to overeat by high-fat or high-carbohydrate diets (Lemmonier, 1972; Faust *et al.*, 1978). Following surgical removal of certain fat depots (lipectomy), fat tissue is slowly regenerated (Faust, Johnson, & Hirsch, 1977a), and even normal growth may be accompanied by an increase in cell number in the aging guinea pig or rat (DiGirolamo & Mendlinger, 1971; Stiles, Francendese, & Masoro, 1975). Considerable debate has thus recently transpired over precursor cells, cell-counting techniques, fat-cell pool size, and size distribution and site variations (see James, 1976; Ashwell, 1978; Stern & Johnson, 1978; Hirsch *et al.*, 1979).

Dietary-induced Obesity

Obesity can be induced in many rat and mouse strains by manipulating the composition and the palatability of the diet. High-fat diets (Mickelsen, Takahaski, & Craig, 1955; Schemmel, Mickelsen, Pierce, Johnson, & Schirmer, 1971), sweetened solutions (Kanarek & Hirsch, 1977), and a supermarket diet consisting of sweetened condensed milk, cookies, and candies in addition to the normal laboratory diet (Sclafani & Springer, 1976) have all been employed to promote obesity in rodents. The severity of obesity produced varies considerably according to rat strain (Faust *et al.*, 1978; Schemmel, Mickelsen, & Gill, 1970), duration of the treatment (Schemmel *et al.*, 1971; Faust *et al.*, 1978), and the age of the animal when the diet is introduced (Kanarek & Hirsch, 1977).

Overeating (e.g., through changes in diet palatability) can, if continued for long-enough periods of time during adulthood, induce various degrees of weight gain and adipocyte proliferation in the various strains of rat. Permanent changes in fatness can be produced (Faust et al. 1978). When the rats are returned to the standard laboratory diet, some elevation in body weight persists. Adipose-cell size returns to control levels while adipose-cell number remains elevated. In this experiment different strains of rats (Osborne–Mendel, Sprague–Dawley, and Zucker) demonstrated differential responsiveness to high-fat feeding; the amount of weight gained and the consequent increases in adipose-cell number were greatest in the Osborne–Mendel and least in the Zucker rat. These results raise the question of whether responsiveness to palatable foods is itself a consequence of some predisposition to overweight. A further question is whether there are thus different degrees of "elasticity" in the control of food intake.

Genetic Obesity

The influence of genetic factors on the development of adipose cellularity in rodents has also been documented (Johnson & Hirsch, 1972; Johnson, Zucker, Cruce, & Hirsch, 1971) in several strains of genetically obese mice and in the genetically obese rat. Two patterns of adipose tissue cellularity are apparent: (1) early-onset hyperplastic–hypertrophic obesity, and (2) later-onset hypertrophic obesity. The majority of obesities in mice (*db/db*, *aA^y*, and NZO) are hypertrophic, but the *ob/ob* mouse and the Zucker rat are hyperplastic as well as hypertrophic. Furthermore, this pattern of obesity is characterized by greater severity and earlier onset as is hyperplastic human obesity. In the Zucker obese rat, adipose-tissue cellularity has been carefully studied in gonadal, retroperitoneal, and inguinal pads between 5 and 52 weeks of age (Johnson et al., 1971; Johnson, Stern, Greenwood, & Hirsch, 1978; Cleary et al., 1978). At all ages studied, adipose-cell size was significantly greater in obese rats than in lean litter mates. Adipose-cell hypertrophy in inguinal pads has even been observed as early as 5–7 days of age in the Zucker obese rat (Boulangé, Planche, & DeGasquet, 1977).

Studies of obese Zucker rats that were underfed or overfed before weaning suggest that a critical adipose-cell size may trigger further adipocyte proliferation (Johnson, Stern, Greenwood, Zucker, & Hirsch, 1973; Johnson et al., 1978). After weaning, overfed and underfed obese rats were allowed *ad libitum* access to standard laboratory chow until

26 weeks of age. At weaning all overfed rats weighed more than underfed rats. Obese rats weighed more than lean rats after *ad libitum* feeding. Early undernutrition did not reduce adipose-cell number in the obese rat, but overnutrition caused it to increase significantly. Adipose-cell size, however, was the same in underfed and overfed obese rats. In contrast, adipose cellularity of the lean rats could be manipulated in either direction. These observations suggest that fat-cell proliferation in the obese rat may be insensitive to early under-nutrition. Other experiments have shown that early and substantial dietary restriction (pair-feeding to lean controls) up to 33 weeks of age fails to protect the animal from obesity (Cleary *et al.*, 1978). Instead, a "stunted" rat with approximately the same proportion of fat (50%) and a mean fat-cell size that is the same as in the unrestricted obese rat is produced. Fat storage is seemingly protected at the cost of decreased skeletal or lean body mass and brain weight.

Hypertrophy (increased cell size) occurs early (5–7 days) in the Zucker rat and is quickly followed by elevation in lipoprotein lipase (LPL, an enzyme of lipid storage) at 7–12 days of age (Cleary *et al.*, 1978; Boulangé *et al.*, 1977). Studies of enzymes associated with cell enlargement and with the transformation of preadipocyte to adipocyte have centered on LPL and glycerol. Lipoprotein lipase is the main enzyme regulating the entrance of plasma FFA into the enlarging fat cell, and hormone-sensitive lipase and glycerol release reflect the breakdown of intracellular triglycerides (TG). A study of milk intake failed to find different intakes in obese and lean rat pups (Boulangé *et al.*, 1977). Furthermore, obese rat pups do not weigh more and are as active as lean siblings (Stern & Johnson, 1977) until 16–18 days. Thus, to date, the earliest known abnormalities in the Zucker rat are adipose-cell hypertrophy followed by elevations in LPL.

The sequence of events in this model of genetic obesity, hypertrophy, a rise in LPL, hyperphagia, and hyperplasia can be contrasted with that seen in dietary-induced obesity. There, observable hyperphagia, a behavioral abnormality, precedes the metabolic and cellular abnormalities. Hypertrophy, and eventually hyperplasia, occur at measurable times later. Faust *et al.* (1978) observed that as adipose tissue enlargement occurs as the result of high-fat or sucrose feeding, adipose cells enlarge to a critical size. Only after this adipocyte hypertrophy occurs are further increases in cell numbers noted. Thus, adipocyte size may have important repercussions in the development of persistent and refractory hyperplastic obesity. The contrast between these two models should provide useful information on behavioral and metabolic antecedents of obesity.

Cellular Patterns of Human Obesity

Investigations of human adipose tissue have been aided by the development of reliable methods for counting adipose-tissue fat cells and measuring their size in isolated fragments of adipose tissue (Hirsch & Gallian, 1968). An early study by Hirsch and Knittle (1970) using this technique documented the occurrence of hyperplasia as well as hypertrophy of adipose depots in severely obese men. In general, cellularity patterns are correlated with age of onset and severity; hyperplastic obesity is most often associated with early onset and severe obesity (Salans, Cushman, & Weismann, 1973; Bjorntop & Sjostrom, 1971).

Hypertrophic obesity is predominantly observed in the moderate obesity of adult onset (Salans, Horton, & Sims, 1971; Hirsch & Batchelor, 1976). An increased number of fat cells, as well as increased fat-cell size, characterizes the adipose tissue of very obese individuals (Hirsch & Knittle, 1970; Salans *et al.*, 1973; Sjostrom & Bjorntop, 1974; Krotkiewski, Sjostrom, Bjorntop, Calgren, Garellick, & Smith, 1977). It has been suggested that excessive fat storage during certain critical periods of adipocyte proliferation in childhood, and, perhaps, adolescence may induce the development of additional fat cells, leading to hyperplastic obesity (Brook, 1972; Knittle, Ginsberg-Fellner, & Brown, 1977). Since early-onset obesity is generally also severe in degree, considerable difficulty has been encountered in separating the effects of age of onset from the degree of obesity or the cellular character of adipose tissue. It seems clear, however, that hyperplastic obesity may develop not only during childhood, but also in the severe obesity of adult onset (Hirsch & Batchelor, 1976; Ashwell, Durrant, & Garrow, 1977).

The newborn, full-term human infant is well endowed with adipose tissue, unlike the newborn of other species. Adipose tissue accounts for 10–15% of body weight. The greater leanness of premature infants suggests that fat accumulation normally occurs during the last trimester of pregnancy. The stored lipid of the newborn has a composition which indicates the likelihood that it is almost exclusively made from carbohydrates within the fetus, rather than by placental transfer of maternal fat (Bagdade & Hirsch, 1966). At birth, stored fat weighs roughly 400 grams, as compared with the 10,000 or more grams found in the average adult. Thus, the newborn has about 1/25 the stored fat it will acquire during growth and maturation. This fat is stored in about 1/5 the number of adult cells and in cells that contain about 1/5 as much lipid as the adipocytes of adult tissue. The adipocytes do not appear unusually small on ordinary histologic study, since an 80% reduction in lipid is accompanied by only about a 40% reduction in cell diameter. Cells smaller than adult cells are seen, but extremely small cells, less than 25 μm in diameter, are generally not found in human-newborn tissue.

Recent findings on human adipocyte growth in infancy support the concept that attainment of a critical adipose-cell size precedes cellular proliferation or differentiation of preadipocytes. Bonnet, Duckerts, and Henskin (1976) demonstrated that while adipose-cell size increased during the first year of life, there were no apparent increases in cell number. An additional study (Dauncey & Gairdner, 1975) noted a steady increase in adipose-cell size from the earliest period studied until 12 months of age in 59 infants ranging from 26 weeks of gestation to 18 months of age. At 12 months, adipose-cell size reached a peak and then declined between 12 and 18 months.

Knittle et al. (1977) and Knittle, Timmers, Ginsberg-Fellner, Brown, and Katz (1979) have reported results on obese and nonobese subjects ranging in age from 2 to 18 years. Adipose-cell number, size, and metabolic fuction were studied. Body composition was measured by determining total body potassium in a whole body counter or calculated on the basis of height and weight using Friis-Hansen nomograms (1961). Obese subjects were defined as individuals who were 130% of ideal weight; nonobese subjects were between 90 and 120%. Absolute amount of fat did not change in the nonobese population during normal growth between the ages of 2 and 10, while obese subjects developed significant increments throughout this age range. During this period, cell sizes were large but unchanging in obese subjects, but a continued increase in cell number occurred. In contrast, nonobese subjects showed increases in adipose-cell size and number only after age 10. At all age levels, however, obese subjects displayed larger fat cells and a greater number of fat cells than the nonobese. A subsequent longitudinal study of younger children 4–48 months of age also found that adipose-cell size increased between 4 and 12 months with a peak cell size at 12 months in normal children. Only after 12 months was there a significant increase in cell number, while adipose-cell size decreased and remained stable between 2 and 4 years. In a longitudinal study of 16 normal children, Hager, Sjostrom, Arvidson, Bjorntorp, and Smith (1977) found that adipose-cell size increased between 1 and 12 months of age, with little change in cell number. Cell number increased from 12 to 18 months. They also found a peak cell size at these ages and by 18 months, adipose-cell size was similar to that of 8- and 22-year-old females. The one obese child studied exhibited a large increase in fat-cell size followed by an increase in cell number from 12 months of age, while one infant who was small for gestational age had a low fat-cell number but normal fat-cell size.

Thus, quantitative and qualitative differences in adipose-cell development occur in obese and nonobese children. By age two, these differences are evident. Further longitudinal studies of adipose-tissue cellularity development are clearly required for a better understanding of normal human adipose-tissue morphological development. Longitudinal studies would allow a better understanding of the development of human obesity—from hypertrophy to hyperplasia and the consequences of intervention.

Feeding Patterns and Obesity

Several studies suggest that infant-feeding practices may be associated with the high prevalence of infantile obesity (Taitz, 1976; Nitzan & Schonfeld, 1976). The decline in breast-feeding, excessive consumption of highly concentrated artificial formulas, and early introduction of nonmilk solids (as early as 20 days of age) have all been cited as promoting early obesity (James, 1976), while a recent report (Taitz, 1976) in Britain has suggested that when these feeding procedures are reversed there are consequent changes in rates of weight gain.

Two studies suggest that early overnutrition can be of long-term as well as of immediate consequence for growth and development. One study showed that the incidence of obesity in 20-year-old men occurred as a function of the timing of the undernutrition during gestation (Ravelli, Stein, & Susser, 1976). Ravelli et al. (1976) studied obesity rates among men after famine exposure in utero and in early infancy during the Second World War. Famine exposure during the last trimester of pregnancy and the first months of life produced significantly lower obesity rates. This finding is consistent with the notion of the importance of nutrition during critical periods of development of adipose tissue. Famine exposure during the first half of pregnancy, however, produced significantly higher obesity rates. Subsequent increased food availability following famine might have led to overnutrition during the important latter part of the pregnancy and the neonatal period.

A second relevant series of studies by Fomon, Owen, and Thomas (1964) and Fomon, Filer, Thomas, Rogers, and Proksch (1969) demonstrated that increasing the caloric value of the formula fed to infants affected the rate of weight gain up to 40 days of age in the newborn infant, while changes in dietary composition (marked changes in fat or carbohydrate components) had little effect. These studies suggest that the newborn child functions primarily as a "volume detector," and is unable to regulate caloric intake. Although infants consume smaller volumes of high-density formulas than more dilute formulas, the reduction in volume is insufficient to prevent higher caloric intake and greater weight gain during the first 40 days.

Weil (1975) has enumerated other variables that can induce infantile obesity: maternal weight and weight gain, infections which may produce decreased activity and maternal anxiety and consequent overfeeding, medical attitudes, and the mother–child relationship. Citing Enzer, he describes the mother who finds that a bottle can quiet the baby and then interprets all the needs of the infant as a need for food. A similar disturbance in early mother–infant interaction has been suggested by Bruch (1970). From her extensive clinical experience with psychiatric treatment of the obese, she believes that obese patients suffer from a "conceptual confusion" with respect to hunger, that is, they are unable to distinguish hunger form other physical or emotional discomforts. This is presumably due to inadequate or inappropriate responses from the social environment, especially the mother, during infancy. The infant who later becomes obese does so because of a failure to learn adequately to recognize and discriminate his own internal states.

Bruch (1969) suggests that awareness of hunger and satiety are not innate biological mechanisms but require learning. For such learning to take place, the infant must experience repeatedly and consistently a definite sequence of events: felt and expressed discomfort, recognition of this signal by the mother, appropriate response, and felt relief. Without the experience of appropriate responses, the infant is assumed to lack the basis for developing self-awareness and self-effectiveness. Bruch observed that many of her obese patients lacked these skills: they responded as if hungry whenever stressed, they felt they were not in charge of themselves, but were "externally" rather than internally controlled. These obese people did not correctly identify hunger or satiety, nor did they differentiate nutritional needs from other physical or emotional discomforts. She has described the families of obese children as encouraging passivity. Food was used as a reward and to relieve anxiety.

Experimental support for this hypothesis has come from the work of Schachter and his students. Moderately obese subjects tend to overeat when food is clearly available and attractive, and undereat when food is unattractive or effort is required to obtain food (Schachter, Goldman, & Gordon, 1968; Nisbett, 1968; Schachter, 1971). These human observations and numerous studies in VMH-lesioned rats led Schachter to a provocative hypothesis. He suggested that the elevated food intake in obese as compared with normal-weight humans resulted from their greater responsiveness to external cues (such as sight, smell, and time of day) and lesser responsiveness to internal physiological cues. These studies have often been difficult to replicate (see Price and Grinker, 1973) and it remains unclear to what degree any excessive reliance on external or sensory cues by the obese is truly an etiologic factor in obesity or merely a secondary or consequential occurrence of the obese state.

An experiment by Stunkard and Koch (1964) examined whether the reported externality of the obese was in fact a deliberate choice rather than an inability to sense internal cues or a denial of their importance. This intriguing study was done by correlating gastric motility and self-reported hunger in obese and normal-weight subjects. Gastric motility was continuously reported over a 4-hour period following an overnight fast. Every 15 minutes subjects reported their hunger. Using signal-detection analysis, it was possible to separate sensitivity, or the ability to detect gastric motility, from criterion, or the willingness to report hunger. Both obese and normal-weight subjects reported feeling hunger only 38% of the time when no contractions were present. However, normal-weight subjects doubled their reports of hunger during the presence of contractions, whereas obese subjects failed to increase their reports. Thus, the inattention to internal events by the obese appeared to be a denial or learned phenomenon, rather than a primary perceptual deficit. This experiment is helpful in providing an alternative explanation for the reported lower responsivity of obese individuals to normal internal cues. In the presence of severe hunger, obese subjects may well utilize a strategy to keep themselves in control and avoid the temptation to overeat. Thus, obese subjects may deny or ignore certain stimuli. This explanation clarifies the seemingly anomalous behavior of obese subjects who in many experimental paradigms eat less than the nonobese.

A serious challenge to hypotheses linking obesity to hyperresponsiveness to external cues, or lessened responsiveness to internal cues, is the finding that the eating behavior of all subjects (including normal-weight subjects) can be markedly controlled by external or cognitive cues (Wooley, 1972; Wooley, Wooley, & Dunham, 1972; Jordan, Stellar, & Duggan, 1968; Spiegel, 1973). Since the testing situation may have quite different meanings for obese and normal-weight subjects, any excessive reliance on external or sensory cues by the obese, even in a covert experiment, cannot be interpreted as a causal factor in obesity. More recent studies (Rodin, 1977) have confirmed the failure of the "external–internal" dichotomy to separate obese and nonobese individuals. High external-responsiveness may exist, but independent of obesity. It may, however, make for a predisposition to obesity in an environment that is especially rich in food cues and where food is highly available.

Ontogeny of Feeding Behavior

The ontogeny of feeding behavior follows similar patterns in man and animals. At birth the organism is virtually parasitic with little active control of patterns of ingestion, but feeding becomes rapidly transformed into a complex phenomenon with multifactorial control (Hall, Cramer, & Blass, 1977; Hall & Rosenblatt, 1977; Hirsch, 1972; Stellar, 1967).

In man there have been studies (Dubignon, Campbell, Curtis, & Partington, 1969; Fomon, 1971) indicating that early in life the human infant is responsive primarily to gastric filling, but after six weeks many more complex factors begin to govern food intake. Fomon and his colleagues (1969, 1975) compared the responses of male and female infants to two levels of caloric densities in formulas (67 or 133 kcal/100 ml; 54 or 100 kcal/100 ml). Infants were studied from day 3 to day 112. While infants at every age level made some adjustment in the total volume of intake (ml/kg/day) to both low- and high-caloric formulas, only after the age of 40 days were infants capable of making adjustments sufficient to control gain in body weight. At this point, there were no differences in daily caloric intake per kilogram body weight (kcal/kg/day) between groups despite the difference in caloric densities of their diets. However, infants who had received the calorically more concentrated formulas were significantly heavier. Further analyses showed that these infants were, in fact, fatter. However, these small differences in weight and fatness were not maintained in later infancy. While weight gain was affected by caloric content in infants until 40 days of age, dramatic differences in dietary components (i.e., carbohydrate and fat) failed to influence intake and rate of weight gain (Fomon, Thomas, Filer, Anderson, & Nelson, 1976).

These data suggest that early in development the infant's food consumption is mainly controlled by gastric filling, or volume, while later on it is also under the control of other cues. These experiments are particularly important since they suggest a possible mechanism for early overfeeding. Fomon et al. (1964) reported that volume of intake per kilogram body weight per day (ml/kg/day) of infants on ad libitum feeding between the ages of 8 and 120 days was positively related to rate of growth as measured by body weights.

Sensory Factors and Obesity

It is clear from animal studies that extraordinary environmental manipulations (e.g., high-fat or supermarket diets) can "uncouple" the apparent control of feeding behavior in the normal lean rat. Additional studies (Faust, Johnson, & Hirsch, in press) have shown that early underfeeding (large litter size) reduces both ultimate adipose-cell number and response to high-fat feeding. Dietary-induced weight gains have also been suggested as a causal factor in human obesity. One hypothesis has been that the obese are qualitatively as well as quantitatively more responsive to sensory or taste cues. One of the most prevalent myths about the factors associated with the genesis of obesity is that obese individuals have a "sweet tooth," that is, they prefer sweet-tasting substances to a greater degree than do normal-weight individuals and thus are unable to restrain themselves in the face of tempting sweet foods (Nordsiek, 1972). If this were true, it would follow that there might be differences in some measurable parameter of taste or actual consumption that would help to provide a physiological clue to the genesis or maintenance of the obese state.

There are few well-controlled observational or questionnaire studies comparing food preferences and intakes of obese and normal-weight subjects. In one study at a County Fair, no differences were found between obese and normal-weight subjects in their preferences for desserts of varying sweetness (Pangborn & Simone, 1958). Self-reports of food consumed by obese teenagers listed fewer bread, sweet, and sugar items than reports by normal-weight children (Kaufman, Poznanski, & Guggenheim, 1974). Similar self-reports of a lower carbohydrate intake by obese adults have also been reported (Keen, 1975). Since self-reports are vulnerable to errors of denial or underestimation, other techniques for assessing food intake are needed. One study directly analyzed the food intake of obese children (4–13 years) in the home (Maaser, 1975). Children averaged 50% overweight. A low proportion (14%) of total caloric intake came from sweet foods. The findings of no significant differences in adipose-tissue fatty acid composition between obese and normal-weight subjects provide further evidence that obese individuals eat roughly the same proportion of fats and carbohydrates as do normal-weight subjects (Hirsch & Goldrick, 1964).

These data suggest that heightened taste responsiveness for sweet foods accompanied by excessive intake are not primary factors in the maintenance of the obese condition (Grinker, 1978). An alternative possibility is that the onset of obesity is dependent upon taste and palatability factors. The suggestion that the obese may rely more heavily on sensory and environmental cues to modulate intake has therefore focused attention on the role of these factors, particularly taste, in the genesis of obesity.

Taste Responses

In our efforts to circumvent the social and cognitive expectations that the obese individual brings to an eating situation, we have examined taste parameters, which are totally independent of food intake, in obese and normal-weight adults and children using appropriate psychophysical procedures (Grinker, Hirsch, & Smith, 1972; Grinker, 1975, 1977; Grinker, Price, & Greenwood, 1976). The separation of taste responses (detection and recognition thresholds, scaling or intensity estimates and preference) from consumption is critical in understanding whether heightened taste responsiveness actually exists and whether it is causally related to obesity (Grinker, 1978).

Using a criterion-free signal-detection procedure, we found no differences between obese and normal-weight subjects in their ability to detect low concentrations of sucrose. We next manipulated the perception of sweetness by addition of a red "cherry" color. With a magnitude-estimation procedure, all subjects rated suprathreshold solutions of sucrose colored red as more sweet than colorless solutions of the same concentration, thus demonstrating equivalent responsivity to an external cue. We obtained marked differences in taste preference. Normal-weight subjects preferred concentrations of medium strength (approximately 6–10% sucrose wt/vol) over more- or less-concentrated solutions, a pattern similar to that reported by Pfaffmann (1961); whereas the preferences of obese subjects were an inverse function of concentration. The more concentrated the solution, the less it was preferred, over the entire range of concentrations.

We examined the reliability and meaningfulness of these taste-preference differences between obese and normal-weight subjects in series of experiments. Differences in taste preferences were found to be specific to the sweet taste (Grinker & Hirsch, 1972). Both obese and normal-weight subjects showed pronounced and equal aversions for sodium chloride which were similar to the aversion pattern reported by Pfaffmann (1961). The findings of a sucrose aversion, so specific to the obese, appeared to be independent of experimental procedures of psychophysical methodology, since we have obtained similar results with hedonic ratings and paired-comparison procedures. Interestingly, the degree of obesity was correlated with sucrose aversion; moderately overweight subjects disliked the sweet solutions less than extremely obese subjects.

Similar findings of lowered taste preference or aversion in obese subjects have been reported (Underwood, Belton, & Hulme, 1973). One recent experiment (Thompson, Moskowitz, & Campbell, 1976) confirms the existence of two distinct preference profiles in both normal-weight and obese subjects. One profile showed progressive decreases in the pleasantness ratings of sucrose concentrations above 0.6M (20%) while the other was characterized by monotonically increasing pleasantness ratings with increasing sucrose concentrations. The pleasantness pattern was not determined by differences in magnitude estimates of intensity or sweetness. Obese and normal-weight subjects did not differ in magnitude estimations of intensity. A negative correlation was reported for hedonic responses (pleasantness) and percent body fat. In other words, degree of overweight was negatively related to preference for sweet concentrations in both the normal-weight and obese samples.

The finding of an aversion to sucrose solutions in the obese is contrary to the popular belief that the obese have a "sweet tooth," yet we find this phenomenon consistently. One hypothesis is that excessive consumption of sweet carbohydrates may lead to a decrease in preference. Preference may reach a maximum value and then decline. This hypothesis has received little support from animal studies. One recent study (Wurtman & Wurtman, 1979) reports that male rats briefly exposed (days 16–30) to sucrose showed no differential preference compared to rats without early exposure. Nevertheless, at least one study finds differences in taste responses in humans as a consequence of diet: Moskowitz, Kumaraiah, Sharma, Jacobs, and Sharma (1975) have reported that Indian workers prefer increasing concentrations of citric acid (label it as pleasant) and low concentrations of quinine. The usual response is an aversion or a rating of unpleasantness. One explanation of these findings is that the diet of these workers is higher in sour foods. Since preference is the only taste parameter which is predictably different in the obese and since it is correlated with the degree of obesity, one must ask whether the ontogeny of sweet aversion and the ontogeny of obesity are related. Accordingly, we have examined the sweet preferences of obese and normal-weight children.

Taste Response in Children and Adolescents

We measured the taste preferences for varying concentrations of sucrose (1.95–19.5% or .057M–0.57M sucrose) in normal-weight and obese children, ages 8–10, by the method of paired comparisons

(Grinker *et al.*, 1976). The taste responses of the obese children were strikingly similar to those of obese adults: the more concentrated the solution, the less frequently it was preferred. The normal and moderately-overweight children responded more like normal-weight adults preferring the most concentrated solutions. Short-term changes in children's metabolic state consistently failed to affect their taste responses. Thus, normal-weight children did not show differences in preferences for sucrose solutions when tested before or after lunch. Obese adolescents tested before and after dinner also did not change the rated attractiveness or percent preference for sweetened Kool-Aid solutions (Grinker *et al.*, 1976).

We have, however, reported significant changes in the taste preference of obese adolescents following weight reduction (Grinker *et al.*, 1976). Ninety adolescent girls and seven boys attending a summer camp for weight reduction made hedonic ratings and magnitude estimates of cherry Kool-Aid solution sweetened with sucaryl (0, 0.5, 1, and 2 times the manufacturer's recommended sweetness) in the first and last weeks of camp. The 0.5× sucaryl solution corresponded to a 5.6% sucrose solution and the 2× solution was equivalent in sweetness to a 22.38% sucrose solution. Subjects were instructed to sip each solution, spit it out, and rinse with water between trials. Subjects rated the pleasantness of each solution on a nine-point scale, which ranged from "tastes great" (+4) to "tastes lousy" (−4) and estimated the sweetness intensity on a scale from 0 to 100. Subjects received one presentation of each solution in random order.

The total sample of girls was divided into thirds on the basis of percent fat. The lightest girls averaged 28.47% fat, the middle third, 37.88% fat, and the heaviest girls averaged 51.37%. Circumference measures (midarm, abdomen, and forearm for boys, and midarm, abdomen, and wrist for girls) were used to calculate percent fat.

Comparisons of magnitude estimates (log transformation) of sweetness intensity showed no differences between heavier and lighter campers. Hedonic ratings, however, were related to the degree of overweight: the heaviest girls liked the most preferred solution (24 ml) significantly less than did the least overweight girls. Age was also significantly related to rated pleasantness; oldest campers, 16 and older liked the solution less. After weight reduction, the obese adolescent showed significant changes in the rated pleasantness for the sweeter solutions. The sweetest solution (2 × the manufacturer's recommended sweetness) increased in pleasantness. The changes were most marked in the heaviest group. Magnitude estimates of sweetness intensity remained unchanged.

Taste Responses in Neonates and Infants

Many of the artifacts which affect the interpretation of the taste response of adolescents and children can be avoided by studying neonatal and infant responses. The human infant is thought to be born with a functional taste system (Bradley, 1974).

The absence of language responses in the newborn restricts the investigator to using feeding reactions such as sucking responses, facial expressions, or respiration for the evaluation of taste preferences. The earliest investigation of newborn humans used facial expressions as the criteria for "liking and disliking" solutions (Peterson and Rainly, 1910; Shinn, 1900; Blanton, 1917; Steiner, 1973). In 1932, Jenson obtained more quantitative information on taste responses by recording volume and pressure changes during sucking. Various concentrations of taste stimuli were presented and the threshold for detection was defined as the concentration that caused a just noticeable distortion of the normal sucking curve. Differential reactions to salt solutions were obtained in two-day-old infants. More recent experiments have reported that neonates prefer solutions of sugar to water and demonstrate a distinct preference for milk over dextrose solutions or corn syrup (Pratt, Nelson, & Sun, 1930; Dubignon & Campbell, 1969; Kron, Stein, Goddard, & Phoenix, 1967). It is uncertain, however, whether the newborn infant accurately differentiates all four taste modalities. There is evidence that infants (like most adults) give positive reactions to sweet and that salt, sour, and bitter may produce negative reactions.

Two studies reported direct ingestive tests of different sweet carbohydrates by newborn infants. Both reported preferences for the sweeter solution. Desor, Maller, and Turner (1973) reported that within short ingestion periods of 3 minutes, newborn infants consumed larger amounts of sugar solutions (glucose, fructose, lactose, or sucrose at .05, .10, .20, and .30M concentrations) than water and consumed larger amounts of the sweeter solutions. Infant anthropometric variables were also related to amount consumed. The lighter infants (below 2722 g) consumed lesser amounts of the sweet solutions than did heavier infants (above 3175 g). Infants were matched for sex, maternal parity, and degree of obstetric sedation.

Nisbett and Gurwitz (1970) reported that during a feeding, neonates consumed more of a sweetened formula (sucrose) than an isocaloric standard formula (lactose). Here, the heavier infants (above 3620 g) consumed more of the sweeter formula than the normal- and lighter-weight infants. Overweight, however, was not related to taste responsiveness. In a replication of this study, Nisbett (1972) again reported no relationship between neonatal overweight and intake. Further studies (Grinker, Jones, & Nowlis, 1977; Grinker, 1978; Grinker & Jones, unpublished) have replicated the findings of Desor *et al.* (1973). Normal-term infants weighing less than 3000 g consumed a lesser amount of a sweet solution (0.125m sucrose) than did heavier infants in a brief 3-minute ingestion test. In these studies intake of a sweet solution (.125M sucrose) was significantly correlated with measures of infant fatness (triceps skinfold or midarm circumference). Smaller and less fat babies, selected from a population of normal-term, healthy neonates, showed a reduced intake compared to larger babies. In preliminary studies similar findings for intake of sweetened formulas have been obtained. Infants received equicaloric lactose or sucrose formulas at regular feedings. The less fat infants (based on measures of triceps skinfold and midarm circumference) consumed a smaller quantity of the lactose formula while consuming equal amounts of the sucrose formula. These findings suggest that smaller infants show greater taste discrimination than larger infants.

One interpretation of these findings is that infants can not only detect a sweet taste at birth, but can also show adult taste preferences. During the neonatal period reliable, meaningful differences in infant responses to sweet solutions occur as a function of infant size. A water taste effect in neonates has also been documented (Grinker *et al.*, 1977). The order in which two taste stimuli, water and a sugar solution, were presented to neonates did affect the amount of the water standard ingested. Less water was ingested when water was presented as the second stimulus following the sweet sugar solution. Bartoshuk (1968) has reported that water has a distinct sour–bitter taste to adult humans after adaptation to sugar. Kobre and Lipsitt (1972) have reported decreased sucking when water follows a sweet carbohydrate. The present data conclusively extend the water taste effect to the human newborn. Thus, infants are capable of discrimination of sweet taste and show evidence of adaptation. These studies should not suggest that early identification of the preobese child is possible. However, matching of infant responsiveness, infant fatness, and maternal and familial obesity may indeed improve the predictability of subsequent obesity.

Activity Patterns

A causal relationship between obesity and decreased activity is difficult to establish. Certainly, underactivity can lead to obesity, and obese and lean animals are often underactive. However, it is also clear that minor shifts in food intake or activity can lead, over long periods of time, to substantial weight gains. Switching from a manual to an electric typewriter with no other changes in activity or food intake could theoretically lead to a weight gain of several pounds per year for the average secretary. Mayer, Marshall, Vitale, Christensen, Mashay-ekhi, and Stare (1954) have documented a direct relationship between food intake and energy expenditure. Increases or decreases in activity are accompanied by appropriate equilibrating changes in food intake. However, the regulation of food intake breaks down at the upper and lower levels of activity and a reduction in weight or an accumulation of fat occurs. Thus farmers pen animals to decrease activity and induce weight gain.

Animal Studies of the Role of Activity in Regulation of Body Weight

There have been many studies documenting the relationship between increased exercise and decreased total body fat (Oscai, 1973, Oscai & Holloszy, 1969). Adult Sprague–Dawley rats forced to exercise are leaner and have smaller fat cells (epididymal depot) than nonexercised controls (Crews, Fuge, Oscai, Holloszy, & Shank, 1969).

A major question concerning the obese state is whether disturbances of feeding patterns or decreases in spontaneous activity precede, coincide with, or are a result of the obesity. Measures of spontaneous activity (wheel running) in genetically obese rats, prior to weaning, immediately postweaning, and in adulthood have been made (Johnson, Stern, & Grinker, 1975; Stern and Johnson, 1977). In these studies, in which obese Zucker rats were given access to activity wheels before weaning, it could be shown that food intake and body weight increased prior to a decrease in wheel running. The inactivity followed soon after hyperphagia. In terms of modifying the genetic–environmental mix, inactivity could further modify long-term development.

It is possible to increase the spontaneous running of young female genetically obese Zucker rats while maintaining the rats' food intake using a technique of Premack (1965) in which eating is contingent on running (Enns, Wecker, & Grinker, 1979). Obese rats on fixed ratio schedules were required to run as many revolutions as lean controls to obtain the amount of food they ordinarily consumed. Under these circumstances, obese experimental rats ran as much as lean controls. When running was discontinued, the obese experimental rats decreased running by 90%.

This study demonstrates a successful technique for increasing activity in obese Zucker rats. The results suggest that activity levels are not defended but that food intake is. Thus, hyperphagia achieves primacy over hypoactivity. This does not mean that activity levels are unimportant. In the natural state, the genetically obese Zucker rat is underactive. These experiments suggest that developmental analyses of the changes in activity and feeding patterns in animals with hypertrophic (increased fat-cell size) as well as hyperplastic–hypertrophic (increased fat-cell number and size) are needed.

Studies of the Role of Activity in Regulating Body Weight in Man

Several studies of human obesity suggest that activity is at least as important as food intake in the genesis of obesity (Bullen, Reed, & Mayer, 1964; Huenemann et al., 1966). Mayer and his associates (Johnson, Burke, & Mayer, 1956; Stefanik, Heald, & Mayer, 1959) have demonstrated an inverse relationship between activity levels and obesity in children and adolescents. Another study (Rose & Mayer, 1968) has documented the complicated interrelationship between activity, body size, and caloric intake in infants. Mack and Kleinheinz (1974) followed activity levels, caloric intakes, and growth curves of five infants from birth to two months of age. Inverse correlations between caloric intake and body activity level and increase in length were reported. None of the infants was followed long enough to determine whether obesity developed. Thus, the few reported studies of infant activity and food intake would seem to indicate that activity may be as important a factor in the overall changes in caloric balance of the obese, or large infant, as is food intake.

PSYCHOLOGICAL EFFECTS OF OBESITY IN CHILDREN

The assignment of deviancy or stigma to obese children and adults is reflected in the negative self-concept of obese adolescents (Monello & Mayer,1963), lower admission to college (Canning & Mayer, 1966), and the negative rankings given to overweight children (Richardson, Hastorf, Goodman, & Dornbusch, 1961; see also Cahnman, 1968; Maddox, 1968; Allon, 1973). Various populations of children and adults were presented with six line drawings depicting children with varying degrees of physical disability and asked to rank them in terms of likability. The drawings included a child with a brace, a child in a wheelchair, a child without a left hand, a child with a harelip, and an obese child. Among these disabilities, overweight was consistently ranked last. One interpretation of these findings is that overweight is a disability for which the overweight child or adult is considered responsible. Failure to correct the deviancy is viewed as irresponsible, criminal, sick, or sinful. The obese child or adult is made to feel mortified and ashamed, is discriminated against, and finally believes that the judgment is correct.

The above discussion of psychological and physiological factors illustrates the complex nature of the etiology of obesity. Other studies indicate how difficult obesity is to treat once it is established. Thus, early identification and particularly prevention should be major focuses of research.

Conclusion

Although the brief discussion of metabolic and behavioral factors in the etiology of obesity has emphasized two theories—regulation of body weight and inreased responsivity to external cues—there are assuredly other theories and other sets of data which do not support these theories. One should not ignore the complexity of the genetic and environmental determinants of human food intake and obesity.

The theory of metabolic regulation suggests that the increase in food intake is secondary or in the service of regulation via adipose tissue or adipose-cell size. This theory suffers from a lack of hard evidence connecting adipose tissue to food intake and to obesity. The externality theory suggests that increased food intake occurs because of sensory or external factors and that the increased adiposity is merely a secondary consequence. Obesity can occur under certain specific external circumstances (such as exposure to palatable diets). The important areas of research, however, are those biochemical, physiological, and psychological factors allowing elasticity in the control of food intake. Infancy may be a "critical period" influencing future elasticity in food intake and cell proliferation and also the development of the behaviors which produce and maintain the obese state.

References

Abraham, S., Collins, G., & Nordsieck, M. Relationship of childhood weight status to morbidity in adults. *HSMHA Health Reports*, 1971, *86:* 273–284.

Allon, N. The stigma of overweight in everyday life. In G. A. Bray (Ed.), *Obesity in perspective*. Bethesda, Maryland: Fogarty International Center Series on Preventive Medicine. Vol. 2, Part 2, Department of Health, Education and Welfare, 1973, pp. 83–102.

Asher, P. Fat babies and fat children. The prognosis of obesity in the very young. *Archives of Disease in Childhood*, 1966, *41*, 672–673.

Ashwell, M. Commercial weight loss groups. In G. A. Bray (Ed.), *Recent advances in obesity research: II, Proceedings of the Second International Congress on Obesity.* London: Newman Publishing, 1978, pp. 266–275.

Ashwell, M., Durrant, M., & Garrow, J. S. How a "fat cell pool" hypothesis could account for the relationship between adipose tissue cellularity and the age of onset of obesity. *Proceedings of the Nutrition Society,* 1977, *36,* 111A.

Bagdade, J. D., & Hirsch, J. Gestational and dietary influences on the lipid content of the infant buccal fat pad. *Proceedings of the Society for Experimental Biology and Medicine,* 1966, *112,* 616–619.

Bartoshuk, L. M. Water taste in man. *Perception and Psychophysics,* 1968, *3,* 69.

Biron, P., Mongeau, J. G., & Bertrand, D. Familial resemblance of body weight and weight/height in 374 homes with adopted children. *Journal of Pediatrics,* 1977, *91,* 555–558.

Bjorntorp, P., & Sjostrom, L. Number and size of adipose tissue fat cells in relation to metabolism in human obesity. *Metabolism,* 1971, *20,* 703.

Bjorntorp, P., Carlgren, G., Isaksson, B., Krotkiewski, M., Larsson, B., & Sjostrom, L. The effect of energy reducing dietary regime in relation to adipose tissue cellularity in obese women. *American Journal of Clinical Nutrition,* 1975, *28,* 445.

Blanton, M. G. The behavior of the human infant during the first 30 days of life. *Psychological Review,* 1917, *24,* 456–483.

Bonnet, F. P., Duckerts, M., & Henskin, A. Subcutaneous adipose tissue growth in normal and obese children: Methodological problems. In Z. Laron (Ed.), *Pediatric and adolescent endocrinology.* Vol. 1. *The adipose child.* Basel Karger, 1976, pp. 104–111.

Borjeson, M. The aetiology of obesity in children. A study of 101 twin pairs. *Acta Paediatrica Scandinavica,* 1976, *65,* 279–287.

Boulangé, A., Planche, E., & DeGasquet, P. Excess fat storage and normal energy intake in the newborn Zucker rat (fafa). Paper presented at the Second International Congress on Obesity, Washington, D.C., 1977.

Bradley, R. M. Development of the taste bud and gustatory papillae in human fetuses. In J. F. Bosma (Ed.). *Third Symposium on Oral Sensation and Perception: The mouth of the infant.* Springfield: C. C. Thomas, 1972, 137–162.

Bray, G. A. To treat or not to treat—that is the question? In G. A. Bray (Ed.), *Recent advances in obesity research: II, Proceedings of the Second International Congress on Obesity.* London: Newman Publishing, 1978, pp. 246–265.

Brook, C. G. D. Evidence for a sensitive period in adipose cell replication in man. *Lancet,* 1972, *3,* 624–627.

Bruch, H. Obesity in childhood. Physical growth and development of obese children. *American Journal of Diseases of Children,* 1939, *8,* 457.

Bruch, H. Hunger and instinct. *Journal of Nervous and Mental Disease,* 1969, *149,* 91–114.

Bruch, H. Juvenile obesity: Its courses and outcome. In C. V. Rowlan, Jr., (Ed.), *Anorexia and obesity.* Boston: Little, Brown, 1970, pp. 231–254.

Bullen, B. A., Reed, R. B., & Mayer, J. Physical activity of obese and nonobese adolescent girls appraised by motion picture sampling. *American Journal of Clinical Nutrition,* 1964, *14,* 211.

Cahnman, W. J. The stigma of obesity. *Sociological Quarterly,* 1968, *9,* 283–299.

Canning, H. & Mayer, J. Obesity—its possible effect on college acceptance. *New England Journal of Medicine,* 1966, *275,* 1172–1174.

Charney, E., Goodman, H. C., McBride, M., Barbro, L., & Pratt, R. Childhood antecedents of adult obesity: Do chubby infants become obese adults? *New England Journal of Medicine,* 1976, *295,* 6–9.

Cleary, M. P., Vasselli, J. R., Jen, C., & Greenwood, M. R. C. Effects of chronic food restriction in the Zucker (fa/fa) rat. *Federation Proceedings,* 1978, *37,* 675.

Cohn, C., & Joseph, D. Influence of body weight and body fat on appetite of "normal" lean and obese rats. *Yale Journal of Biological Medicine*, 1962, *34*, 598–607.

Cox, J. E., & Powley, T. L. Development of obesity in diabetic mice pairfed with lean siblings. *Journal of Comparative and Physiological Psychology*, 1977, *91*, 347–358.

Crews, E. L., Fuge, K. W., Oscai, L. B., Holloszy, J. O., & Shank, R. E. Weight, food intake and body composition. Effects of exercise and of protein deficiency. *American Journal of Physiology*, 1969, *216*, 351.

Dauncey, M. J., & Gairdner, D. Size of adipose cells in infancy. *Archives of Disease in Childhood*, 1975, *50*, 286–290.

Desor, J. A., Maller, O., & Turner, R. E. Taste in acceptance of sugars by human infants. *Journal of Comparative and Physiological Psychology*, 1973, *84*, 496–501.

DiGirolamo, M., & Medlinger, S. Role of fat cell size and number in enlargement of epididymal fat pads in three species. *American Journal of Physiology*, 1971, *221*, 859–864.

Dorner, G., Grychtolik, H., & Julitz, M. Overfeeding in the first three months of life as a significant risk factor for the development of obesity and resulting disorders. *Deutsche Gesundheitswesen*, 1977, *32*, 6–9.

Drenick, E. J. Weight reduction by prolonged fasting. In G. A. Bray (Ed.), *Obesity in perspective.* Bethesda, Maryland: Fogart International Center Series on Preventive Medicine, Vol. 2, Part 2, Department of Health, Education and Welfare, 1973, pp. 341–360.

Dubignon, J., & Campbell, D. Discrimination between nutriments by the human neonate. *Psychosomatic Science*, 1969, *16*, 186–187.

Dubignon, J., Campbell, D., Curtis, M., & Partington, M. W. The relation between laboratory measures of sucking, food intake, and perinatal factors during the newborn period. *Child Development*, 1969, *40*, 1107–1120.

Eid, E. E. Follow up study of physical growth of children who had excessive weight gain in first six months of life. *British Medical Journal*, 1970, *2*, 74–76.

Enns, M. P., Wecker, J., & Grinker, J. A. An examination of the circadian distribution of schedule induced activity and food intake in lean and obese Zucker rats. Paper presented at the Eastern Psychological Association Meeting, Philadelphia, 1979.

Faust, I. M., Johnson, P. R., & Hirsch, J. Adipose tissue regeneration following lipectomy. *Science*, 1977a, *197*, 391–393.

Faust, I. M., Johnson, P. R., & Hirsch, J. Surgical removal of adipose tissue alters feeding behavior and the development of obesity in rats. *Science*, 1977b, *197*, 343–396.

Faust, I. M., Johnson, P. R., Stern, J. S., & Hirsch, J. Diet-induced adipocyte number increase in adult-rats: A new model of obesity. *American Journal of Physiology*, 1978, *235*, E279–E286.

Faust, I. M., Johnson, P. R., & Hirsch, J. Long-term effects of early nutritional experience on the development of obesity in the rat. *Journal of Nutrition*, in press.

Fomon, S. J. A pediatrician looks at early nutrition. *Bulletin of the New York Academy of Science*, 1971, *47*, 569–578.

Fomon, S. J., Owen, G. M., & Thomas, L. N. Milk or formula volume ingested by infants fed ad libitum. *American Journal of Diseases of Children*, 1964, *108*, 601.

Fomon, S. J., Filer, L. J. Jr., Thomas, L. N., Rogers, R. R., & Proksch, A. M. Relationship between formula concentration and rate of growth of normal infants. *Journal of Nutrition*, 1969, *98*, 241–254.

Fomon, S. J., Filer, L. J., Jr., Thomas, L. N., Anderson, T. A., & Nelson, S. E. Influence of formula concentration on caloric intake and growth of normal infants. *Acta Paediatrica Scandinavica*, 1975, *64*, 172–181.

Fomon, S. J., Thomas, L. N., Filer, L. J., Jr., Anderson, T. A., & Nelson, S. E. Influence of fat and carbohydrate content of diet on food intake and growth of male infants. *Acta Paediatrica Scandinavica*, 1976, *65*, 136–144.

Friis-Hansen, G. Body water compartments in children: Changes during growth and related changes in body composition. *Pediatrics*, 1961, *28*, 69.

Garn, S. M. Aspects of growth and development. In V. C. Vaughan, III (Ed.), *Issues in human development*. Washington, D.C.: United States Government Printing Office, 1971, pp. 52–58.

Garn, S. M., & Clark, D. C. Trends in fatness and the origins of obesity. *Pediatrics*, 1976, *57*, 443–456.

Garn, S., Bailey, S., Cole, P., & Higgins, I. T. T. Evidence for the social inheritance of obesity in childhood and adolescence. In L. Gedda and P. Parisi (Eds.), *Auxology: Human growth in health and disorder*. London: Academic Press, 1977, pp. 217–223.

Goldblatt, P. B., Moore, M. E., & Stunkard, A. J. Social factors in obesity, *Journal of the American Medical Association*, 1964, *192*, 1039–1044.

Greenwood, M. R. C., & Hirsch, J. Postnatal development of adipocyte cellularity in the normal rat. *Journal of Lipid Research*, 1974, *15*, 474.

Grinker, J. Behavioral and metabolic consequences of weight reduction. *Journal of the American Dietetic Association*, 1973a, *62*, 31.

Grinker, J. Obesity and taste: Sensory and cognitive factors in food intake. In G. A. Bray (Ed.), *Obesity in perspective*. Bethesda, Maryland: Fogarty International Center Series on Preventive Medicine. Vol. 2, Part 2, Department of Health, Education and Welfare, 1973b, pp. 73–80.

Grinker, J. Obesity and taste: Human and animal studies (presented at Fogarty International Conference on Obesity, 1973). Washington: U.S. Government Printing Office, 1975.

Grinker, J. Behavioral and metabolic factors in the etiology of obesity. *Weekly Psychiatry Update Series*, *31*, 1977, 2–5.

Grinker, J. Obesity and sweet taste. *American Journal of Clinical Nutrition*, 1978, *31*, 1078–1087.

Grinker, J., & Hirsch, J. Metabolic and behavioral correlates of obesity. In J. Knight (Ed.), *Physiology, emotion, and psychosomatic illness*. Amsterdam: A CIBA Foundation Symposium 8, ASP, 1972, pp. 349–374.

Grinker, J., Hirsch, J., & Smith, D. V. Taste sensitivity and susceptibility to external influence in obese and normal weight subjects. *Journal of Personality and Social Psychology*, 1972, *22*, 320–325.

Grinker, J., Hirsch, J., & Levin, B. The affective responses of obese patients to weight reduction: A differentiation based on age at onset of obesity. *Psychosomatic Medicine*, 1973a, *35*, 57.

Grinker, J., Glucksman, M. L., Hirsch, J., & Viseltear, G. Time perception as a function of weight reduction: A differentiation based on age at onset of obesity. *Psychosomatic Medicine*, 1973b, *35*, 104.

Grinker, J., Price, J. M., & Greenwood, M. R. C. Studies of taste in childhood obesity. In D. Novin, W. Wyrwicka, & G. A. Bray (Eds.), *Hunger: Basic mechanisms and clinical implications*. New York: Raven Press, 1976, pp. 441–457.

Grinker, J., Jones, S., & Nowlis, G. Sweet preference in neonates: Effects of type of sugar, concentration and birth weight on ingestion. Paper presented at the Eastern Psychological Association meeting, New York, 1977.

Hager, A., Sjostrom, L., Arvidson, B., Bjorntorp, P., & Smith, U. Adipose tissue cellularity in infancy. Paper presented at the Second International Congress on Obesity, Washington, D.C., 1977.

Hall, W. G., & Rosenblatt, J. S. Suckling behavior and intake control in the developing rat pup. *Journal of Comparative and Physiological Psychology*, 1977, *9*, 1232–1247.

Hall, W. G., Cramer, C. P., & Blass, E. M. Ontogeny of suckling in rats: Transitions toward adult ingestion. *Journal of Comparative and Physiological Psychology*, 1977, *91*, 1141–1155.

Hammer, S. L., Campbell, V., & Wooley, J. Treating adolescent obesity: Long range evaluation of previous therapy. *Clinical Pediatrics*, 1971, *10*, 46–52.

Hammond, W. H. Measurement and interpretation of subcutaneous fat, with norms for children and young adult males. *British Journal of Preventive and Social Medicine*, 1955, *9*, 201–211.

Heald, F. P., & Hollander, R. J. The relationship between obesity in adolescence and early growth. *Journal of Pediatrics*, 1965, *67*, 35–38.

Hernesniemi, I., Zachmann, M., & Prader, A. Skinfold thickness in infancy and adolescence. A longitudinal correlation study in normal children. *Helvetica Paediatrica Acta*, 1973, *29*, 523.

Hirsch, J. Regulation of food intake: Discussion. In F. Reichsman (Ed.), *Advances in psychosomatic medicine*. Vol. 7. *Hunger and satiety in health and disease*. Basel: Karger, 1972, pp. 229–242.

Hirsch, J., & Batchelor, B. Adipose tissue cellularity in human obesity. *Journal of Clinical Endocrinology and Metabolism*, 1976, *5*, 299–311.

Hirsch, J., & Gallian, E. Methods for the determination of adipose cell size in man and animals. *Journal of Lipid Research*, 1968, *9*, 110.

Hirsch, J., & Goldrick, R. B. Serial studies on the metabolism of human adipose tissue. I. Lipogenesis and free fatty acid uptake and release in small aspirated samples of subcutaneous fat. *Journal of Clinical Investigation*, 1964, *43*, 1776–1792.

Hirsch, J., & Han, P. W. Cellularity of rat adipose tissue: Effects of growth, starvation and obesity. *Journal of Lipid Research*, 1969, *10*, 77–82.

Hirsch, J., & Knittle, J. L. Cellularity of obese and nonobese human adipose tissue. *Federation Proceedings*, 1970, *29*, 1516–1521.

Hirsch, J., Faust, I. M., & Johnson, P. R. What's new in obesity: Current understanding of adipose tissue morphology. In N. Freinkel (Ed). *Contemporary Metabolism*, Vol. 1, New York: Plenum, 1979, pp. 385–399.

Huenemann, R. L. Environmental factors associated with preschool obesity. *Journal of the American Dietetic Association*, 1974, *64*, 480–487, 488–491.

Huenemann, R. L., Hampton, M. C., Shapiro, L. R., & Behnke, A. R. Adolescent food practices associated wih obesity. *Federation Proceedings*, 1966, *25*, 4–10.

Illingworth, R., Harvey, C., & Gin, S. T. Relation of birth weight to physical development in childhood. *Lancet*, 1949, *2*, 598.

James, W. P. T. (Ed.). *Research on obesity. A Report of the DHSS/MRC Group*. London: Her Majesty's Stationery Office, 1976.

Jenson, K. Differential reactions to taste and temperature stimuli in newborn infants. *Genetic Psychology Monographs* 1932, *12*, 361–479.

Johnson, P. R., & Hirsch, J. Cellularity of adipose depots in six strains of genetically obese mice. *Journal of Lipid Research*, 1972, *13*, 2–11.

Johnson, M. L., Burke, B. S., & Mayer, J. Relative importance of inactivity and overeating in the energy balance of obese high school girls. *American Journal of Clinical Nutrition*, 1956a, *4*, 37–43.

Johnson, M. L., Burke, B. S., & Mayer, J. The prevalence and incidence of obesity in a cross-section of elementary and secondary school children. *American Journal of Clinical Nutrition*, 1956b, *4*, 231–238.

Johnson, P. R., Zucker, L. M., Cruce, J. A. F., & Hirsch, J. Cellularity of adipose depots in the genetically obese Zucker rat. *Journal of Lipid Research*, 1971, *12*, 706–714.

Johnson, P. R., Stern, J. S., Greenwood, M. R. C., Zucker, L. M., & Hirsch, J. Effect of early nutrition on adipose cellularity and pancreatic insulin release in the Zucker rat. *Journal of Nutrition*, 1973, *103*(5), 738–743.

Johnson, P. R., Stern, J. S., & Grinker, J. Patterns of activity and food intake in the genetically obese Zucker rat (fafa). In A. Howard (Ed.), *Recent advances in obesity research: I, Proceedings of the First International Congress on Obesity*. London: Newman Publishing, 1975, p. 111.

Johnson, P. R., Stern, J. S., Greenwood, M. R. C., & Hirsch, J. Adipose tissue hyperplasia and hyperinsulinemia in Zucker obese female rats: A developmental study. *Metabolism*, 1978, *27*, 1941–1954.

Jordan, H. A., Stellar, E., & Duggan, S. Z. Voluntary intragastric feeding in man. *Communications in Behavioral Biology*, 1968, *1*, 65–67.

Kanarek, R. B., & Hirsch, E. Dietary-induced overeating in experimental animals. *Federation Proceedings*, 1977, *36*(2), 154–158.

Kaufmann, N. A., Poznanski, R., & Guggenheim, K. Teenagers dieting for weight control. *Nutrition and Metabolism*, 1974, *16*, 30.

Keen, N. The incomplete story of obesity and diabetes. In A. Howard, (Ed.), *Recent advances in obesity research: I, Procedings of the First International Congress on Obesity*. London: Newman Publishing, 1975, pp. 116–127.

Knittle, J. L. In *Proceedings of Serono Symposium No. 17 on Obesity in Childhood*, Bologna, Italy, 1977.

Knittle, J. L., & Hirsch, J. Effect of early nutrition on the development of rat epididymal fat pads: Cellularity and metabolism. *Journal of Clinical Investigation*, 1968, *47* (9), 2091–2098.

Knittle, J. L., Timmers, K., Ginsberg-Fellner, F., Brown, R. E., & Katz, D. P. The growth of adipose tissue in children and adolescents. *Journal of Clinical Investigation*, 1979, *63*, 239–246.

Knittle, J. L., Ginsberg-Fellner, F., & Brown, R. E. Adipose tissue development in man. *American Journal of Clinical Nutrition*, 1977, *30*, 762–766.

Kobre, K. R., & Lipsitt, L. P. A negative contrast effect in newborns. *Journal of Experimental Child Psychology*, 1972, *14*, 81–91.

Kron, R. E., Stein, M., Goddard, K. E., & Phoenix, M. D. Effect of nutrient upon the suckling behavior of newborn infants. *Psychosomatic Medicine*, 1967, *29*, 24–32.

Krotkiewski, M., Sjostrom, L., Bjorntorp, P., Calgren, C., Garellick, G., & Smith, U. Adipose tissue cellularity in relation to prognosis for weight reduction. *International Journal of Obesity*, 1977, *1*, 395–416.

Lawrence, W. C. M. A study of overweight school children. *Health Bulletin* (Edin.), 1970, *28*, 44–46.

Lemonnier, D. Effect of age, sex, and site on the cellularity of the adipose tissue in mice and rats rendered obese by a high-fat diet. *Journal of Clinical Investigation*, 1972, *51*, 2907–2915.

Lloyd, J. K., Wolff, O. H., & Whalen, W. S. Childhood obesity: Long term study of height and weight. *British Medical Journal*, 1961, *2*, 145.

Maaser, R. Analyse der Nahrungsaufnahme adiposer Kinder. (Analysis of the food intake of obese children.) *Monatsschrift für Kinderheilkunde*, 1975, *123*, 284–285.

Mack, R. W., & Kleinheinz, M. E. Growth, caloric intake and activity levels in early infancy: A preliminary report. *Human Biology*, 1974, *46*(2), 345–354.

Maddox, G. L., Back, K. W., & Liederman, V. R. Overweight as a social deviance and disability. *Journal of Health and Social Behavior*, 1968, *9*, 287–298.

Mayer, J. Genetic factors in human obesity. *Annals of the New York Academy of Science*, 1965, *131*, 412–421.

Mayer, J., Marshall, N. B., Vitale, J. J., Christensen, J. H., Mashayekhi, M. B., & Stare, F. J. Exercise, food intake and body weight in normal rats and genetically obese adult mice. *American Journal of Physiology*, 1954, *177*, 544–548.

McCance, R. A., & Widdowson, E. M. Nutrition and growth. *Proceedings of the Royal Society, London*, Series B, 1962, *156*, 326.

Mellbin, T., & Vuille, J. C. Physical development at 7 years of age in relation to velocity of weight gain in infancy with special reference to incidence of overweight. *British Journal of Preventive and Social Medicine*, 1968, *27*, 225.

Mellbin, T., & Vuille, J. C. Weight gain in infancy and physical development between 7 and 10½ years of age. *British Journal of Preventive and Social Medicine*, 1976, *30*, 233–238.

Mellbin, T., & Vuille, J. C. The relative importance of rapid weight gain in infancy as a precursor of childhood obesity. In Z. Laron (Ed.), *Pediatric and adolescent endocrinology*. Vol. 1. *The adipose child*. Basel: Karger, 1976, pp. 78–83.

Metropolitan Life Insurance Company. New Weight Standards for Men and Women. *Statistical Bulletin*, 1959, *40*, 1–4.

Mickelsen, O., Takahaski, S., & Craig, C. Experimental obesity I: Production of obesity in rats by feeding high fat diets. *Journal of Nutrition*, 1955, *57*, 541–554.

Monello, L. J., & Mayer, J. Obese adolescent girls: An unrecognized "minority" group? *American Journal of Clinical Nutrition*, 1963, *13*, 35–39.

Moskowitz, H. R., Kumaraiah, V., Sharma, K. N., Jacobs, H. L., & Sharma, S. D. Cross-cultural differences in simple taste preferences. *Science*, 1975, *190*, 1217–1218.

Mossberg, N. Obesity in children. A clinical–prognostical investigation. *Acta Paediatrica* (Uppsala), 1948, *35*, Supp. 2, 1.

Mullins, A. G. The prognosis in juvenile obesity. *Archives of Disease in Children*, 1958, *33*, 307–314.

Neyzi, O., Saner, G., Binyildiz, P., Yazicioglu, S., Emre, S., & Gurson, C. T. Relationships between body weight in infancy and weight in later childhood and adolescence. In Z. Laron (Ed.), *Pediatric and adolescent endocrinology*. Vol. 1. *The adipose child*. Basel: Karger, 1976, pp. 89–93.

Nisbett, R. E. Taste, deprivation and weight determinants of eating behavior. *Journal of Personality and Social Psychology*, 1968, *10*, 107–116.

Nisbett, R. E. Hunger, obestiy and the ventromedial hypothalamus. *Psychological Review*, 1972, *79* (6), 433–453.

Nisbett, R. E., & Gurwitz, S. B. Weight, sex and the eating behavior of human newborns. *Journal of Comparative and Physiological Psychology*, 1970, *73* (2), 245–253.

Nitzan, N., & Schonfeld, T. M. Excessive weight gain during early infancy as related to breast feeding versus bottle feeding. In Z. Laron (Ed.), *Pediatric and adolescent endocrinology*. Vol. 1. *The adipose child*. Basel: Karger, 1976, pp. 66–69.

Nordsiek, F W. The sweet tooth—The search for safe means of satisfying the universal craving for sweets continues unabated but so far with limited success. *American Scientist*, 1972, *41*, 45.

Oscai, L. B. The role of exercise in weight control. *Exercise and Sport Sciences Review*, 1973, *1*, 103.

Oscai, L. B., & Holloszy, J. O. Effects of weight changes produced by exercise, food restriction or overeating on body composition. *Journal of Clinical Investigation*, 1969, *48*, 2124.

Ounsted, M., & Sleigh, G. The infant's self-regulation of food intake and weight gain. *Lancet*, June 28, 1975, 1393–1397.

Pangborn, R. M., & Simone, M. Body size and sweetness preference. *Journal of the American Dietetic Association*, 1958, *34*, 924–928.

Peterson, F., & Rainly, L. N. The beginning of the mind in the newborn. *Bulletin Lying-in Hospital, City of New York*, 1910, 7, 99.

Pfaffmann, C. The sensory and motivating properties of the sense of taste. In M. R. Jones (Ed.), *Nebraska Symposium on Motivation* (vol. 9). Lincoln: University of Nebraska Press, 1961, pp. 71–110.

Prader, A., Hernesniemi, I., & Zachmann, M. Skinfold thickness in infancy and adolescence. A longitudinal correlation study in normal children. In Z. Laron (Ed.), *Pediatric and adolescent endocrinology*. Vol. 1. *The adipose child*. Basel: Karger, 1976, pp. 84–88.

Pratt, K., Nelson, A., & Sun, K. *Contributions in psychology*. Ohio State Unversity Press, 1930, 105, No. 10.

Premack, D. Reinforcement theory. In M. R. Jones (Ed.), *Nebraska Symposium on Motivation*. Lincoln: University of Nebraska Press, 1965, pp. 123–180.

Price, J. M., & Grinker, J. Effects of degree of obesity, food deprivation and palatability on eating behavior of humans. *Journal of Comparative and Physiological Psychology*, 1973, 85, 265.

Ravelli, G. P., Stein, J. A., & Susser, M. W. Obesity in young men after famine exposure in utero and early infancy. *New England Journal of Medicine*, 1976, 295, 349–353.

Richardson, S. A., Hastorf, A. H., Goodman, N., & Dornbusch, S. M. Cultural uniformity in reaction to physical disabilities. *American Sociological Review*, 1961, 26, 241–247.

Rodin, J. Has the distinction between internal versus external control of feeding outlived its usefulness? In G. A. Bray (Ed.), *Recent advances in obesity research: II, Proceedings of the Second International Congress on Obesity*. London: Newman Publishing, 1977, pp. 75–85.

Rose, H. E., & Mayer, J. Activity, calorie intake, fat storage, and the energy balance of infants. *Pediatrics*, 1968, 41, 18–29.

Salans, L. B., Horton, E. S., & Sims, E. A. H. Experimental obesity in man: Cellular character of the adipose tissue. *Journal of Clinical Investigation*, 1971, 50, 1005–1011.

Salans, L. B., Cushman, S. W., & Weismann, R. E. Adipose cell size and number in nonobese and obese patients. *Journal of Clinical Investigation*, 1973, 52, 929–941.

Schachter, S. Some extraordinary facts about obese humans and rats. *American Psychologist*, 1971, 26, 129.

Schachter, S., Goldman, R., & Gordon, A. Effects of fear, food deprivation and obesity on eating. *Journal of Personality and Social Psychology*, 1968, 10, 91–97.

Schemmel, R., Mickelsen, O., & Gill, J. L. Dietary obesity in rats: Body weight and body fat accretion in seven strains of rats. *Journal of Nutrition*, 1970, 100, 1041–1048.

Schemmel, R., Mickelsen, O., Pierce, S. A., Johnson, J. T., & Schirmer, R. G. Fat depot removal, food intake, body fat and fat depot weight in obese rats. *Proceedings of the Society for Experimental Biology and Medicine*, 1971, 136, 1269–1273.

Schiele, B. C., & Brozek, J. "Experimental neurosis" resulting from semistarvation in man. *Psychosomatic Medicine*, 1948, 10, 31–50.

Sclafani, A., & Springer, D. Dietary obesity in adult rats: Similarities to hypothalamic and human obesity syndromes. *Physiology and Behavior*, 1976, 17, 461–471.

Shenker, I. R., Fisichelli, V., & Lang, J. Weight differences between foster infants of overweight and nonoverweight foster mothers. *Journal of Pediatrics*, 1974, 84, 715–719.

Shinn, M. M. *The biography of a baby*. Boston: Houghton, Mifflin & Co., 1900.

Silverstone, J. T., Gordon, R. P., & Stunkard, A. J. Social factors in obesity in London. *Practitioner*, 1969, 202, 682–688.

Sjostrom, L., & Bjorntorp, P. Body composition and adipose tissue cellularity in human obesity. *Acta Medica Scandinavica*, 1974, 195, 201–211.

Spiegel, T. A. Caloric regulation of food intake in man. *Journal of Comparative and Physiological Psychology*, 1973, *84*, 24.

Stefanik, P. A., Heald, F. P., & Mayer, J. Caloric intake in relation to energy output of obese and non-obese adolescent boys. *American Journal of Clinical Nutrition*, 1959, *7*, 55–62.

Steiner, J. E. The human gustofacial response: Observation on normal and anencephalic newborn infants. In *Fourth Symposium on Oral Sensation and Perception: Development in the fetus and infant.* Department of Health, Education and Welfare, 1973, pp. 254–278.

Stellar, E. Hunger in man: Comparative and physiological studies. *American Psychologist*, 1967, *22*, 105–117.

Stern, J. S., & Johnson, P. R. Spontaneous activity and adipose cellularity in the genetically obese Zucker rat (fafa). *Metabolism*, 1977, *26*, 371–380.

Stern, J. S., & Johnson, P. R. Size and number of adipocytes and their implications. In H. Katzen & R. Mahler (Eds.), *Advances in modern nutrition.* (Vol. 1). New York: Halstead Press, 1978, pp. 303–340.

Stiles, J. W., Francendese, A. A., & Masoro, J. Influence of age on size and number of fat cells in the epididymal depot. *American Journal of Physiology*, 1975, *229*, 1561–1568.

Stunkard, A. J. Obesity and the social environment. In A. Howard (Ed.), *Recent International Congress on Obesity.* London: Newman Publishing, 1975, pp. 178–190.

Stunkard, A. & Koch, C. The interpretation of gastric motility 1. Apparent bias in the reports of hunger by obese persons. *Archives of General Psychiatry*, 1964, *11*, 74–82.

Stunkard, A. J., & McLaren-Hume, M. The results of treatment for obesity. A review of the literature and report of a series. *Archives of Internal Medicine*, 1959, *103*, 79–85.

Stunkard, A. J., d'Aquili, E., & Filion, R. D. L. Influence of social class on obesity and thinness in children. *Journal of the American Medical Association*, 1972, *221*, 579–584.

Svenger, T., Lindberg, T., Weibull, B., & Olsson, V. L. Nutrition, overnutrition, and obesity in the first year of life in Malmo, Sweden. *Acta Paediatrica Scandinavica*, 1975, *64*, 635–640.

Taitz, L. S. Infantile over-nutrition among artificially fed infants in the Sheffield region. *British Medical Journal*, 1971, *1*, 315.

Taitz, L. S. Relationship of infant feeding patterns to weight gain in the first weeks of life. In Z. Laron (Ed.), *Pediatric and adolescent endocrinology.* Vol. 1. *The adipose child.* Basel: Karger, 1976, pp. 60–65.

Tanner, J. M. Standards for subcutaneous fat in British children. *British Medical Journal*, February, 1962a, 446–450.

Tanner, J. M. *Growth at adolescence.* Oxford: Blackwell Scientific Publications, 1962b.

Tanner, J. Variability of growth and maturity in newborn infants. In M. Lewis & L. Rosenblum (Eds.), *The effect of the infant on its caregiver.* New York: Wiley, 1974, pp. 77–103.

Ten State Nutrition Survey 1968–1970. Department of Health, Education and Welfare No. (HSM) 72-8131, 1972.

Thompson, D. A., Moskowitz, H. R., & Campbell, R. G. Effects of body weight and food intake on pleasantness ratings for a sweet stimulus. *Journal of Applied Physiology*, 1976, *41*, 77.

Underwood, P. J., Belton, E., & Hulme, P. Aversion to sucrose in obesity. *Proceedings of the Nutrition Society*, 1973, *32*, 93a.

Weil, W. B., Jr. Infantile obesity. In M. Winick (Ed.), *Childhood obesity.* New York: Wiley, 1975, pp. 61–72.

Weil, W. B. Current controversies in childhood obesity. *Journal of Pediatrics*, 1977, *91*, 175–187.

Whitelaw, A. G. L. The association of social class and sibling number with skinfold thickness in London school boys. *Human Biology*, 1971, *43*, 414–420.

Whitelaw, A. G. L. Influence of maternal obesity on subcutaneous fat in the newborn. *British Medical Journal*, 1976, *2*, 985–986.

Withers, R. R. J. Problem in the genetics of obesity. *Eugenics Review*, 1964, *55*, 81.

Wolff, O. H. Obesity in childhood. A study of birth weight, height and onset of puberty. *Quarterly Journal of Medicine*, 1955, *24*, 109.

Wooley, S. C. Physiological versus cognitive factors in short term food regulations in the obese and nonobese. *Psychosomatic Medicine*, 1972, *34*, 62–68.

Wooley, O. W., Wooley, S. C., & Dunham, R. B. Can calories be perceived and do they affect hunger in obese and nonobese humans. *Journal of Comparative and Physiological Psychology*, 1972, *80*, 250–258.

Wurtman, J. J., & Wurtman, R. J. Sucrose consumption early in life fails to modify appetite of adult rats for sweet food. *Science*, 1979, *205*, 321–322.

Zucker, L. M., & Zucker, T. F. Fatty, a new mutation in the rat. *Journal of Heredity*, 1961, *52*, 275–278.

7

Developmental Consequences of Malnutrition in Early Childhood

Henry N. Ricciuti

The past ten years have witnessed a heightened and continuing concern with malnutrition as a serious public health problem which constitutes a threat to the normal growth and development of many thousands of poor children in various regions of the world, including the United States. Malnutrition tends to occur primarily in poor families confronting the adverse socioeconomic and environmental conditions typically associated with poverty, including poor housing and sanitation, exposure to infectious and parasitic disease, inadequate health care, large family size, very limited educational and occupational opportunities, poor feeding and child care practices, etc. Under such circumstances, it is well known that malnutrition may lead to increased early childhood mortality and morbidity, and to substantial impairment of physical growth and brain development, particularly if the nutritional deficits are early, severe, and long-lasting without treatment. The possibility that malnutrition may also result in a significant and long-lasting impairment of the development of intellectual and social competence, and of adaptive behavior generally, has been a matter of continuing widespread concern during the past ten years. This issue is obviously not only a matter of substantial scientific importance but one with tremendous social and public-policy implications as well.

In the late 1960s and early 1970s in the atmosphere of heightened

HENRY RICCIUTI • Department of Human Development and Family Studies, Cornell University, Ithaca, New York 14850.

public concern about malnutrition as a public health problem in this country and elsewhere, there was a rather widespread tendency to assume somewhat uncritically that there was a direct causal relationship between early malnutrition and impaired learning and intellectual development, leading in some instances to irreversible mental retardation (Ricciuti, 1970; Scrimshaw & Gordon, 1968). This assumption was based in large part on human as well as animal studies indicating retarded brain development and brain function resulting from early malnutrition (Dobbing, 1968; Winick & Rosso, 1969), and on the frequent observation that children having suffered obvious malnutrition tend to show reduced levels of intellectual functioning and school achievement. During the past few years, however, it has become increasingly recognized that the relationships between nutritional deprivation and psychological development in children are quite complicated ones which are methodologically difficult to investigate and are not yet clearly understood.

A substantial body of research has shown quite clearly, for example, that it is extremely difficult, if not impossible, to make a meaningful evaluation of the independent effect of malnutrition *as such* on mental development in children, apart from the influence of various adverse social and environmental conditions typically associated with malnutrition, and capable of having a substantial impact on children's behavior and intellectual development in their own right (Pollitt & Thomson, 1977; Ricciuti, 1977). There has been a tendency, therefore, to move away from the assumption of a direct causal relationship between early malnutrition, altered brain development, and impaired intellectual functioning, toward a focusing of greater attention on the following issues:

(a) More systematic analysis of the ways in which the child's nutritional status and aspects of his social environment and early experience may interact in jointly influencing the course of psychological development, with more precise assessment of nutritional status as well as behavioral outcomes.

(b) A fuller understanding of the mechanisms through which altered nutritional status may affect behavior and psychological development.

(c) Evaluation of the effectiveness of systematic efforts to prevent or ameliorate the potentially adverse behavioral consequences of early malnutrition.

Since there have been a number of recent extensive reviews of the substantial research literature on malnutrition and behavioral development (Brozek, 1978; Pollitt & Thomson, 1977; Latham, 1974), this paper will not attempt to present another exhaustive review of this literature. Rather, it will endeavor to critically summarize and evaluate the present state of our knowledge in this area, and to delineate in some detail some of the major research issues and priorities which currently represent topics of prime concern to a good many investigators in the field. Attention will be focused primarily on protein–calorie malnutrition, the most common nutritional problem occurring worldwide in poor populations. Space limitations preclude discussion of such issues as iron deficiency anemia, and the problem of obesity, which is generally considered the most widespread nutritional problem in this country.

We turn first to a brief discussion of the nature of protein–calorie malnutrition and how it is typically assessed, followed by an overview of the major research strategies that have been employed in studies of malnutrition and psychological development.

Protein–Calorie Malnutrition

Definition and Assessment

The major concern of this paper is with malnutrition resulting essentially from an insufficiency of protein and calories in the child's diet, commonly referred to as "protein–calorie malnutrition" (PCM), although more recently alluded to under the generic rubric of "protein and energy deficits". Protein–calorie malnutrition includes the conditions of *nutritional marasmus*, or starvation, usually beginning in the earliest months of life and continuing for an extended period, producing infants whose physical growth and motor development are grossly impaired; and *kwashiorkor*, due primarily to an insufficiency of protein, typically occurring as a rather acute illness toward the end of the first year or in the second year of life, frequently after the birth of a younger sibling. Many combinations or mixtures of these two conditions are found in practice, and they vary greatly in severity and duration (Scrimshaw, 1963).

The most severe clinical forms of marasmus or kwashiorkor typically occur in combination with various infectious or parasitic diseases, and require hospitalization and treatment to ensure the child's survival. Although early and severe malnutrition occurs with considerable frequency in the poorer populations of developing countries (up to 20% in some instances), the most widespread type of malnutrition is that of mild-to-moderate chronic undernutrition, which is most readily noted in some retardation of physical growth and development.

One of the important methodological problems in this area is that it is difficult to secure accurate assessments of nutritional status in children, particularly if one is concerned with measurement throughout a broad range of nutritional variation and not simply with clinically obvious and severe malnutrition. Three types of measures are usually employed: assessment of food intake from detailed dietary information; clinical or physical evaluations, including various anthropometric measures, particularly height, weight, and head circumference; and biochemical evaluations of specific nutrients from blood and urine samples. The interpretation of such measures is considered quite difficult, particularly if one attempts to judge the adequacy of an individual's nutritional status from a single index, and many nutritionists feel that these assessments are most valid when used in combination with one another (Ten State Nutrition Survey, 1972).

A final definitional comment has to do with the importance of distinguishing between hunger and malnutrition. The schoolchild who frequently misses breakfast or lunch may perform poorly because of inattentiveness and distractability associated with hunger. However, these potential influences on school performance and learning, about which we know very little, clearly need to be differentiated from those effects which are the result of long-term protein–calorie malnutrition. Many severely malnourished children are characterized by apathy, withdrawal, and loss of appetite, rather than by the increased activity and restlessness associated with hunger (Cravioto, DeLicardie, & Birch, 1966).

Major Research Strategies

Most studies of protein–calorie malnutrition have been based on samples of children from poor populations in Latin America, Asia, and Africa. The general strategy has usually involved a comparison of developmental or intelligence test scores, school performance, or other behavioral assessments of children with a known or presumed history of malnutrition, with those of children from the same general population but with a more favorable nutritional history. In the case of early malnutrition serious enough to warrant hospitalization or special treatment, comparative assessments of behavior and development status have sometimes been made during treatment and recovery, as well as a number of years later when the children are of school age. Most studies of school-age children have been retrospective, involving a comparison of children with and without a history of hospitalization for severe malnutrition in the first two or three years of life.

Studies of the more common mild-to-moderate, chronic malnutrition have usually employed anthropometric indices of growth, such as stature or head circumference, as indices of the preschool or school-age child's nutritional history, and correlated these indices with various behavioral outcome measures.

A second research strategy which has been employed more frequently in recent years involves the use of various types of experimental intervention. Children considered at risk of malnutrition are provided with added health care and nutritional supplementation, and an evaluation is made of the behavioral consequences of such intervention, along with the effects on physical growth, nutritional status, and health. More recently, we are beginning to see various forms of environmental stimulation included as an added intervention aimed at promoting behavioral development and physical growth.

A third strategy, less common but potentially extremely valuable, involves the ecologically oriented, detailed longitudinal study of the growth and development of samples of children from birth, in settings where chronic malnutrition is endemic. This approach is best illustrated by Cravioto's recent studies in a rural Mexican village (Cravioto, Birch, DeLicardie, Rosales, & Vega, 1969). The assumption underlying this approach is that the natural variation occurring in such a population will make it possible to study prospectively those conditions which lead to the development of malnutrition in some children and not in others in the same environment.

Studies of Severe Malnutrition

There have been a number of studies indicating that infants examined during and shortly after rehabilitation from severe protein–calorie malnutrition requiring hospitalization in the first several years of life, are substantially retarded in physical growth and motor development, and show appreciably reduced performance on developmental and cognitive tests (Cravioto & Robles, 1965; Chase & Martin, 1970; Brockman & Ricciuti, 1971). The severity of the malnutrition and the associated developmental delay involved here is reflected in the fact, for example, that many of these children might have body weights when hospitalized for treatment at 5 or 6 months of age which are no greater or even less than their birthweights, and have made little or no gain in length; or, they may have body weights at 10 months which are no greater than that of a normal 1-month-old. At the same time, these children may have Developmental Quotients on standard infant tests that are well below 60. Preschool and school-age children 5–11 years of age having experienced severe malnutrition in the first 2 or 3 years of life have also frequently been found to perform substantially less well than controls on a variety of intelligence and perceptual–cognitive tests and do less well in school (Cravioto &

DeLicardie, 1970; Hertzig, Birch, Richardson, & Tizard, 1972; Champakam, Srikantia, & Gopalan, 1968).

It is interesting to note that a number of the investigators reporting these results caution against uncritical interpretation of the findings as evidence of a direct causal relationship between malnutrition and mental subnormality, since the same socioenvironmental factors which contribute to the development of marasmus or kwashiorkor in some children and not in others in the same environment may well contribute directly to the reduced intellectual performance observed (Chase & Martin, 1970; Champakam et al., 1968). Moreover, those children who continue to manifest subnormal levels of intellectual functioning six to ten years after treatment for early, severe malnutrition have typically returned to the same adverse environments which contributed to the severe malnutrition in the first place, and which may be a major determinant of the child's current intellectual functioning.

The importance of variations in the quality of the home environments among very poor families is illustrated in recent work by Richardson (1976) in Jamaica, indicating that children with early, severe malnutrition whose families scored relatively high on several social-background factors showed only a minimal reduction in IQ at six to ten years of age relative to comparison cases. On the other hand, children whose families were characterized by more adverse social conditions showed a substantially greater IQ reduction. Thus, the potential effects of even severe early malnutrition on intellectual functioning in the early elementary school years may be considerably attenuated by relatively more favorable social-background conditions in the generally very poor families. Somewhat more dramatic evidence of the potential for amelioration of long-term effects of severe, early malnutrition is suggested in the recent work of Winick, Meyer, and Harris (1975). Korean orphan girls with a history of malnutrition, as judged by retarded physical growth at two to three years of age, shortly before adoption by primarily middle-class American families, were found to have IQs and school achievement within the normal range for American children when followed up in grades 1 to 8.

In summary, then, there is reasonably good evidence that severe protein–calorie malnutrition in the first several years of life may have substantial adverse effects on children's intellectual development. The effects appear to be more marked the more severe the nutritional deprivation, and the longer it continues without treatment. If·nutritional treatment and rehabilitation occur early in the first year, the chances of recovery of normal or near normal intellectual functioning appear quite good. There is some evidence, although not entirely consistent, to suggest that severe malnutrition beginning in the second year of life or later, often taking the form of kwashiorkor, appears to produce effects which are not as severe and seem to be more amenable to treatment and remediation. It is still not clear whether malnutrition *as such* is the primary determinant of impaired intellectual functioning, since it is so inextricably intertwined with adverse social and environmental circumstances. Recent studies suggest that the potential long-term effects of early, severe malnutrition may be greatly attenuated, or virtually eliminated, by favorable developmentally supportive later environments, or compounded by less favorable environmental conditions. Considerable effort is being made to understand more clearly the mechanisms through which severe malnutrition may exert its influence on behavior and development, as well as to determine which psychological processes are more vulnerable to its potential impact. These topics will be discussed more fully somewhat later in the paper.

Studies of Mild-to-Moderate Chronic Malnutrition

There have been a good many studies of the intellectual development of children who have presumably experienced the very widespread mild-to-moderate chronic malnutrition which is endemic in many poor populations, as judged primarily on the basis of some physical growth retardation, particularly in height, weight, or head circumference. While these shorter children often tend to show somewhat reduced levels of intellectual function, these findings are particulary difficult to interpret because of the problems involved in using simple anthropometric indices like height or head circumference as the principal indices of nutritional status and history. It is well known, for example, that while variations in height may well reflect children's nutritional histories, particularly under conditions of nutritional adversity, these height variations may also reflect a variety of other social characteristics of the environment, or biological characteristics of the individual (including genetic factors), which are themselves capable of influencing the child's intellectual development (Ricciuti, 1977; Pollitt & Ricciuti, 1969).

Several studies of the intellectual competence of tall and short children in Latin America illustrate these interpretive difficulties. In a study of 6- to 11-year-old children living in a Guatemalan village, for example (Cravioto *et al.*, 1966), tall children tended to make fewer errors than short children in identifying geometric forms on the basis of integrating visual, haptic, and kinesthetic information. Although the tall and short children came from families with generally equivalent socioenvironmental backgrounds, maternal education was markedly higher in the case of the tall children, who may thus have had substantially more intellectual stimulation and opportunities for learning. Similarly, in a Chilean study of 1- to 5-year-old poor children considered at risk of mild-to-moderate malnutrition (Monckeberg, Tisler, Toro, Gattas, & Vegal, 1972), a substantial correlation was found between mothers' IQ and the children's growth in height ($r = .71$). Thus, the lower IQs found in the shorter children may well be attributable to genetic factors or to reduced levels of intellectual stimulation provided by the less competent mothers.

A number of more recent studies of mild-to-moderate malnutrition have endeavored to evaluate the relative influence of social or environmental factors, and the nutritional variations reflected in physical growth measures, with the use of correlational and multiple-regression analyses. In a Guatemala study of 3- to 6-year-old village children, for example, Klein, Freeman, Kagan, Yarbrough, and Habicht (1972) found that physical growth measures and a composite of social factors showed generally equivalent correlations with tests of language and memory (mostly .20 to .40). On the other hand, insofar as the development of perceptual competence is concerned, their data suggest that nutritional background (height and head circumference) may play a somewhat greater role than social experience (r's were .33 vs. .18 for boys, and .33 vs. .25 for girls).

Working with considerably younger children in Bogota (6–30 months), Christiansen, Vuori, Mora, and Wagner (1974) found that Griffiths Developmental Quotients (DQs) were substantially more highly correlated with physical growth (multiple R for height and weight = .57) than with a composite socioeconomic index (multiple R = .43). Moreover, the predictability of DQs from height and weight alone was increased by only .05, from .57 to .62, when the social factors were added. Klein, Yarbrough, Lasky, and Habicht's study of 24-month-old children (1974) also suggests a somewhat greater influence of nutritional or growth factors rather than social factors on developmental test scores, particularly with regard to motor development.

On the other hand, in Richardson's (1976) previously mentioned study of 6- to 10-year-old Jamaica boys who experienced severe malnutrition early in life, a composite family social background index was much more predictive of IQ levels than was the occurrence of the previous history of severe malnutrition. These and other studies indicate that it is very difficult to arrive at any firm, consistent estimates of the magnitude of the independent contributions of nutritional and associated socioenvironmental influences to the growth of intellectual competencies. As will be argued more fully somewhat later in this paper, a more fruitful approach would involve a closer examination of the potential interactions between these two major sources of influence, as they jointly shape the course of intellectual development.

In summary, when we consider the chronic, mild-to-moderate malnutrition which is endemic in many economically disadvantaged populations, the research evidence suggesting adverse effects on children's psychological development is substantially weaker and less clear than that dealing with early and severe malnutrition. Generally speaking, the reserch thus far suggests that mild-to-moderate malnutrition appears to play a relatively minor role in determining children's intellectual development, in comparison with the substantial ifluence exerted by various social and environmental factors.

CURRENT RESEARCH DEVELOPMENTS, NEEDS, AND PRIORITIES

Having briefly reviewed some of the major findings of recent research bearing on the relationship between malnutrition and behavioral development in children, we turn next to a somewhat more analytical consideration of contemporary research issues and priorities which appear to this reviewer to represent important directions for continued investigation.

As indicated in the foregoing summary, there is a large body of literature indicating that malnutrition tends to be associated with reduced levels of intellectual functioning in children. In my view, there would be very little to be gained by additional studies which again simply showed that malnourished children perform less well on various intellectual tests than adequately nourished children from the same general population, or even from families with approximately equivalent educational backgrounds. Generally speaking, what is needed at present is a much sharper delineation and analysis of these relationships, with more precise assessments of nutritional status as well as behavioral outcomes. More specifically, as mentioned at the outset, we need to direct our efforts toward a fuller understanding of how malnutrition and other environmental influences interact in combination to influence development, a more complete explanation of the mechanisms or channels of influence through which variations in nutritional status may affect the course of mental development and cognitive functioning, and further studies of the effectiveness of various forms of experimental interventions, including health care, nutritional supplementation, enrichment of the child's social and learning environment, etc. In the long run, these lines of inquiry should not only substantially enhance our understanding of the basic scientific issues involved, but at the same time provide a sounder knowledge base on which to build systematic and effective field programs of prevention and remediation.

In the paragraphs which follow, research issues and needs which seem to this reviewer to be of particularly high priority in each of the three areas just mentioned will be discussed briefly, along with suggested research strategies.

Analyses of Patterns of Interaction between Malnutrition and Socioenvironmental Influences

As mentioned in the initial summary, in recent years there has been an increased recognition of the significant role played by various social and environmental conditions typically associated with malnutrition as important determinants of psychological development in children. Various research and analytic strategies have been employed in an effort to evaluate the relationship between nutritional status and intellectual competencies, independent of those socioenvironmental influences associated both with malnutrition and behavioral outcomes. These efforts have sometimes taken the form of comparing the performance of malnourished and better nourished children from the same neighborhoods or general socioeconomic levels. Such a strategy, however, does not take into account the likelihood that those poor families whose children are better-nourished may also be living under less adverse socioeconomic circumstances than the experimental families, and may be providing a social and learning environment which is more facilitative of their children's intellectual development (Monck-eberg et al., 1972). Other investigators have employed somewhat more refined but still relatively simple indices of variations in family and home environment (type of housing, income, education of parent) and incorporated them in partial correlation or regression analyses aimed at determining how much of the variance in cognitive performance can be accounted for by nutritional status alone, by socioenvironmental variations alone, and by the two combined (Klein et al., 1972; Christiansen et al., 1974).

From this reviewer's perspective, these kinds of analyses are heuristically useful up to a point, but they are of rather limited value in advancing our understanding of the interactive influences of nutritional and socioenvironmental variations on intellectual development. First, the indices of nutritional status and of the family and home environment are typically quite simplistic and hence may be capturing only a small portion of the developmentally relevant variations in each domain. Moreover, obtained estimates of the independent contribution of nutritional versus socioenvironmental factors will vary greatly depending on various characteristics of the samples employed (such as age, homogeneity or heterogeneity with respect to environmental and nutritional variation), and also depending on the particular outcome measures utilized (Ricciuti, 1977). Most studies employing this analytic approach typically find that simple indices of nutritional status (ht., wt., h.c.) and of socioeconomic background are positively correlated (r's in the .20s to .30s), with correlations of about the same order of magnitude being found between each of these predictors and measures of intellectual competence. Regression analyses tend to show that both social factors and nutritional history make some independent contribution to intellectual competence, with the percentages of variance presumably attributable to each source of influence varying substantially from study to study (e.g., 29% for social factors vs. 5% for severe early malnutrition in the previously mentioned study of 6- to 10-year-old Jamaican boys [Richardson, 1976]; 18% vs. 32% in a study of 6- to 30-month-old Colombian children [Christiansen et al., 1974]).

At this point in time, there would appear to be little value in further studies concerned primarily with the question of how much of the variation in intellectual competence can be attributed to nutritional status alone or to socioenvironmental factors alone. Rather, we need to go beyond such analytic strategies and systematically direct our research at increased understanding of how malnutrition and the child's social environment interact in jointly influencing the development of intellectual competencies, employing more refined measures of nutritional status, as well as more precise and detailed analyses of relevant features of the social and physical environment in the home, neighborhood, or community.

The potential value of this line of approach is strongly suggested by several recent studies indicating that within very poor populations where children are known to be generally at risk of early malnutrition, variations in particular features of the child's home and family environment may either increase or reduce substantially the likelihood of severe malnutrition occurring in specific families (DeLicardie & Cravioto, 1974; Richardson, 1974). It is important to note also, that these features of the child's social environment associated with the occurrence of malnutrition include environmental influences which can have a substantial direct effect on the child's mental development (e.g., mother's competence, degree to which child-care practices provide nurturance and support for psychological development). For example, in a longitudinal study of several hundred infants born in a poor rural Mexican village (DiLicardie & Cravioto, 1974), those children who experienced severe malnutrition in the first three years of life were found to have lower IQs than controls at five years of age, and tended to come from homes which, as early as the first year of life, were observed to be lower in the quantity and quality of social, emotional, and cognitive stimulation provided to the child. Moreoever, these same features of the early home environment were also related to IQ at five years of age among children without a history of severe malnutrition.

In the present context, it is particularly important to note, as mentioned earlier, that once a child has suffered from early malnutrition, even of the severe type, the risk of subsequent impairment of mental development will also depend very much on the quality of the child's home and family environment. On the basis of both human and animal studies, it has become increasingly apparent that a developmentally facilitative social environment may substantially attenuate or even prevent the potentially unfavorable consequences of early, severe malnutrition (Richardson, 1976; Winick et al., 1975; Lloyd-Still, Hurwitz, Wolff, & Shwachmann, 1974; Levitsky, 1979).

The studies just summarized clearly emphasize the importance of our directing more systematic attention toward more precise evaluations of those aspects of the family environment or family functioning which make some families less vulnerable to the occurrence of severe malnutrition than others in the same "at risk" population, and also more capable of "buffering" or attenuating the potentially adverse behavior effects of malnutrition when it does occur. The approach suggested here involves going beyond the well-known demographic indicators of increased biosocial stress and risk such as maternal age or health history, family size, parental education, income, exposure to infections or parasitic disease, accessibility of health care, etc. What is needed is a more refined analysis of the coping strengths and strategies used by families, as well as their capacity to provide developmentally facilitative child care or child-rearing environments which are supportive of both physical growth and psychological development, in the face of generally adverse socioenvironmental circumstances. The identification of these intrafamilial strengths or vulnerabilities should certainly enhance significantly our basic understanding of important interactions between nutritional and socioenvironmental influences on growth and development. At the same time, from the perspective of prevention and remediation, this added knowledge should provide helpful guidelines or avenues of approach in the development of effective programs of intervention and support for families coping with adversity.

Another example of important interrelationships between malnutrition and salient aspects of the child's social environment or early experience is reflected in the growing evidence that the infant or young child's altered nutritional status, as reflected in physical appearance and behavior, may affect the manner in which primary caregivers respond to or care for the child, thus potentially altering his early experience in developmentally significant ways (Chavez, Martinez, & Yachine, 1975; Graves, 1978). Further systematic investigation of these interrelationships should shed additional light on the question of why some children in a given family are severely malnourished while siblings are spared. As our knowledge concerning these developmentally significant patterns of child care and parent–child relationships expands, we should better be able to plan effective preventive or remedial approaches to families where the risk of malnutrition is particularly high.

While the emphasis in the discussion thus far has been upon the interaction of malnutrition and *social* factors in the child's experience and environment, it would similarly be very important to examine more carefully the manner in which malnutrition of various types and degrees of severity might combine with other biological risk factors, such as low birth weight, prematurity, congenital or genetic anomalies, etc., adversely affecting the development of intellectual competecies.

Identification of Mechanisms through Which Altered Nutritional Status May Affect Intellectual Competencies

One of the most important research questions still confronting us in this field is the problem of specifying the mechanisms, or channels of influence, through which malnutrition might exert its impact on the development of various behavioral competencies. In human studies, this problem is being approached in part by efforts to assess a wider array of potential behavioral outcomes of malnutrition in order to determine whether various specific perceptual–cognitive, learning, or motivational processes might be particularly vulnerable to the impact of nutritional deficits (Klein, 1979; Hoorweg, 1976; Pollitt, Greenfield, & Leibel, 1978). The same general approach is being followed in much of the recent animal research, where investigators have also been able to manipulate experimentally the conditions of nutritional deprivation, recovery, and treatment (including added experience) (Levitsky, 1979; Frankova, 1974).

When the concerns about malnutrition as a possible major cause of mental retardation reached a peak in the late 1960s and early 1970s it was assumed by many that the brain changes produced by malnutrition led directly to an impairment of learning ability and thus to retarded intellectual development, which was often irreversible. On the basis of much human as well as animal research since that time, however, most investigators have tended to discard this view in favor of the hypothesis that malnutrition may exert its major influence on behavioral competencies through dysfunctional changes in attention, responsiveness, motivation, and emotionality, rather than through a more direct impairment of basic ability to learn. In short, the malnourished child's interaction with his environment may be altered in ways that make him less likely to seek out, utilize, and respond to opportunities for learning and social interaction available in his environment. This state of events would imply quite hopeful prospects for reversibility or remediation, since it may be possible to manipulate the environment so as to make the child's interaction with it more intellectually facilitative (to be discussed more fully later in this review).

This general problem of more precise identification of the mechanisms through which the behavioral effects of malnutrition might be mediated certainly deserves much more systematic attention with human subjects at different age levels, and with different types and severity of nutritional deficits. As indicated earlier, one approach to this problem is to broaden our behavioral assessments so as to include measures specifically intended to determine which psychological processes or competencies are particularly vulnerable to various kinds of malnutrition. Although a good many recent studies have indeed gone beyond general IQ or DQ assessments, particularly with preschool or school-age children, it is difficult to find consistent patterns of differential nutritional vulnerability for various perceptual–cognitive functions across studies. Much of this inconsistency is to be expected, since the particular competencies or skills which seem most affected by malnutrition are likely to vary with the age of the children, the severity of the malnutrition, the particular tests used, the degree to which sociocultural or environmental influences on performance have been controlled, etc.

Nevertheless, perhaps the most common suggestion derivable from much of the research, but particularly from studies of early and severe malnutrition, is that the nutritional deficits seem to alter the child's attentional competencies and responsiveness to the environment. For example, the commonly reported clinical observations of reduced activity or apathy in severe early malnutrition, particularly of the marasmic type, are supported by recent experimental studies indicating reduced alerting or orienting responses to simple auditory stimuli (Lester, Klein, & Martinez, 1975). On the other hand, while these malnourished infants or toddlers seem less responsive to low or moderate levels of stimulation, they appear to be hyperreactive to higher stimulus levels that are more "intrusive." Nonsupplemented young infants, for example, responded more irritably to a moderately stressful stimulus than did supplemented infants (Vuori, de Navarro, Christiansen, Mora, & Herrera, 1978), a finding paralleling reports of heightened "emotionality" and difficulty in extinguishing conditioned responses in malnourished animals. It is interesting to note that this same pattern of reduced attention to moderate stimuli and hyperreactivity to more intense stimuli is also being found in very recent studies of premature or low-birth-weight infants in this country (Rose, Schmidt, & Bridger, 1976). Accompanying this pattern of altered responsiveness in children with early malnutrition are reports of reduced curiosity and exploratory behavior in infants and toddlers (Chavez et al., 1975; Graves, 1978).

Although the data are much less consistent and clear, there are some suggestions from studies of preschool and school-age children that tasks which require the capacity to mobilize and sustain attention may be particularly affected by malnutrition—e.g., simple tasks of short-term memory, or tasks in which incidental learning is possible. These suggestive findings, which need much more systematic replication, come both from studies of mild-to-moderate malnutrition (Klein, 1979; Irwin, Klein, et al., 1979; McKay, McKay, & Sinisterra, 1974), as well as a recent study of teenage children with history of clinical malnutrition in the first two years of life (Hoorweg, 1976). The importance of further systematic research directed at the impact of malnutrition on the child's attentional and motivational competencies is also supported by recent reports of altered work styles, or responses to cognitive demands shown by preschool children having experienced early clinical malnutrition (DeLicardie & Cravioto, 1974), as well as less favorable performance on tasks requiring sustained attention by Boston children with iron deficiency (Pollitt, Greenfield, & Leibel, 1978).

Virtually all the research just discussed has involved behavioral assessments of children performing in structured test or experimental situations. There is great need to extend systematically the beginning efforts that have been made recently to examine the potential consequences of malnutrition on various adaptive, intellectual, or learning competencies manifested in various real-life settings (Hoorweg, 1976; Nerlove, Roberts, Klein, Yarbrough, & Habicht, 1974; Richardson, Birch, & Hertzig, 1973). Assessments of functional competence based on observations of performance in these natural settings would complement the more common test or laboratory assessments in important ways, not the least of which would be to shed some light on the ecological or functional validity of these more controlled measurements. It is interesting to note that current early-intervention research in this country strongly reflects a similar movement away from a heavy dependence on psychological tests or laboratory observations, toward more utilization of evaluations of competence manifested in natural situations.

Effectiveness of Nutritional and Social Interventions in Fostering the Development of Intellectual Competence

The systematic utilization of experimental intervention strategies represents one of the most potent research approaches in this field. The hospitalization and treatment of clinically ill children with severe malnutrition obviously represents a basic and widely used form of intervention, which could be more fully exploited for systematic behavioral research purposes than it has been thus far. It is encouraging to note that in the past few years there has been an increasing utilization of nutritional intervention as a research strategy, particularly in connection with efforts to prevent malnutrition in populations where the problem is a chronic and endemic one. Because such studies are carried out within a longitudinal, prospective framework, they provide the opportunity to follow the physical growth and psychological development of children whose nutritional histories have been systematically influenced through the provision of added health care and nutritional supplementation, beginning prenatally in some instances (Irwin et al., 1979; Brozek, Coursin, & Read, 1977). One of the major advantages of the intervention strategy is that changes or contrasts in children's dietary intake and nutritional status can be monitored prospectively as they occur, along with concurrent social and environmental factors, so that their relationships to contemporary or subsequent developmental outcome measures can be more meaningfully evaluated. This contrasts rather sharply with the situation characterizing many retrospective studies of malnourished children, in which information about previous nutritional and developmental histories is often very limited and unclear.

A few recent nutritional-intervention studies have begun to incorporate procedures for enrichment or enhancement of the child's social and learning environment as components of the intervention program, along with nutritional supplementation and health care. This intervention has sometimes been provided as an enrichment of experience, or "stimulation" during treatment for severe malnutrition, sometimes as a preschool program for children typically exposed to chronic undernutrition, and sometimes in the form of a home visiting program to support the mother as a caregiver and promoter of her infant or toddler's development (Brozek et al., 1977). In my view, this general strategy represents an extremely important approach since it recognizes the fact that the child's health and nutritional status, and his opportunities for learning and social development represent integral components of developmentally supportive child-care or child-rearing environments.

Let us briefly consider some of these recent intervention studies in somewhat more detail. With regard to severe and early malnutrition, as previously mentioned, it has been apparent for some time that the earlier the treatment and rehabilitation, the less the risk of severe developmental impairment (Pollitt & Thomson, 1977). Also, ensuring that the child is not deprived of adequate social and physical stimulation during treatment and rehabilitation, or providing added experiences during this period, seems to offer some facilitation of the recovery process (McLaren, Yaktin, Kanawati, Sabbagh, & Kadi, 1973; Monckeberg & Ruimallo, 1979). The long-term benefits of these early treatments and interventions, of course, are very much influenced by the nature of the enduring environments to which the children return after hospitalization. As indicated earlier, the importance of the later developmental environments of children having experienced early and severe malnutrition is emphasized by recent findings indicating that if these environments are favorable and supportive of development there may be a substantial recovery of both physical growth (Winick *et al.*, 1975; Graham, 1972), as well as intellectual development (Winick *et al.*, 1975; Lloyd-Still *et al.*, 1974).

Insofar as mild-to-moderate malnutrition is concerned, research thus far suggests that the provision of freely available nutritional supplementation to children and families at risk of mild-to-moderate undernutrition in rural Guatemalan villages has relatively little impact on the enhancement of mental development, particularly when compared with the role played by socioenvironmental influences (Klein, 1979; Irwin *et al.*, 1979). In an experimental intervention study with urban poor families in Bogota, during the first 18 months of life children who had received either nutritional supplementation *or* home visiting to promote maternal encouragement of intellectual development showed rather slight advantages in developmental-test scores over control children receiving only health care (Mora, Christiansen, Ortiz, Vuori, & Herrera, 1979). Children who received both treatments showed somewhat more favorable gains in both physical growth and developmental-test performance.

While the results just summarized and a few other behavioral advantages reported for supplemented infants early in the first year of life can be considered somewhat promising, they represent quite modest effects, considering the scope and cost of the interventions involved. On the other hand there may be more subtle but important effects on the families provided with the combined health-care, supplementation, and home-visiting program, which have not yet been fully assessed.

The recent report from the Cali, Colombia project (McKay, Sinisterra, McKay, Gomez, & Llorenda, 1978) indicates that some facilitation of cognitive functioning can apparently be produced by a highly structured, cognitively oriented all-day preschool program, which also provides health care and nutritional supplementation. As is the case with many preschool intervention programs in this country, it is not clear at this point to what extent these apparent benefits will be maintained when the children continue on in the public school system, particularly if no systematic efforts have been made to enhance the continuing environment of the home and family.

In considering the general implications of these recent intervention studies one is inclined to conclude, on the other hand, that the results thus far are mildly promising, at least in the case of the studies which have included social or environmental intervention as well as health care and nutritional supplementation. At the same time, however, these studies also reflect the difficulties of designing and implementing effective early-intervention programs which can be shown to produce functionally meaningful enhancement of intellectual competencies. Nevertheless, this reviewer remains convinced that more of our research efforts must be aimed directly at the issue of intervention strategies for optimizing the growth and development of children who live in adverse environments and are at risk of both malnutrition and suboptimal intellectual development, or have already experienced severe malnutrition. Obviously, in the long run the most effective forms of "intervention" would involve major improvements of the developmentally threatening economic, social, and physical conditions under which large populations of the poor live. Short of these long-term political, social, and economic changes, however, and working within the framework of resources potentially available in the immediate future, we need to continue to develop and systematically evaluate the effectiveness of various forms of intervention which could eventually be incorporated into realistic, ongoing social programs.

It seems highly possible that the most effective intervention strategies are likely to be those which are simultaneously concerned not only with nutritional and health needs, but also with ensuring necessary socioenvironmental supports for optimal psychological development. Our major research goal, then, should be to determine how best to combine these elements in programs which meet the special needs of particular groups of children and families, given our goal of facilitating cognitive development. It seems reasonable to assume, also, that intervention is most likely to be effective, as well as more feasible economically, if it can be focused so as to reach particularly those children and families considered to be at greatest biological or socioenvironmental risk of impaired development.

SUMMARY AND CONCLUSIONS

It is quite clear that protein–calorie malnutrition represents a significant threat to the normal growth and development of many thousands of children living under the adverse conditions associated with poverty in many regions of the world. While protein–calorie malnutrition may produce substantial retardation of physical growth and brain development, there is relatively little evidence thus far that it has a direct and independent effect in producing intellectual or learning deficits in children, apart from the adverse social and environmental conditions typically associated with malnutrition. Nevertheless, severe and extended malnutrition beginning in the first two years of lfe may well be implicated as one important determinant of suboptimal development, particularly if combined with a developmentally unfavorable social and learning environment in the home. Even in such instances, however, it appears that the long-term effects of severe malnutrition may be substantially attenuated or minimized by a more favorable, developmentally supportive later environment. Mild or moderate malnutrition appears to play a relatively minor role in determining children's intellectual development, in comparison with the substantial influence exerted by various social and environmental factors.

Much current research is quite properly directed at a fuller understanding of the interactions between malnutrition and specific features of the child's social and physical environment in the home and neighborhood, in order to determine how these two major sources of potential influence may combine to produce either heightened or attenuated risk to normal psychological development. At the same time, considerable research has been focused on a better understanding of the mechanisms through which malnutrition may exert its influence on behavior, through both human and animal studies. Considerable evidence thus far suggests that malnutrition may alter the child's attentional strategies and competencies, responsiveness to the environment, and emotionality, rather than directly impairing the basic ability to learn.

There has also been a substantial increase in experimental intervention studies concerned with evaluation of the effectiveness of broadly based nutritional-supplementation and health-care programs in enhancing both physical and mental development. Some of these programs have begun to incorporate efforts to provide added enrichment or enhancement of the child's early social and learning environments as well. While the results of these efforts to enhance children's intellectual development have not been particularly encouraging so far, continued research along these lines is very much needed. Such intervention research should add significantly to our basic understanding of the influence of malnutrition and early experience on behavioral development, while at the same time strengthening the knowledge base required for planning effective social programs aimed at prevention and remediation of suboptimal development.

REFERENCES

Brockman, L.M., & Ricciuti, H.N. Severe protein–calorie malnutrition and cognitive development in infancy and early childhood. *Developmental Psychology,* 1971, *4,* 312–319.

Brozek, J. Nutrition, malnutrition, and behavior. *Annual Review of Psychology,* 1978, *29,* 157–177.

Brozek, J., Coursin, D.B., & Read, M.S. Longitudinal studies on the effects of malnutrition, nutritional supplementation, and behavioral stimulation. *Bulletin of the Pan American Health Organization,* 1977, *11,* 237–249.

Champakam, S., Srikantia, S.G., & Gopalan, C. Kwashiorkor and mental development. *American Journal of Clinical Nutrition,* 1968, *21,* 844–852.

Chase, H.P., & Martin, H.P. Undernutrition and child development. *New England Journal of Medicine,* 1970, *282,* 933–939.

Chavez, A., Martinez, C., & Yachine, T. Nutrition, behavioral development, and mother–child interaction in young rural children. *Federation Proceedings,* 1975, *34,* 1574–1582.

Christiansen, N., Vuori, L., Mora, J.O., & Wagner, M. Social environment as it relates to malnutrition and mental development. In J. Cravioto *et al.* (Eds.), *Early malnutrition and mental development.* Uppsala: Almquist and Wiksell, 1974, pp. 186–199.

Cravioto, J., & DeLicardie, E.R. Mental performance in school age children. *American Journal of Diseases of Children,* 1970, *120,* 404.

Cravioto, J., & Robles, B. Evolution of adaptive and motor behavior during rehabilitation from kwashiorkor. *American Journal of Orthopsychiatry,* 1965, *35,* 449–464.

Cravioto, J., DeLicardie, E.R., & Birch, H.G. Nutrition, growth and neuro-integrative development: An experimental and ecologic study. *Pediatrics,* 1966, *38,*319–372.

Cravioto, J., Birch, H.G., DeLicardie, E., Rosales, L., & Vega, . The ecology of growth and development in a Mexican pre-industrial community. *Monographs of the Society for Research in Child Development,* 1969, *34,* 1–65.

DeLicardie, E.R., & Cravioto, J. Behavioral responsiveness of survivors of clinically severe malnutrition to cognitive demands. In J. Cravioto *et al.* (Eds.), *Early malnutrition and mental development.* Uppsala: Almquist and Wiksell, 1974, pp. 134–153.

Dobbing, J. Efects of experimental undernutrition on development of the nervous system. In N.S. Scrimshaw & J.E. Gordon (Eds.), *Malnutrition, learning and behavior.* Cambridge: Massachusetts Institute of Technology Press, 1968, pp. 181–202.

Frankova, S. Interaction between early malnutrition and stimulation in animals. In J. Cravioto *et al.* (Eds.), *Early malnutrition and mental development*. Uppsala: Almquist and Wiksell, 1974, pp. 202–209.

Graham, G. Environmental factors affecting the growth of children. *American Journal of Clinical Nutrition*, 1972, *25*, 1184–1188.

Graves, P.L. Nutrition and infant behavior: A replication study in the Katmandu Valley, Nepal. *American Journal of Clinical Nutrition*, 1978, *31*, 541–551.

Hertzig, M.E., Birch, H.G., Richardson, S.A., & Tizard, J. Intellectual levels of school children severely malnourished during the first two years of life. *Pediatrics*, 1972, *49*, 814–824.

Hoorweg, J.C. *Protein–energy malnutrition and intellectual abilities*. The Hague/Paris: Mouton, 1976.

Irwin, M.H., Klein, R.E., & others Effects of food supplementation on cognitive development and behavior among rural Guatemalan children. In J. Brozek (Ed.), *Behavioral effects of energy and protein deficits*. Bethesda: Department of Health, Education and Welfare (NIH), 1979, pp. 239–254.

Klein, R.E. Malnutrition and human behavior: A backward glance at an ongoing longitudinal study. In D.A. Levitsky (Ed.), *Malnutrition, environment, and behavior: New perspectives*. Ithaca: Cornell University Press, 1979, pp. 219–237.

Klein, R.E., Freeman, H.E., Kagan, J., Yarbrough, C., & Habicht, J.P. Is big smart? The relation of growth to cognition. *Journal of Health and Social Behavior*, 1972, *13*, 219–225.

Klein, R.E., Yarbrough, C., Lasky, R.E., & Habicht, J.P. Correlations of mild to moderate protein–calorie malnutrition among rural Guatemalan infants and preschool children. In J. Cravioto *et al.* (Eds.), *Early malnutrition and mental development*. Uppsala: Almquist & Wiksell, 1974, pp. 168–181.

Latham, M.C. Protein–calorie malnutrition in children and its relation to psychological development and behavior. *Physiological Review*, 1974, *54*(3), 541–565.

Lester, B.M., Klein, R.E., & Martinez, S.J. The use of habituation in the study of the effects of infantile malnutrition. *Developmental Psychobiology*, 1975, *8*, 541–546.

Levitsky, D.A. (Ed.). *Malnutrition, environment, and behavior: New perspectives*. Ithaca: Cornell University Press, 1979.

Lloyd-Still, J.D., Hurwitz, I., Wolff, P.H., & Shwachmann, H. Intellectual development after severe malnutrition in infancy. *Pediatrics*, 1974, *54*, 306–311.

McKay, H., McKay, A., & Sinisterra, L. Intellectual development of malnourished preschool children in programs of stimulation and nutritional supplementation. In J. Cravioto *et al.* (Eds.), *Early malnutrition and mental development*. Uppsala: Almquist and Wiksell, 1974, pp. 226–233.

McKay, H., Sinisterra, L., McKay, H.G., Gomez, H., & Lloreda, P. Improving cognitive ability in chronically deprived children. *Science*, 1978, *200*, 270–278.

McLaren, D.S., Yaktim, U.S., Kanawati, A.A., Sabbagh, S., & Kadi Z. The subsequent mental and physical development of rehabilitated marasmic infants. *Journal of Mental Deficiency Research*, 1973, *17*, 273–281.

Monckeberg, F., & Ruimallo, J. Psychomotor stimulation in recovery of early severe marasmic malnutrition: Experience in recovery centers. In J. Brozek (Ed.), *Behavioral effects of energy and protein deficits*. Bethesda, Md.: Department of Health, Education and Welfare (NIH), 1979, pp. 121–130.

Monckeberg, F., Tisler, S., Toro, S., Gattas, V., & Vegal, L. Malnutrition and mental development. *American Journal of Clinical Nutrition*, 1972, *25*, 766–772.

Mora, J.O., Christiansen, N., Ortiz, N., Vuori, L., & Herrera, M.G. Nutritional supplementation, early environment, and child development during the first 18 months of life. In J. Brozek (Ed.), *Behavioral effects of energy and protein deficits.* Bethesda: Department of Health, Education and Welfare (NIH), 1979, pp. 255–269.

Nerlove, S.B., Roberts, J.M., Klein, R.E., Yarbrough, C., & Habicht, J.P. Natural indicators of cognitive development: An observational study of rural Guatemalan children. *Ethos,* 1974, 2, 265–295.

Pollitt, E., & Ricciuti, H. Biological and social correlates of stature among children living in the slums of Lima, Peru. *American Journal of Orthopsychiatry,* 1969, 39, 735–747.

Pollitt, E., & Thomson, C. Protein–calorie malnutrition and behavior: A view from psychology. In R.J. Wurtman & J.J. Wurtman (Eds.), *Nutrition and the brain* (Vol. 2). New York: Raven Press, 1977, pp. 261–306.

Pollitt, E., Greenfield, D., & Leibel, R. Behavioral effects of iron deficiency among preschool children in Cambridge, Massachusetts. Paper presented at the 62d Annual Meeting of the Federation of American Societies for Experimental Biology, Atlantic City, New Jersey, April 1978.

Richardson, S.A. The background histories of school children severely malnourished in infancy. In I. Schulman (Ed.), *Advances in pediatrics, 21.* Chicago: Yearbook Medical Publications, 1974, pp. 167–192.

Richardson, S.A. The relation of severe malnutrition in infancy to intelligence of school children with differing life histories. *Pediatric Research,* 1976, 10, 57–61.

Richardson, S.A., Birch, H.G., & Hertzig, M.E. School performance of children who were severely malnourished in infancy. *American Journal of Mental Deficiency,* 1973, 77, 623–632.

Ricciuti, H.N. Malnutrition, learning and intellectual development: Research and remediation. In *Psychology and the Problems of Society.* Washington, D.C.: American Psychological Association, 1970.

Ricciuti, H.N. Adverse social and biological influences on early development. In H. McGurk (Ed.), *Ecological factors in human development.* Amsterdam: North Holland Press, 1977, Chapter 12.

Rose, S.A., Schmidt, K., & Bridger, W.H. Cardiac and behavioral responsivity to tactile stimulation in premature and full-term infants. *Developmental Psychology,* 1976, 12, 311–320.

Scrimshaw, N.S. Malnutrition and the health of children. *Journal of the American Dietetic Association,* 1963, 42, 203–208.

Scrimshaw, N.S., & Gordon, J.E. (Eds). *Malnutrition, learning and behavior.* Cambridge: MIT Press, 1968.

Ten State Nutrition Survey 1968–1970. Department of Health, Education and Welfare Publication No. (HSM) 72-8131, 1972.

Vuori, L., de Navarro, L., Christiansen, N., Mora, J.O., & Herrera, M.G. Food supplementation of pregnant women at risk of malnutrition and newborn responsiveness to stimulation. Unpublished manuscript. Harvard School of Public Health, Dept. of Nutrition, Boston, 1978.

Winick, M., & Rosso, P. Head circumference and cellular growth of the brain in normal and marasmic children. *Journal of Pediatrics,* 1969, 74, 774–778.

Winick, M., Meyer, K., & Harris, R.C. Malnutrition and environmental enrichment by adoption. *Science,* 1975, 190, 1173–1175.

8

Clinical Perspectives on the Sick and Dying Child

Ursula Thunberg

Introduction

Development in the medical sciences has resulted in a marked shift in the pattern of disease in children. One-hundred years ago the chances of reaching old age were much poorer than they are today. Improvement of health care with vaccination against many potentially fatal childhood diseases, antibiotics, and improved hygienic and nutritional conditions have changed this picture. More children in this society die today of accidents and chronic, fatal, and malignant diseases than in earlier times. Though in our society the death of a child is considered a rare event, there still are many cultures in which less than half of all newborn infants will complete their first year of life.

The emergence of the psychological and biological sciences with their various techniques and related systemic conceptualizations has led to a more complete but also more holistic view of the sick individual.

The direct implications of these scientific developments for the understanding of the ill child are a better awareness of developmental problems, respect for the specificity of response in the individual child, and for the complexity of interaction between the child and his family, the child and the medical staff.

URSULA THUNBERG • Chief, Child Adolescent Service, Bedford/Stuyvesant Community Mental Health Center, 1360 Fulton Street, Brooklyn, New York 11216.

The Sick Child

General Reactions

The reactions of a child to acute or chronic illness and perhaps resultant hospitalization will vary according to attained developmental state, level of emotional and physical stress, subjective significance of those, capacity to communicate stress or distress and thus be able to modify it actively, feeling about self, and quality of relationship to the family system.

In general the cognitive appraisal of a situation with its conscious and unconscious reactions, symbolic values, and the child's past experience will condition the youngster's responses.

In acute illness or injury children show reactions that could be directly related to the occurring insult by illness or injury. More general concomitants of physical illness are pain and discomfort, nausea, restless behavior, or very frequently disturbances in sleep pattern and appetite. Some children become whiny and clingy when feverish. Some may show signs of depression, anxiety, and confusion, many regress to a developmentally earlier stage of development, perhaps presenting loss of speech, or loss of bladder and bowel control. Chronic illness or a handicapping illness may have long-standing effects on personality development and feeling about self. The type of illness, physiological concomitants of illness such as fever and metabolic disturbances, and the type of treatment received will all have an influence on the behavioral expression of the child.

Even more than adults, children are helplessly exposed to the special characteristics of the hospital setting with its guidelines for interpersonal relationships that are quite different than the interaction the child is used to at home. They rarely have an understanding of the exact reasons that have led to their separation from home and many times do not equate illness with reason for hospitalization. In childhood, many events have a magical and symbolic "other than actually is" quality.

> A 6-year-old boy who was hospitalized for acute appendicitis felt that he was hospitalized because he was bad, as he had pushed his younger sister a few days earlier after she broke one of his favorite toys.

Development Stages

In trying to understand the range of responses that may occur, it is essential to be aware of the developmental stage of the child, his basic endowment with its specific motor, verbal, emotional, intellectual, and perceptual characteristics, the sociocultural background from which he has emerged and the emotional quality of his family, the type and length of illness, the characteristics of the hospital staff and unit in which the child is treated, and the type of treatment received. The above-mentioned studies and the resultant shift in understanding of developmental stages in the healthy child provide us with the basic frame of reference for understanding the reactions of the ill child.

A child of about 6–8 months perceives the mother already as the first permanent object and will protest separation with anger, followed by depression.

> A bright and alert 10-month-old boy needed hospitalization for a period of about two weeks for an acute abdominal illness. Because of illness of another child, his mother was prevented from seeing him. He initially screamed a lot, and later on appeared to be withdrawn. On follow-up, after the baby returned home, the mother reported that when he first came home, he reacted with a smile to the present family members. He refused to relate to her during the first 36 hours. When he finally did, he was tearful and clingy, a behavior pattern that continued in an exaggerated manner compared with his prehospital behavior, for a period of about two weeks.

> A 12-month-old boy underwent surgery following a diagnosis of unilateral Wilms Tumor. He reacted to his mother's leaving with angry screaming. He resisted any kind of physical examination with kicking and screaming while during the three-times-a-week visits with the play therapist he was receptive to physical and emotional contact.

Children under five years of age often interpret hospitalization and separation from the family, especially the mother, as abandonment and punishment and frequently may regress to an earlier developmental level of psychophysiological functioning. Thus an already verbal child may decide to stop speaking, or a toilet-trained child under the impact of unconscious anxiety may begin wetting or soiling himself. Initial protest of separation may be followed by withdrawal behavior with depressed affect. Child and parent may start a vicious cycle of misunderstanding with resultant disturbed interaction.

> A 4-year-old boy was hospitalized with a leg fracture. The nursing staff requested a child psychiatrist consultation following his unusually withdrawn and depressed behavior. Child and mother were observed in their interaction, showing a mother who attempted to get her son's attention and a 4-year-old boy with a sad facial expression, who shook his head and half-turned his back on her. She became angry after her repeated attempts to make contact led to the same response. Finally she threatened to go home and not to return. At that point the child psychiatrist intervened and spent some time exploring the mother's feelings about the situation. She felt anger at his negativistic response in the past days, which was quite different from his outgoing and friendly behavior at home. She was so

irritated that she did not feel like coming back. The psychiatrist explained to her her son's reaction in terms of his feeling himself abandoned and punished. Regular visits from his mother and the verbal assurance that she always would return were recommended. Following this intervention the mother appeared less tense. Follow-up showed improvement in the affective and social functioning of the child.

Though the younger school child, 6–8 years of age, has a good understanding of the reasons for separation, this age group, based on unconscious dynamic processes related to the resolution of the oedipal phase of development, generally presents with a heightened fear of and preoccupation with bodily mutilation. Pain-producing treatment procedures are often interpreted as punishment and may lead to increased anxiety and occasionally to regression.

> An 8-year-old boy from a large family, in which the mother generally managed the interaction by ordering or threatening her children, was placed in a pelvic cast after an open fracture of both legs following a collision of his bicycle with a car. The child psychiatrist was called as he exhibited nearly a panic level of anxiety postoperatively. He presented with an extremely anxious facial expression and pressured speech when seen. He experienced great guilt, as his mother had forbidden him to ride the bike downhill and as his friend, who had stood behind him during the ride, had received a bad head injury. He felt that the accident had occurred as punishment for disobeying his mother. He was very worried that his legs had disappeared and felt that his genitalia were damaged. Via a drawing the child psychiatrist explained the relationship between his pelvis, legs, genitalia, and the cast. Operative procedures were explained to him as were future therapeutic plans. After this his anxiety abated. He was closely followed up and improved rapidly, in spite of very few and inconsistent visits by his somewhat harsh mother.

Depending on the age of the child, an impairment in physical skill and capacity can have different implications. A toddler who just started to experience the world and the movement of his body in space with intensity and just began to integrate his body movements into balanced motor skill would be affected differently than an older child with already well-integrated movements.

Bergman and Freud (1965) described the reaction of a 5-year-old girl to restraint as that of protest and anger.

> A 10-year-old boy had an amputation of his entire right leg following the diagnosis of a malignancy of the femur. He was seen pre- and postoperatively by the child psychiatrist with a ten-day follow-up postoperatively. As the pediatric surgeon and his parents had discussed the reason for the operation, he was well aware of it and explained to the psychiatrist in his words, "If they don't take my leg away it is going to spread all over my body and it will kill me." He expressed fantasies of receiving a bionic leg like the Six Million Dollar Man, a television character with atomically

powered artificial limbs surgically created following an accident, which placed him among the supermen. He was somewhat depressed when it was explained to him that his new leg would not be of that quality. He was prepared for surgery by discussing anesthesia and postoperative procedures with him. He wondered if he would feel pain and if he would be able to run or swim again. He spontaneously expressed that he was afraid, but he did not try to show it. In spite of his anxiety he was autonomous and spontaneous in his activities on the ward preoperatively.

On the second day postoperatively he looked very depressed, was nonverbal, showed general motor retardation and expressed on questioning that he felt "very, very sad—I am sad because they took my leg away."

On the fourth day after surgery, he was found sitting up in bed, watching television and at the same time was coloring in a book. He was talkative and showed a lighter mood, complained about his wound itching and a feeling as if his leg was still there.

On the eighth postoperative day he was moving around in a wheelchair and talked about having tried his crutches in preparation for going home. His affect was normal with no nonverbal signs of depression. He commented on the visit of two friends during which he warned them that if they laughed at him having just one leg, he was going to beat them up.

The adolescent, who is in the midst of an intense process of finding his place among his peers and gaining their recognition, who is experimenting with autonomy and sexual competence, has difficulties in dealing with illness and related sequelae.

A nearly 14-year-old girl with a long-standing painful history of bilateral bone disease of the femur which increasingly had forced her to be on crutches and isolated her from the social activities of her peers underwent bilateral replacement of the hip joints without any complaints. She had been followed by the psychiatrist over several years and intermittently had expressed anger and tearful resentment at her handicap. She mobilized enormous emotional resources for this sequential operation and, in contrast to her past reactions to medical intervention, was hopeful and cheerful throughout. The operation succeeded without other complications and the adolescent completed hospitalization without difficulties. During the therapeutic sessions she fantasized about being able to go out with her girlfriends, to have dates like other girls and to go dancing.

Adolescents have a tendency, if they are handicapped in one area of their functioning, to compensate in others. The above-described girl, in spite of a chronic deteriorating disease pattern and frequent absences from school because of illness, was able to function as an A student throughout her grades.

To what degree illness has a long-term influence on the personality of the child will vary according to type and length of trauma imposed, developmental age of the child, and related integration of feeling of self- and body image.

Body Image and Feelings of Self

The evolution of the body image is seen (Fisher & Cleveland, 1968) as the resultant of (1) a learning process, "in which the individual experiences his body in manifold situations"; (2) the perceived reactions of others; and (3) self-exploration of the body. This leads to an internalized hierarchy of values assigned to the body's principal areas. This process we can see reflected in the boy who is worried about damaged genitalia or the girl who would like to have improved functioning of her legs.

> A beautiful 16-year-old adolescent girl who had to undergo dialysis reacted to loss of weight and change of skin tonus and quality with increased attention to her clothing. Her dresses were always impeccably neat and ironed and she focused much psychic energy on making herself look beautiful. Her anxiety increased as physical deterioration did not allow her to continue in these efforts.

A group of 27 boys and 32 girls, age 7–15 years with diabetes for at least 1 year, were studied. A most significant finding was that body image was disturbed in most of the children (Fällström, 1974).

The above-described case of the 10-year-old boy with amputation of the femur reflects postoperative disturbances of the body image, described generally as phantom pain. This phenomenon is ascribed to radical body mutilation and a persistence of the individual in viewing his body as intact, until gradual integration of the occurred mutilation into the body scheme brings about a shift of feeling (Fisher & Cleveland, 1968). The perception of the world around us emerges via complex processes of a psychological nature and with the help of our genetically and developmentally conditioned sensory organs. Studies into the nature of altered states of consciousness have only increased the puzzles that have to be answered to clarify the relationship between sensory organ, world, and perception of the world in the psychological arena of conscious and unconscious awareness. Handicapped children with a disturbance of the sensory organs may not experience normal development of this process and the resultant sensory distortions may lead to disturbance of the body image and a constricted or distorted perception of the world as compared to so-called normal perception. There has been an increase in the awareness of the professional therapist about the implications of such sensory deficiencies and active attempts have been made to enrich such handicapped children via increased utilization of other sensory organs, like training a blind child toward an increased use of the tactile or auditory sense of perception or a motorically handicapped one in the increased use of the visual and tactile sense. There has been an increasing recognition that chronic lack of stimulation in physically and mentally handicapped children may lead to general retardation in physical, intellectual, and psychic functioning of the child.

Physical deformities that differentiate a youngster from others, that may be visible to himself or others may, unless dealt with in a therapeutic manner at an early age, lead to disturbed emotional reactions in the child. Gross physical differences, as facial deformities, cleft palate, or absence or deformities of limbs which lead to unpredictable reactions of the world around him may be very traumatizing to the child. Children with ambiguous genitalia should be seen at the earliest age with their families for diagnosis, intervention, and clarification of the related identity and social issues. The congenital defect of hypospadia which requires surgical repair of the penis may lead to pre- and postoperative psychological trauma and will need special therapeutic intervention. The reaction can be especially severe in cases of unsuccessful repair. Chronic and debilitating illnesses with associated deformities will necessitate ongoing emotional support of the child and family. Deformed children more so than others will be in danger of withdrawal and social isolation to avoid the stigma of human curiosity and reaction.

Acute versus Chronic Illness

Generally, milder illness in the child is treated by the private pediatrician or the neighborhood health center with the child only incapacitated for a few days and generally staying at home with his mother and family. Beyond the physical discomfort of illness no changes should be expected.

Acute Hospitalization

When illness leads to hospitalization, in most cases the illness is acute, and the child is very ill, distressed, or in pain. The parents will be worried, show agitation or fearfulness. Sometimes arrival at the hospital can be climactic. The strangeness and unfamiliarity of an emergency room with its confusion adds distress. Exposure to unfamiliar medical diagnostic emergency procedures, like drawing of blood or application of an intravenous set, may overwhelm the child with fears. Though there has been an increasing theoretical awareness of children's emotional reactions to distress in the medical training programs, little of it has been applied at the point of acute medical intervention with its technical focus on immediate and pragmatic physical treatment. Many times emergency rooms are staffed by young personnel with no children of their own, and only the spontaneous and accidental empathy of the treating physician or nurse would safeguard a proper handling of the emotional needs of the child.

The child will have to adjust to a change in major habitual patterns. Special diets may not allow for the consumption of familiar foods. Unknown people with different human qualities interact with the youngster. Though children may respond with severity of emotional reaction to the cited stress, most will readjust quickly when returned to their natural habitat.

Chronic Hospitalization

The problems become somewhat more complex and may have more serious implications when we deal with chronic illness, or with perhaps intermittent acute crises like diabetes, cystic fibrosis, or sickle cell anemia, illnesses of a chronic nature with potentially serious implications. Some of these illnesses may only lead to intermittent acute hospitalizations, some may lead to chronic hospitalization. Because of the poor sense of time in the child, who measures time more in the urgency of need gratification than in the objective measurements by watch and calendar, long-term hospitalization may be particularly difficult to experience for children.

The uniformity of social patterns in the hospital, with a certain paucity of events and narrowness of human interaction, may limit the chronically hospitalized child's range of psychosocial responses and flexibility and may limit his capacity to cope appropriately outside of the known and predictable hospital world. This can lead to the syndrome of the hospital child.

> A 12-year-old boy since age 7 needed repeated surgical interventions and hospitalizations for sequelae to an acute trauma to the upper alimentary tract. An unhappy home situation with a conflicted and ambiguous mother was not able to satisfactorily compete with the attention given by a young, committed, and interested nursing staff. The boy had increased difficulties adjusting to the home situation and returned to the hospital both for relevant medical reasons and under various excuses. Attempts to intervene therapeutically on an outpatient basis failed because of nonattendance. Some improvement occurred during later adolescence apparently spontaneously, when the youngster began volunteer work in the hospital, allowing him to continue his contact with the gratifying hospital structure.

Parent and Child

In our child-oriented society, good parental care implies healthy children. Frequently when children get ill, parents feel that they have neglected their duty and become anxious and defensive. Worry about the child's welfare, unfamiliarity with the hospital, and a feeling of impotence often augment the parents' anxiety. Depending on the specific personality of the respective parent, this stressful situation may lead them to interact in an anxious or angry manner with the child or hospital staff. The present crisis may trigger memories of unrelated past events that may color the reaction of the parent inappropriately. The child's leaving the family, the preoccupation of the parent with the needs of the sick child, the disturbance of the normal daily living routines have implications for the other members of the family. The father's reaction may range from annoyance and anger to quiet withdrawal from involvement, siblings may misunderstand the parents' preoccupation and respond with jealousy and acting-out behavior to the mother's absence and unavailability. These responses in their turn may intensify the feelings of guilt and worry in the parent and start a vicious circle of stressful interpersonal relationships. Some parents flood a hospitalized child with gifts, hoping in some concrete sense to compensate the ill child for whatever suffering or deprivation he has to experience.

Unusual behavior of the parent sometimes increases the anxiety in the ill child. Some parents by giving many gifts may increase their financial worries and this may lead among other things to tension among the marital partners. Some parents may avoid a sick child, as in the above-described case of the 10-year-old boy with fracture of the legs, whose mother came rarely and irregularly. In many single-parent families the pressures that the sudden illness of a child can create may be quite difficult to tolerate for the mother and may necessitate professional support. In the course of many years of relating to parents with ill children, I have been amazed at the patience with which many single mothers tried to satisfy the needs of the ill child and the children at home. The impact that the illness of a child has on the family system will vary depending on whether the child is acutely ill or chronically ill. The length of stay in the hospital, as it lasts, will drain the emotional resources of the parent and family members.

> In an intact family with one chronically ill oldest adolescent boy, the worried focus was on his problems. As the parents did not encourage discussion of the existing medical illness, the three younger siblings responded with anger and resentment to the apparent special attention the older one was receiving. In the course of several years, the other siblings responded with various forms of disturbed behavior, ranging from poor school performance in an otherwise very bright youngster to stealing and drinking in the others.

Return of chronically ill children into the home situation can be associated with problems. Bergmann and Freud (1965) pointed out that some of the hospitalized children were clearly ambivalent about going home. Sometimes parents have difficulties in having a chronically ill or handicapped child return to the home setting. A study of adolescent cystic fibrosis patients (Rosenlund & Lustig, 1973) pointed out some of the difficulties the parents had to allow for age-appropriate autonomy and behavior in their children and how overindulgence and denial of reality intervened in the proper treatment process.

> Sometimes the overindulging behavior of parents can increase the anxiety level in the child. A 12-year-old girl complained that she felt it was very creepy at home since she returned, as in contrast to the other children in the family she was allowed to get away with everything, was not scolded like the others, and got more things than they did. She reported that the siblings reacted with anger and behaved in an obnoxious manner when the mother was absent. She stated that she did not like the situation at all but was hesitant to tell her mother as she did not want to hurt her feelings.

An interesting study done on the modifiability of maternal anxiety as it related to children's cooperative behavior in dental care showed a marked relationship between the anxiety of the mother and the child patient's behavior on the first dental visit in children aged 3–6 years (Wright, Alpern, & Leake, 1973).

Many parents with chronically ill children generally are not aware what they can or can't do unless so informed by professional staff. Even if such information is provided, in many cases the projected fears of the parents may not allow them properly to grasp what was said to them. In my experience with chronically and potentially fatally ill children and their parents, psychotherapists in close interaction with the medical staff have to go through a somewhat prolonged process of repetition of giving information on how much and what type of activity the child should have and the fears of the parent gradually have to be elicited and worked through therapeutically. Parents who are struggling with unconscious guilt feelings not related to the illness have particular difficulties in this area.

The professional medical staff are not aware of how little the usual parent knows about medical matters and do not bother to give detailed information to the parents to help them in better understanding the problems related to their children. In spite of this, especially parents of children with chronic diseases gradually become quite sophisticated in their medical knowledge and occasionally can present, after repeated hospitalizations of the child, an embarrassment to a young physician. It appears that the parent by gaining intellectual knowledge on the disease feels somewhat more in control over an otherwise not controllable situation.

As a general ground rule, as near to normal functioning of the child in the personal, interpersonal, and social areas should be attempted in a realistic evaluation of the child's possibilities and capacity to function. Again this evaluation may have to go through a process of interaction between parent and professional, as only time and a developing trusting relationship will elicit the proper information and allow for relevant adjustments.

Professional Staff

This brings us to the role the medical and other professional staff has to play in interaction with the child. Many times staff members that come into first contact with the child are young and do not have firsthand experience with children. In hospital wards the stay of young physicians is transitory and rarely can long-term relationships be established between the child and the physician. The nursing staff provides the primary continuity of contact to the children and their parents. Good pediatric services have already developed an awareness that frequent changing of nurses increases the anxiety level in children from the infant onward and where possible assign to each nurse a group of children for which she is responsible. This approach is to be welcomed though it is not yet generally applied.

As indicated earlier, though the professional-training programs include child development in the curricula of both the physician and nurse, many times the practical implications for the clinical situation are not taught. The professional staff many times experiences the parent as a disturbing and alien factor and the intense behavior of an anxious and worried parent sometimes will be misinterpreted as aggression. This occurs especially in situations where hospital staff and parents do not belong to the same sociocultural background and requests of the parent and associated nonverbal expression are misrated and misinterpreted. Generally the medical stance is to be somewhat impersonal and detached while functioning as a physician or nurse. If then an anxious parent from a culture in which love and concern for the child is expressed in weeping and agitation relates to a stoic physician, this behavior might trigger off anxiety and anger in the medical staff and lead to inappropriate, reactive responses.

Occasionally the cultural background of the parents makes them concerned about the type of food the child will eat in the hospital. A family with a Hindu background may want their child only to receive vegetarian foods, or an orthodox Jewish parent may request kosher food. Some Hispanic parents may want certain foods given to their children out of a belief that certain foods are good for some illness symptoms and not good for others. The medical intellectual approach may clash with the parents' wishes unless moderated by awareness of and respect for cultural differences.

Our increasing knowledge of the close bond existing between

children and their families has practical implications for the way we should deal with family members even if their presence in the hospital situation is experienced as an intrusion. Many modern hospitals, recognizing this reality, have already utilized the parent as an important teammate in improving the welfare of the child. So we will find frequent visiting hours on the pediatric wards, especially at mealtimes, and in some more advanced and affluent hospitals sleep-in possibilities for the parents of younger children (Lindheim, Glaser, & Coffin, 1972).

Psychophysiological Disorders

Psychosomatic illnesses like asthma, colitis ulcerosa, anorexia nervosa and many others with psychosomatic features in the disease process present special problems which in the course of more than a century have led to complex theoretical formulations.

Group, and especially family, therapy provides a particular frame of reference for experiencing and describing the psychic functioning of the individual human being and for targeting those influences that improve or diminish his functioning in health or illness. A recent very interesting sequence of studies focuses on the child's position in the family structure and the implications of the family dynamics for disease etiology and treatment process in psychosomatic illness (Minuchin, Rosman, & Baker, 1978). By using an open systems model, Minuchin explores the implications of such an approach for the treatment of anorexia nervosa, labile juvenile diabetes, and asthma. He and his coworkers find that there seem to exist three necessary related conditions for the development and maintenance of severe psychosomatic problems in children: (1) a certain type of family organization that encourages somatization; (2) involvement of the child in the parental conflict; and (3) physiological vulnerability. In his model the families show four outstanding characteristics: enmeshment, overprotectiveness, rigidity, and lack of conflict resolution. The sick child is considered to play a central role in family-conflict avoidance, and family conflict is thought to be one important feeder source for reinforcement of the symptoms.

THE DYING CHILD

In a culture where aging and death are deemphasized and much attention is given to youth and children, the unexpected death of a child creates serious emotional reactions in those around him.

Dying is considered the final phase in human life, and death-related reflections are generally postponed until a personal crisis or death in the family forces an adult to deal with death-related issues.

Imagery of Death

There has been ongoing interest in the way in which normal children are aware of the existence of death. Gregory Rochlin (1969) interviewed young children of the ages 3 to 5 in play-therapy sessions on what they thought about death. They related it to being punished for disobeying their parents, for instance leaving the house without boots. Death was perceived by them as cyclically interchanging with life—people would die, be in a grave, and then be alive again. There was an animistic quality of thinking in these youngsters as according to them dead people were able to hear what was said and went on eating and growing in the grave.

In my clinical encounters with normal healthy children, I have heard a 3½-year-old talk about having lived before. Similarly a 4-year-old once commented on the death of an older person: "Don't worry, his mommy and daddy will make a new body for him." Repeated interactions with youngsters in difficult situations provide many examples of the effort to cope with the idea of death.

A 5-year-old on a beach walk with his mother found the skeletal remains of a fish and involved her in a complex discussion about the difference between being alive and being dead. There was an attempt to intellectually grasp what actually happens when something dies. A 6-year-old and a 7½-year-old, in reaction to the fatal illness of a close family member, celebrated the death of two young moles that had been killed by the house cat with a solemn funeral including burial, plants on the grave, and accompanying music, without ever having been exposed to any such ceremony, except possibly on TV.

Sylvia Anthony (1940), in England, studied schoolchildren. According to her findings, children understood the biological essentials of death after age eight. Thoughts on death would intrude into the fantasies of schoolchildren and invaded their games at home and at school. Dying for them was often associated with lying helplessly on one's back or going to the hospital.

Maria Nagy (1948), in Budapest, Hungary, studied 378 schoolchildren of the ages 6 to 10 years as to their fantasies on death. They drew pictures and discussed them with her. According to her findings children under 5 did not perceive death as final, but as sleep or departure. After the age of 5 it seemed children were able to perceive death as final and universal; 6- and 7-year-olds were more aware of the personal immediacy of death and were able to imagine their own and others' deaths. The concept of a soul that lived on after death was expressed. As these studies were done in a cultural setting with dominant religions representing Christian faith, the answers probably were conditioned by that sociocultural background. Also, the described imagery of death as a person or skeleton may have been reflecting the frequent presentation of death in a personalized form in the churches and art of that culture. Thus, Nagy found that the older children frequently perceived death as a person with frightening features. To what degree cultural background influences death imagery of children is not well studied to date and could only be clarified by cross-cultural studies with a developmental focus.

Robert Kastenbaum (1959), in a study on time and death in adolescence, found that most adolescents place thoughts about death far into the future. In one study (Middleton, 1936), 90% of the adolescents said that thoughts about death in a personal way rarely were on their minds.

Although there has been considerable discussion of the degree to which children of various ages show an awareness that they may have to die or are dying, few concrete data have yet emerged. There has been a tendency when dealing with fatally ill children to interpret their responses according to what was believed regarding children developmentally. It is generally held that older children are aware of death and experience death-related anxiety. However, the scarcity of studies on what occurs in the case of young children dying is most significant.

It may be essential to reflect on how the death of a young child usually occurs in the hospital. Generally the parent is present, perhaps the nursing staff, and rarely or never the medical professional. If the medical professional is present, it is in order to deal with acute medical distress and treatment. Since a child is in such close interaction with his or her family, the emotions of parents who know that their child is dying will influence the behavior of a child. In the course of working for more than seven years with the children of the pediatric oncology clinic in a major-hospital setting, I have observed very varied reactions of parents and children.

In the professional literature very few cases of young children expressing an awareness of their own death or dying have been reported.

Green (1967) reported the case of one 4-year-old boy with metastasized neuroblastoma who, 24 hours before his death, expressed awareness of his impending death.

Raimbault and Roger (1967), who worked with very young children with fatal diseases and were interested in their ideas about their illness, were surprised at the frequency with which the young children spontaneously approached the death theme.

Gesell (1940) finds very little or no understanding of death up to the age of 4.

Hinton (1968) stated that "on the whole children are not unduly evasive of the thought of death and they are usually quite prepared to speak of it."

Natterson and Knudson (1960) felt that the doctors detected signs of anxiety of dying in young children, but that it was largely overshadowed by the fear of separation and painful procedures.

That children with fatal diseases have a very clear-cut awareness of their own impending death is very poignantly shown in Vernich's unpublished "conversations" with leukemic children (Vernich, 1973).

From my own experience, my impression is that the rarity of these data reflects more the absence of the professional from the deathbed than the lack of awareness in young children of their impending demise.

E. was an only child, who was nearing her sixth birthday. I knew her for more than three years. She was in the final relapse of her illness and was dying of leukemia. Following a regular pattern, once a day I would visit her on the ward, generally in the mornings or evenings. One day at noontime her mother called and requested that I come over to the ward. She stated that E. had requested my coming immediately. I went and saw her in bed in no apparent distress or pain but looking exhausted. We had a few short exchanges: "How do you feel?"—"Not good."—"You'll get better"; and her response was "No, I won't." As she said nothing else, I conversed at the bedside with her mother. She informed me that E. also had requested that the father should leave work and visit her now. The father visited. Around five o'clock that evening she went into coma following a brain bleeding. She never regained consciousness and died six days later.

D. was an extremely beautiful 14-year-old girl with leukemia who over several years had weekly clinic contacts. She had consistently resisted becoming involved with the child psychiatrist. During the last four weeks of her life she actively searched out the therapist and spontaneously began to express her worries about her mother, who was upset, as her grandmother was seriously ill with diabetes in the hospital. D. relapsed two weeks later and needed hospitalization She deteriorated rapidly. On the day before she died, her mother and I rode the elevator together to visit her. The mother began asking questions about another child in the clinic who was in good shape, at home, and attending school. The mother wondered why D. told her that this girl was very ill and dying. When coming to the room, it was obvious that D. had some bleeding in the brain with associated neurological signs. She was still verbal and able to recognize and to relate to her surroundings. The mother was extremely upset and proclaimed her own inability to cope with the situation rather loudly. D. died that evening surrounded by her family. The mother was seen after the funeral and told me that D. had told her before losing consciousness that she was going to die and had to leave her. The mother said that this communication from her daughter enabled her to stay with her daughter until she had died, though initially she thought she could never tolerate such a reality.

It is extremely difficult for parents to realize that their child is going to die, to be supportive to the youngster while they themselves go through an extremely painful process of separation. Parents' capacity to cope with the situation notwithstanding consistent psychotherapeutic support varies greatly. Some parents hover over the dying child and are barely able to take off time for sleep and eating.

H. was a 10-year-old girl with leukemia, who had difficulties separating from her mother when hospitalized. Her mother would be on the ward day and night, in spite of having several younger children at home and being pregnant again. The relationship had a symbiotic quality and both mother and child were mutually reinforcing it. The mother believed in spirits and began to increase the anxiety level in the child. Therapist and nursing staff had major difficulties in influencing the mother to normalize her attendance on the ward so that she would get some rest. The mother finally had a major portion of the ward staff supportively revolving around her physical needs. She refused contact with the therapist in a passive–hostile manner in spite of repeated attempts to involve her in a therapeutic relationship. H. died in an acute bleeding crisis. The mother was upset to the point that the medical staff had to sedate her. Follow-up on the case via relatives gave the incidental information that at the funeral the mother jumped into the grave and wanted to be buried with her daughter.

Other parents have disappeared from the ward a few days before their child died and left the dying child in the care of the nursing staff.

G. was a 9-year-old girl from a very deprived family, who, following a brain tumor and increasing paralyzation, had to be hospitalized for medical care. Two younger children and a very demanding maternal grandmother shared the household. As G. deteriorated, to finally become nonverbal, the mother's infrequent visits became fewer, until two months before her death she was left only with the nursing staff and the therapist to care for her.

Generally, though, I have found parents from varied economic and sociocultural backgrounds supportive and available to the children and focused on diminishing their emotional and physical discomfort.

S. was one of two children and the only girl in the family. After months of treatment for leukemia and accelerating relapses, she finally had to be hospitalized in another hospital to attempt to save her life with a new medication. Her mother was consistently supportive to her and the sibling. She kept in close contact with the therapist. At the time when it became obvious that S.'s life could not be saved, she called the therapist daily. As the mother had never seen anybody die, she requested the therapist to tell her what happens when somebody dies. The physiological sequence of death as observed was described to her as well as the terminal states of consciousness. Supported by the priest of her religion, she stayed with her child until the end, later reflecting that if she had not had some prior information on what happens when people die, she would not have been able to tolerate staying with her child throughout.

A. was the youngest of three children who, following an operation for hepatoblastoma at age eight months, at age four was rehospitalized with advanced metastasis to the lungs. As the professionals communicated to the parents that no further medical intervention could be done, the parents decided to take her home so she could die there. It seems that in spite of respiratory distress and pain she appeared to be more comfortable in the home setting. A. died in peace at home a few days after leaving the hospital.

This child was one of two young children whom the parents requested to take home so that they would be more at ease. In both cases the decision was made by black families.

Children that attend a tumor clinic regularly are aware of one another's state of health or the absence of another child because of illness or death. A 6-year-old girl who went home after a hospital stay stated spontaneously that one of her friends was very sick. The girl she was referring to was in the last phase of a malignant disease and at this time was bedridden, emaciated, and nearly helpless. When asked how sick this child was, she stated, "She is so sick she might die."

A 12-year-old boy who generally did not talk about the children who had left the clinic during the time that he attended, in the context of a filming session, which was made for the purpose of letting medical students know what a boy with a serious disease does experience and has to go through, spontaneously began to remember all the children who had never come back to the clinic because they had died. He said that occasionally he and some other children in the clinic used to talk about their death but he also volunteered: "I do not like to do this because it makes me feel creepy and sad." He related that to being worried about his own future. An older friend of his from the clinic had only died recently after many years of illness and he described how upset he was when he had heard his friend had died. He described how his mother told him about it. He talked about the reactions of the neighborhood boys on the death of his friend: "They behaved funny. They could not believe it. They all stayed home and did not talk to one another. Nobody felt like talking."

Adolescents generally have an awareness of the seriousness of their illness. This does not mean that they will communicate this knowledge to their parents. Depending on the openness in communication that the parents have established, they may or may not find out the preoccupations of their adolescent child.

Death during adolescence is an especially painful process for children and parents. The adolescent is a person who is going through a rapid shift in physical status, feelings, feeling of self, and values and finds himself in a process of exploring life toward a formulation of meaningful life goals. Developmentally, thoughts on death are far away. The adolescent would like to be accepted by his peers and the emaciation and loss of muscles that go with chronic malignant disease are very poorly accepted by him.

> T. was a 16-year-old boy with many years of a malignant lymph node disease. Being the oldest of several boys, he had a hard time accepting that as a result of medication and radiation treatment he was physically thinner and less muscular than his younger siblings. He sometimes was mistaken for being the younger brother of his sibling which made him quite angry. T. was extremely well informed about his disease and had accumulated in the course of the years a rich and sophisticated knowledge about it. At times in discussions with young residents he could provide an embarrassment for them. He was beset by many fears and worries which he had difficulty expressing, especially as his parents seemed to discourage any discussion of his medical problems and gradual deterioration.

The dying teenager highlights special problems that dying children present for the medical staff. Medical professional ethics emphasize the saving and prolongation of life, and dying and death unconsciously are experienced as a mistake or failure on the physician's part. In many cases the medical team most likely in charge of the medical care of the dying child or adolescent consists of interns and residents, young nurses and social workers. These health-team members frequently identify with the adolescent who is relatively close to their age. This may lead to emotional overreaction of the staff. As many teenagers like to reason and to provoke, with the skills of an adult, they frequently threaten the role identification and the sense of security of the medical personnel. Not infrequently when we had a very upset medical staff on the ward, it was in reaction to the severe illness or death of an adolescent boy or girl. It is clear, then, that the impending death of an adolescent or young child is an unusually difficult process for the medical staff as well as the patient and family.

Because of the emotional difficulties involved in helping a dying child and his family members, because of the demands made on the insight and emotional stamina of medical personnel, learning how to handle human crisis around death should be built into an early stage of clinical training. For the benefit of the physician's patients and in the long run for the benefit of his own psychological health such training is crucial, so that the physician does not have to turn away when death takes the control out of his hands.

REFERENCES

Anthony, S. *The child's discovery of death.* London: Kegan-Paul, French & Truber, 1940

Bergmann, T., & Freud, A. *Children in the hospital.* New York: International Universities Press, 1965

Fällström, K. *On personality structure in diabetic schoolchildren aged 7–15 years. Acta Paediatrica Scandinavica,* 1974, Supplement 25.

Fisher, S., & Cleveland, S. E. *Body image and personality.* New York: Dover, 1968.

Gesell A. *The first five years.* New York: Harper, 1940.

Green, M. Care of the dying child and psychosocial aspects in the care of children with cancer. *Pediatrics,* 1967, *140* (suppl.), 496.

Hinton, J. *Dying.* Aylesbury, England: Hunt, Barnard & Co., 1968, p. 22.

Kastenbaum, R. Time and death in adolescence. In H. Feifel (Ed.), *The Meaning of Death.* New York: McGraw-Hill, 1959.

Lindheim, R., Glaser, H. H., & Coffin, C. *Changing hospital environments for children.* Cambridge, Mass.: Harvard University Press, 1972.

Middleton, W.C. Some reactions towards death among college students. *Journal of Abnormal and Social Psychology,* 1936, *31,* 2.

Minuchin, S., Rosman, B., & Baker, L. *Psychosomatic families: Anorexia nervosa in context.* Cambridge, Mass.: Harvard University Press, 1978.

Nagy, M. H. The child's theories concerning death. *Journal of Genetic Psychology,* 1948, *73,* 3.

Natterson, J. M., & Knudson, A.G. Observations concerning fear of death in fatally ill children and their mothers. *Psychosomatic Medicine,* 1960, *22,* 456.

Raimbault, G., & Roger, P. L'enfant et son image de la maladie. *Archive Française Pediatricque,* 1967, *24,* 445–462.

Rochlin, G. How younger children view death and themselves. In E. A. Grollman (Ed.), *Explaining death to children.* Boston: Beacon Press, 1969.

Rosenlund, M., & Lustig, H. S. Young adults with cystic fibrosis: Problems of a new generation. *Annals of Internal Medicine,* 1973, *78,* 959–961.

Vernich, J. Unpublished 'conversations' in the editorial comment by James Anthony. In E. J. Anthony and C. Koupernik (Eds.), *The child in his family: The impact of disease and death.* New York: Wiley, 1973, pp. 103–104.

Wright, G. Z., Alpern, G. D., & Leake, J. L. Modifiability of maternal anxiety as it relates to children's cooperative dental behavior. *Journal of Dentistry for Children,* 1973, *40,* 265–271.

9

Peer Behavior and Mother–Infant Interaction in Maltreated Children

MICHAEL LEWIS AND STEPHANIE SCHAEFFER

Our interest in maltreated infants stems from two concerns: one theoretical, the other practical. From a theoretical point of view we are interested in the interdependence of early social experiences, more specifically, the effect of the mother–child relationship on other social relationships. From a practical point of view, we are interested in how one might intervene in the lives of maltreated children so as to ameliorate the potentially harmful effects of a poor parent–child relationship.

In this paper, we will first present various theoretical positions now available which touch upon the issue of social development and, in particular, the development of social relations. Our concerns center around the role of the mother–infant relationship on subsequent social relationships, more precisely, on peer relationships. Having presented these various positions, we shall move to a general review of the literature on maltreated children presenting first the various theoretical approaches offered to explain maltreatment and then a review of the characteristics of maltreated children. Having reviewed this literature, our own study of maltreated children–parent interactions and peer behavior will be presented. The data available from this study will be

MICHAEL LEWIS AND STEPHANIE SCHAEFFER • Institute for the study of Exceptional Children, Educational Testing Service, Rosedale Road, Princeton, New Jersey 08541. We wish to thank the staff of the Millhill Family and Child Care Center of Trenton, New Jersey for their cooperation, and in particular Ms. Andree Newsome, Director.

used to return to our original concerns: the implications for a theory of social development and intervention.

Two Views of Social Relations

Two views of the development of social relationships have been articulated: an epigenetic and a social-network model. The most prevalent model is the epigenetic one which has as its central thesis the assumption that there is a direct relationship from one set of social experiences to the next. More specifically, the epigenetic model argues for a linear relationship suggesting that the infant first adapts to one relationship and from this primary relationship subsequent ones follow. The attachment theories of Bowlby (1969) and Ainsworth (1969) all have this epigenetic model as one of their basic propositions. Simply stated, this model holds that subsequent social relations are dependent upon the attachment relationship between mother and infant. In particular, peer relationships should be affected by the mother–child attachment. While there are several studies which suggest a relationship between mother–child and peer relationships (Matas, Ahrend, & Sroufe, 1978; Waters, Wippman, & Sroufe, in press), the reasons for this are confounded and may have to do with issues unrelated to the epigenetic model. For example, the finding that secure attachment and peer relations are related leaves open the possibility that either or both of these early social experiences lead to the later results. Unless we can separate out the effects both of early peer contact and secure maternal attachment, we cannot logically conclude which is at work; as Hartup (in press) and Lewis (1979) have suggested, there may be a relationship between mothers who provide secure attachment and mothers who provide early peer experiences.

Alternative models of social development are possible and have been proposed. In these, functional relationships between different systems remain relatively independent and while being capable of mutual affect, do not have a linear feature as their key assumption. In particular, Harlow (Harlow & Harlow, 1965) and more recently Hartup (in press) and Lewis (Lewis, 1979; Lewis & Feiring, 1978, 1979; Lewis, Young, Brooks, & Michalson, 1975) have made this point. Lewis (Edwards & Lewis, 1979; Lewis, 1979) has argued for a social-network model in which multiple social objects occupy simultaneous rather than sequential importance since they satisfy multiple and differential social needs. The articulation of the matrix formed by social objects and needs is an important task in the study of social development (Edwards & Lewis, 1979; Lewis & Feiring, 1979) and suggests the child's social relationships center around the child's needs and the culturally determined method of meeting these needs. For example, some cultures promote the use of multipe caregiving in the form of both mother and older female sibling or friend (Whiting & Whiting, 1975), others support day-care settings with multiple adults, while others support the more traditional mother–infant relationship. The particular goals and values of a culture will determine the nature of the social network—the number and nature of the people and the tasks they perform. In a culture where only the mother interacts with the infant for the first 2 or 3 years, it must be the mother who is assigned both a caregiving and playmate function. This culture will differ from those in which the mother is the caregiver but peer experience is available, and will differ still more from one in which the older female sibling takes care of the child.

In this culture, the articulation of the relationship between function and people in 3-year-old children clearly indicates a separation of function and person, with adults assigned the role of caretaking, older peers that of teaching, and similar-age peers that of play (Edwards & Lewis, 1979). Thus, the social-network model argues that children have multiple needs which are satisfied by both mother and peers. Moreover, while one system will affect another, the development of social relationships is not sequential. Thus, while the mother–infant attachment may affect the child's peer relationship, these peer relationships are not determined by the attachment relationship. Two ways in which the maternal–infant attachment relationship may affect peer relationships, although not determine them in the epigenetic sense, are (1) peer availability, and (2) generalized fear. Mothers who are inadequate in terms of "mothering" and who are unable to facilitate an attachment relationship may at the same time prevent the infant from having peer experience. Given that it is the mother who in our culture must facilitate early peer contact, her failure to do so will result in the absence of contact and the development of inadequate peer-interaction skills. In this case, poor attachment and poor peer relationships are related although the failure of the attachment relationship to the mother is not the cause of the poor peer relationships; the cause is lack of experience with peers. Poor "mothering" resulting in a poor attachment relationship also may produce general fearfulness which has the effect of inhibiting contact with peers. It is this lack of contact, caused by fear, which affects peer relationships. This may explain why younger rather than same-age or older peer therapists are better able to help depressed children; the younger peer may be less fearful for the "patient" since its skills are less advanced. Notice, in both cases, it is not the poor interpersonal relationship with the mother that leads to poor subsequent relationships, but rather a more indirect effect. These are then alternatives to the epigenetic view which have not been eliminated and which prevent us from determining causal relations.

The epigenetic and social-network views can be tested around the relationship between mother–infant attachment and peer relationships. The epigenetic model would hold that poor attachments should lead to poor peer relationships while the social-network model would allow for the independence of these two relationships *provided* that the mutual interactions as discussed above could be controlled. The work with nonhuman primates provides some support for this social-network model. Harlow (1969) looked at infants raised by mothers with no peers and another group raised with peers but without mothers. Although there are some difficulties with this study, the general findings that peer behavior was facilitated by early peer raising and *not* maternal raising suggest an independence of peer and maternal relations. Additional support for this view has been supplied by Suomi and Harlow (1972) and Novak and Harlow (1975) who found that one could use peers to overcome depression caused by the absence of the infant's mother. However, the work of Furman, Rake, and Hartup (in press) is more relevant. These investigators located socially-withdrawn preschool children and assigned them to two peer-therapy and one control condition. The therapy conditions worked and these children's peer behavior appeared normal. Since the mother–child attachment system was not manipulated, and since we can assume that the attachment in these isolates was inadequate, these results would appear to support the peer system as independent from maternal attachment since the peer system can be altered without altering the attachment relationship. These results, taken together, indicate that there is no reason to suppose that maternal attachment *per se* will lead to successful peer relationships *without* peer experience although early peer experience can overcome poor parental interaction (as in the case of the isolates) in its effect on subsequent peer behavior.

A more direct approach (one which would not make any assumption about mother–child attachment) would be to locate a group of children who had inadequate attachment and at the same time had adequate peer experience. If we could demonstrate that inadequate maternal–infant relationship did not affect peer relationships when peer relationships were available, we would have more support for the social-network rather than the epigenetic model. Moreover, the demonstration that concurrent peer experience in the presence of poor mother–infant relationship can protect the child against poor subsequent peer relationships would provide support for an intervention program. The use of a sample of maltreated infants who attend a day-care program provides the conditions to consider these issues. However, before turning to our study, a review of what is known about maltreated children is necessary.

A Review of Maltreated Children

Theoretical Approaches

The bulk of research on child maltreatment has its theoretical underpinnings in one of three basic orientations: psychodynamic, sociological, or social learning. While all three approaches view child abuse and neglect as multiply determined, they differ substantially in causative emphasis and analysis. These orientations focus on parental factors. Having presented them, we will turn our attention to the child factors which are associated with maltreatment.

Psychodynamic Model. Psychodynamic approaches locate the primary cause of child maltreatment in the personality disorders of abusive parents. Investigators have utilized a variety of clinical and standardized testing procedures to delineate these personality characteristics specifically implicated in abuse. The resulting lists of traits and typologies have tended to be general, inconclusive, and nondifferentiating. Abusing adults have been variously characterized as immature, impulsive, self-centered, hypersensitive, quick to react with poorly controlled aggression (Kempe, 1973); aimless, psychopathic, antisocial, hostile, passive, dependent, depressed (Young, 1964); subject to episodic outbursts of loss of control, reason, and judgment (Kaufman, 1962, as cited in Gil, 1970); low in self-esteem, the ability to empathize, and the need to give nurturance (Melnick & Hurley, 1969); having intense feelings of self-hatred and worthlessness (Galston, 1966, as cited in Gil, 1970); and exhibiting a low threshold for frustration (Elmer, 1977).

However, recent evidence has indicated that fewer than 10% of child abusers can be diagnosed as mentally ill (Kempe, 1973), and further, that the degree and range of personality disturbance found in abusing parents exist in nonabusing parents as well (Gil, 1970; Walters, 1975). The systematic search for personality attributes unique to child abusers has yielded, in fact, only one clear-cut conclusion, that "a general defect in character—from whatever source—is present in the abusing parent allowing aggressive impulses to be expressed too freely" (Spinetta & Rigler, 1972, pp. 300–301). Parke and Collmer (1975) question the tautological nature of these psychiatric explanations and "the usefulness of re-describing the abusive parent as being low in aggression control"; they go on to state that "relabeling is not a substitute for adequate explanation" (p. 520). Other criticisms of these studies refer to methodological considerations and include the lack of representative samples, the failure to use comparison groups for empirical validation, and the reliance on *ex post facto* analyses (Spinetta & Rigler, 1972).

The psychodynamic approach has been successful in identifying factors in parental histories and child-rearing beliefs that are associated with child maltreatment. There is overwhelming evidence that abusing parents were themselves subjected to abuse and neglect as children; in their comprehensive review of the literature, Spinetta and Rigler (1972) cite 22 studies confirming this finding. Parental histories show that physical maltreatment was frequently combined with emotional abuse running the gamut from severe deprivation or loss of mothering to excessive criticism and denigration (see, for example, McHenry, Girdany, & Elmer, 1963; Steele & Pollock, 1968; Young, 1964). Disagreement exists regarding the psychodynamic mechanisms responsible for the translation of these childhood experiences into child-abusing behaviors in adulthood. In general, however, explanations for abuse rely upon complex interrelationships among intrapsychic conflicts, defensive structure, and superego functioning which, under stress, are "acted out" in aggression (see, for example, Galdston, 1965; Green, Gaines, & Sangrund, 1974). The result is what Kempe has termed "a cycle of abuse," where an aggressive pattern of parenting is repeated from one generation to the next.

Aggressive parenting behaviors are frequently supported by child-rearing attitudes. Many abusive parents consider physical punishment an appropriate and necessary disciplinary technique (Kempe & Kempe, 1978; Wasserman, 1967). In addition, many have inadequate knowledge of the behaviors and needs that are age-appropriate for their children (Galdston, 1965; Johnson & Morse, 1968) and hold unrealistic expectations for their performance (Steele & Pollock, 1968). Often coupled with misconceptions regarding development is a gross insensitivity to individually-expressed needs and desires of their offspring (Jacobs & Kent, 1977; Steele & Pollock, 1968). Several investigators have described a role reversal in abusing and neglecting relations in which the child is treated as an adult and expected to satisfy parental needs for nurturance and "good mothering" (see, for example, Blumberg, 1974; Galdston, 1965; Green et al., 1974; Steele & Pollock, 1968). Moreover, there may exist a general attitude of resentment and rejection toward the child's whole person, or feelings that the child is unlovable or bad (Kempe & Kempe, 1978; McHenry et al., 1963; Young, 1964). In some abusing families, one child is selected to be the main or exclusive victim of maltreatment; in most two-parent families, one parent is the active abuser or most obvious neglecter, while the other serves to condone the maltreatment by his or her passivity (Brown & Daniels, 1968; Kempe, Silverman, Steele, Droegemueller, & Silver, 1962).

Sociological Model. The sociological approach defines child maltreatment as a social problem caused by a combination of cultural and socioeconomic factors. The use of force against children in America is seen as a widespread, socially sanctioned child-rearing practice embedded in a culture with a tradition of interpersonal violence (for fuller expositions see Bakan, 1971; Chase, 1975; Gil, 1970; Walters, 1975). As a consequence, child maltreatment exists on two levels in society: the institutional and the familial (Garbarino, 1977; Gil, 1970). The effects of institutional maltreatment have received much speculation but little direct exploration; it may well be that "society, as a whole, by permitting millions of children to grow up under conditions of severe deprivation" is the major abuser today (Gil, 1970, p. vii). On the familial level, studies clearly show that physical punishment is used by parents of all occupations against children of all ages in families at each social-class level (for a review of this research, see Parke & Collmer, 1975). According to the sociological view, what distinguishes the child abuser from the nonabuser is the excessive and inappropriate use of this culturally-acceptable disciplinary technique due, in large part, to environmental stresses that increase the strains and frustrations of daily living and weaken mechanisms of self-control (Gil, 1970). That these stress factors operate with greatest impact and rapidity on the lower socioeconomic classes is a long-held supposition, recently receiving substantial support from demographic studies of child abuse and neglect.

Gil (1970) concluded from a nationwide survey of nearly 13,000 reported abuse cases that child abuse was more likely to occur among low-income and minority groups. More recent studies have continued to document the link between poverty and abuse (e.g., Elmer, 1977; Garbarino & Crouter, 1978; National Academy of Sciences, 1976), calling into question the commonly advanced argument that biased reporting of cases accounts for this relationship. Other socioeconomic variables implicated in child maltreatment include under- or unemployment (Galdston, 1965; Gil, 1970), low levels of education (Gil, 1970), and poor housing conditions (Light, 1973).

Demographic descriptions of abusing and neglecting adults suggest that mothers and younger parents are more likely to be the perpetrators of maltreatment (Gelles, 1975; Jacobs & Kent, 1977). In addition, some investigators report that abusive parents tend to show some deviation in social, behavioral, physical, or intellectual functioning prior to the abusive incident (Gil, 1970; Kempe & Kempe, 1978).

Specific aspects of family structure and organization seem to be particularly stressful and play a role in child maltreatment. Family size, as well as the spacing of children within the family, are associated with both abuse and neglect. Abusive families are more likely to be larger (Elmer, 1977; Young, 1964). Gil (1970) found that the proportion of families with four or more children was twice as high for his abusive sample as for the population in general, and conversely that the proportion of small families (one or two children) was much larger in the general population than in his sample. Moreover, families wth children born in very close succession (Kempe *et al.*, 1962) and families headed by females (Gil, 1970; Giovannoni & Billingsley, 1974) are more likely to be involved in maltreatment.

Internal characteristics of family functioning have been implicated in child maltreatment. Recurrent parental separation and reconciliations (Elmer, 1977; Young, 1964) and frequent disagreements over child-rearing and other issues (Jacobs & Kent, 1977) are common occurrences in abusing and neglecting homes. Moreover, decision-making power tends either to be concentrated in the hands of only one parent (Geles, Straus, & Steinmetz, 1979) or to be avoided by both (Young, 1964). These families are often disorganized with respect to household routines (Elmer, 1977) and suffer from chronic transience (Gil, 1970; Jacobs & Kent, 1977). In essence, they lead what Garbarino (1977) refer to as "lives out of control," created by a basic "asynchrony" or mismatch between reality demands and consequent coping strategies.

The relationship of the family unit to support systems in the environment (i.e., those systems that in some way support the parenting function) has recently received attention from an ecological perspective as an important determinant of child maltreatment. Support systems fulfill a number of social functions which relate directly to child abuse: (1) they provide feedback to parents about themselves and their children and monitor levels of disturbance in parent–child relationships; (2) they supply whatever additional services and resources are necessary for the effective management of family life; and (3) they provide for the satisfaction and control of emotional needs and impulses in acceptable channels (Garbarino, 1977). Support systems operate through the establishment of large social networks which connect the smaller-network family to its environment.

Drawing on the well-established finding that abusing and neglecting families tend to be socially isolated, without community, church, club, group, friendship, or extended family ties (Elmer, 1967; Green *et al.*, 1974; Young, 1964), several investigators have suggested that child maltreatment is a direct function of an inavailability, inadequacy, and underutilization of support systems which could ameliorate the effects of disruptive socioeconomic forces on the family (Bronfenbrenner, 1974). Research by Garbarino and his associates (Garbarino, 1976; Garbarino & Crouter, 1978) has provided evidence for this hypothesis; the addition of factors reflecting the presence of support systems in the environment (for example, enrollment in day care, stability of neighborhood) accounted for much more of the variance in rates of child maltreatment than economic indices alone. A study by Giovannoni and Billingsley (1974) on the extended family relationships of neglecting and adequate low-income mothers also bears on the issue of support systems in operation. They found that neglecting mothers had few, if any, contacts with relatives during the previous year, while adequate mothers had seen all their relatives during the same time span. The authors concluded that "relationships with extended kin were highly salient features of the lives of the women in this study, and when absent or impaired, a matter that impinged upon maternal adequacy" (p. 74). Further confirmation of the association between abuse and lack of support is provided by Green *et al.* (1974). Their sample of 60 abusive mothers complained of alienation from spouses and extended family members, and a corresponding acute lack of help with child rearing.

Social-Learning Model. From a social-learning approach, child maltreatment is conceptualized as a learned pattern of parent–child interaction defined as abusive or neglectful by the social context. Two features are stressed in this analysis: (1) because child maltreatment is viewed as learned behavior, it is explained by, and subject to, the same laws of learning that apply to other social behaviors; and (2) because child maltreatment is seen as a pattern of interaction, the roles of both parent *and* child in creating and maintaining conditions of abuse are stressed.

The well-supported finding that abusing and neglecting parents were themselves maltreated as childrn suggests that these parents are using the same techniques that their own parents used to control and care for them. A social-learning analysis indicates a number of factors that makes this outcome likely. Exposure to aggressive or neglecting models of parenting in childhood is a powerful source for learning, through observation, patterns of abusive caretaking that may be utilized in adulthood. Extensive research on imitative learning in children has demonstrated that "mere observation of aggressive models, regardless of the quality of the model–child relationship, is a sufficient condition for producing imitative aggression in children" (Bandura & Huston, 1961, p. 317). Exposure to abusing models also serves an informative function by legitimizing and sanctioning the use of violence against children (for a review of aggressive modelng, see Stein & Freidrich, 1975). It is likely that in the absence of alternative child-rearing models, adults from abusive homes will repeat the only parenting model they know.

Apart from serving as role models for aggressive behavior, punitive and neglectful parents provide highly frustrating, often painful, experiences for their children. Observational and experimental research on aggression indicates that frustration and physical attack are potent elicitors of aggressive reactions in children (see Feshbach, 1970). Studies on parental punishment have consistently found positive relationship between physical punishment and aggressive behavior in children (Feshbach, 1973). Moreover, aggression apears to have a negative effect on the production of empathic responses in children (Feshbach & Feshbach, 1969), which may in turn encourage increased aggressiveness. Longitudinal data point to the stability of aggressive behaviors over time, at least for males (e.g., Kagan & Moss, 1962), suggesting that aggressive children become aggressive adults.

Once established in the adult's behavioral repertoire, aggressive responses must compete with nonabusive responses designed to control children's behavior. But the use of force often gains ascendancy in the response hierarchy because it is reinforced by the cessation, if only temporarily, of the child's aversive behavior. As Parke and Collmer note, "a number of studies (e.g., Davitz, 1952) have shown that, under conditions of stress and frustration, predominant responses are likely to be emitted; in short, the typical use of physically punitive responses in disciplinary contexts makes it more likely that these same types of response will be employed in anger-eliciting situations" (1975, p. 537).

Both sides of the parent–child equation have been implicated in the escalation of aggressive behavior to abusive levels. Experimental studies of punishment indicate that inconsistent administration of punishment tends to be ineffective in controlling children's present behaviors, and more importantly, may engender more resistance to behavioral extinction or inhibition in the future (Deur & Parke, 1970; Parke & Deur, 1972). Clinical studies of abusive families have noted the marked degree of inconsistency in parental dsciplining (Elmer, 1977) and its "lack of corrective purpose" (Young, 1964, p. 181). Either alone, or paired with intermittent reinforcement, inconsistent punishment may serve to maintain or increase the child's aversive behaviors, and consequently, to intensify parental punitiveness. Patterson and Cobb (1971) describe a coercion process wherein the behavior of each member of a dyad is an aversive stimulus to the other, eliciting aversive responses designed to terminate the aversive stimulus, and ultimately creating a spiraling pattern of increasingly aversive inter-action. For example, a whining child may instigate parental yelling, which in turn elicits tantrum behavior from the child, which conse-quently provokes parental hitting.

A study by Parke, Sawin, & Kneling (1974), as cited in Parke & Collmer, 1975) indicates the importance of the child's reactions to discipline in determining his subsequent punishment. Adults were instructed to discipline, via a closed-circuit videotape, a misbehaving child who then reacted in one of four ways: by ignoring the adult, making reparations, pleading with the adult, or defying the adult. Children who behaved defiantly received the harshest punishment following subsequent misbehavior, and children who behaved repar-atively received the least.

Characteristics of the Maltreated Child

Age. The most severe cases of child abuse and neglect are seen in children under 3 years of age (Blumberg, 1974; Elmer, 1977, Gald-ston, 1965; Green, 1978; Kempe et al., 1962; Walters, 1975). Although maltreatment has been documented through adolescence (Gelles, Straus, & Steinmetz, 1979; Gil, 1970), one-half to two-thirds of reported cases involve children under 6 years of age (Gil, 1970; Johnson & Morse, 1968). Many factors have been linked to this finding. Evidence of maltreatment in younger children may be more obvious or medically serious due to the higher levels of physical and developmental vulner-ability in early life. In addition the preverbal child is unable to provide information to others about his life experiences or to significantly alter, through his own initiatives, the amount of contact he has with maltreating adults. Finally, maltreating parents are particularly associ-ated with daily living with younger children, whose "normal" behav-iors can include sustained crying, feeding disruptions, demands for attention, toilet-training accidents, temper tantrums, irritability, and unreasoned disobedience (Blumberg, 1974; Kemp & Kempe, 1978; Weston, 1974). Exacerbated by socioeconomic, marital, or personal stresses, the frustrations inherent in raising young children may be potent elicitors of abusive reactions from parents.

Sex. In those studies where sex differences have been found, boys are more often reported to be targets of abuse than girls (Gelles et al., 1979; Gil, 1970; Green, 1978). This may be due to the fact that boys 3 months or younger sleep considerably less, and cry and fuss significantly more than girls (Moss, 1967). Other sex differences in behavior appearing in the preschool years that may have impact on children's manageability and consequently on child maltreatment include differences in aggression and in compliance. Maccoby and Jacklin (1974) conclude that boys from as early as 2 years of age are more aggressive both physically and verbally, more likely to engage in bursts of strenuous physical activity, and less compliant to the demands and directions of adults than are girls. These behaviors may function directly as elicitors of parental violence or they may indirectly encourage child abuse by heightening parental stress and loss of control.

Birth History. The prenatal and neonatal histories of maltreated children suggest several factors that may contribute to child abuse and neglect. Although rates of illegitimacy do not appear to differentiate abused from nonabused children (Johnson & Morse, 1968), investigators agree that children resulting from unplanned or unwanted pregnancies are more likely to be maltreated (Blumberg, 1974; Gelles, 1973; Jacobs & Kent, 1977).

In addition, the incidence of prematurity found in samples of abused and neglected children, typically ranging from 22% to 30%, is significantly higher than the 7–8% average for the population at large (Elmer, 1977; Jacobs & Kent, 1977; Klein & Stern, 1971). Elmer (1977) reports that low-birth-weight infants are "known to be more difficult to care for than full-term babies" (p. 49) for a number of reasons: because of immature digestive systems, they eat less and must be fed more frequently; and because of immature nervous systems, they tend to be more irritable and to cry more often. That excessive crying may be extremely stressful to adults is suggested by Frodie, Lamb, Leavitt, and Donovan (1978). They presented parents with 6-minute videotapes of crying and smiling infants and found that infantile crying elicited significant increases in automatic arousal and negative feelings such as anger, distress and discomfort in the adults. In addition to problems in management, low birth weight increases the likelihood of neonatal medical complications. Prematurity continues to be associated with the delayed development of intellectual, verbal, social, and physical skills and the increased likelihood of behavior problems such as hyperactivity through infancy and early childhood (Caputo & Mandell, 1970; Elmer, 1977).

Beside its effects on the appearance and behaviors of the neonate, prematurity has ramifications for the earliest interaction between mother and child because it necessitates extended periods of mother–infant separation. Evidence from both animal and human studies that early postpartum separation may indeed produce disturbances in the later development of parent–child attachment (Kennell, Gordon, & Klaus, 1970; Liefer, Lederman, Barnett, & Williams, 1972). After their review of research on the premature infant, Parke and Kollmer (1975) conclude that "the burden, stress, and disappointment associated with the birth and care of a low birth weight infant could increase the probability of abuse" (p. 552).

Individual Differences. There is evidence from a variety of sources that the maltreated child is often developmentally or physically different from siblings and peers. It is unclear whether these differences are a significant cause, rather than largely the result, of child abuse and neglect. Gil (1970) reported that during the year preceding the abusive incident, 29% of abused children showed disturbances in social interaction and general functioning, 14% displayed physical handicaps of some degree, and an additional 8% revealed impairments in intellectual functioning. Similarly, Johnson and Morse (1968) reported that 70% of their samples of abused, inner-city children had shown physical or developmental deviation prior to their injury. These findings strongly suggest that deviation in the child is a precursor to maltreatment; and in some cases, where congenital defects, deformities, or other inborn impairments are present from birth, it is clearly so (Blumberg, 1974; Green *et al.*, 1974). However, in most instances, the etiology of the deviation is not obvious, and most probably involves the interplay of both hereditary and environmental factors.

Research on neonates and infants indicates that, even within normal limits, there are large hereditary individual differences in such temperamental qualities as activity level, adaptability, irritability, soothability, and preferred modes of interaction (e.g., Carey & McDevitt, 1978; Korner, 1974; Moss, 1967). It appears that those infants who are more difficult to care for—who are colicky, irritable, demanding, poor feeders, resistive to physical contact, less adaptable, and hard to satisfy—run an increased risk of being maltreated (Blumberg, 1974; Green *et al.*, 1974). The relationship between difficulty in management and child maltreatment continues through childhood, with extremely active, restless, and aggressive children reported to be more vulnerable to abuse and neglect (Dubanoski, Evans, & Higuchi, 1978; Green *et al.*, 1974; Johnson & Morse, 1968). Several investigators (e.g., Elmer, 1977; Green *et al.*, 1974) conclude that certain otherwise normal characteristics of the child seem to hold special significance and triggering potential for the abusive parent; these characteristics include biologically-determined attributes (e.g., the sex or ordinal position of the child), particular age-appropriate behaviors (e.g., sexual behavior), selected physical traits (e.g., facial resemblance to the parent), or physcial unattractiveness.

Regardless of the source of the behaviors, abused and neglected children have been described as whining, fussy, listless, chronically crying, restless, demanding, stubborn, resistive, unresponsive, pallid, sickly, emaciated, panicky, fearful, and unsmiling (Johnson & Morse,

1968); apathetic, unappealing (Galdston, 1965); particularly prone to develop violent behavior as a character trait (Galdston, 1971); shy, hypervigilant, either highly compliant or extremely aggressive, untrusting, withdrawn, severely depressed, negative, hyperactive (Kempe & Kempe, 1978); frequently sad, dejected, self-deprecatory, self-destructive, low in self-esteem and frustration tolerance, engaging in provocative, belligerent, and limit-testing behavior which elicits beatings and punishment from parents, other adults, and peers (Green, 1978); and anxious, hostile, and low in empathy (Feshbach, 1973). In addition, Kempe and Kempe (1978) estimate that 20% to 50% of abused children are significantly neurologically damaged so that they lag behind age mates in language development and the attainment of physical skills. Other investigators have noted the higher incidence of mental retardation, cognitive deficits, and aberrant or defective speech patterns (Elmer, 1977; Green, 1978). By school age, the number of abused and neglected children placed in grades below their age level, in mental institutions, and in special educational classes for the learning disabled, emotionally disturbed, or mentally retarded is noteworthy (Gil, 1970; Green, 1978; Kline, 1977).

However, the same serious methodological criticisms that can be made of the research aimed at isolating the distinctive personality characteristics of abusive parents apply with even greater strength to these studies of maltreated children. The lack of representative samples and the failure to use control or comparison groups or to conduct statistical tests of significance on observed differences render the reported findings tentative and inconclusive; when, in fact, research is properly designed, the results are often remarkably at variance with the majority of the literature. Elmer (1977), in a follow-up study of traumatized children, compared abused subjects with a comparison group of accident children and with a control group of subjects with no history of trauma; subjects were matched with regard to age, sex, race, socioeconomic language development, self-concept, intellectual functioning, and various personality characteristics. She found that "when pertinent demographic variables were taken into account, the abused children differed significantly from their peers only in weight and in some measures of impulsivity. Each of these differences was in relation to *either* [control or accident children, respectively], not to both groups, a fact that tends to weaken the results" (p. 107). The majority of all the children studied showed some degree of disturbance, but this was evenly distributed across the groups. Thus, 70% of the entire sample experienced speech problems and 39% were doing poorly in school; in addition, all the children looked sad, fearful, and anxious. The author concluded that "lower-class membership, with the stresses produced by grossly insufficient income, poor housing, poor health, etc., may be as potent as abuse for the subsequent development of the child" (pp. 108–109).

The review indicates several important factors which can be summarized as follows: (1) economically disadvantaged children are more maltreated that those from higher social classes; (2) maltreated children are more likely to have some individual difference which marks them off from other children—for example, they are premature; and (3) maltreating parents were likely themselves to have been maltreated.

What is needed in addition to the work already undertaken is a study of the patterns of social behavior among maltreated children and their parents and the consequences of that maltreatment in terms of the child's other social relations. In the study to follow, such an analysis is undertaken.

Study of Mother–Child and Child–Peer Behavior

Design of Research

The present research explored the effects of child maltreatment on young children's social interactions with mothers and peers. The subjects were 26 children ranging in age from 8 to 32 months attending a full-day child-care center in New Jersey. Most of the subjects were from minority groups and all were from families in the lower socioeconomic categories. None of the children suffered from serious physical impairments. Twelve of the children had been identified by the New Jersey Division of Youth and Family Services as abused/neglected; the 14 children in the control group had no history of maltreatment. Table 1 presents the number of subjects in each of the groups. A check for differences between the control and abused/neglected groups revealed little difference betwen the groups on such variables as SES level, family income, father present or absent, number of other siblings and

TABLE 1. Subjects in Mother–Child and Peer Behavior Study

Group	Control	Abuse/neglect	Total
Younger (under 18 months)	6	4	10
Older (over 18 months)	8	8	16
Total	14	12	26

birth order. Thus, except for abuse and neglect, these groups were quite similar.

All data were collected by observation of the children interacting with their mothers and peers in the context of the day-care center. Mother–child interaction was observed in three situations which are commonly used to experimentally investigate the mother–child relationship: departure, separation, and reunion. In the present study, a naturally occurring separation took place when the mother dropped her child off at the center in the morning (departure) and was no longer present (separation). Similarly, reunion occurred when the mother returned to the center to pick her child up at the end of the day (reunion). Maternal behaviors were recorded during departure and during reunion. The child's behaviors during departure, separation (the first two minutes following the mother's departure), and reunion

TABLE 2.   MATERNAL AND INFANT BEHAVIORS OBSERVED DURING DEPARTURE, SEPARATION, AND REUNION

Condition	Mother's behaviors		Child's behaviors	
Departure	1.	Look	1.	Look
	2.	Vocal	2.	Vocal
	3.	Leave-taking (says bye, waves to child)	3.	Leave-taking (says bye, waves to M, follow M)
	4.	Proximity	4.	Proximity (prox to M, goes to M)
	5.	Caretaking (dress)	5.	——
	6.	Positive affect (soothe, praise, kiss, sm/laugh)	6.	Positive affect (sm/laugh)
	7.	Negative affect (scold, ignore)	7.	Negative affect (fret, cry, protest)
	8.	——	8.	Play (play with toys, play with peers or caregiver)
Separation	(Mother not present)		1.	Goes to door
			2.	Calls to mother
			3.	Plays with peer
			4.	Cries, frets, protest, anger
Reunion	1.	Look	1.	Look
	2.	Vocal	2.	Vocal
	3.	Greeting (name child, greet)	3.	Greeting (left arms, call to M)
	4.	Proximity	4.	Proximity
	5.	Positive affect	5.	Positive affect
	6.	Negative affect	6.	Negative affect
	7.	——	7.	Play

were recorded. Table 2 lists some of the mother and child behaviors recorded in each condition. Three different occasions of departure/separation and reunion were obtained for each mother–child dyad. The data presented are the sum of the values over the three observations.

Peer interaction was recorded during free and structured play which occurred throughout the day in the center. Each subject was observed for twelve 5-minute periods across different days for a total of 60 minutes. Observation periods were randomly assigned with the following constraints: for each child, data were gathered over different days and different situations (e.g., free play, play in teacher-organized activities, etc.); and a target child was observed at his assigned time as long as he was in a situation where social interaction was possible, whether or not he was actually engaged with a peer. A variety of proximal, distal, affective, and play behaviors were recorded (see Table 3).

Behavioral check-sheets were constructed which listed the specific behaviors applicable to the type of interaction to be observed. The check-sheets were divided into six 10-second time periods, representing 1 minute per sheet. Each instance of observed behavior was recorded either by a check to designate its occurrence (for example, smile), or by a symbol to specify its social referent, "p" for peer, "m" for mother, or "c" for caregiver (for example, "p" in kiss row when child kisses peer). More than one response for each participant could be scored in each 10-second period, but only one instance of each response could be noted. A small timing device which signaled 10-second periods was attached to an earplug so that the observer could score behavior by time period.

For all data analyses, the unit of measurement was the number of

TABLE 3. CHILDREN'S PEER-DIRECTED BEHAVIORS DURING FREE PLAY

		Free play categories
1.	Proximal	prox, touch, hold/pick-up, lie/lean, hold hands
2.	Distal	look, gesture to, imitate
3.	Vocal	vocal to
4.	Affectionate	hug, kiss
5.	Play	play
6.	Positive play	offer, share, show, accept, throw, follow
7.	Negative play	take, resist take, pull hair, bite, hit, push/pull
8.	Play self	play self
9.	Play object	play object
10.	Positive affect	smile/laugh
11.	Negative affect	fret, cry, frown, protest/anger
12.	Activity	clap, movement, throw nondirected

10-second periods in which a given behavior occurred summing over episodes for each condition. Although the total amount of time a child was observed in separation and in free play was fixed by experimental design, the time of departure and reunion varied in each episode for each mother–child pair. Because our interest was predominantly in those responses made specifically to the situations of mother leaving and reuniting with her child, only the last 30 seconds prior to the mother's exit for departure, and the first 30 seconds following the mother's perceived (by the child) entry into her child's room for reunion, were analyzed. After initial frequency counts were computed for each behavior according to condition, related behaviors were grouped into broader categories (for example, children's proximal-behavior category in free play included the behaviors of proximity, touch, hold, lie/lean, hold hands). Interobserver reliabilities were obtained on one-third of the sample. The reliabilities were quite high, determined by number of agreements over number of agreements plus disagreements and ranging in value from .76 to .98 with an average of .85.

Research Findings

The results in terms of the mother–infant interaction and peer–peer play will be presented as they occurred in four situations: maternal departure/separation, maternal reunion, and free play in the nursery. Because of the few age differences, the age variable will not be considered in this analysis.

Maternal departure and separation have been considered separately since Weinraub and Lewis (1977) have reported important differences between these situations. Maternal reunion, used by Ainsworth, Blehar, Waters, and Wall (1979) as a situation to measure infant attachment, can be viewed as one method of testing whether maltreated infants, in fact, do appear to be insecurely attached. Finally, the free-play situation can be used to assess the child's behavior toward other people, both peers and adult.

Mother–Infant Relationship

Maternal Departure (see Table 4). Maternal behavior toward her infant prior to her leaving showed marked differences as a function of whether or not the mother was a maltreating parent. In general, maltreating mothers were less positive and more negative toward their children. A MANOVA indicated a significant difference between the groups when all behavioral categories were considered ($p < .04$) and

TABLE 4. MEAN NUMBER OF 10-SECOND PERIODS OF OCCURRENCE OF MOTHER'S BEHAVIOR TOWARD CHILD AND CHILD'S BEHAVIOR TOWARD MOTHER IN DEPARTURE SITUATION

	Age group	Mother's behavior		Child's behavior	
		Control (14)	A/N (12)	Control	A/N
Look	Y	2.00	2.50	4.00	1.25
	O	3.63	3.63	3.75	3.00
	Tot	2.93	3.25	3.86	2.42
Vocal	Y	.50	.25	.00	.00
	O	1.00	.63	.13	.25
	Tot	.79	.50	.07	.17
Leave-taking	Y	1.67	.25	.67	.00
	O	1.50	.50	.50	.13
	Tot	1.57	.42	.57	.08
Proximity	Y	2.50	.50	2.50	.50
	O	2.25	1.88	2.50	2.00
	Tot	2.36	1.42	2.50	1.50
Caretaking	Y	.17	1.75		
	O	.88	.38		
	Tot	.57	.83		
Positive affect	Y	.67	.25	.33	.25
	O	.13	.88	.00	.25
	Tot	.93	.67	.14	.25
Negative affect	Y	.00	.00	1.17	2.25
	O	.00	.50	.75	.38
	Tot	.00	.67	.93	1.00
Play	Y			1.83	.25
	O			.75	1.50
	Tot			1.21	1.08

individual MANOVA's and chi squares showed similar results. Maltreating mothers spoke to their children less often and showed less leave-taking behavior ($p < .02$). For example, they waved goodbye and said "bye-bye" significantly less than the control mothers. While control mothers engaged in more proximal behavior ($p < .09$, chi square), maltreating mothers engaged in somewhat more distal behavior, especially looking.

In terms of emotional tone, control mothers showed more positive behavior but, of particular importance, they showed significantly less negative behaviors than did the abusing/neglectful mothers ($p < .05$, chi square). It is interesting to note that the maltreating mothers showed more caregiving behaviors than the controls, especially for the younger age group ($p < .03$, chi square). Investigation of the reasons for this indicated that this greater frequency, rather than reflecting more concern, is another measure of neglect. The maltreating mothers were less likely to change or clean their infants at home and because nursery school policy is such, were required to change and dress their children prior to their departure. Thus, all together, the two groups— control and maltreating mothers—determined by the Division of Youth and Family Services, do reflect real differences in terms of these mothers' behavior toward their children.

Children's behavior as a function of these two types of mothers showed little significant difference. The MANOVA was not significant, although the differences that do appear indicate that maltreated children looked significantly less at their mothers than normally treated children ($p < .05$), that they stayed further from them ($p < .09$), and they they failed to wave goodbye and follow them as they left ($p < .08$). Interestingly, maltreated infants also showed more positive behavior toward their mothers as they left although this was not significant.

Maternal Separation. Once gone, the effect of the mother's absence on the child's behavior could be assessed and differences based on the maltreatment determined. There were no significant differences in the infant's behavior between the two groups in those behaviors directed toward the absent mother; although the maltreated children showed less upset than the normally treated children ($\bar{x} = 3.43$ vs. 2.17) and less movement toward the door ($\bar{x} = 1.00$ vs. 0.25).

There was no difference in the amount of time the children played with peers although maltreated children played with objects more than the control children ($p < .04$, chi square). One can only conclude that there are relatively few differences between these two groups of children when they are left by their mothers in the nursery school. This should not be terribly surprising since the mothers' separation, unlike the laboratory situations, is not accompanied by the child being left alone. To the contrary, they are left in the care of known adults and in the company of familiar peers!

Maternal Reunion (see Table 5). The mother's and child's response to the return of the mother is a useful measure of the mother–infant relationship since it has been thought to be the major situation in which to assess the nature of the attachment relationship. The situation as it occurs here is unlike the laboratory setting in many ways since there are not multiple 3-minute episodes of different people moving in and out of an unfamiliar room (Ainsworth & Wittig, 1969). Nevertheless, observation of maternal and infant behavior in this situation may give us some idea as to the nature of the parent–child relationship. Of particular importance are the maternal behaviors of greeting, proximity

Table 5. Mean Number of 10-Second Periods of Occurrence of Mother's Behavior toward Child and Child's Behavior toward Mother during Reunion

	Age group	Maternal behavior		Child behavior	
		Control	A/N	Control	A/N
Look	Y	6.00	6.00	6.83	7.50
	O	5.50	4.63	5.88	6.38
	Tot	5.71	5.08	6.29	6.75
Vocal	Y	1.50	.50	.00	.00
	O	1.88	1.00	1.38	.00
	Tot	1.71	.83	.79	.00
Greeting	Y	3.00	.75	.33	.00
	O	1.38	.63	.75	.25
	Tot	2.07	.67	.57	.17
Proximity	Y	1.17	1.25	2.33	1.75
	O	2.13	1.50	4.63	3.63
	Tot	1.71	1.42	3.64	3.00
Positive affect	Y	1.67	1.00	1.17	1.00
	O	.88	.13	.75	.75
	Tot	1.21	.42	.93	.83
Negative affect	Y	.00	.00	1.17	.50
	O	.00	.00	.00	.38
	Tot	.00	.00	.50	.42
Play	Y			.00	.25
	O			.00	.00
	Tot			.00	.08

seeking, verbal interaction, and positive affect. Infant behaviors indicative of secure attachment include greeting and movement toward mother and degree of positive and negative affect.

Overall, all behaviors of maltreating mothers are different from the controls (MANOVA $p < .10$) and indicate that the abusing/neglectful mothers show less engagement with their children when they are reunited with them at the end of the day. Control mothers show more looking behavior, more verbal interaction, more proximity seeking, and more positive affect. In particular, they show significantly more greeting behavior ($p < .05$). Maltreated children in turn greet their mothers less ($p < .05$, chi square) stay in less proximity, and play more, vocalize less to them ($p < .09$, chi square) and show less positive affect ($p < .05$, chi square). Taken together, these group data for both mother and child would appear to indicate that the maltreated children are insecurely attached in agreement with George and Main's observation (1979) of the attachment of these children.

In summary, then, the observation of maternal departure, separation, and reunion reveals several interesting findings: (1) there are significant differences in maternal behavior toward their infants between mothers classified as maltreating by the State's Division of Youth and Family Services and a matching group of mothers not so classified; (2) maltreating mothers are more abusive (scold more) and less positive, maintain and initiate less proximity, speak less to their children, greet them less upon meeting, and say goodbye less during departure; and (3) maltreated infants look at their mothers less, say "goodbye" less, and follow them less upon departure, greet them less upon departure, greet them less upon reunion, and stay in less proximity when they are present. In terms of the attachment literature, as a group they appear to be insecurely attached.[1]

Peer–Peer Relationships

Play Situation. Peer relationships were explored by watching the children at play during the course of several weeks. Casual observation of these two groups of children revealed little difference. An observer, not knowledgeable about the abuse/neglect classification, would not be able to tell the children apart. In none of the classrooms did the maltreated children stand out as different, either in their sociability or play with peers. There were no obvious signs of withdrawn, overly hostile, or passive behavior which could be used to identify these children. Two casual observers were unable to differentiate children on the basis of the maltreatment dimension. More refined observations were obtained for each child. Sixty minutes of 10-second observations over a wide variety of free-play and structured-play situations, a total of 360 10-second periods, were collected for each child and the data for the control and maltreated children are presented in Table 6. These formal observations agree with our impressions; there are few differences over a wide range of behaviors in children's peer interaction as a function of maltreatment. In fact, a MANOVA was not significant and only one behavior showed any difference between the two groups. Maltreated children showed less positive play than the control children ($p < .08$). Positive play is a composite of six different play behaviors including share, show, offer, accept, throw to, and follow peer. For

---

[1]No analysis on individual subjects was undertaken given the small number of subjects and the wide age range. While it is not appropriate to talk of attachment for a group as a whole, this analysis gives us some information on this variable which might be useful.

Table 6. Mean Number of 10-Second
Periods of Occurrence of Child's
Behavior toward Peers in Free Play

Child's behavior	Age group	Peers Control	A/N
Proximal	Y	210.67	177.50
	O	269.75	263.50
	Tot	244.43	234.83
Distal	Y	199.17	197.25
	O	231.13	218.63
	Tot	217.43	211.50
Vocal	Y	4.67	3.75
	O	25.13	26.50
	Tot	17.14	18.00
Affectionate	Y	.83	.25
	O	1.00	1.13
	Tot	.93	.83
Play with person	Y	2.00	1.25
	O	66.25	44.13
	Tot	38.71	29.83
Positive play	Y	10.00	4.00
	O	31.25	17.13
	Tot	22.14	12.75
Negative play	Y	12.50	15.50
	O	14.75	14.75
	Tot	13.79	15.00
Play with self	Y	9.83	16.50
	O	12.13	14.25
	Tot	11.14	15.00
Play with object	Y	241.17	231.25
	O	206.75	226.00
	Tot	221.50	227.75
Positive affect	Y	13.83	12.25
	O	26.88	21.38
	Tot	21.29	18.33
Negative affect	Y	8.83	10.25
	O	9.38	6.75
	Tot	9.14	7.92
Activity	Y	47.17	40.75
	O	88.38	62.25
	Tot	70.71	55.08

share, throw to, and follow, the control infants had higher scores while for show, offer, and accept, the maltreated children had higher scores. Thus, even within the positive-play category, the particular behaviors show no consistent result.

CONSISTENCY OF FINDINGS: A REVIEW OF OTHER STUDIES

Before discussing the implications of these results, both for a theory of social development and as a means of intervention into the lives of maltreated infants, it is necessary to compare these findings with data available in the literature. Our findings, especially on the reunion behavior of both mother and child in the maltreated group, would seem to support George and Main's (1979) suggestion that abused children are most similar to the insecurely attached, mother-avoidant children in that they were somewhat less likely to approach their mothers and more likely to avoid proximity with them. We did not find, however, that the children showed any aggression toward them.

A study by Hyman and Parr (1978) found significant differences in the interactive patterns that abused and nonabused children displayed with their mothers. The authors compared an abused group of twelve mother–child dyads ranging in age from 6 to 24 months to a control group pair-matched for sex, age, ordinal position, parental age, home accommodations, and ethnic group, in a strange-situation procedure based on Ainsworth and Wittig (1969). The results revealed some similarities in that the maltreated children showed more negative behavior toward their mothers and interacted with them less than controls. There were no differences during separation and reunion, although the maltreated infants vocalized less and played more than the control children. Maltreating mothers were less responsive to their infants, a finding we observed but have no formal data for. That mothers scolded more and were more abusive to these children is also supported by clinical studies (see, for example, Young, 1964).

Burgess and Conger (1978) observed abusive, neglecting, and control families matched on pertinent demographic variables while performing experimentally-created tasks in their homes. The results indicated that abusive and neglecting families differed significantly in patterns of interaction from control families, these differences largely determined by maternal behaviors. Overall, neglecting parents were the most negative and least positive in their family interactions across the three groups; abusive parents, compared with controls, had less contact both physically and verbally with family members and relatively more aversive interactions. The behaviors of mothers were particularly significant. Although their rates of physical and verbal responding to their children were similar, neglecting mothers directed substantially more negative, and less positive, contacts to their children than did control mothers. Abusing mothers, on the other hand, had less verbal, as well as less positive, interactions with their children than did controls. Contrary to the authors' expectations, no remarkable differences were found among the children from the three family types, a finding consistent with our results. Patterns of interaction between siblings did not differ over the three family types, nor did interactions between the spouses. These data suggest that child maltreatment affects mother–child interactive behaviors directly but may not disturb the interactions of other family members. The similarity between these results and the present study are clear: mother–infant interaction may not affect other social relations. These results support the social-network model in that they suggest interdependence of negative relations even within the same family.

Systematic information concerning the peer interactions of abused and neglected children is almost nonexistent; available findings are clincally-based and largely anecdotal (Galdston, 1971; Green, 1978). In both these studies, peer interactions were negatively affected, a finding quite different from the one reported by Seay, Alexander, and Harlow (1964). They compared the peer behaviors of normal, ferally-reared monkeys with those of monkeys raised by mothers who subjected them to life-threatening levels of maltreatment. In general, the infant–infant social interactions were quite similar in the abused and normal groups, with both groups developing and maintaining effective contact-play patterns. As we have tried to indicate, poor peer relations may be a function of other factors than poor mother–infant interactions. The findings of Galdston (1971) and Green (1978) cannot be understood until we know more about the children's total social experience.

IMPLICATIONS FOR A THEORY OF SOCIAL DEVELOPMENT AND INTERVENTION STRATEGIES

The results of this study of maltreated children lead to the belief that poor infant–maternal relationships do not of necessity lead to poor peer relationships. These findings together with the work of Harlow (Harlow, 1969; Harlow & Harlow, 1965; Novak & Harlow, 1975; Suomi & Harlow, 1972) and Hartup (Furman et al., in press; Hartup, in press) raise serious questions about the epigenetic view of social development. Even though others (for example, Lieberman,

1977; Matas *et al.*, 1978) have found an association between attachment and peer relations, the possible reasons for this have not been fully articulated. As we have suggested, there are three reasons why maternal attachment has been associated with poor peer relations: (1) the epigenetic view—poor early maternal relations result in subsequent poor interpersonal relations; (2) poor maternal relations are associated with limited other interpersonal contacts which do not allow for the rehearsal of interpersonal behavior; or (3) poor maternal relations leads to general fearful behavior which in turn leads to poor interpersonal relations.

That appropriate peer behavior is exhibited when infants are raised by peers alone (Harlow, 1969), when treated by peer therapists (Suomi & Harlow, 1972; Furman *et al.*, in press) or when placed in a day-care setting, suggests that peer relations are not predicated on successful maternal relations. In the present study, the maternal–infant relation was poor, in fact, the maltreated children appeared to be insecurely attached. Nevertheless, they were able to engage in successful peer relations as long as they were able to engage in peer behavior. Harlow's studies of monkeys reveal the same finding—as long as infants were allowed peer contact, they had normal peer relations independent of the maternal–infant relation. The epigenetic view does not receive support from these data; however, it is not possible to separate out which of the other two factors may be involved. Certainly, maltreated children appear fearful when first introduced into the day-care setting, but it is equally likely that part of the maltreatment has been their isolation from other interpersonal relations.

We feel that these data support a broader model of social development, a view we have called the social-network model (Lewis & Feiring, 1978, 1979; Lewis & Weinraub, 1976). The social network is best characterized by a matrix of social objects and functions. The objects that people the young child's world, the functions that the child needs to survive and develop, and the relationship between objects and functions, are culturally determined and vary considerably. For some children, the mother may be the sole object in the infant's world; as such, she must satisfy all functions and needs. In such a matrix, the outcome of this single relationship will determine all others. However, if the matrix includes others such as fathers, siblings, and peers, then the complex arrangement of object–function relations may result in widely different consequences. The findings on early peer and maternal relations, both in humans and monkeys, suggest that the social network of the young child has some flexibility and that the relation between objects and functions is more fluid than originally suggested. Parents may have functions which are different from peers.

Data from a variety of sources suggest that parents (adults) are associated with security and dependency while peers are associated with teaching and play (Edwards & Lewis, 1979; Whiting & Whiting, 1975). The social-network model allows us to consider a wide set of important functions or needs, attachment being just one. Play and learning may be others which have a different course of development and which may be facilitated by other social objects. Objects and functions within the matrix are related in that they form part of the social context of the child. Moreover, difficulties and rewards in one area are bound to affect others. However, rather than rigid, sequential, and linear models, the social-network model allows for a more flexibile system. Difficulties in one area do not necessarily produce difficulties in another, as long as the flexibility of the system is maintained. It breaks down only when cultural values force a constricted system. Thus, poor maternal relationship will lead to a subsequently poor peer relationship only if the poor maternal relationship leads to early peer isolation.

The treatment of maltreated children has, of necessity, to be multifaceted. The complex array of difficulties created by maltreatment cannot be overcome by a single prescription. Moreover, maltreatment is not a single entity. Child neglect and child abuse are two widely different parental behaviors which have different etiology. For example, among poor inner-city families, the ability to locate a babysitter is difficult; thus, many parents, especially single parents, are confronted with the choice of either not going out at all in the evening or else leaving their child alone. This form of child neglect has to be quite different from the parent who beats the child until bones are broken or internal damage caused.

Given these difficulties, any general prescription must be used with some caution. Even so, the results of this study and a reading of the literature suggest that part of the problems in interpersonal relations that result from a maltreated child stem not solely from the poor child–parent attachment, but also from secondary effects such as social isolation from other people and from general fearfulness which also may have the effect of producing social isolation. This social isolation can be treated through requiring that the child be placed in a social milieu which contains other people, including adults, and same-aged and older peers. As long as we hold to the epigenetic view, the experience of other people, while potentially important, could not be justified from a theoretical view. If all subsequent social relations depended on the mother–child relationship and if that relationship was one of maltreatment, there was little hope of altering this course of development. The use of a social network approach is, therefore, an optimistic view arguing for greater flexibility in social behavior since, although the mother–child relationship is important for some aspects, it is not the sole determinant *per se* of all other social relations. Specifically, day-care settings are important for these children and their use is recommended. Day care offers the child other social objects, in particular, peers, and it is this experience which will aid it in forming and maintaining friendships and close interpersonal relations throughout the life cycle. Moreover, the day-care setting, especially if accompanied by support for the mother, will allow the family itself a larger social network. This support system can be useful to the parent(s) as well since, as Garbarino (1977) and Bronfenbrenner (1974) have suggested, the absence of a larger network for the family may be an important cause of the maltreatment itself. The social network, both of the child and of the family, is an important aspect of development. No theory of social development or intervention should ignore its impact.

REFERENCES

Ainsworth, M. D. Object relations, dependency, and attachment: A theoretical review of the infant–mother relationship. *Child Development*, 1969, *40*, 969–1026.

Ainsworth, M. D. S., & Wittig, B. A. Attachment and exploratory behavior of one-year-olds in a strange situation. In B. M. Foss (Ed.), *Determinants of infant behavior* (Vol. 4). London: Methuen, 1969.

Ainsworth, M. D., Blehar, M. C., Waters, E., & Wall, S. *Patterns of attachment: A psychological study of the strange situation.* New York: Halsted Press, 1978.

Bakan, D. *Slaughter of the innocents: A study of the battered child phenomenon.* San Francisco: Jossey-Bass, Inc., 1971.

Bandura, A., & Huston, A. Identification as a process of incidental learning. *Journal of Abnormal and Social Psychology*, 1961, *63*, 311–318.

Blumberg, M. L. Psychopathology of the abusing parent. *American Journal of Psychotherapy*, 1974, *28*, 21–29.

Bowlby, J. *Attachment and loss.* Vol. 1. *Attachment.* New York: Basic Books, 1969.

Bronfenbrenner, U. *Is early intervention effective? A report on longitudinal evaluations of preschool programs* (Vol. 2). Washington, D. C.: Department of Health, Education and Welfare, Office of Child Development, 1974.

Brown J. A., & Daniels, R. Some observations on abusive parents. *Child Welfare*, 1968, *47*, 89–94.

Burgess, R. L., & Conger, R. D. Family interaction in abusive, neglectful, and normal families. *Child Development*, 1978, *49*, 1163–1173.

Caputo, D. V., & Mandell, W. Consequences of low birth weight. *Developmental Psychology*, 1970, *3*, 363–383.

Carey, W. B., & McDevitt, S. C. Stability and change in individual temperament diagnoses from infancy to early childhood. *Journal of the American Academy of Child Psychiatry*, 1978, *17*, 331–337.

Chase, N. F. *A child is being beaten: Violence against children, an American tragedy.* New York: McGraw-Hill, 1975.

Deur, J. L., & Parke, R. D. The effects of inconsistent punishment on aggression in children. *Developmental Psychology*, 1970, *2*, 403–411.

Dubanoski, R. A., Evans, I. M., & Higuchi, A. A. Analysis and treatment of child abuse: A set of behavioral propositions. *Child Abuse and Neglect,* 1978, *2,* 153–172.

Edwards, C. P., & Lewis, M. Young children's concepts of social relations: Social functions and social objects. In M. Lewis & L. Rosenblum (Eds.). *The child and its family: The genesis of behavior* (Vol. 2). New York: Plenum, 1979.

Elmer, E. Follow-up study of traumatized children. *Child Abuse and Neglect,* 1977, *1,* 105–109.

Feshbach, N. The effects of violence in childhood. *Journal of Clinical Child Psychology,* 1973, *2,* 28–31.

Feshbach, N., & Feshbach, S. The relationship between empathy and aggression in two age groups. *Developmental Psychology,* 1969, *1,* 102–107.

Feshbach, S. Aggression. In P. H. Mussen (Ed.), *Carmichael's manual of child psychology* (Vol. 2). New York: Wiley, 1970, pp 159–259.

Frodie, A. M., Lamb, M. E., Leavitt, L. A., & Donovan, W. L. Fathers' and mothers' responses to infant smiles and cries. *Infant Behavior and Development,* 1978, *1,* 187–198.

Furman, W., Rake, D. F., & Hartup, W. W. Rehabilitation of socially-withdrawn children through mixed-age and same-age socialization. *Child Development,* in press.

Galdston, R. Observations on children who have been physically abused and their parents. *American Journal of Psychiatry,* 1965, *122,* 440–443.

Galdston, R. Violence begins at home: The Parent's Center project for the study and prevention of child abuse. *American Academy of Child Psychiatry,* 1971, *10,* 336–350.

Garbarino, J. A preliminary study of some ecological correlates of child abuse: The impact of socio-economic stress on mothers. *Child Development,* 1976, *47,* 178–185.

Garbarino, J. The human ecology of child maltreatment: A conceptual model for research. *Journal of Marriage and the Family,* 1977, *39,* 721–736.

Garbarino, J., & Crouter, A. Defining the community context for parent–child relations: The correlates of child maltreatment. *Child Development,* 1978, *49,* 604–616.

Gelles, R.J. Child abuse as psychopathology: A sociological critique and reformulation. *American Journal of Orthopsychiatry,* 1973, *43,* 611–621.

Gelles, R. J. The social construction of child abuse. *American Journal of Orthopsychiatry,* 1975, *45,* 363–371.

Gelles, R. J., Straus, M., & Steinmetz, S. In mixed views: A national conference on child abuse. *APA Monitor,* 1979, *10.*

George, C., & Main, M. Social interactions of young abused children: Approach, avoidance, and aggression. *Child Development,* 1979, *50*(2), 306–318.

Gil, D. *Violence against children: Physical child abuse in the United States.* Cambridge, Mass.: Harvard University Press, 1970.

Giovannoni, J. M., & Billingsley, A. Child neglect among the poor: A study of parental adequacy in families of three ethnic groups. *Child Welfare,* 1974, *49,* 196–204.

Green, A. H. Psychopathology of abused children. *American Academy of Child Psychiatry,* 1978, *17,* 92–103.

Green, A. H., Gaines, R. W., & Sangrund, A. Child abuse: Pathological syndrome of family interaction. *American Journal of Psychiatry,* 1974, *131,* 882–886.

Harlow, H. F. Age-mate or peer affectional system. In D. S. Lehrman, R. A. Hende, E. Shaw (Eds.) *Advances in the study of behavior* (Vol. 2). New York: Academic Press, 1969.

Harlow, H. F., & Harlow, M. D. The affectional systems. In A. M. Schrier, H. F. Harlow, & F. Stollnitz (Eds.), *Behavior of nonhuman primates* (Vol. 2). New York: Academic Press, 1965.

Hartup, W. W. Two social worlds: Family relations and peer relations. In M. Rutter (Ed.), *Scientific foundations of developmental psychiatry.* London: Heinemann, in press.

Hyman, C. A., & Parr, R. A controlled video observational study of abused children. *Child Abuse and Neglect*, 1978, *2*, 217–222.

Jacobs, R. A., & Kent, J. T. Psychosocial profiles of familes of failure to thrive infants—preliminary report. *Child Abuse and Neglect*, 1977, *1*, 469–477.

Johnson, B, & Morse, H. A. Injured children and their parents. *Children*, 1968, *15*, 147–152.

Kagan, J., & Moss, H. *Birth to maturity.* New York: Wiley, 1962.

Kempe, C. H. A practical approach to the protection of the abused child and rehabilitation of the abusing parent. *Pediatrics*, 1973, *51*, 804.

Kempe, R. S., & Kempe, C. H. *Child abuse.* Cambridge, Mass.: Harvard University Press, 1978.

Kempe, H. C., Silverman, F. N., Steele, B. F., Droegemueller, W., & Silver, H. K. The battered child syndrome. *Journal of the American Medical Association*, 1962, *181*, 17–24.

Kennell, J. H., Gordon, D., & Klaus, N. H. The effect of early mother–infant separation on later maternal performance. *Pediatric Research*, 1970, Abstract 150.

Klein, M., & Stern, L. Low birth weight and the battered child syndrome. *American Journal of Diseases of Childhood*, 1971, *122*, 15–18.

Kline, D. F. Educational and psychological problems of abused children. *Child Abuse and Neglect*, 1977, *1*, 301–107.

Korner, A. F. The effect of the infant's state, level of arousal and ontogenetic stage on the caregiver. In M. Lewis & L. A. Rosenblum (Eds.), *The effect of the infant on its caregiver.* New York: Wiley, 1974.

Lewis, M. *The social nexus: Toward a theory of social development.* Invited address, Eastern Psychological Association meetings, Philadelphia, April 1979.

Lewis, M., & Feiring, C. The child's social world. In R. M. Lerner & G. D. Spanier (Eds.), *Child influences on marital and family interaction: A life-span perspective.* New York: Academic Press, 1978.

Lewis, M., & Feiring, C. The child's social network: Social object, social functions and their relationship. In M. Lewis & L. Rosenblum (Eds.), *The child and its family: The genesis of behavior* (Vol. 2). New York: Plenum, 1979.

Lewis, M., & Weinraub, M. The father's role in the infant's social network. In M. Lamb (Ed.), *The role of the father in child development.* New York: Wiley, 1976.

Lewis, M., Young, G., Brooks, J., & Michalson, L. The beginning of friendship. In M. Lewis & L. Rosenblum (Eds.), *Friendship and peer relations: The origins of behavior* (Vol. 4). New York: Wiley, 1975.

Lieberman, A. F. Preschoolers' competence with a peer: Relations with attachment and peer experience. *Child Development*, 1977, *48*, 1277–1287.

Liefer, A. D., Leiderman, P. H., Barnett, C. R., & Williams, J. A. Effects of mother–infant separation on maternal attachment behavior. *Child Development*, 1972, *43*, 1203–1218.

Light, R. Abused and neglected children in America: A study of alternative policies. *Harvard Educational Review*, 1973, *43*, 556–598.

Maccoby, E. E., & Jacklin, C. N. *The psychology of sex differences.* Stanford, Ca.: Stanford University Press, 1974.

Matas, L., Ahrend, R. A., & Sroufe, L. A. Continuity of adaptation in the second year: The relationship between quality of attachment and later competence. *Child Development*, 1978, *49*, 547–556.

McHenry, T., Girdany, B. R., & Elmer, E. Unsuspected trauma with multiple skeletal injuries during infancy and childhood. *Pediatrics*, 1963, *31*, 903–908.

Melnick, B., & Hurley, J. Distinctive personality attributes of child-abusing mothers. *Journal of Consulting and Clinical Psychology.* 1969, *33*, 746–749.

Moss, H. A. Sex, age, and state as determinants of mother–infant interaction. *Merrill–Palmer Quarterly*, 1967, *13*, 19–36.

National Academy of Sciences. *Toward a national policy for children and families*. Washington, D. C.: United States Government Printing Office, 1976.

Novak, M. A., & Harlow, H. F. Social recovery of monkeys isolated for the first year of life: Rehabilitation and therapy. *Developmental Psychology*, 1975, *11*, 453–465.

Parke, R. D., & Collmer, C. W. Child abuse: An interdisciplinary analysis. In E. M. Hetherington (Ed.), *Review of child development research* (Vol. 5). Chicago: University of Chicago Press, 1975, pp. 509–590.

Parke, R. D., & Deur, J. L. Schedule of punishment and inhibition of aggression in children. *Developmental Psychology*, 1972, *7*, 266–269.

Patterson, G. R., & Cobb, J. A. A dyadic analysis of "aggressive" behavior. In J. P. Hill (Ed.), *Minnesota symposia on child psychology* (Vol. 5). Minneapolis: University of Minnesota Press, 1971.

Seay, B., Alexander, B. K., & Harlow, H. F. Maternal behavior of socially deprived rhesus monkeys. *Journal of Abnormal and Social Psychology*, 1964, *69*, 345–354.

Spinetta, J. J., & Rigler, D. The child-abusing parent: A psychological review. *Psychological Bulletin*, 1972, *77*, 296–304.

Steele, B. F., & Pollock, D. A psychiatric study of parents who abuse infants and small children. In R. F. Helfer & C. H. Kempe (Eds.), *The battered child*. Chicago: University of Chicago Press, 1968.

Stein, A. H., & Friedrich, L. K. Impact of television on children and youth. In E. M. Hetherington (Ed.), *Review of child development research* (Vol. 5). Chicago: University of Chicago Press, 1975.

Suomi, S. J., & Harlow, H. F. Social rehabilitation of isolate-reared monkeys. *Developmental Psychology*, 1972, *6*, 487–496.

Walters, D. R. *Physical and sexual abuse of children: Causes and treatment*. Bloomington: Indiana University Press, 1975.

Wasserman, S. The abused parent of the abused child. *Children*, 1967, *14*, 175–179.

Waters, E., Wippman, & Sroufe, L. A. Social competence in preschool children as a function of the security of earlier attachment to the mother. *Child Development*, in press.

Weinraub, M., & Lewis, M. The determinants of children's responses to separation. *Monographs of the Society for Research in Child Development*, 1977, *42*(4, Serial No. 172).

Weston, J. T. The pathology of child abuse. In R. E. Helfer & C. H. Kempe (Eds.), *The battered child*. Chicago: University of Chicago Press, 1974.

Whiting, B. B., & Whiting, J. W. M. *Children of six cultures: A psychocultural analysis*. Cambridge, Mass.: Harvard University Press, 1975.

Young, L. *Wednesday's children*. New York: McGraw-Hill, 1964.

10

The Infant's Effort to Cope with Separation

Leonard A. Rosenblum and Edward H. Plimpton

The social setting within which the human and nonhuman primate develops has been a pivotal element in the evolution of the order. Except in a few species (e.g., orangutan), relatively elaborate social structures have emerged based on kinship, gender, age, and status factors, each attuned to particular environmental demands (Eisenberg, Muckinhirn, & Rudran, 1972; Gartlan, 1968). The crucial role of primate adaptation through disparate forms of social organization is perhaps best reflected in the fact that wild primates of the same or closely related species living under different ecological conditions develop dramatically different forms of social organization (Struhsaker & Leland, 1979). It is perhaps not surprising then that the abrupt loss or chronic absence of the network of social support normally available to primates often results in quite serious behavioral debilitation. In light of the relatively prolonged period of infantile dependency in these higher forms, such loss of social support is particularly disruptive in infants. The loss of social support may vary from episodic, relatively brief disruptions in contact with attachment figures, an everyday event, to the trauma of abrupt, complete, and sustained loss. On the other hand, the social structure and its contact with the developing

LEONARD A. ROSENBLUM AND EDWARD H. PLIMPTON • State University of New York, Downstate Medical Center, Department of Psychiatry, Brooklyn, New York 11203. This research was supported by NIMH grant No. 22640 infant can vary from elaborated kinship and troop systems common to wild primates and many human cultures, to the nuclear family, the single parent, or the isolation provided by unfortunate societal or planned experimental conditions. While relatively few may suffer the most traumatic forms of loss, virtually all confront some form of these experiences during their lives, and hence the study of these phenomena has provided considerable scientific as well as literary interest throughout our history.

But the significant question remains: how shall we attempt to understand the reactions we see when one form or another of these experiences is incurred? Typically, the interpretation of behavior seen during separation has been framed in terms of the consequences of psychological loss (e.g., Bowlby, 1969; Kaufman, 1977). The emphasis of these ballistic theories of separation response is to view the sequelae of separation as the unfolding of a preprogrammed sequence of response which has evolved to cope with the loss experience. Such views pay little heed to the physical and social environmental circumstances in which the separated infant finds itself, a factor of likely importance. Indeed, some investigators have questioned whether any long-term consequences can be attributed directly to the influence of the separation *per se* (Rutter, 1972). Furthermore, the problematic relationship between the behavioral effects of social-bond disruption versus those of possible social and sensory diminution or deprivation has also been addressed by several previous workers at both the human- and nonhuman-primate level (Mineka & Suomi, 1978; Rutter, 1972; Yarrow, 1961).

Our purpose in the material that follows is to attempt to redress the imbalance of attention provided by the more traditional theories regarding the role of the infant's attempts during separation, not only to respond to the loss or deprivation experience, but actively to adapt to the particular environmental circumstances within which it continues to live. Inasmuch as ethical and practical constraints have made controlled information of this type quite limited in humans, we shall attempt to elaborate these views through discussion of material developed in our studies of laboratory-reared nonhuman primates.

THE MOTHER'S ROLE IN INFANT REGULATION

In most nonhuman primates, as in man, the primary source of inital socialization as well as sustenance is the biological mother of the infant. Acting as the primary interface between the infant and the social and physical world, the mother plays many roles in guiding the course of infant development. In protecting and restraining the infant's activities through various behaviors the mother acts as a filter for the huge array of stimuli impinging upon the developing infant. However, in addition to modulating external stimuli, the mother often provides a source of stimulation herself by grooming, playing, and otherwise interacting with her infant during periods of environmental quiescence. As the infant grows older, more coordinated, and capable of coping with an increasingly rich and diversified environment, the mother actively encourages movement from her through weaning and a variety of other contact-deterring behaviors.

Throughout the period of early maturation, the mother also serves as the target of many of the infant's developing response patterns. Primarily, she serves as the fulcrum of the infant's attempts to modulate the degree of affective arousal at levels which facilitate interactions with the social and physical environment. The older primate infant moves to and from the mother at its own pace, making physical contact, oral contact with the breast, resting, sleeping, and leaping free to engage the outside world when it is able and ready. In these early periods the infant depends upon the constant availability of the attachment figure as the safe base to which it can return and from which it can depart when arousal has been reduced and energies renewed. As in human societies, for most nonhuman primates, as the infant grows older, others may supplement and ultimately replace the mother in playing these roles. Adult males, other females, and peers and siblings of both sexes all play a part in providing the structure within which the normal infant gradually emerges as an adult (e.g., Lewis & Rosenblum, 1979).

THE INFANT'S ROLE IN SELF-REGULATION

From the beginning of life onward, however, the infant must play an active role in eliciting the supportive properties of the mother. The newborn primate infant, although held tightly to the mother's ventrum following birth, must depend upon its own strong clinging and rooting reflexes present at birth, to establish and maintain nutritive contact with the mother's nipple. Monkey mothers never "give the breast" to their young infants. Thus, the handicapped infant brain-damaged since birth may be held by the mother, but not in a fashion which allows survival when the infant's reflex system fails to function properly (see Figure 1). Mother and infant must each play their part, synchronizing their actions simultaneously to the changing needs of both members of the dyad. A disruption in the temporal synchrony of infant

FIG. 1. A brain-damaged pigtail newborn being held by its mother. The infant's face and body are oriented away from mother. Unlike a normal infant, this unresponsive neonate is not actively grasping its mother; and mother fails to orient her body toward her.

and maternal behavior patterns may also affect the infant's survival. A striking example of the adverse effects of infant–mother dyssynchrony occurred several years ago in our laboratory. A multiparous bonnet macaque developed a prolapsed uterus during the birth of one of her infants. As a result of this event, extreme physical debilitation and fatigue left the mother initially unable to respond to her newborn infant. The infant was then removed and maintained with human care until it reached 25 days of age. At this point the infant, quite strong and healthy, was returned to its mother who eagerly retrieved it to her ventrum. Despite the fact that upon palpation this mother showed evidence of continued lactation, the infant, while still clinging to her ventrum, starved to death three days later. The infant no longer possessed the neonatal reflexes which enable the newborn to attain the nipple immediately, and lacked the learning experience which supplants the decaying reflexive patterns during the first several weeks of life in the normal infant (Mowbray & Cadell, 1962). In addition, the mother was incapable of providing the extra compensation needed to correct the deficit in the infantile nursing patterns. Our hand-reared infant could not survive the disruption in behavioral coordination with its mother that resulted from the unusual way in which it spent the first several weeks of life. Although previous studies (Rosenblum & Youngstein, 1974) have indicated a range of compensatory potential in both the infant's and the mother's response repertoire, the range of such potential has definite limits.

BEHAVIORAL RESPONSES TO DEPRIVED ENVIRONMENTS

In light of the complex social environment within which most primate species live, it is perhaps not surprising that infant monkeys, reared in the complete absence of the opportunity to interact with mother and others, display a range of disordered patterns of behavioral development. Thus, a series of classic studies carried out in the Wisconsin Primate Laboratory over a period of many years indicated that rhesus monkey infants reared from birth to at least the first six or nine months of age in complete social isolation manifest diverse forms of behavioral disturbance, including autisms of various types, withdrawal from relatively mild forms of social and physical stimulation, and unusually high levels of aggressive behavior (reviewed in Sackett, 1968).

Although recent evidence suggests that the effects of isolation rearing may vary depending upon the species (Sackett, Holm, Ruppenthal, & Fahnenbruch, 1976), infants reared in this manner are profoundly disturbed. Attempts to substitute peer contact, which under normal circumstances becomes an important source of stimulation during the first year, result in infants that are less permanently and profoundly disordered, but still retarded in their social development. The so-called "together–together" animals (i.e., infant rhesus reared from birth in the absence of the biological mother, but in the continued presence of one or more peers of the same age) manifest socially inhibiting prolongation of sustained clinging patterns between rearing partners (Chamove, Rosenblum, & Harlow, 1973). The intense clinging normally would have been directed toward the mother and partly through her encouragement would have gradually diminished over time. However, under the together–together rearing conditions, each infant clings vigorously to the other, neither assisting nor pushing the other in making excursions into the outer world; as a consequence the infantile clinging pattern remains at very high levels into the second half-year of life. This pattern of sustained mutual clinging apparently serves to inhibit the development of other patterns of social and nonsocial behavior such as play and environmental exploration.

Nonetheless this research on restricted rearing reflects several basic features of the infant's efforts to establish and maintain a degree of affective equilibrium under various circumstances. As Berkson (1968) has pointed out, the compensatory efforts seen in altered rearing conditions primarily involve the active elements of the infant's behavioral repertoire at the time the conpensatory demand is made. Thus, an infant placed into a restricted environment during the first month of life develops strong clasping patterns toward itself or, if possible, toward peers. This type of compensatory effort may be unusually intensified and prolonged during development for three reasons. First, the compensatory actions may only partially fulfill the infant's emotional needs. Second, if the behaviors toward a particular compensatory target (whether self or other) compete with or exclude its direction toward more suitable objects, then behavioral retardation becomes increasingly severe. Third, we suggest that if the demand quality of the environment is extreme or if the infant is required to meet a given level of demand with insufficient time or opportunity (cf. emergence trauma, Scott, 1971) to organize its behavioral efforts toward compensation, more severe debilitation will occur.

The infant can, however, attempt to make some adjustment to unusual rearing conditions when given a more gradual and supportive opportunity. Squirrel monkey infants reared alone with their mothers, thus lacking the opportunity to engage in peer interactions, primarily those of social play, show essentially normal decrements in filial contact with mother as they grow older (see Figure 2). Hence, unlike the motherless together–together animals, infantile clinging to mothers under relatively deprived social conditions follows a relatively normal developmental path. However, these single-dyad infants, lacking peer-contact and play opportunities, show appreciably higher levels of other forms of contact with their mothers as they mature, as compared to levels observed in normal group-reared infants. Thus the infant's effort to compensate for the lack of a complete social network results in an intensification and prolongation of close contacts with mother.

When infants are removed from the biological mother at birth and raised in partial isolation on artificial mother-surrogates but offered relatively brief and frequent opportunities to interact freely with age mates, adequate social compensation is achieved and apparently normal infant development can result. In an early study (Rosenblum, 1961), infant rhesus were reared with cloth-covered surrogates in open cages within the colony room where opportunities to see and hear other animals were present but contact was prevented. These infants

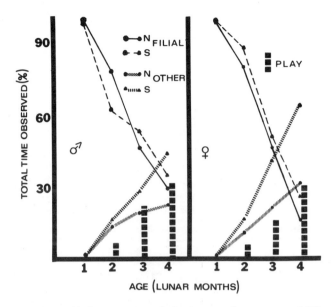

FIG. 2. A comparison of infant contact and play in normal-group-reared (N) and single-dyad-reared (S) squirrel monkeys. The primary form of physical contact during the first three months, *filial*, involves ventral–dorsal contact between infant and mother. *Other* involves all other forms of dyadic contact. Social peer *play* is graphed only for th group-reared subjects.

were placed together as groups of four (two males and two females), 20 minutes each day from the first week of life onward, in a complex, toy-filled playroom. Infants reared in this manner, despite the limited opportunity to interact with peers, developed an essentially normal social pattern. Social play as well as homo- and heterosexual dominance and reproductive behaviors developed normally. As adults these infants showed reproductive capabilities and apparently normal maternal behavior.

Of course, under the complex and demanding circumstances of the natural environment, a primate infant deprived for even a relatively short time of the diverse forms of care and support provided by the biological mother could never survive. However, these various studies of uncommon rearing circumstances show that when placed within a carefully controlled and modified physical environment, and offered regular opportunities to interact with other members of their species which do not overwhelm them (i.e., appropriate peers, or adoptive adults), such infants are subsequently capable of at least normal social and reproductive behavior.

BEHAVIORAL RESPONSE TO SEPARATION

A major separation experience, potentially involved in a hospital stay for a human mother or her infant, or a parallel laboratory manipulation for their nonhuman-primate counterparts, is a relatively uncommon, but often calamitous event. Investigators from various disciplines studying both human and nonhuman primates have stressed that at a certain developmental level the distress seen upon separation is the direct result of the absence of a specific individual, i.e., the attachment figure (e.g., Spitz, 1946; Rosenblum & Kaufman, 1968). Indeed, the apparent focus of separation distress upon the absence of a specific individual is one criterion often used in determining the presence of a prior attachment (e.g., Ainsworth, 1972).

In a recent review of the nonhuman-primate literature on separation, Mineka and Suomi (1978) have pointed out that although all species which have been investigated show at least a biphasic reaction to separation, there is tremendous variability in the form of the total response. Whereas all nonhuman primates studied to date show what has been termed a "protest reaction" upon separation from mother (or peers) characterized by heightened vocalization and locomotion, not all species nor all individuals within a species subsequently show a "depressed" or "despair" phase. Figure 3 presents a summary of the separation literature in this regard. It is striking that despite the tremendous variation in methodology, in approximately 92% of the studies subjects showed increases in locomotion and vocalization immediately upon separation. In addition to the protest behaviors, the only other behavior which reliably changed in the separation was social play. A decrease in social play occurred in 81% of the studies where social partners were available during the separation. The various behaviors used to describe the "despair" phase have included increased postural collapse and self-directed activities as well as decreases in activity level, play, and exploration. As Figure 3 illustrates, the behaviors used to describe "despair" occur less reliably than those for protest. A "detachment phase" (Bowlby, 1969) upon reunion of mother and infant has not been observed to occur in nonhuman primates under most circumstances, although some evidence has emerged (Mitchell, personal communication; Rosenblum, 1971). Several potential sources of this variability in response to separation have been identified in the literature and include such factors as species, number and length of separations, preseparation history, and the nature of the separation environment Mineka & Suomi, 1978). However, the amount of individual variation that remains even when these variables are taken into account is impressive. In fact, some investigators have questioned the utility of using nonhuman-primate mother–infant sep-

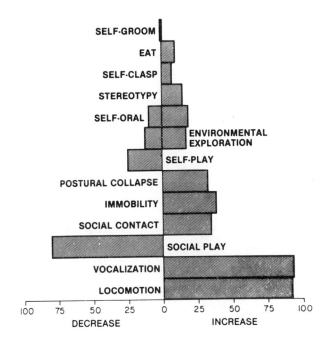

FIG. 3. The percentage of nonhuman-primate separation studies which show for a given behavior a change from preseparation to separation. The graph is based on 23 studies, listed in the bibliography, published from 1962–1978. As might be expected, these studies differed from each other on a wide number of variables: (1) *species;* 13 studies used the rhesus while the other 10 used the pigtail, bonnet, java, patas, and squirrel monkey, (2) *rearing environment;* in 16 studies infants were reared with their mothers, 4 with age-mate peers, 1 with a surrogate, and 2 compared different rearing environments, (3) *separation environment;* in 14 studies infants were separated in a social setting, 7 in social isolation, and 2 had groups with both social and nonsocial separations, and (4) *length of separation;* varied from 2–3 days to several weeks.

For a study to be included in this literature graph three criteria had to be met: (1) separations had to last longer than 2 hours, (2) subjects were under 2 years of age, and (3) subjects had to be observed during both the preseparation and separation period. Changes from preseparation to separation were based on either reported statistical changes or descriptive comments. When there was no mention of a behavior, we assumed that no change occurred with respect to it. If a study had more than one experimental group then each was considered separately. When the subjects were repeatedly separated and reunited, only changes which occurred in the first separation were considered.

aration as a model of depression because of the large variability in response (Lewis, McKinney, Youngs, & Kramer, 1976).

Undoubtedly, many questions concerning the manner in which an infant will respond to maternal loss could be answered in a large study which systematically manipulated the previously mentioned variables. Unfortunately, given the current cost and limited numbers of available nonhuman primates, it is unikely that such a large parametric study will be undertaken. However, the difficulty in understanding the range of response to the loss of attachment figures may involve a conceptual bias as well as a deficit in data. The problem in current conceptualization lies in viewing the forms of behavior seen during the separation in terms of a single unfolding process triggered by the loss of the attachment figure. On both logical and empirical grounds, we suggest that there is a need to expand our conceptualization on the determinants of separation distress.

The Unitary-Process View of Separation

An underlying assumption in many theories which attempt to explain the nature of the infant's separation response is that the initial and subsequent responses seen are tied together as a unitary process. The infant, upon losing its mother, is seen as embarking on basically a predetermined journey in which the route has been chartered by either evolution or some homeostatic mechanism, with only minor characteristics of the trajectory effected by variables such as the separation environment or prior experience.

Although the explanatory perspectives developed in Bowlby's ethological, Kaufman's conservation–withdrawal, and Solomon and Corbitt's opponent-process theories deal with different dimensions of the separation phenomena, they are all in essence, unitary, ballistic models. Bowlby has explained the patterns of protest, despair, and detachment as "phases of a single process and . . . only when they are treated as such is their true significance grasped" (1973, p. 27). To the degree that separation responses reflect a unitary process, one would expect positive correlations in the intensity of expression between each phase of the separation response. Infants who protest the most vigorously upon separation should become the most depressed and subsequently the most detached and the slowest to recover. This would seem to be the most reasonable expectation if each one of these three phases is a successive adaptation in dealing with the loss of the attachment figure.

The conservation–withdrawal interpretation of the separation response (Kaufman, 1977; Kaufman & Rosenblum, 1967) views the infant's behavior in terms of a succession of presumptively "adaptive responses." The initial agitated reaction of the separated infant is presumably aimed at regaining its mother. However, after a certain length of time, continued engagement in the agitated patterns threatens exhaustion. In order to conserve energy and prevent complete exhaustion, the infant becomes inactive and assumes a hunched-over or "collapsed" posture. It is contended that the conservation–withdrawal process involved in the collapsed posture enables the infant to survive by preventing fatigue and decreasing visibility to predators. In a similar vein to Bowlby's position, one would predict from the conservation–withdrawal model that the infant who protests the most vigorously will be in greatest need of conservation. Only those infants who have put their resources in danger by engaging in vigorous protest will subsequently need to conserve them.

The opponent-process theory of acquired motivation hypothesizes that the response to separation is similar in mechanics to the process of giving up an addiction (Solomon & Corbitt, 1974). In this view, many affective states are opposed in the central nervous system by other ones of opposite value. The function of these opponent-processes is to bring the organism back into a state of emotional neutrality. A nonseparated infant would be in what is termed State A (no distress, pleasure). Upon separation, the B State is gradually activated and is strengthened by repeated use. Unfortunately, the somewhat broad and abstract nature of this theory means that the behavioral features of the B process, the manner in which a separated infant regains emotional neutrality, and the meaning of "emotional neutrality" are not entirely clear. In Hoffman's (1974) analysis of inprinting in ducks, the initial distress vocalization recorded upon separation is viewed as the B process. However, Mineka and Suomi (1978) have suggested from separation studies with peer-reared monkeys that the despair state is the B state. While the identification of A and B processes is a critical problem for opponent-process theory (e.g., Rajecki, Lamb, & Obmascher, 1978) they are nonetheless tied together as a unitary function. The behavior seen during separtion, whether protest or despair (or perhaps both), is intended to bring the infant back into its preseparation state of emotional equilibrium which has been disrupted by the abrupt removal of the attachment figure.

Although the theories of Bowlby, Kaufman, and Solomon and Corbitt deal with different mechanisms, they view the infant's behavior during separation in terms of one unified process. Strong correlations between all phases of the separation with each other are predicted from these unitary models.

SOME CONCEPTUAL AND EMPIRICAL PROBLEMS WITH UNITARY MODELS

We have now come to question on both empirical and conceptual grounds whether the response to separation is a unitary, continuous process. The most basic conceptual problem concerns the difficulty in indentifying behavorial adaptations which have been brought about through natural selection. Both Bowlby and Kaufman have couched their explanations in terms of evolutionary adaptations to loss. While it is easy to see how protest behavior may have evolved, the subsequent despair or conservation–withdrawal response is not as obvious. A separated infant may have a better chance to survive if it makes vigorous efforts by vocalizing and moving to regain contact with the lost mother. Indeed, following a review of pertinent human and nonhuman literature regarding initial responses to separation, Cairns (1977) has recently suggested that "the distress induced by separation may indeed be a homology across related mammalian forms" (p. 15). However, if an infant does not relocate its mother or get adopted within a day or so, what are the chances for survival? In the natural environment of most nonhuman primates, the danger from predators and the need to forage for food and water would make the chances of survival of a young infant in the absence of the mother and social group quite minimal. Thus, it is unlikely that a separated infant which did not regain contact with its mother or get adopted within two or three days would survive long enough to reproduce. If the separated infant did not subsequently reproduce, it is difficult to see how any particular pattern of response to prolonged separation could be selected for in an evolutionary sense. For example, van Lawick-Godall (1971), in describing chimpanzees of the Gombe National Park, mentions that even a four-year-old (Merlin) died after losing his mother when he was not adopted. Even in separation studies in the laboratory, infants sometimes die both during the separation period (Rosenblum, 1971) and even following reunion with mother (Spencer-Booth & Hinde, 1971). We therefore have serious doubts whether the depressed posture or other altered patterns of response of the separated infant can be interpreted as having evolved as a relatively closed genetic program (Mayr, 1961) in the same sense as may have occurred for protest behavior. Indeed it is possible that the determinants of the depressive reaction (however broadly or narrowly we define it) may be an entirely different set of variables from those involved in protest.

There is empirical evidence which indicates that the reaction seen immediately upon separation may be part of a different process than that operating during the ensuing separation. Weinraub and Lewis (1977) have compared the behavior of two-year-old nursery school children during their mother's departure and subsequent absence. They found that only passive distress during the mother's departure was found to correlate with separation distress. In view of their findings, Weinraub and Lewis (1977) argue that the response during departure and separation may be determined by a different set of variables. They suggest that response during departure will be heavily influenced by the manner in which the mother leaves and the child's cognitive understanding of the departure event. The response during the separation period itself will be more strongly affected by a wider set of variables such as gender, social class, and so on.

Review of the nonhuman-primate separation literature provides similar indications of a discontinuity between the initial ("protest") and subsequent ("despair") patterns of response to separation. For example, removal of an infant to a novel environment in conjunction with a significant separation seems to result in relatively heightened levels of protest, but minimal indications of subsequent depression (Hinde & McGinnis, 1977; Chappell & Meier, 1975). However, repeated four-day peer separations are reported to result in a diminution of initial protest and an increase in some measures of despair (Mineka & Suomi, 1978). In contrast to predictions from unitary-process models, it is experimentally possible to independently alter either protest or despair. The relative absence of correlation between departure-protest and the behavior of the separation state suggest that they are not connected as a single process.

PROBLEMS OF ADAPTATION DURING SEPARATION

Although obvious, it is important to reiterate that both human- and nonhuman-primate mothers provide their infants with many things ranging from physical necessities such as food and warmth, to a psychologically and physically secure base from which the infant may explore and to which it may return. In addition, as Cairns has pointed out, "stimuli distinctive to the mother may also serve a more general role in the support of response patterns of the young in which she was not directly involved" (Cairns, 1972, p. 45). An infant which has been separated from its mother may be responding not only to the psychological loss but also to the disruption in the entire social network. Following Cairns further, in a later paper he suggests, "The problem has been that primate investigators focused initially on what the young animal was deprived of but gave little attention to what he was exposed to and the conditions where he was placed" (Cairns, 1977, p. 7).

A clear example of some problems of regulation and adaptation during separation is found in the rat, which does not form an attachment in the typical usage of the term (Mendoza, Coe, Smotherman, Kaplan, & Levine, in press). Hofer (1978) has found that in rats mothers play a significant role in regulating the physiological status of their offspring. Two-week-old rat pups that are separated from their mothers among other things experience a 40% decrease in cardiac rate. It was subsequently shown, however, that cardiac rate was tied to the amount of milk received by the infants. By feeding the separated infants as frequently and with equivalent amounts of food as nonseparated ones, heart-rates remained at preseparation levels. This relationship between cardiac rate and milk consumption is explained in part by the fact that each day a two-week-old rat consumes about 30–40% of its body weight in milk. The variations in heart-rate are geared to accommodate changes in the need to absorb and transport the nutrients contained in the milk.

> This unexpected regulatory phenomenon of the early social relationship in the rat was revealed by the use of mother–infant separation, followed by analytic studies based on a concept of the relationship as a regulator, rather than on the concept of attachment and social-bond formation. To have inferred that the low heart rates were a reflection of an emotional state precipitated by disruption of the pheromonal bond would have been wrong and could have obscured other processes from view. (Hofer, 1978, p. 145.)

In the primate order, the disruption of a social bond is clearly an important component to the separation reaction. However, as both Cairns and Hofer have suggested, the mother is both a direct and indirect source of regulation for the infant. The separated infant is faced with the problem of how to reestablish, within itself and/or through its interactions with others, the range of regulation which the mother has provided. Isolation-rearing studies have provided one example of how an infant will attempt to establish an equilibrium within itself. Stereotyped motor acts are frequently observed in both human and nonhuman primates, raised under various levels of deprivation. Berkson (1968) has suggested that stereotyped behaviors are infantile patterns which have been redirected as a consequence of deprivation rearing. When infants are placed into social isolation at birth, at a point when sucking and clasping reflexes are strong, high levels of self-sucking and self-clasping almost always develop (Berkson, 1968). If no other alternative objects are available, the oral and physical contact a normally reared infant has with its mother is directed on to the self in the form of self-sucking and self-clasping. However, infants placed into isolation at six months, when sucking and clasping reflexes have declined in strength, do not develop stereotyped patterns which incorporate these two behaviors. While the development of some stereotyped behaviors such as self-clasping appears to depend on the age at which the infant was placed into isolation, others such as self-rocking depend more on particular qualities of the environment. Thus, Mason and Berkson (1975) have found that self-rocking could be eliminated in isolation-reared infants if they were raised on a mobile mother-surrogate as opposed to a stationary one. Stereotyped body-rocking and the self-stimulation it provides appears to develop in the absence of appropriate amounts of vestibular stimulation which the mother normally provides the infant in carrying it around.

The nature of infant–environment transactions is critical to the understanding of separation behavior. A separated infant not only loses a social bond but is also forced thereby to engage in an atered set of transactions with the social and nonsocial environment. While transactional models have been proposed in other areas of developmental research (e.g., Sameroff & Chandler, 1975), many experiments in primate behavior operate under the unitary-process or main-effect model. As a result the nature of the environment and its demand qualities for the separated infant receive at best only limited attention. For example, it is not uncommon in primate studies of social separation to place the subject into isolation during the separation (e.g., Suomi, Harlow, & Domek, 1970; Suomi, Seaman, Lewis, Delzio, & McKinney, 1978; Young, Suomi, Harlow, & McKinney, 1973). In these experiments one cannot distinguish between the response to the loss of a social partner versus those patterns which emerge as a result of social isolation.

IMMEDIATE AND LONG-TERM RESPONSE TO SEPARATION

In a recent study conducted in our laboratory, we attempted to analyze the pattern of the infants' response to separation using two temporal perspectives. First, infants were observed every 90 minutes during the first 24 hours following the removal of mother. Second, observations were carried out during a fairly long, six-week separation.

Subjects were six pigtail macaque infants *(macaca nemestrina)* which had been housed as three pairs of mother–infant dyads for two months prior to separation (see Figure 4). At the time of separation, in each pair of dyads one infant was 4 months old and the other 7 months old. In two of the pairs, the infants were females while the third pair consisted of a male and a female. Subjects were housed in pens measuring 11 × 8 × 4 ft with three shelves spaning the width of the pen. One window consisting of one-way-vision glass measuring 24 × 42 in. was located in the front of the pen. Food and water were continuously available. Separations were carried out by simultaneous removal of both mothers from each group, leaving the infants behind in the familiar setting. The mothers were housed together in another part of the laboratory during the separation period.

FIG. 4. Pigtail mother–infant dyads prior to separation.

In order to trace the transition from the initial protest reaction to the possible onset of depression, infants were observed during the first hour following separation and then for 5 minutes at 90-minute intervals for the next 24 hours. The method of observations and taxonomy of behavior are described in Table 1. For nighttime observations the lights in the subjects' pen were turned off as usual (12-hour light–dark cycle). However, the lights of an adjacent pen were left on at night. This allowed for a low-level illumination which permitted sufficient light for observations and yet did not overtly disturb the animals. Subjects had been habituated to this modification in the lighting prior to separation.

It is germane to point out that prior work by Reite and his coworkers using an implantable biotelemetry system has identified a number of important physiological changes in separated pigtail infants during the first 24 hours (Reite & Short, 1978; Reite, Kaufman, Pauley, & Stynes, 1974; Reite, Short, Kaufman, Stynes, & Pauley, 1978; Seiler, Cullen, Zimmerman, & Reite, 1979). Initially, heart rate and body temperature elevate as the infant vigorously moves about and vocalizes. However, during the first night of separation and also to some degree in subsequent nights, there is a significant drop in both body temperature and heart rate. In addition, there are more frequent sleep disturbances on the first night of separation in the form of alterations in sleep latency, number of arousals, REM latency, and number of REM periods. In general, only the amount of REM remained consistently altered on subsequent separation nights. Physiological correlates of depression remain suggestive but not entirely clear. In one study (Reite et al., 1974), two infants who experienced a severe drop in body temperature on the first night of separation showed complete posture collapse the following morning. However, in another study, Reite and Short (1978) found that behavioral measures of depression (in this case decreased play and locomotion) on day 3 and 4 of separation correlated only with sleep disturbances and not with body temperature and heart rate.

Although these changes in certain physiological measures have

TABLE 1. BEHAVIORAL TAXONOMY

Posture	In an attempt to provide a more subtle picture of the infant's affective state, posture was divided into two parts: (1) forward flexion of the *back* in which the shoulders were lowered to the height of knees; (2) forward flexion of the *neck* in which either the chin rested on the chest or the back of the head was parallel to the floor. In the data discussed in this chapter only measures of back flexion are used because *neck* did not occur with sufficient frequency.
Location change	A measure of activity based on any change in pen location from the preceding time sample.
Limbs	Curling inward of one or both feet without any objects being grasped.
Self-oral	Any part of infant's body in contact with mouth.
Self-clasp	Active clasping of body with either hands or feet.
Self-groom	Careful picking through and brushing of subject's own fur or scratching of self.
Eat/drink	Presence of either active eating or drinking
Coo vocalizations	A prolonged sound, low in intensity and pitch, observed during periods of disturbance.
Peer contact	Any form of physical contact.

Behaviors were sampled once every 10 seconds for 20 minutes a day, 4 days a week.

been recorded during the first 24 hours of separation, comparable behavioral measures in equivalent detail do not exist. The current study was conducted in the belief that behavioral observations may be crucial in providing important clues concerning the psychological significance of any concomitant physiological change.

The simultaneous removal of the infants' mother in our double-dyad situation produced behavioral response patterns in the infants similar to those found in previous studies (e.g., Rosenblum & Kaufman, 1968). Immediately upon removal of the mothers, all infants began vigorous cooing and rapid movement about the pen. Somewhat surprisingly, the 7-month-old infants tended to coo-vocalize with greater frequency than the 4-month-olds ($\bar{x} = 16.9$ vs. $\bar{x} = 7.4$). While most of the movement consisted of rapid pacing back and forth across the pen, two of the 4-month-old infants made several attempts to achieve contact with their older partners. In one instance, for example, the older was hanging from the ceiling and the younger from its position on the top shelf repeatedly attempted to grasp the other's foot. On other occasions, the young infants moved to the older and attempted to press their body against the other. This effort to establish contact with others immediately following loss of the primary attachment figure has been demonstrated repeatedly in separation studies in our laboratory involving bonnet macaques (Rosenblum & Kaufman, 1968) in which rather complete adoption of separated infants by group members is a frequent occurrence. Similar, rapid adoptions have also been seen in other species including squirrel monkeys and langurs (Dolhinow, 1978). The speed with which a separated monkey infant will attempt to be fostered was also quite dramatically illustrated by Mason and Kenney (1974). In their study rhesus infants were separated from their mothers and placed with a friendly dog. Virtually all infants made contact with their dog within 2 hours and were subsequently adopted by the dogs. These contact-seeking adoption data suggest that even in the period immediately following maternal loss, i.e., the protest phase, infants were attempting to respond to the particular qualities of the separation environment and to effect some adaptation to it by moving toward other social objects.

Following separation from mother in our 6 pigtail infants, the initial response of coo-vocalizations and vigorous locomotion rapidly diminished, so that by the afternoon of the first day, i.e., 3–5 hours after separation, there were significant decreases in both vocalizations (Friedman, $\chi r^2 = 27.5$, $df = 3$, $p < .01$) and locomotion (Friedman, $\chi r^2 = 12.2$, $df = 3$, $p < .01$) (see Figure 5). It should be pointed out that in other separation settings, such as those in which an infant is placed in an unfamiliar environment, high levels of protest behavior (vocaliza-

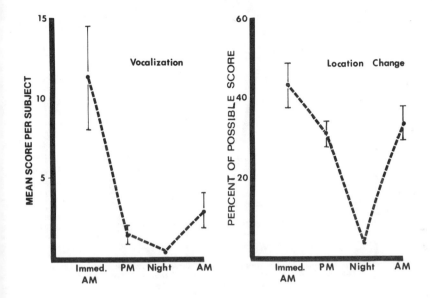

FIG. 5. Protest behaviors durng the first 24 hours of separation.

tion and locomotion) last much longer than the first few hours, sometimes continuing for several days (Hinde & McGinnis, 1977).

The protest behavior observed in our separated pigtail subjects was, however, effectively terminated when the lights were turned off. Although there was some brief cooing immediately after the lights went out, for the remainder of the first night of separation the infants virtually never vocalized. In addition, although the infants were not in complete darkness, locomotion dropped dramatically at night. Coincident with the decrease in these protest behaviors was a significant increase in posture-drop (hunching over), one of the primary measures of the despair phase (Friedman, $\chi r^2 = 7.47$, $df = 3$, $p < .05$) (see Figure 6). Thus, in the perspectives of both previous studies, these pigtail infants were markedly depressed on the first night, i.e., 12–15 hours after separation. This nominally depressive state thus appeared appreciably earlier than previously suggested (see above).

However, although these infants appeared to be depressed on the first night, it is important to question whether this is the most appropriate interpretation of these observations. Indeed, although these subjects showed an increase in postural changes which reached their highest values in days 3–7 of separation (in keeping with prior reports), after their first night, none of these subjects was subsequently observed in comparably sustained periods of posture collapse during

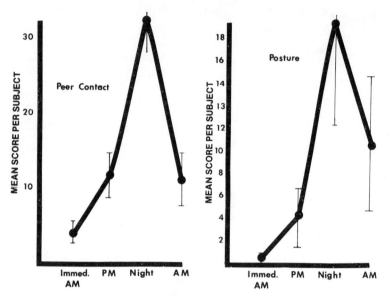

FIG. 6. Peer contact and posture during the first 24 hours of separation.

FIG. 7. Separated pigtail infants, older infant on the top shelf, younger on the middle. The back of the younger infant is flexed forward, although not sufficiently to be scored in our scoring system.

the daylight hours of observations. (see Figure 7). Whether we view the first night's pattern and its disappearance as initial evidence of conservation, lack of stimulus support or control, emergence of a "B" state, the efforts of the infants to regulate total stimulus input while at rest or an effort at thermoregulatory control (as the Reite data might suggest), these diurnal and day-1 to day-2 shifts in behavior are not readily interpretable within current formulations of the reaction to separation.

We had questioned earlier theories which attempted to explain the behavior of the separated infant exclusively in terms of a unified mechanism, triggered initially by the disruption of an attachment. While we cannot clearly point out the needed additions to the unified models, the lacunae appear to be in the consideration of the degree to which the behavior of the infant represents an effort to cope with the separation environment. In keeping with the transactional view, we suggest that behavioral change during separation may reflect the infant's coping attempts as much as the response to maternal loss.

One further perspective on the infants' response in this regard may be gained by looking at the distribution of salient behavior over the course of the entire separation. In order to facilitate an understanding of the relative distribution of given behaviors over time and their temporal patterning with respect to each other, we have used the peak or maximal separation value as the base from which to compute changes in their relative frequencies over the course of the entire separation, since the absolute frequency of each behavior differs markedly.

Within the larger context of the six-week separation, as anticipated, vocalization reached its highest level immediately upon separation and then quickly declined (see Figure 8). Locomotion peaked immediately, dropped during days 3–7, but then gradually rose again to preseparation levels by the fourth week. Coincident with the drop in activity on days 3–7, posture scores reached their highest level and gradually declined to minimal levels by the third and fourth week (see Figure 9). The combined oral measure of eat/drink (Figure 9) was quite interesting. These behaviors were at their highest relative level during the second week of separation. Considering that the levels of eat/drink were appreciably lower from the third week on while health was maintained, it seems likely that the earlier separation scores for this behavior are not easily interpreted as a direct function of nutritional needs, but rather were meeting other psychological needs as well. Whereas peer contact fluctuated somewhat over the course of the entire separation, the importance of the presence of a familiar peer during these separations should not be understated (see Figure 9). In addition

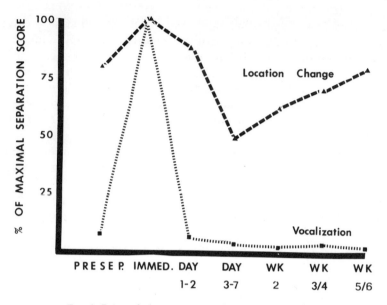

Fig. 8. Protest behaviors across the entire separation.

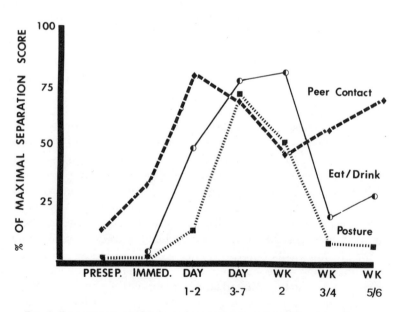

Fig. 9. Peer contact, eat/drink, and posture across the entire separation.

to the social initiatives noted above, in one of the dyads, we observed on several occasions that as the younger infant dropped into a hunched posture, the older infant came over and tried to initiate a play bout (see Figure 10). Although it may be premature to suggest that the postural changes have communicative significance, these peer interactions undoubtedly played a significant role in influencing the course of the separation reaction.

Three behaviors, self-oral, curling of the hind limbs (limbs), and self-groom, appear to be the most overt and frequent efforts by the infant at self-regulation (see Figure 11). While the three behaviors might all be considered as self-regulatory efforts, they appear to serve different functions. The self-oral part of the preseparation repertoire and with interindividual variations in frequency, remains basically

FIG. 10. Separated pigtail infants. Older infant initiating a play bout with the younger one

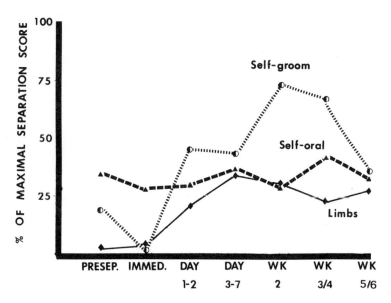

FIG. 11. Self-groom, self-oral, and limbs across the entire separation.

unchanged across the separation. In contrast, the inward curling of the hind limbs was never detected during the preseparation period but emerged relatively rapidly during the separation and stayed at fairly constant levels thereafter. The precise function of limb curling is unclear but like postural changes in the trunk (posture drop) may be related to thermoregulation. Finally, self-groom slowly increased to peak levels during the second week of separation and then only gradually declined. While grooming is a form of stimulation when normally done by the mother (or others), it also functions to soothe and cleanse the infant as well. In self-grooming both the focus of motor-engagement and the receipt of stimulation may form part of the infant's benefits from this activity. The gradual increase and decrease of self-grooming during the separation suggests subtle, perhaps changing motivation for its instigation in the separated infant.

Response to Mother across a Separation

We have emphasized that over the course of a separation the infant must restructure its behavior in order to meet the new demands of the environment. However, even the eventual return of most behaviors to their preseparation level does not necessarily reflect the dissolution of the infant's bond to the mother. Assessment of the infant's response to the mother compared to the other familiar female with whom it had lived across the separation was made in this study by periodically returning the mothers to the home pen in a wire-mesh cage for 30 minutes (see Rosenblum, 1978, for other applications of this technique). In the current mother-return manipulation, evidence of the association of the protest pattern with the departure aspect of separation was in evidence. When tested on days 2, 6, 10, and 14 of separation, infants who were no longer vocalizing or locomoting actively showed exceptionally high vocal levels to the returned mother; on the first of these trials, the familiar female also evoked high levels of vocalization, but these decreased rapidly on subsequent trials. Removal of the mother from the pen after the first four returns immediately resulted in renewed and prolonged bouts of vocalizing, locomotion, and eat/drink. This departure-protest did not generally appear after removal of the familiar female, but some "protest" patterns did emerge intermittently. Paradoxically, during the first return trial, on day 2 of separation, although high levels of protest were evoked by the partially returned but incompletely available mother, infants were reluctant to approach the mother, although they moved to the familiar female quite readily (all infants were previously habituated to the empty mesh cage in which the adult females were returned). Within several return trials however, infants were moving quickly to the returned mother, and protest behavior on her return diminished although renewed, but increasingly brief protest was produced by her departure for several subsequent trials.

TRIPHASIC ADJUSTMENT TO SEPARATION

The results of these current and past studies on separation have led us to hypothesize that the three phases of the separation reaction which have been observed in nonhuman primates (i.e., "protest," "despair," and "recovery") have a number of distinguishing characteristics. It must be stressed that the speculations presented below reflect both existing data and, at times, somewhat precarious inductive leaps, whose theoretical adequacy cannot be determined until a number of new, carefully focused studies are carried out. As is true of all "phase" or "stage" hypotheses, we must be wary of allowing this heuristic device to result in viewing the predominant behaviors of a phase as mutually exclusive. Depending upon the temporal window through which behavior is observed, any or all components of each phase may be seen during other periods. The phase descriptors reflect the relative preponderance of behavior types in terms of the probability of viewing each one in a given time period.

In keeping with these constraints, we suggest the following.

Protest

(a) This pattern, largely involving specific vocalizing behaviors and heightened locomotion, reflects a *closed genetic pogram* (Mayr, 1961) subject to the laws of natural selection.

(b) The pattern is triggered by the sudden event of maternal departure or the initial recognition of the loss of visual or physical contact with mother, rather than the sustained state of separation. The protest pattern emerges and declines quite rapidly in most circumstances, and its active presence in the behavioral repertoire is limited to the period in which reestablishment of contact has the maximum probability.

(c) The overt expression of protest behaviors may itself help to reduce distress; external feedback and/or internal reinforcement seem unnecessary for the relatively short-term mainenance of these behaviors. Thus, in laboratory environments, in which total space is extremely limited, as in a small cage, or in which visual access to all areas is accessible from any point, "searching" could be executed with little effort; despite this fact infants in these settings nonetheless engage in very high levels of undirected locomotion. In short, the behavior lacks the organized qualities of a "search." Indeed the agitated infant appears to incorporate little information from the environment in determining the form of its movement during this phase. However, despite the relatively high stimulus thresholds of the infant during the protest phase, expression of protest may also serve to increase the infant's knowledge of salient environmental features such as sources of food and social support which may facilitate successful adaptation to its new circumstances.

(d) As with other more common unconditioned responses, the protest UCR may be suppressed by other events (e.g., a hostile social group that threatens or attacks the protesting infant). These protest behaviors may also be extinguished (albeit with difficulty) through repeated unsuccessful elicitation.

Despair

(a) The diverse patterns of behavior used somewhat interchangeably to define this stage include, among others, decreases in activity and social play and increases in self-orality and posture collapse.

(b) These patterns, while appearing intermittently from the onset of separation, reach peak levels during the days 2–8 of separation and decline subsequently.

(c) Inasmuch as survival of young infants separated for several days is doubtful in the natural environment, it is unlikely that the behavioral response patterns observed in these phases are the product of natural selection to prolonged separation. Instead they reflect the idiosyncratic employment of a group of behaviors which serve to promote affective equilibrium in a variety of circumstances and were evolved to meet these other basic needs.

(d) The combination and preponderance of elements in this phase, unlike those of protest, show marked individual differences and may reflect the confluence of genotypic variations and individual reinforcement histories. Infants of rejecting or neglectful mothers ("insecurely attached") may have more frequent experience in the expression of these behaviors followed by reestablishment of contact with the mother as a part of their preseparation experience and may as a consequence express them more fully during separation.

Recovery

(a) The elements of this phase, including the achievement of affective stability and the concomitant reemergence of age-normal levels of activity, body maintenance, exploration, and play, reflect the relative success of the infant at returning to the path of psychological, social, and physical development along which it was progressing when the separation intervened.

(b) These behaviors are inextricably tied to the social and physical environment within which the infant has been and continues to function; as such they are quite idiosyncratic in their form, structure, and temporal patternings.

(c) Reflections of the recovery process can be seen relatively early in the separation period, even when other phase-related behaviors predominate, but recovery does not generally emerge strongly until 7–10 days have elapsed.

(d) Recovery, or at least the rapidity with which it emerges, may depend upon the successful deployment of behaviors of protest and despair. This rather circular statement implies that repeated experience in passing through the protest–despair–recovery cycle may enhance the "effective" or coping ability of the infant and result in a diminution of the more malleable despair phase with relatively more rapid recovery following subsequent separation.

SOME TRIPHASIC MODELS

In an attempt to describe the interplay of these phases more graphically, and to suggest some possible outcomes of future research in this area, we present the following descriptive models based on the materials presented above.

In Figure 12, Part A illustrates the course of behavior following separation in a normally, "securely" attached young monkey infant. Behaviors involved in protest are assumed to have a low frequency of occurrence prior to separation. In this type of infant, despair-related behaviors are assumed to occur with somewhat greater frequency before separation. The behaviors asociated with the recovery phase are those which form the major part of the age-appropriate behaviors in such infants prior to separation.

It will be noted that these models assume that phases are designated in terms of the predominant, not the exclusive appearance of behaviors of each type. Thus in Figure 12, Part B describes the pattern we suggest might be seen in infants less securely attached. Although

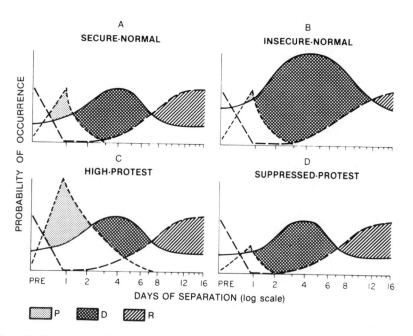

FIG. 12. The hypothesized course of protest, P, despair, D, and recovery, R, under various conditions: (A) secure–normal, (B) Insecure–normal, (C) high-protest, (D) suppressed-protest.

the preseparation history of insecurely attached infants may involve the more frequent evocation of protest, this pattern appears at the same time as with "secure normals." However, despair behavior begins earlier and lasts longer for the "insecure normals" as opposed to the secure normals.

Parts C and D similarly reflect the likely course of infant response in the period following separation under conditions which either enhance or suppress the expression of protest behavior. When the infant is placed in a strange environment as an accompaniment to separation, the protest patterns are heightened and subsequent patterns of despair lessened. Conversely when protest behaviors are actively suppressed, which might occur when the separated infant is in the presence of a hostile social group, the despair phase emerges more rapidly.

Figure 13, Parts A, B, and C, reflect hypothesized changes in the separation response when the infant has had a previous history of repeated separations. It is suggested that repeated brief separations (i.e., less than 1 day) should result in a relative enhancement of the

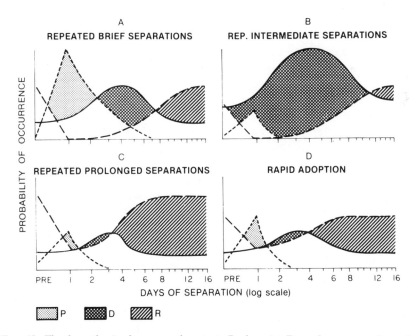

FIG. 13. The hypothesized course of protest, P, despair, D, and recovery, R, under various conditions: (A) repeated brief separation, (B) repeated intermediate separation, D, rapid adoption.

protest pattern with a concomitant submersion of the despair patterns. This particular manipulation has not yet appeared in the literature. However, repeated separations intermediate in length (3–8 days) have been done and result in the earlier appearance of the despair patterns and the parallel submersion of the protest patterns. Finally, repeated prolonged separations, in which the infant has repeated opportunities to "work through" the separation experiences (also a manipulation not yet carried out) is hypothesized to be characterized by minimal protest and despair behaviors and the rapid emergence of recovery patterns.

Part D of Figure 13 illustrates the patterns generally observed when a young infant is rapidly adopted by a foster caretaker following separation from the primary attachment figure. In this instance, although some short-lived protest appears, minimal evidence of despair patterns emerges, and evidence of recovey emerges quite rapidly. The reader will note the similarity between those models proposed for repeated separation experiences and those separations which occur under conditions which influence the expression of the unconditioned protest behaviors.

Summary

In this chapter, we have argued that explanations of the separation response in terms of a unitary process are inadequate. The available evidence suggests that the protest, despair, and recovery patterns are not connected together as phases of a single process. Protest behaviors are geared toward reestablishing contact with mother or finding a potential caretaker and have evolved as a product of natural selection. However, separation from mother, in addition to psychological loss, also involves a disruption in a system of behavioral and physiological regulation. We emphasized the infant's initiating role in response to the natural mother, and its efforts to compensate for the inadequacies of environments devoid of mother or peers. The separated infant undertakes similar efforts, not merely to respond to the loss it has experienced but also to respond to the ongoing features and events of the environment it now faces.

References

Ainsworth, M.D.S. Attachment and dependency: A comparison. In J. L. Gewirtz (Ed.), *Attachment and dependency.* Washington, D.C.: V.H. Winston & Sons, 1972, pp. 97–137.

Berkson, G. Development of abnormal stereotyped behaviors. *Developmental Psychobiology*, 1968, *1* (2) 118–132.

Bowlby, J. *Attachment and loss.* Vol 1. *Attachment.* New York: Basic Books, 1969.

Bowlby, J. *Separation: Anxiety and anger.* New York: Basic Books, 1973.

Cairns, R.B. Attachment and dependency: A synthesis. In J.L. Gewirtz (Ed.), *Attachment and dependency.* Washington, D.C.: V.H. Winston & Sons, 1972, pp. 29–80.

Cairns, R.B. Beyond social attachment: The dynamics of interactional development. In J. Alloway, P. Pliner, & L. Krames (Eds.), *Attachment behavior.* New York: Plenum, 1977, pp. 1–24.

Chamove, A.S., Rosenblum, L.A., & Harlow, H.F. Monkeys *(Macaca mulatta)* raised only with peers. A pilot study. *Animal Behavior,* 1973, *21,* 316–325.

Chappell, P.F., & Meier, G.W. Modification of response to separation in the infant rhesus macaque through manipulation of the environment. *Biological Psychiatry,* 1975, *10* (6), 643–657.

Dolhinow, P. Commentary on Rajecki *et al.:* Infantile attachment theory. *The Behavioral and Brain Sciences,* 1978, *3,* 443–444.

Eisenberg, J.F., Muckinhirn, N.A., & Rudran, R. The relation between ecology and social structure in primates. *Science,* 1972, *176,* 863–874.

Gartlan, J.S. Structure and function in primate society. *Folia Primatologica,* 1968, *8,* 89–120.

Hinde, R.A., & McGinnis, L. Some factors influencing the effects of temporary mother–infant separation: Some experiments with rhesus monkeys. *Psychological Medicine,* 1977, 197–212.

Hofer, M.A. Hidden regulatory processes in early social relationships. In P.P.G. Bateson & P.H. Klopfer (Eds.), *Perspectives in ethology* (Vol. 3). New York: Plenum, 1978, pp. 135–166.

Hoffman, H.S. Fear-mediated processes in the context of imprinting. In M. Lewis & L.A. Rosenblum (Eds.), *The origins of behavior.* Vol. 2. *The origins of fear.* New York: Wiley, 1974, pp. 25–48.

Jones, B.C., & Clark, D.L. Mother–infant separation in squirrel monkeys living in a group. *Developmental Psychobiology,* 1973, *6* (3), 259–269.

Kaplan, J. The effects of separation and reunion on the behavior of the mother and infant squirrel monkey. *Developmental Psychobiology,*, 1970, *3* (1), 43–52.

Kaufman, I.C. Developmental considerations of anxiety and depression: Psychobiological studies in monkeys. In T. Shapiro (Ed.), *Psychoanalysis and contemporary science.* New York: International Universities Press, 1977, pp. 317–363.

Kaufman, I.C., & Rosenblum, L.A. The reaction to separation in infant monkeys: Anaclitic depression and conservation-withdrawal. *Psychosomatic Medicine,* 1967, *29,* 649–675.

Kaufman, I.C., & Stynes, A. Depression can be induced in a bonnet macaque infant. *Psychosomatic Medicine,* 1978, *40* (1), 71–75.

Lewis, J.K., McKinney, W.T., Youngs, L.D., & Kraemer, G.W. Mother–infant separation in rhesus monkeys as a model of human depression. *Archives of General Psychiatry,* 1976, *33,* 699–705.

Lewis, M., & Rosenblum, L. (Eds.). *Genesis of Behavior.* Vol. 2. *The Child and Its Family.* New York: Plenum, 1979.

Mason, W.A., & Berkson, G. Effects of maternal mobility on the development of rocking and other behaviors in rhesus monkeys: A study with artificial mothers. *Developmental Psychobiology,* 1975, *8*(3), 197–211.

Mason, W.A., & Kenney, M.D. Redirection of filial attachments in rhesus monkeys: Dogs as mother surrogates. *Science,* 1974, *183,* 1209–1211.

Mayr, E. Cause and effect in biology. *Science,* 1961, *134,* 1501–1506.

Mendoza, S.P., Coe, C.L., Smotherman, W.P., Kaplan, J., & Levine, S. Functional consequences of attachment: A comparison of two species. In R.W. Bell & W.P. Smotherman (Eds.), *Maternal influences and early behavior*. Spectrum Press, in press.

Meyer, J.S., Novak, M.A., Bowman, R.E., & Harlow, H.F. Behavioral and hormonal effects of attachment object separation in surrogate-peer-reared and mother-reared infant rhesus monkeys. *Developmental Psychobiology*, 1975, *8* (5), 425–435.

Mineka, S., & Suomi, S.J. Social separation in monkeys. *Psychological Bulletin*, 1978, *85* (6), 1376–1400.

Mowbray, J.B., & Cadell, T.E. Early behavior patterns in rhesus monkeys. *Journal of Comparative and Physiological Psychology*, 1962, *55*, 350–357.

Preston, D.G., Baker, R.P., & Seay, B. Mother–infant separation in the patas monkey. *Developmental Psychology*, 1970, *3* (3), 298–306.

Rajecki, D.W., Lamb, M.E., & Obmascher, P. Towards a general theory of infantile attachment: A comparative review of aspects of social bond. *The Behavioral and Brain Sciences*, 1978, *3*, 17–464.

Reite, M., & Short, R. Nocturnal sleep in separated monkey infants. *Archives of General Psychiatry*, 1978, *35*, 1247–1253.

Reite, M., Kaufman, I.C., Pauley, J.D., & Stynes, A.J. Depression in infant monkeys: Physiological correlates. *Psychosomatic Medicine*, 1974, *36* (4), 363–367.

Reite, M., Seiler, C., & Short, R. Loss of your mother is more than loss of a mother. *American Journal of Psychiatry*, 1978, *135* (3), 370–371.

Reite, M., Short, R., Kaufman, I.C., Stynes, A.J., & Pauley, J.D. Heart rate and body temperature in separated monkey infants. *Biological Psychiatry*, 1978, *13* (1), 91–105.

Reite, M., Short, R., & Seiler, C. Physiological correlates of maternal separation in surrogate-reared infants: A study in altered attachment bonds. *Developmental Psychobiology*, 178, *11* (5), 427–435.

Rosenblum, L.A. *The development of social behavior in the rhesus monkey*. Unpublished Ph.D. thesis, University of Wisconsin, 1961.

Rosenblum, L.A. Infant attachment in monkeys. In H.R. Schaffer (Ed.), *The origins of human social relations*. New York: Academic Press, 1971, pp. 85–108.

Rosenblum, L.A. Affective maturation and the mother–infant relationship. In M. Lewis & L.A. Rosenblum (Eds.), *The development of affect*. New York: Plenum, 1978, 275–292.

Rosenblum, L.A., & Kaufman, I.C. Variations in infant development and response to maternal loss in monkeys. *American Journal of Orthopsychiatry*, 1968, *38* (3), 418–426.

Rosenblum, L.A., & Youngstein, K.P. Developmental changes in compensatory dyadic responses in mother and infant monkeys. In M. Lewis & L.A. Rosenblum (Eds.), *The origins of behavior*, Vol. 1. *The effect of the infant on its caregiver*. New York: Wiley, 1974, pp. 141–162.

Rutter, M. *Maternal deprivation reassessed*. Harmondsworth, England: Penguin Books, 1972.

Sackett, G.P. Abnormal behavior in laboratory-reared rhesus monkeys. In M.W. Fox (Ed.), *Abnormal behavior in animals*. Philadelphia: W.B. Saunders, 1968, pp. 293–331.

Sackett, G.P., Holm, R.A., Ruppenthal, G.C., & Fahnenbruch, C.E. The effect of total social isolation rearing on the behavior of rhesus and pigtail macaques. In N.E. Walsch & W. Greenough (Eds.), *Environments as therapy for brain dysfunction*. New York: Plenum, 1976, pp. 115–131.

Sameroff, A.J., & Chandler, M.J. Reproductive risk and the continuum of caretaking casualty. In F.D. Horowitz, M. Hetherington, S. Scarr-Salapatek, & G. Siegel (Eds.), *Review of child deveopment research*. Chicago: University of Chicago Press,1975.

Schlottman, R., & Seay, B. Mother-infant separation in the java monkey *(macaca irus)*. *Journal of Comparative and Physiological Psychology*, 1972, *79* (2), 334–340.

Scott, J.P. Attachment and separation in dog and man: Theoretical propositions. In H.R. Schaffer (Ed.) *The origins of human social relations*. New York: Academic Press, 1971, pp. 227–243.

Seay, B., & Harlow, H.F. Maternal separation in the rhesus monkey. *The Journal of Nervous and Mental Disease*, 1965, 140(6), 434, 441.

Seay, B., Hansen, E., & Harlow, H.F. Mother–infant separation in monkeys *Journal of Child Psychology and Psychiatry*, 1962, 3, 123–132.

Seiler, C., Cullen, J.S., Zimmerman, J., & Reite, M. Cardiac arrhythmias in infant pigtail monkeys following maternal separation. *Psychophysiology*, 1979, 16 (2), 130–135.

Singh, M. Mother–infant separation in rhesus monkey living in natural environment. *Primates*, 1975, 16 (4), 471–476.

Singh, S.D. Effects of infant–infant separation of young monkeys in a free-ranging natural environment. *Primates*, 1977, 18 (1), 205–214.

Solomon, R.L., & Corbitt, J. An opponent-process theory of motivation: I. Temporal dynamics of affect. *Psychological Review*, 1974, 81 (2), 119–145.

Spencer-Booth, Y., & Hinde, R.A. Effects of 6 days separation from mother on 18- to 32-week-old rhesus monkys. *Animal Behavior*, 1971, 19, 174–191.

Spitz, R.A. Anaclitic depression. *Psychoanalytic Study of the Child*, 1946, 2, 313–342.

Struhsaker, T.T., & Leland, L. Socioecology of five sympathic monkey species in the Kibale Forest, Uganda. In J.S. Rosenblatt, R.A. Hinde, C. Beer, M. Busnel (Eds.), *Advances in the study of behavior*. New York: Academic Press, 1979, pp. 159–228.

Suomi, S.J., Harlow, H.F. & Domek, C.J. Effects of repetitive infant–infant separation of young monkeys. *Journal of Abnormal Psychology*, 1970, 76 (2), 161–172.

Suomi, S.J., Collins, M.L., & Harlow, H.F. Effects of permanent separation from mother on infant monkeys. *Developmental Psychology*, 1973, 9 (3), pp. 376–384.

Suomi, S.J., Collins, M.L., Harlow, H.F., & Ruppenthal, G.C. Effects of maternal and peer separations on young monkeys. *Journal of Child Psychology and Psychiatry*, 1976, 17, 101–112.

Suomi S.J., Seaman, S.F., Lewis, J.K., Delizio, R.D., & McKinney, W.T. Effects of imipramine treatment on separation-induced social disorders in rhesus monkeys. *Archives of General Psychiatry*, 1978, 35, 321–325.

van Lawick-Goodall, J. Some aspects of mother–infant relationships in a group of wild chimpanzees. In H.R. Schaffer (Ed.), *The origins of human social relations*. New York: Academic Press, 1971, pp. 115–123.

Weinraub, M., & Lewis, M. The determinants of children responses to separation. *Monographs of the Society for Research in Child Development*, 1977, 42 (4, Serial No. 172).

Yarrow, L.J. Maternal deprivation: Toward an empirical and conceptual re-evaluation. *Psychological Bulletin*, 1961, 58, 459–490.

Young, L.D., Suomi, S.J., Harlow, H.F., & McKinney, W.T. Early stress and later response to separation in rhesus monkeys. *American Journal of Psychiatry*, 1973, 130 (4), 400–405.

11

The Transmission of Incompetence
The Offspring of Mentally Ill Women

ARNOLD J. SAMEROFF AND RONALD SEIFER

The ways in which parents influence the development of their children are many, some quite obvious and direct, others quite subtle and elusive. Socialization and educational practices produce the diversity of human cultural differences in fairly straightforward ways. However, the transmission of the individual differences which characterize mental illness is far from clear.

Schizophrenia, of all the mental disorders, has generated the most interest. Whereas most other disorders can be viewed as an extreme variation of some normal psychological characteristic, schizophrenia has been striking in its seeming abnormality, its alienation from typical modes of functioning. As research in this disorder multiplied, clear familial influences were found with apparent hereditary transmission (Kallmann, 1938). Large numbers of the offspring of schizophrenic parents were found to have mental disturbances.

While the rate of schizophrenia in the general population is about 1%, about 10% of children with a single schizophrenic parent become schizophrenic (Hanson, Gottesman, & Meehl, 1977). However, schizophrenia is not the only risk to which the offspring of schizophrenic parents are vulnerable, although the degree of risk is uncertain. For

---

ARNOLD J. SAMEROFF AND RONALD SEIFER • Institute for the Study of Developmental Disabilities, University of Illinois, Chicago Circle, Chicago, Illinois 60680.

example, Higgins (1976) found only 25% of these children to be free of psychiatric disturbance, Reisby (1967) found 84% to have no mental-illness, and Kallmann (1938) found over 40% to be either borderline or definitely schizophrenic with no mention of neurotic disorders.

The early studies of the transmission of schizophrenia used adult psychiatric diagnoses as their outcome measure. In contrast, studies of the outcomes of children of parents with nonpsychotic mental disturb-ances have centered on symptomatology during childhood and did not address the issue of ultimate psychiatric outcome (Cooper, Leach, Storer, & Tonge, 1977; Buck & Laughton, 1959). More recently, research on the offspring of schizophrenics has come to deal directly with the developmental progress of these high-risk children (see Garmezy, 1974, for a summary).

Attentional processes have been a major focus of research with diagnosed schizophrenics (Garmezy, 1978). A number of studies have now examined attention in high-risk samples from infancy through adolescence (Cohler, Grunebaum, Weiss, Gamer, & Gallant, 1977; Erlenmeyer-Kimling & Cornblatt, 1978; Mednick & Schulsinger, 1968). Similarly, general cognitive ability, e.g., intelligence, has been a focus of both adult and high-risk studies (Cohler et al., 1977; Rieder, Broman, & Rosenthal, 1977; Worland, Lander, & Hesselbrock, 1979; Mednick & Schulsinger, 1968). Another major target of high-risk studies has been the reported adjustment of children in school by teachers (Wein-traub, Neale, & Leibert, 1975), peers (Rolf, 1972), and in the home by parents (Landau, Harth, Othnay, & Scharfhertz, 1972). In addition, obstetric complications (McNeil & Kaij, 1978), physiologic responsivity (Janes, Hesselbrock, & Stern, 1978; Itil, Hsu, Saletu, & Mednick, 1974), and clinical status of the children (Worland et al., 1979) have been assessed.

In general the children of mentally ill parents show greater social, behavioral, and psychiatric disturbance than the children of normal parents, but not decreased general cognitive ability. However, these differences have not been demonstrated to be clinically significant, and appear to be less severe than disturbances exhibited by children identified as having psychological and behavioral problems. Worland et al. (1979) found that children of schizophrenics and manic-depres-sives demonstrated more general psychopathology on a battery of clinical tests, and produced more primitive Rorschach responses, compared with children of physically ill parents and children of parents with no physical or mental illness. However, no differences were found on intelligence tests, "good" Rorschach responses, or Rorschach pro-ductivity. Rolf (Rolf, 1972; Rolf & Garmezy, 1974) has found that children identified by the school system as having problems showed more disturbance on peer and teacher ratings than did children of schizophrenic or neurotic mothers. However, all of these groups differed to some extent from classmates on peer ratings. The children of schizophrenics were, in general, more disturbed than children of neurotics. Weintraub et al. (1975) found little difference between the children of schizophrenic and depressed mothers, but they did find substantial differences between these children and controls. They report differences on the Devereux teacher rating scales of classroom disturbance, impatience, disrespect, comprehension, inattention–withdrawal, creative initiative, and need for teacher closeness.

Since the adult manifestation of schizophrenia includes disorders of attention, association, ability to comprehend reality, and thought processes, one might expect to find precursors of these disorders in high-risk children. For example, Worland et al.'s (1979) finding of more primitive Rorschach responses, and Garmezy's (1978) summary of findings of decreased attention are symptomatic of, though probably qualitatively different from, well-developed forms of schizophrenia.

In sum, studies of the transmission of mental disorder have historically focused on familial incidence of schizophrenia. Only recently have developmental studies begun to identify early forms of nonpsychotic behavioral disturbance in the young offspring of schizophrenic parents. At this point, however, a more elaborate discussion of the source of those higher rates of mental disturbance is necessary. While it is clear that there is a familial risk for schizophrenia, it is not clear whether that risk is a biological one or a social one.

HEREDITY STUDIES OF SCHIZOPHRENIA

The biological approach to familial transmission received significant support from the early studies of Kallmann (1938, 1946). Work by supporters of the notion that stressful psychological experience contributes heavily to schizophrenia's emergence (e.g., Lidz, 1973; Wynne & Singer, 1963) has lent support to the social view.

Kallmann's original surveys assessing familial concordance for schizophrenia, and particularly the high rates reported for identical twins, have undergone considerable reassessment. Rosenthal (1962, 1970) pointed out that Kallmann's studies, based as they were on a resident state-hospital population, included primarily chronic schizophrenics. Furthermore, Gottesman and Shields (1966) and Rosenthal have raised questions about Kallmann's broad diagnostic criteria. When Gottesman and Shields established careful diagnostic procedures in a study of consecutive hospital admissions, they were able to show impressive but far lower concordance rates for schizophrenia among identical twins than did Kallmann.

While twin studies gave comfort to the genetic camp, they were not free of sniping from the environmentalists. Jackson (1960) led an early assault on the value of the twin studies, charging, among other things, that in virtually all such studies the twins involved share the same psychological environment for a significant portion of their lives. The finding that monozygotic twins have higher concordance rates than dizygotic twins was attributed to a more similar environment for the identical twins, who, for example, are more often mistaken for each other than fraternal twins. Further, dizygotic twins have consistently shown higher concordance than full sibs, although these concordance rates should be identical under a genetic hypothesis (Kringlen, 1976).

In recent years, several studies have used an ingenious technique to separate constitutional from environmental etiological factors. By studying offspring of schizophrenics adopted by nonschizophrenics, and therefore reared in a nonschizophrenic environment, one could determine which was the dominant influence—having a schizophrenic heredity or a schizophrenic environment.

In the first of the adoptee studies, Heston (1966) compared the psychological status of 47 adoptees whose biological mothers were schizophrenic to 50 adoptees whose biological mothers had no history of psychiatric disorder. All had been separated from their mothers within two weeks of birth. Heston found five schizophrenics among the adoptees, all of whom had schizophrenic mothers. He also found a disproportionate number of psychopaths in the group with schizophrenic biological mothers.

A more elaborate series of adoptee studies has been done by Rosenthal, Kety, Wender and their associates (Rosenthal, Wender, Kety, & Welner, 1971; Kety, Rosenthal, Wender, Schulsinger, & Jacobson, 1975; Wender, Rosenthal, Kety, Schulsinger, & Welner, 1974). In one study, Rosenthal et al. (1971) identified 69 index cases who were given up for adoption at an early age, who had at least one biological parent diagnosed as schizophrenic, and who were raised by adoptive parents with no obvious mental disorder. They also identified 67 matched control subjects, adoptees whose biological and adoptive parents manifested no obvious mental disorder. They found that the only subject hospitalized for schizophrenia in the entire sample of 136 was an index case; two others were diagnosed as schizophrenic and both were index cases; 10 out of 17 who were seen as borderline schizophrenics were index cases; and 9 out of 14 who were described as schizoid or borderline paranoids were index cases.

These findings by Heston and the Rosenthal–Kety–Wender group seem to lend strong support to the idea that genetic factors contribute significantly to the development of schizophrenia. Yet, even these studies fail to control for certain potentially relevant factors, and their findings only reach statistical significance on occasion.

The genetic position in regard to schizophrenia fits well with a current return to nativism to explain other kinds of deviant development. Attributing low IQs to racial differences (Jensen, 1973) and hyperactivity in schoolchildren to constitutional factors (Wender, 1971) also fits the etiological model that is used to explain schizophrenia's emergence. All that remains in any of these disorders is to trace the biological connections between the genetic or constitutional factors and the actual resultant dysfunction.

It is at this point that our problems really begin. As Jackson (1960) so neatly pointed out in his critique of genetic hypotheses:

> Until the ill-defined concept of "personality" can be broken down into enduring traits that are shown to have a genetic basis, it is surely fruitless to look for a genetic mechanism behind the symptomatic disorder of schizophrenia.

Jackson identifies two central problems in his statement. The first is to define schizophrenia in terms of some enduring, or at least clearly identifiable, personality traits, and the second is then to trace the connections between these traits and some constitutional variable.

ETIOLOGICAL MODELS

Five possible models need to be considered for understanding the development of a schizophrenic disorder, two with specific constitutional factors, two with specific environmental factors, and the last with neither specific constitutional nor specific environmental factors (see Table 1).

The single-factor views posit a condition that produces schizophrenia (or some distortion of it, e.g., spectrum disorders) in all individuals having that condition. In the constitutional form (Model 1) one view would be that one, or several, genes produce schizophrenia. In the environmental form (Model 2), certain schizophrenogenic social situations, for example, living with specific types of impossible conflicts, would produce schizophrenia in any child.

There is insufficient evidence today to support these single-factor views and most investigators have moved to some multifactor position. In two of the multifactor positions (Models 3 and 4) schizophrenia can

TABLE 1.   ETIOLOGICAL MODELS OF SCHIZOPHRENIA

		Component causes	
		Constitution	Environment
A.	*Single-factor views*		
	Model 1. Constitutional:	Schizophrenia	Irrelevant
	Model 2. Environmental:	Irrelevant	Schizophrenogenic
B.	*Multifactor views*		
	Model 3. Constitutional:	Specific predisposition	Nonspecific stress
	Model 4. Environmental:	Nonspecific vulnerability	Special disposition
	Model 5. Transactional:	Nonspecific vulnerability	Nonspecific stress

still be clearly specified as resulting from some specific constitutional or environmental cause, but that cause is more predisposing than disposing. In other words, either defects in a child's nature or nurture may produce schizophrenia but either requires fertile soil for its development.

On the constitutional side (Model 3), the defects may reside in a genetic diathesis or in a specific area of brain damage (Rosenthal, 1970). Individuals with these defects need not become schizophrenic, if they grow up in an environment with low stress levels. It is only when their resistance drops below a certain threshold that they "catch" schizophrenia. On the environmental side (Model 4) the interactional position would argue that the germ resides in the caretaking environment either in the form of deviant communication patterns or family interactions (Lidz, 1973; Wynne & Singer, 1963). Not every child subject to these environments would become schizophrenic. A heightened susceptibility through some constitutional vulnerability would be required. Such general vulnerabilities might consist of physical deviancies resulting from delivery complications, temperamental variations in attentional distributions, or perceptual hypersensitivities.

The difference between the first four models and the fifth view (Model 5) is that each of the former posits a specific cause for a schizophrenic outcome. The transactional view does not argue for any *specific* developmental precursor, either constitutional or environmental. Rather, schizophrenia is treated as one of a full range of potential "normal" outcomes of development (cf. Kringlen, 1976). The use of the word normal here may seem out of place, but from a developmental point of view, normality resides in the ability of the organism to adapt to its environment. To the extent that a schizophrenic outcome is the result of the transactions of a specific child coping with his own specific environment, then an outcome that permits functional survival within that environment can be considered both adaptive and normal. This view can be seen in the cross-cultural writings of Erikson (1963) and intracultural speculations of Laing (1964). It has also been elaborated elsewhere in a more general form (Sameroff, 1975).

The five models reduce to two foci for research investigation. Whether one conceives of a constitutional factor as producing some form of schizophrenia in every carrier or merely predisposing the carrier toward schizophrenia, one must be able to identify some unique difference between such individuals and their peers. Similarly whether one considers an environmental factor as producing schizophrenia in any individual raised in that environment or merely acting as a predisposing agent, one must be able to identify some unique characteristic of that environment.

ROCHESTER LONGITUDINAL STUDIES

In 1968, we (Sameroff & Zax, 1973a) initiated a study applying the high-risk approach developed by Mednick and Schulsinger (1970) in Denmark to the age group used earlier by Fish and her associates (Fish, Shapiro, Halpern, & Wile, 1965). Our study differed in several important respects from the previous studies.

Where Fish and her colleagues provided a clinical picture of the development from birth of a group of children, some of whom were born to schizophrenic women, the absence of control groups made it impossible to determine if the outcomes were the result of the mother's schizophrenia alone. Since a diagnosis of schizophrenia is usually associated with chronic and severe mental disturbance, high anxiety, social incompetency, and a variety of demographic variables, and since all these factors may have an effect on the newborn condition and later development of a child, they must be adequately controlled in any study devoted to understanding the singular effect of a schizophrenic heritage.

While Mednick and Schulsinger did include a nonschizophrenic control group in their study, they assessed the offspring of these women only after they had reached adolescence. This strategy enabled them to follow these children through early adulthood, making an actual diagnosis of schizophrenia a realizable outcome measure during the investigators' lifetimes. In contrast, we felt that the ideal point in time to search for constitutional differences would be at birth, when the infant had not yet been subject to the social consequences of life with a schizophrenic mother. Accordingly, we began our study with pregnant schizophrenic women and planned to follow their offspring through the first four years of life.

In addition, we felt that it was necessary to use additional control groups. As Mednick and McNeil (1968) pointed out in their original justification of the high-risk strategy for studying schizophrenia, many of the characteristics which have been attributed to schizophrenia have really been the *consequences* of the diagnosis rather than of the disorder itself. These consequences include the effects of labeling and institutionalization. Similarly, we felt that a schizophrenic mother might influence her offspring in many ways that might be a consequence of the chronicity or severity of her mental illness *per se*, rather than something specifically related to her diagnosis. In short, our strategy was to include control populations that would allow us to assess the effects of separate aspects of psychiatric diagnosis, chronicity of disturbance, severity of disturbance, and social competency, as well as the general characteristics of social class, race, educational level, and family constellation.

For our study 337 pregnant women were recruited over a four-year period. Before delivery the women underwent a clinical interview. From the interview and case records each woman was given a diagnosis, a chronicity rating, a severity of illness rating, and a social competence score.

The chronicity of psychological disturbance was defined by the frequency of psychiatric contact plus the need for, and length of, institutionalization. The least chronic category involved subjects who had had no previous psychiatric contact and were diagnosed as having no mental illness on the basis of the interview. The most chronic category included cases which had in excess of four psychiatric contacts or more than one year of institutionalization.

The severity of mental illness score was based on an evaluation of emotional state, current functioning at home, at work, and the general level of social adjustment. Our social competence score, developed by Barbara Fox (1975), was based on six measures similar to those used in the Zigler and Phillips (1962) scale.

For our analysis of the effects of a schizophrenic mother on the development of her child, four groups were formed from the total sample based on the psychiatric diagnosis: (1) a schizophrenic group, with 29 mothers, (2) a neurotic–depressive group, with 57 mothers, (3) a personality-disordered group, with 41 mothers, and (4) a no-mental-illness group, with 80 mothers. The no-mental ilness control group was matched to the other groups on the basis of age, race, socioeconomic status, number of children, education, and sex of child.

When the four groups were compared on mental-health criteria other than diagnosis, it was found that the schizophrenic women as a group were more chronically ill, more severe in their current symptomatology, and more socially incompetent.

As a control for chronicity all the women in our sample were divided into four groups based on their psychiatric histories. Similarly four groups were formed based on the severity of psychopathology rating. Any differences between the schizophrenic and other diagnostic groups could then be evaluated in terms of either chronicity or severity of mental illness independent of diagnosis, in order to determine which factor was making the greatest contribution to the outcome measures.

Outcome Measures

The assessments in the longitudinal study were made during pregnancy, at birth, and then at 4, 12, 30, and 48 months of age both in the home and in the laboratory. At each age assessment variables were divided into four sets, each focused on domains of behavior related to potential mental-illness outcomes. These are (1) perceptual–motor functioning, (2) cognitive functioning, (3) affective functioning, and (4) social functioning.

Perceptual–Motor Functioning

Perceptual–motor functioning was tested at birth with the Brazelton (1973) Neonatal Behavioral Assessment Scales. The newborns were also monitored for autonomic responsivity in a sensory stimulation task. At 4, 12, and 30 months of age they were tested with the Bayley Infant Development Scales which included scores for psychomotor performance. Physical health was assessed from birth records and also from a medical history form filled out by the mothers when the children wre 30 and 48 months of age.

Cognitive Functioning

Cognitive performance at birth was measured by tests of alertness and habituation on the Brazelton scales. At 4, 12, and 30 months the mental-development index of the Bayley scales was used and at 48 months the Verbal Scales of the Wechsler Preschool and Primary Scale of Intelligence (WPPSI). The Peabody Picture Vocabulary Test (PPVT) was also given at both 30 and 48 months of age.

Affective Functioning

The child's emotional responsivity was assessed at birth from irritability and associated scores on the Brazelton scale. At 4 months, mood, threshold to stimulation, and intensity of response were scored from a maternal questionnaire. Emotionality was recorded during observations of mother–infant interactions in the home at 4 and 12 months of age. During the psychometric testing in the laboratory, the examiner scored measures of emotional responsivity during the 4-, 12-, 30-, and 48-month laboratory sessions. At 30 and 48 months of age additional information was obtained from the Rochester Adaptive Behavior Inventory (RABI), a detailed maternal interview designed by Fredric Jones (1977).

Social Functioning

The social behavior of a newborn is hard to define but we judged alertness and consolability measured by the Brazelton Scales to be its primary constituents. At 4 and 12 months, the mother–infant social interactions were observed and recorded in the home setting. At 4, 12, 30, and 48 months, ratings of the child's social responsiveness were made by the examiner during the psychometric evaluation. At the later testings, the child's reactions to separation from his or her mother were scored. A social history and the results of the RABI provided us with additional sources of information on the child's social behavior.

DEVELOPMENTAL FINDINGS

Pregnancy and Birth Complications

Mednick and his coworkers (Mednick & Schulsinger, 1970) originally reported that of the 20 children who had become disturbed among the 200 offspring of schizophrenic women in their longitudinal study many had suffered "severe perinatal distress." This report stimulated us, as well as others, to focus on delivery complications as a source of the diathesis leading to schizophrenia.

When the four diagnostic groups in our study were compared on a broad spectrum of pregnancy and delivery conditions only two variables differentiated the schizophrenic group from the other groups. First, during pregnancy the schizophrenic women were more likely to be taking chronic medication than the other three groups. Second, schizophrenic offspring had lower birth weights than no-mental-illness controls. This paucity of findings in our study related to the effects of schizophrenia on childbirth is reflected in revised findings, showing fewer differences, by Mednick and his coworkers (Mednick, Mura, Schulsinger, & Mednick, 1971), a similar study by Hanson, Gottesman, and Heston (1976), the Swedish investigations of McNeil and Kaij (1973), and the conclusions of a thorough review by McNeil and Kaij (1978). McNeil and Kaij did find in their sample a tendency for process-schizophrenic women to have lower birth weights.

When we changed our focus from comparisons between the diagnostic groups to comparisons based on severity and chronicity of mental disorder, we found that, irrespective of diagnosis, the lowest-birth-weight babies were born to women who had the severest or the most chronic mental illnesses. Thus, it would appear that the birth-weight difference can be better attributed to the effects of a severe and lengthy mental disturbance rather than schizophrenia *per se.*

Condition of the Infant

The previous work of Fish and Mednick had produced several suggestions for directions in which to seek differences in the behavior of our newborn infants. Fish postulated that early inactivity and poor postural–motor developments were important risk factors, while Mednick argued that autonomic hyperactivity was a key ingredient in risk for schizophrenia.

To test Mednick's hypothesis we measured changes in cardiac and respiratory rate to a variety of stimuli. No differences in newborn reactivity were found using either the diagnostic, the severity, or the chronicity comparison groups. Our findings are in accord with those of Schachter and his coworkers (Schachter, Kerr, Lachin, & Faer, 1975) in Pittsburgh who were also unable to find differences in cardiac reactivity in a comparison between offspring of schizophrenic, low-certainty schizophrenic, and nonschizophrenic women. If hyperreactivity is a characteristic of high-risk offspring of schizophrenic women, it is either at such a low base rate that it is statistically undetectable during the newborn period or it emerges later in the course of the child's development.

The study of the newborn's activity, tonus, and reflex behavior as suggested by Fish was a far more fruitful approach. Our newborn examination utilized the Brazelton Scales which include interactive variables such as alertness, cuddliness, and consolability, motoric variables such as activity and tonus, and state-control variables such as irritability, arousal, and self-quieting behavior.

The only variables to effectively discriminate the diagnostic groups was a tonicity cluster composed of reflex strength and the tonus and activity scales. The group that did poorest on this cluster was the offspring of neurotic–depressive women. This group of infants was the worst off in most other diagnostic comparisons. Depressed women had infants with lower Apgar scores at one and five minutes, and who required more respiratory resuscitation.

The use of severity and chronicity of mental illness comparisons to help understand differences found between diagnostic groups can be seen in Figure 1. In the case of birth weights, where offspring of schizophrenics were found to weigh significantly less than control offspring, the effect can be seen to be determined by a combination of severity and chronicity factors. In the case of the Apgar test scores, in which the offspring of neurotic–depressives scored lower than both the controls and the personality disorders, the effect can be seen to be a function of severity but not chronicity. And finally in the case of

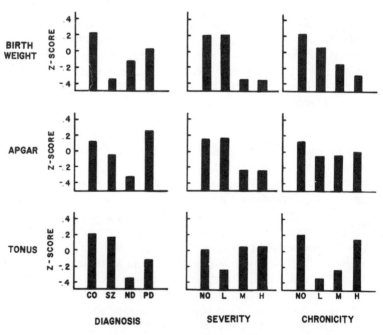

FIG. 1. A comparison of birth weight, Apgar scores, and tonus measures for groups based on psychiatric diagnosis (CO = no mental illness, SZ = schizophrenic, ND = neurotic–depressive, PD = personality disorder), severity of symptoms (NO = no symptoms, L = one symptom, M = moderate symptoms, H = many symptoms), and chronicity of illness (NO = no illness, L = single contact, M = more than one contact, H = hospitalization).

muscle tonus, in which the offspring of the neurotic–depressives were more hypotonic than the control offspring, the effect could not be attributed to either severity or chronicity of mental illness dimensions. These conclusions were further supported in a series of regression analyses comparing the relative influences of diagnosis, severity, and chronicity on these three infant outcome measures.

The offspring of the neurotic–depressive women also suffered more fetal and neonatal deaths than any of the other groups. Of the five infants in the study who died during the perinatal period, four were born to women in the neurotic–depressive group, and one was born to a woman in the no-mental-illness control group. The control mother's prenatal assessment scores were examined, and she was found to have had a prenatal anxiety score comparable to the women in the neurotic–depressive group (see Table 2).

The high infant mortality rate found in our sample of pregnant neurotic–depressives (4 out of 56 or 70 per 1000) and other newborn differences lend some credence to the possible existence of intrauterine biochemical factors in depressed women. Much further work would be necessary to discover whether the mother's depression is causal to the infant's illness, the infant's illness is causal to the mother's depression, even though they are not schizophrenic (Wender *et al.*, 1974).

Moreover, these differences between the depressive and other groups were not explained by the severity or chronicity comparisons. Though the Apgar scores were related to severity of disturbance, the mean score of the depressive group was lower than the mean score for the high-severity group. In contrast to the birth weight differences in the schizophrenic group, the characteristics of the newborn offspring of depressive women appear to be unique to a diagnosis of depression and are not as readily explainable by the severity or chronicity of the mother's mental illness. It is possible that the differences other studies

TABLE 2.   MATERNAL CHARACTERISTICS AND CAUSE OF DEATH FOR DECEASED NEWBORNS

Diagnostic group	Chronicity	Severity	SES	Marital status	Cause of death
Neurotic–depressive	Low	Medium	3	Married	Pneumonia following respiratory distress syndrome
Neurotic–depressive	Low	Medium	3	Separated	Stillborn, intrauterine fetal death after 42 weeks
Neurotic–depressive	Medium	Medium	1	Married	Congenital heart disease from trisomy-18
Neurotic–depressive	High	High	5	Separated	27-week-old premature unable to sustain respiration
Control	None	Low	5	Married	Stillborn, intrauterine fetal death after 36 weeks

have reported in the newborn offspring of schizophrenic women may be a consequence of the higher levels of depression among schizophrenics compared with normals. Our data emphasize the importance of utilizing an adequate range of control groups in such studies.

Adoption and Foster Placement

Another interesting set of data to emerge from our study concerns the issue of adoption and foster placement. Of the infants in the study, six were given up by their mothers during the neonatal period for either adoption or foster placement. An analysis of these six cases is of interest to the interpretation of the studies which have shown higher rates of psychopathology in the adopted offspring of schizophrenic women when compared to the adopted offspring of normal women.

The six infants given up in our study all came from schizophrenic women. No mother in any of the other diagnostic groups gave up a child in the newborn period. Comparison between the characteristics of the 23 schizophrenic mothers who kept their infants and the six mothers who gave up their infants for placement in either adoptive (N = 3) or foster homes (N = 3) are listed in Table 3.

The placement mothers were significantly older and of lower SES than those keeping their children. Neither birth order nor race were reliably different for the two groups. Not unexpectedly, a greater proportion of the placement mothers were either single, separated, or divorced than home-rearing mothers. Comparisons of the Home-Rearing and Placement groups on mental-health measures indicate that the six Placement mothers were more socially incompetent, were judged to have been more anxious and severely disturbed when interviewed in their last month of pregnancy, and had longer histories of emotional disturbance than Home-Rearing mothers.

The prenatal and newborn condition of the infants given up for placement was compared with the condition of the home-reared infants in Table 4. The course of the pregnancy and the condition of the infants was worse for the placement group. Their mothers had significantly more illnesses during pregnancy and the infants had more problems after birth, and the infants significantly differed in birth weight. Not one of the six placement babies was over 2800 grams at birth, while four of the six spent the newborn period in the special-care nursery.

These findings indicate that schizophrenic mothers who gave up their infants for adoption or foster placement were not a random sample of schizophrenic mothers, contradicting at least one basic assumption of adoption studies. Rather, they were a selected sample

Table 3. Social and Mental-Health
Characteristics of Schizophrenic Mothers

	Home-Rearing	Placement
N	23	6
Age***	25.0	33.2
Socioeconomic status**	4.0	5.0
Birth order:		
First born	6(26%)	3(50%)
Late born	17(74%)	3(50%)
Race:		
White	17(74)	4(67)
Nonwhite	6(26%)	2(33%)
Marital status:*		
Married	16(70%)	1(17%)
Single, separated, or		
divorced	7(30%)	5(83%)
Social incompetency*	31.9	36.5
Severity (CAPPS)***	2.9	4.5
Anxiety (CAPPS)***	2.5	4.0
Anxiety (IPAT)	38.4	41.8
Chronicity*		
Hospitalized > 6 months	8(35%)	5(83%)
Hospitalized < 6 months	10(43%)	1(17%)
Not hospitalized	5(22%)	0(0%)

* p < .05   ** p < .01   *** p < .001

of severely and chronically disturbed women who were older and less
likely to be in an intact marriage than those schizophrenic mothers
who chose to rear their infants. In this light, the proportion of their
offspring expected to show emotional disorder, based on a diathesis
model, should be much higher than the proportion of emotionally

Table 4. Newborn Status and Research
Obstetrical Scale (ROS) Scores (High
score indicates more complications)

	Home-reared	Placement
N	23	6
ROS Prenatal score***	1.08	2.66
ROS delivery score	2.47	2.66
ROS infant score***	0.39	2.33
ROS total score***	3.94	7.65
Birth weight***	3317	2394

***p < .001

disturbed offspring from the schizophrenics who rear their own children. Indeed, researchers in the Rosenthal–Kety–Wender group have
made a similar point about their own control sample. They have grown
suspicious that there is a far higher degree of pathology among mothers
giving their children up for adoption than among mothers in general,
even though they are not schizophrenic (Wender et al., 1974).

Not only are the schizophrenic mothers who gave up their infants
for placement not a random sample of schizophrenic mothers, but their
offspring are not a random sample of schizophrenic offspring, contradicting another basic assumption of adoption studies. In our sample,
these infants were more premature and had more physical problems
than the home-reared sample. Wender et al. (1974) previously found
that children who were somehow deviant prior to adoption, such as
weak, difficult, or small, showed higher incidence of later mental
illness, further highlighting the need to document the joint status of
mothers and infants in adoption research. The adopted *infant* of a
schizophrenic biological parent was thought to bring nothing to its
new family other than its schizophrenic genes. Sameroff and Zax
(1973b) suggested that the infant might bring other things along with
him such as a difficult temperament. The adoption data from the
current study, although derived from a small sample, suggest that the
infant may bring with him far more concrete evidence of his deviancy
than his schizophrenic genes. He also may bring an underweight, tiny
body which places extra caretaking demands on his new adoptive
parents. These extra caretaking demands and deviant physical appearance have been demonstrated to affect mother–infant interaction (Field,
1977), and have the potential of beginning a negative chain of transactions which could produce a deviant outcome irrespective of whether
the infant carried schizophrenic genes (Sameroff, 1975).

To summarize our adoption data, this report is a cautionary tale.
From our small sample of six placement babies, one cannot generate
strong conclusions despite the highly significant differences we found.
What can be said is that generalizations from other studies of schizophrenia which use adoptees must also limit their conclusions since
both the mothers and children associated with adoption appear to be
an unusual and special sample.

Cognitive Functioning

At 4, 12, 30, and 48 months of age each child was given a
psychometric evaluation. In Figure 2 the IQ scores at each age have
been converted to Z-scores (mean of 0 and standard deviation of 1) to

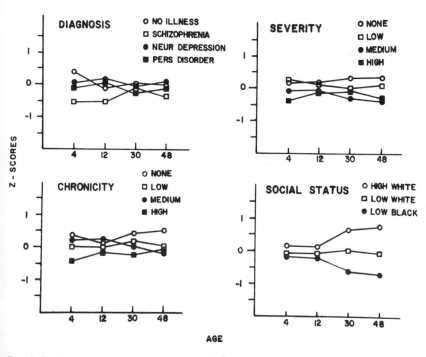

FIG. 2. Intelligence quotients, expressed as Z-scores, for offspring in relation to maternal diagnosis, chronicity of illness, severity of symptoms, and social class. Scores at 4 and 12 months are based on the Bayley Mental Development Index, and at 30 and 48 months on the Peabody Picture Vocabulary Test.

improve visual comparability across age. At 4 and 12, the scores are from the Bayley Mental Development Indices, while at 30 and 48 months they are from the Peabody Picture Vocabulary Test.

Early differences in developmental scores disappear by thirty months of age for the mental illness comparisons of diagnosis, severity, and chronicity of disturbance. These early differences are related to the lower birth weights in the more disturbed groups.

However, when the same data are viewed from the perspective of socioeconomic status completely opposite results appear. There are no differences during the early sensory–motor period but during the third year when language becomes relevant to IQ performance, the effects of social-class differences are enormous, as one would expect.

Social–Emotional Adaptation

At 30 months of age a global rating was obtained for each child from the RABI. The ratings were on a scale ranging from a low score of 1, reflecting a happy child with superior relationships, to a score of 5, reflecting a child with extreme or bizarre behavior and intense adjustment problems.

In Figure 3 one can see the distribution of 30-month global ratings based on either mother's diagnosis, the severity and chronicity of her mental illness, or her socioeconomic status.

In the diagnostic group analysis no group had scores significantly different from the controls. The schizophrenic offspring had higher than average scores but not significantly so. When we examined the severity groups, the effects were much clearer both in the figure and statistically. The more symptomatic the mother's illness, the less adaptive the child. The socioeconomic-status graph is similar. A powerful linear effect is evident, showing that children of lower-class mothers scored as being significantly less competent than higher SES groups.

What we can conclude from the analysis of both cognitive and social–emotional adaptiveness at 30 months of age is that the effects of social milieu appear to match the effects of maternal psychopathology in the social–emotional sphere, and to overpower it in the cognitive sphere.

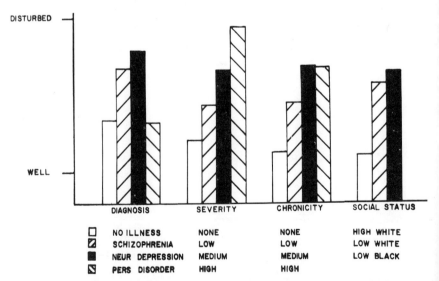

FIG. 3. Mean RABI global ratings (4 years) for diagnosis, severity of illness, chronicity of illness, and social-status groupings.

SUMMARY

The ways in which personality might be passed from generation to generation, though long studied, is still little understood. An examination of the transmission of extreme patterns of behavior, such as found in mental illness, was thought to be a reasonable strategy for illuminating the transmission of more typical psychological characteristics. Most of the research in this area has centered on the offspring of schizophrenics, since this group is a potential model for both biological and social heredity. The work we have reported has been in this area.

To summarize the results of our longitudinal study to date, we have not found that offspring of schizophrenic women are a healthy, happy, intelligent lot. Our measures have shown that they have high levels of illness, fearfulness, sadness, retardation, and social maladaptiveness. However, this does not make them uniquely different from the offspring of women with other severe or chronic mental disorders, or even children of psychiatrically normal women from the lower socioeconomic strata of our society. Without the appropriate control groups built into our study, we might have been led into the error of attributing these differences to the effects of a schizophrenic heritage alone.

In short, caretaking environments in which high levels of stress exist, whether through economic or emotional instability, produce young children with high levels of incompetent behavior. Whether or not these early manifestations of aggressiveness or fearfulness will express themselves in later mental illness will only be determined by further longitudinal research. In the interim, our findings have identified a population of vulnerable children toward which early-intervention studies might fruitfully be directed.

REFERENCES

Brazelton, T. B. *Neonatal Behavioral Assessment Scale.* London: Heinemann, 1973.

Buck, C. W., & Laughton, K. B. Family patterns of illness: The effect of psychoneurosis in the parent upon illness in the child. *Acta Psychiatrica et Neurologica Scandinavica,* 1959, *34*, 165–175.

Cohler, B. H., Grunebaum, H. U., Weiss, J. L., Gamer, E., & Gallant, D. A. Disturbance of attention among schizophrenic, depressed and well mothers and their young children. *Journal of Child Psychology and Psychiatry,* 1977, *18*, 115–135.

Cooper, S. F., Leach, C., Storer, D., & Tonge, W. L. The children of psychiatric patients: Clinical findings. *British Journal of Psychiatry,* 1977, *131*, 514–522.

Erikson, E. H. *Childhood and society* (2nd Ed). New York: Norton, 1963.

Erlenmeyer-Kimling, L., & Cornblatt, B. Attentional measures in a study of children at high-risk for schizophrenia. In L. C. Wynne, R. L. Cromwell, & S. Mathysse (Eds.), *The nature of schizophrenia: New approaches to research & treatment.* New York: Wiley, 1978.

Field, T. M. Effects of early separation, interactive deficits, and experimental manipulations on infant–mother face-to-face stimulation. *Child Development,* 1977, *48,* 763–771.

Fish, B., Shapiro, T., Halpern, F., & Wile, R. The predication of schizophrenia in infancy: III. A ten-year follow-up report of neurological and psychological development. *American Journal of Psychiatry,* 1965, *121,* 768–775.

Fox, B. A. *Socioeconomic status, psychopathology, and socialization.* Unpublished master's dissertation, University of Rochester, 1975.

Garmezy, N. Children at risk: The search for the antecedents of schizophrenia. Part II: Ongoing research programs, issues, and intervention. *Schizophrenia Bulletin,* 1974, No. 9, 55–125.

Garmezy, N. Attentional processes in adult schizophrenia and in children at risk. *Journal of Psychiatric Research,* 1978, *14,* 3–34.

Gottesman, I. I., & Shields, J. Schizophrenia in twins: 16 years' consecutive admissions to a psychiatric clinic. *British Journal of Psychiatry,* 1966, *112,* 809–813.

Hanson, D. R., Gottesman, I. I., & Heston, L. L. Some possible childhood indicators of adult schizophrenia inferred from children of schizophrenics. *British Journal of Psychiatry,* 1976, *129,* 142–154.

Hanson, D. R., Gottesman, I. I., & Meehl, P. H. Genetic theories and the validation of psychiatric diagnosis: Implications for the study of children of schizophrenics. *Journal of Abnormal Psychology,* 1977, *86*(86), 575–588.

Heston, L. L. Psychiatric disorders in foster home reared children of schizophrenic mothers. *British Journal of Psychiatry,* 1966, *112,* 819–825.

Higgins, J. Effects of child rearing by schizophrenic mothers: A follow up. *Journal of Psychiatric Research,* 1976, *13,* 1–9.

Itil, T. M., Hsu, M., Saletu, B., & Mednick, S. Computer EEG and auditory evoked potential investigations in children at high risk for schizophrenia. *American Journal of Psychiatry,* 1974, *131,* 892–900.

Jackson, D. D. *The etiology of schizophrenia.* New York: Basic Books, 1960.

Janes, C. L., Hesselbrock, V., & Stern, J. A. Parental psychopathology, age, and race as related to electrodermal activity of children. *Psychophysiology,* 1978, *15,* 24–34.

Jensen, A. R. *Educability and group differences.* New York: Harper & Row, 1973.

Jones, F. H. The Rochester adaptive behavior inventory: A parallel serves as instruments for assessing social competence during early and middle childhood and adolescence. In J. Strauss, H. Babigian, & M. Roff (Eds.), *The origins and course of psychopathology: Methods for longitudinal research.* New York: Plenum, 1977.

Kallmann, F. J. *The genetics of schizophrenia.* New York: J. J. Augustin, 1938.

Kallmann, F. J. The genetic theory of schizophrenia: An analysis of 691 schizophrenic twin index families. *American Journal of Psychiatry,* 1946, *103,* 309–322.

Kety, S. S., Rosenthal, D., Wender, P. H., Schulsinger, F., & Jacobson, B. Mental illness in the biological and adoptive families who have become schizophenic: A preliminary report based on psychiatric interviews. In R. R. Fieve, D. Rosenthal, & H. Brill (Eds.), *Genetic research in psychiatry.* Baltimore: Johns Hopkins University Press, 1975.

Kringlen, E. Twins—still our best method. *Schizophrenia Bulletin,* 1976, *2,* 429–433.

Laing, R. D., & Esterson, A. *Sanity, madness, and the family.* New York: Basic Books, 1964.

Landau, R., Harth, P., Othnay, N., & Sharfhertz, C. The influence of psychotic parents on their children's development. *American Journal of Psychiatry*, 1972, *129*(1), 38–43.

Lidz, T. *The origin and treatment of schizophrenic disorders*. New York: Basic Books, 1973.

McNeil, T. F., & Kaij, L. Obstetric complications and physical size of offspring of schizophrenic, schizophrenic-like, and control mothers. *British Journal of Psychiatry*, 1973, *123*, 341–348.

McNeil, T. F., & Kaij, L. Obstetric factors in the development of schizophrenia. Complications in the births of preschizophrenics and in reproduction by schizophrenic parents. In L. C. Wynne, R. L. Cromwell, & S. Mathysse, (Eds.), *The nature of schizophrenia: New approaches to research & treatment*. New York: Wiley, 1978.

Mednick, S. A., & McNeil, T. F. Current methodology in research on the etiology of schizophrenia: Serious difficulties which suggest the use of high-risk-group method. *Psychological Bulletin*, 1968, *70* (6), 681–693.

Mednick, S. A., & Schulsinger, F. Some premorbid characteristics related to breakdown in children with schizophrenic mothers. In D. Rosenthal, & S. S. Kety (Eds.), *The transmission of schizophrenia*. Oxford: Pergamon Press Ltd., 1968, pp. 267–291.

Mednick, S. A., & Schulsinger, F. Factors related to breakdown in children at high risk for schizophrenia. In M. Roff & D. F. Ricks (Eds.), *Life history research in psychopathology* (Vol. 1). Minneapolis: University of Minnesota Press, 1970, pp. 51–93.

Mednick, S. A., Mura, E., Schulsinger, F., & Mednick, B. Perinatal conditions and infant development in children with schizophrenic parents. *Social Biology*, 1971, *8*, 5103–5113.

Reisby, N. Psychoses in children of schizophrenic mothers. *Acta Psychiatrica et Neurologica Scandanavica*, 1967, *43*, 8–20.

Rieder, R. O., Broman, S. H., & Rosenthal, D. The offspring of schizophrenics. II: Perinatal factors and I. Q. *Archives of General Psychiatry*, 1977, *34*, 789–799.

Rolf, J. E. The social and academic competence of children vulnerable to schizophrenia and other behavior pathologies. *Journal of Abnormal Psychology*, 1972, *80*(3), 225–243.

Rolf, J. E., & Garmezy, N. The school performance of children vulnerable to psychopathology. In D. F. Ricks, A. Thomas, & M. Roff (Eds.) *Life history research in psychopathology* (Vol. 3). Minneapolis: University of Minnesota Press, 1974.

Rosenthal, D. Problems of sampling and diagnosis in the major twin studies of schizophrenia. *Journal of Psychiatric Research*, 1962, *1*, 116–134.

Rosenthal, D. *Genetic theory and abnormal behavior*. New York: McGraw-Hill, 1970.

Rosenthal, D., Wender, P. H., Kety, S. S., Welner, J., & Schulsinger, F. The adopted-away offspring of schizophrenics. *American Journal of Psychiatry*, 1971, *128*(3), 87–91.

Sameroff, A. J. Early influences on development: Fact or fancy? *Merrill–Palmer Quarterly*, 1975, *21*, 267–294.

Sameroff, A. J., & Zax, M. Perinatal characteristics of offspring of schizophrenic women. *Journal of Nervous and Mental Diseases*, 1973a, *157*, 191–199.

Sameroff, A. J., & Zax, M. Schizotaxia revisited: Model issues in the etiology of schizophrenia. *American Journal of Orthopsychiatry*, 1973b, *43*, 744–754.

Schachter, J., Kerr, J., Lachin, J. M., & Faer, M. Newborn offspring of a schizophrenic parent: Cardiac reactivity to auditory stimuli. *Psychophysiology*, 1975, *12*, 483–492.

Weintraub, S., Neale, J. M., & Leibert, D. C. Teacher ratings of children vulnerable to psychopathology. *American Journal of Orthopsychiatry*, 1975, *45* (5), 838–845.

Wender, P. H. *Minimal brain dysfunction in children*. New York: Wiley, 1971.

Wender, P. H., Rosenthal, D., Kety, S. S., Schulsinger, F., & Welner, J. Cross-fostering: A research strategy in clarifying the role of genetic and experiential factors in the etiology of schizophrenia. *Archives of General Psychiatry*, 1974, *30*, 121–128.

Worland, J., Lander, H., & Hesselbrock, V. Psychological evaluation of clinical disturbance in children at risk for psychopathology. *Journal of Abnormal Psychology,* 1979, *88*(1), 13–26.

Wynne, L. C., & Singer, M. T. Thought disorder and family relations of schizophrenics. *Archives of General Psychiatry,* 1963, *9,* 191–198.

Zigler, E., & Phillips, L. Social competence and the process-reactive distinction in psychopathology. *Journal of Abnormal and Social Psychology,* 1962, *65,* 215–222.

12

The Child in the
Nonconventional Family

BERNICE T. EIDUSON

BACKGROUND

In this volume on nonconventional children, the question repeatedly raised is what factors produce a nonconventional child? In some cases mutant chromosomes have been implicated, in others biochemical dysfunctions. Discovery of such clear-cut indices for certain childhood conditions that make for nonconventional growth has intensified the search for other biological markers. However it has not diminished the question of whether or not, in the absence of such biological pathogenicities, unusual external environmental or milieu conditions will also produce nonconventional children and childhoods.

The role early environment plays in developmental outcomes has not lost interest for psychologists. However, the heredity–environment polemic has become less lively since the interactionist position has seemed increasingly appropriate to the understanding of the genesis of development, even prenatally (Eiduson, Eiduson, & Geller, 1971).

BERNICE T. EIDUSON • University of California, Los Angeles, School of Medicine, The Center for the Health Services, Los Angeles, California 90024, This work is supported in part by the National Institute of Mental Health Research Scientist Career Award No. 5 K05 MH 70541-08 to Bernice T. Eiduson, Ph.D., and by the United States Public Health Service Grant No. 5 R01-06 MH 24947 and Carnegie Corporation Grant B 3970-06. Project coinvestigator, Thomas S. Weisner, Ph.D., and senior investigators Jannette W. Alexander, MSW, Jerome Cohen, Ph.D., Irla Lee Zimmerman, Ph.D., and Max R. Mickey, Ph.D., have also been responsible for directing the project.

Yet the role of postnatal psychological events—relationships, interactions, and experiences, for individual differences that seem to have no critical biological markers or associated phenomena, continues to encourage the search for salient environmental variables, or groups of variables that promise a predictable relationship to developmental outcome.

Twin and sibling studies have been one major thrust in this search, permitting some opportunity to look at growth (Shields, 1962). The contribution of psychological or experiential variables as distinguished from genetic and biological precursors can be systematically, and statistically, approached. Other data derive from comparative studies of psychological development, given some knowledge, and at times, control of certain environmental phenomena. Studies of institutionalized children or of growth in a distinctive culture are cases in point (Whiting & Whiting, 1975).

Such knowledge is often cross-sectional, obtained at single chronological points, or at a number of points so widely spaced that information about relationships between psychological events, or between certain environmental and certain outcome variables, is spotty and tenuous. Longitudinal research has been instructive in elucidating the vagaries of apparent continuities and discontinuities obtained by cross-sectional data, though not as yet contributing definite data on the sequences, factors, and interactions in development—even in those areas where clinical data suggest they should lie.

The present research describes a longitudinal effort which aspires to make a contribution in this regard: it proposes to study development as a function of the family setting in which a child grows (Eiduson, 1974). The family has been assumed to be the primary socializing agent for the child (Brim, 1966). Family is hypothesized to be the milieu which is most formative for personal and social relationships, interactions, networks, early exposure and cognitive stimulation, instilling of values, attitudes, beliefs, and preferences, the genesis of components of self-identity.

By and large the family has been viewed with the conventional two-parent nuclear family as the modal unit (Herzog & Sudia, 1968). Statistically this has been so in most Western European countries, and even in the variety of diverse anthropological cultures, a nuclear family unit emerges regularly as the basic family entity (Skolnick, 1975).

Furthermore, the child-development literature has generally assumed that the traditional two-parent nuclear family is the family paradigm which provides the most optimal milieu for the growth and development of the cognitive and socioemotional resources of the child (Greenfield, 1974). Other family models, such as one-parent families or group care, have been thought to be deficient or deficit units, with the socialization experiences for a child less than adequate for growth. For example, a one-parent family has been hypothesized as inadequate for providing the child with some of the support needed for good use of cognitive abilities, for appropriate models for psychosexual identity, etc. (Pederson, 1976); a group family unit has been thought to be less than optimal for intensive 1 : 1 early bonding experiences, and later object relationships (Spiro & Spiro, 1975). Empirical studies of father absence in the one-parent family and studies of children reared in groups have reinforced these assumptions to some extent. Work on minority populations whose families have often been one-parent or mother-headed and which showed that children often lack the sufficient cognitive stimulation or the opportunities for developing close affective needs between parent and child have also been used as evidence supporting the notion that a two-parent nuclear unit is the family of choice when a child's development is at stake (Deutsch, 1967). Indeed when severe sociopathological conditions such as delinquency also became implicated with some of the deviances in family structure, the importance of a two-parent traditionally structured family for healthy growth seemed to receive further support (Reissman, Cohen & Pearl, 1964).

The body of work on children growing up in variants of the two-parent nuclear family has in recent years been questioned in terms of its methodological sophistication (Pederson, 1976). Longitudinal studies of kibbutz youngsters particularly have suggested that some of the negative anticipated consequences of group care may have been hasty and overdrawn (Beit-Hollahmi & Rabin, 1977).

Furthermore, as the implications of child rearing in nonnuclear units are being reviewed, questions are also raised about whether the socioemotional and cognitive consequences are also inevitable when a variant family lifestyle has not come about by default, as by death, divorce, or desertion, but rather when the lifestyle has been consciously selected or opted for by the family and for them, at least, is the family unit of choice. It is to this issue that the UCLA interdisciplinary Family Styles Project has addressed its research into nontraditional families (Cohen & Eiduson, 1975).

Nonconventional family styles such as single-mother households, two-parent social-contract marriages, and communes, communities, and living groups are characteristic of some of the variant family styles that were developed by young people in the late 1960s and 1970s who wanted to live in ways that they thought were more in line with their values, attitudes, and perspectives, and so rejected the two-parent traditional nuclear unit in which they had been raised (Eiduson, Cohen

& Alexander, 1976). They espoused a strengthening of interpersonal ties and relationships within the family structure, a greater respect for individual needs of each member, and a recasting of traditional roles and responsibilities within the family. In the search for ways of daily living in which such values might be realized, they chose to depart from the two-parent nuclear family structure, thinking it could no longer offer the potential they desired; and, indeed, they proceeded to develop family units which were more in line with their attitudes and beliefs. In setting up these alternative family units, they offered our research group a naturalistic opportunity to study the socialization attitudes and behaviors that emerged as new child-rearing values were put into practice, and the impact of these nontraditional families on the infant and young child.

Three groups of alternatives, social contract families (families who live as two-parent nuclears but are not legally wed), single-mother households, (one-parent families in which the woman is household head without having a husband available), and living groups or communities (families which have three or more adult members whose family essentially is larger than the traditional two-parent unit and wedded together by common goals or philosophies) were selected for study, along with 52 families representing each of these three experimental family styles (Eiduson, 1978b). Fifty children born into the two-parent traditionally married family served as a comparison group. Populations are Caucasian, parents aged 18–35, from families of origin that had been middle-class or stable working-class in background. Mothers had to be pregnant with a first child (in two-thirds of the cases), or a second (in one-third of the cases). The 150 children in families comprising the alternative population were obtained throughout the indigenous network in California. Referrals were sought through La Maze teachers, physicians who perform home birth, ecology centers, and social and educational agencies which alternatives frequented. This snowball sample contrasted with the random sample of traditional marrieds, the comparison group, who were obtained through randomly sampling the list of obstetricians in the AMA directory. Each physician was asked to nominate one woman from his practice who met criteria; she was encouraged then to contact the project.

Starting with the third semester when parents were engaged in the study, assessment of socialization processes in the child's family proceeds through interviews, questionnaires, and home visits permitting naturalistic observations of children, parents, and others (Eiduson & Weisner, 1978). In addition studies of the social and physical milieu of the home provide an ecological focus through the variety of field techniques.

Child development is assessed through pediatric and neurological examinations conducted at birth; home observations initiated at 6 months; intelligence testing at 8 months; cognitive, physical, nutritional, and emotional assessments at 1 year; home observations again at 18 months and so on, through the first 6 years of life. This multimethod, multitrait longitudinal research strategy involves the administration of standardized and semistandarized tests and standard experimental situations either in the home setting or in project offices at periodic intervals. Studies will be carried forth until the child passes his sixth birthday and has spent some time in the first grade so that the impact of family socialization processes and development to date on the child's subsequent adjustment to a mainstream institution like the school can be examined.

The research strategy considers the child as a cohort in the study rather than the family. Therefore he is followed whatever the changes in family lifestyle or residence. Family incentives for participating are of two kinds: $5 per procedure to cover expenses; plus $80 per year in pediatric or dental services for each child, if the provider of services sends to the subject codifiable information concerning the nature of illness, reason for referral, and disposition of the case (Eiduson, 1979a).

BACKGROUND CHARACTERISTICS OF PARENTS

To understand whether the persons attracted to alternative lifestyles differed in significant ways from those parents who were attracted to the traditional two-parent nuclear family, a large number of demographic and social-background variables such as place of birth, birth order, years of education completed, present perception of past relationships with parents and siblings, previous drug history, and alternative experiences were examined (Cohen & Eiduson, 1975).

In general, results support findings by other investigators who have shown that young Caucasian parents who had opted for variations from the nuclear family during the counterculture period of the 1960s and 1970s were in the main no different from their peers of like socioeconomic class (Keniston, 1965).

Some general characteristics of the population may be summarized as follows:

1. The mothers in the study comprised a group of 208 women whose mean age was 25.4 ± 3.8, with a range of 18–33. The fathers' average age was 27.9 ± 4.9, with a range of 19–49. The single mothers and single fathers were the youngest of the population and the

traditional marrieds the oldest group, but these differences were not significant.

2. The largest group of mothers and fathers were born in the Pacific states. The Northeast and the Mid-Atlantic states contributed the second and third most sizable contingents.

3. At the time they entered the study 50% of families lived in Los Angeles and environs, with the remainder fairly evenly divided between San Diego and Northern California (San Francisco up to the Oregon border).

4. Of the study population, 83% were currently residing in urban and 17% in semirural settings.

5. Both parents had an average of slightly more than three siblings, and came from families with as many as seven children. Mothers were most often second-oldest children, while half of the fathers were eldest children.

6. The socioeconomic status (SES) of the population in terms of the mother's family of origin showed that 17% were from upper-class families, 18% upper-middle class, 31% middle-class, 27% working-class, and 7% lower-class (although we had not planned to include this group in our population). The father's family origin showed a similar SES distribution.

7. The SES of parents at time of entry in the study was of course very different, for the nontraditional families, by and large, had become downwardly mobile, i.e., were living at a level one or two SES steps "below" that of their own parents, while the traditionals were more on a par with their previous backgrounds. With the nontraditionals, downward mobility was often a chosen departure in line with their distaste for materialism as a goal in life, their divestment of conventional kinds of possessions, and their more casual attitude to goal-oriented employment.

8. The alternative group more frequently interrupted their education than did the traditionals, as would be expected from the literature on young adults attracted to the counterculture movement in the late 1960s. The total population of mothers reported completion of 13.9 ± 2.2 years (mean) of formal schooling, with single mothers the lowest and traditional marrieds and domestic living groups almost 1 year above the mean. Fathers averaged 14.5 ± 2.6 years of schooling. Women in emergent family variations are underrepresented in the group achieving college-level degrees, while traditional fathers had on an average one more year of college. The difference in years of education completed is significant.

In comparing the traditional parents to those living in one of the alternative lifestyles, we found relatively few background variables and attitudes which seemed to differentiate the two groups; however, the factors which were significant contributed to our understanding of the motivations for seeking a variant family form (Cohen & Eiduson, 1975):

1. The parents of alternative-family participants had moved from one residence to another much more frequently than did those in the traditional lifestyles.
2. Also, alternatives had parents who had remarried significantly more often.
3. Additionally, self-perception related to earlier life experiences and collected retrospectively showed that, as a group, alternatives viewed their early childhoods as unhappy, whereas most of the traditionally married parents perceived this period of life as happy.
4. There was a general tendency for project traditional mothers to have maintained better relationships with their own mothers during childhood and adolescence than did those women who chose to live in an alternative lifestyle.

Interview data obtained from fathers in separate sessions showed the same trends. Mothers who were currently in living groups and in social-contract marriages appeared to have had the most difficulty with their own parents, especially in early adolescence. Among the alternatives, the single mothers seemed to have maintained the best relationship with their own parents during their growing-up years.

The Family Groups

We had hypothesized that family environments of our four lifestyle groups would present different functional and interactional settings to the child (Eiduson & Weisner, 1978). To establish the differences we obtained detailed information on the specific characteristics of each of the family environments by meticulously documenting the structure, composition, organization, and neighborhood and community involvement of each household. For example, in one study (Weisner & Martin, 1979) in which the most conventional and common family unit under study, the traditional marrieds, was compared with the most nonconventional, the living group, the traditional two-parent nuclear unit was found to be a (1) smaller and more restricted social unit, one that was also (2) more stable in terms of residential mobility, and (3) in terms of family membership. The traditional family also is maintaining (4) significantly more emotional and physical involvement with own kin.

This finding is of interest because it suggests that this variable, relationships with own parents and siblings, which we showed in a previous study (Cohen & Eiduson, 1975) to be one of the few characteristics distinguishing parents who sought an alternative versus a traditional family unit prior to the birth of the child, seems to remain an important difference after the child is born. The traditional family also provides a setting in which the mother herself undertakes more of the total household duties, although her overall workload appears lighter than that borne by her counterpart in the extended group (Eiduson, 1978a).

Pilot work had suggested that there was no "typical" or representative living group, single-mother family, or social-contract unit (Eiduson et al., 1976). Therefore in sample selection, an effort was made to introduce as much variation in family style in each of our groups as possible. Some within-group differences then proved of interest. Living groups that were religious in orientation, or led by a charismatic leader, and sometimes called creedal groups, were able to be distinguished from domestic household living groups along ideological, as well as certain functional (Berger, 1971) and structural dimensions, as number of caretakers for the child, daily routines, and attitudes toward parenting. Similarly, "circumstantial" social contracts could be differentiated from "committed" social contracts, in terms of the motivations for entering a nonlegal family unit; and within the single-mother group, a typology of "nest-builders," "post-hoc adaptors," and "unwed mothers" appeared to distinguish maternal attitudes toward the newborn, as well as residential arrangements and maternal caretaking practices once the child was born (Kornfein, Weisner, & Martin, 1976).

It is hard to convey some appreciation of the range of differences in families we are studying, particularly in areas influential on the child's development, without giving some précis of family styles. Each précis (these have been published elsewhere in Eiduson, 1979d) depends on systematic empirical quantitative analyses of value systems, social and physical characteristics of the household, parental aspirations and expectations for the child, observations and other documentation of caretaking practices, assessment of support systems available to the mother and significant persons in the household during the child's first year of life, etc. (Eiduson & Alexander, 1978).

Communes are the families whose lifestyle is most divergent from the conventional. They can be small or large, rural or urban, creedal (i.e., having an ideological commitment) or merely social or proximal domestic units. In size they range from triadic (two like-sex parteners mated to one spouse—we have two of these) to combinations of kin and nonkin "extended families" of hundreds, seen in the more popular religious groups. Our creedal groups range from 10 to 100 members.

We have found it useful to distinguish between the creedal, or religious groups, and the domestic groups (Eiduson, 1979b). The former are based mainly upon either Eastern philosophies and culture, or the new "Jesus Movement" which seeks a new way to live out traditional Judeo–Christian convictions. A smaller group of creedal-groups are derived from allegiance to a charismatic leader with a more or less formalized philosophical system. The domestic group, by contrast, is a less formally organized unit, often formed spontaneously around shared crafts, political convictions, or identification with the natural rural environment or the small contemporary farm. In the latter, people who like each other decide to live in a small household or in close proximity, and share some quarters and tasks, and some social and domestic activities, often child care.

The Christian Religion as a Family Group

The fundamentalist Christian groups have found a new impetus from young people who joined them during the late 1960s and early 1970s in order to find a way back from a drug-ridden and unstructured and meaningless counterculture life.

Christian groups to which our participants were attracted were spotted up and down the California coast. Members live in individual nuclear-family units, usually apartments, or small houses, if married and with a child, so there was some private family existence even though many of its details were determined by the common practices of the group. When people arose, their time of prayer, the place and nature of their activities, who they worked with, and where and what they ate were determined by the group. However, our families almost invariably ate noontime meals, napped and slept, dressed and played in their tiny private quarters. They were interviewed and observed at periods of home observations in these quarters, even though their participation could not have proceeded had the elders not agreed to it. When members from one group within a sect would come to project offices in Los Angeles, arrangements for housing them would be made with elders in the local groups.

Children have a special place when reared in these Christian homes. Since the were they future evangelists, tomorrow's truth-sellers, their own activities, growth, and development were governed with this in mind. They would pledge themselves to the Lord usually by six, but prior to this time each had regularly attended and partici-pated in prayer service. Being part of a group helped make expectations of assuming some assigned responsibilities from the time they were two or three palatable. Similarly, prayer rituals at meals, service attendance and the like were prescribed behaviors.

Parents considered the Lord's will as dictating the child's personality and his response to parenting practices. It was then up to the parent to work with the child to make him able to be responsive to the Lord's teachings. Spanking was a common disciplining tool in line with the Biblical "spare the rod and spoil the child"; invariably it would be followed by hugging to show the child that the real intent was punishing the child, with the parent as God's representative of love and care. It was not uncommon for a child to be lightly spanked three or four times during an assessment in our offices—with parent showing none of the guilt that a less righteously and ideologically supported parent would show.

Children, like parents, lived modestly, wore castoffs from older children in the group, played with brothers and sisters or other children in the group in the fields or in an informally-developed play area. They were also expected to be responsive to whoever took care of them—for from their first year, their own parents would be assigned to tasks that took them away from home, while other women would be caretakers. Child caretakers changed from time to time, and the child was expected to adjust regardless. The caretaker had complete responsibility, but knew where the parent was if necessary. A preschooler might report to his mother that he had been hurt on a wire fence, and that an older boy had taken care to bandage the wound. The mother would assume an appropriate intervention had been taken as indeed it usually was.

Children assumed that their lives would be regulated from the outside. Even when children went to public school (since church schools were not always viable alternatives), the patterns of scheduled activities at home were also adhered to before and after school. The times for fun, or play, for school, for meals, and for prayers were set. Activities proceeded along sex-stereotypic lines. Like parents, children learned what was expected of them early.

The Eastern Religions as a Family Group

Doctrines of various Eastern religions differ, rituals differ, and relationships and involvement with the outside community differ. However, the family structures within each of those being studied have certain common components (Weisner & Martin, 1979).

Like the Christian religious family groupings, the Eastern religious families have a family life that is private and outside the group experience as well as a family domain that is group-shared.

The family structure for a child is usually nuclear—father, mother, child(ren); but families do separate with one parent then remaining in the group. In most communities, nuclear families have separate quarters or a private space—an apartment, duplex, or bedroom upon occasion. Quarters are austere, but beautiful. A feeling of calmness, dignity, and care pervades. Meals are generally eaten with the group— for like the Christian groups, these have ritualistic features; sometimes dietary restrictions, or conventions about prayer or interpersonal communication. Children are introduced to these early, for like parents, they participate in both the private and group-shared family practices.

Parents are usually expected to nurture their own young, with supports from group members, who may baby-sit, run a preschool program, or carry out those activities that make it possible for the mother to play a role in the common activities of the group. In some families, mothers are heavily involved in community functions; in others, more minimally so, when children are very young. Fathers who are more traditionally in novice or priestlike roles assume both economic and religious tasks that make their family involvements very much like those seen in the traditional middle-class families, i.e., they are present for meals, occasionally also in the evenings, but they are expected to be mainly occupied with the work that makes the religious family go.

Parents then support the larger group by some assigned tasks, and in turn are freed from the need of individual supports; these are provided by the group. They have food, shelter, friends who share spiritual and personal commitments, and who provide all manner of personal assistance and resources. Depending on the extent to which a religious group is closed or has involvement in the larger community, close friends can also exist outside the family group.

Eastern religions offer few definite principles to guide young parents in childrearing (Kornfein, 1975). Food regimens define kind of diet and times of eating, but not necessarily eating habits. Even in those religions in which children are isolated alone with mother in days following birth in order to protect the newborn from unwanted influences, creedal rules do not cover later, less ritualistic aspects of mother–child interactions or child-rearing practices in regard to discipline or toilet-training. At many intervention points parents make their own decisions, and thus a child sees a model in which the belief system provides the general outlines for life, and the parent gives it his interpretation. One can visit a group of children in a religious group who are easily distinguished by dress and aspects of physical appearance and find them playing with wagons and tricycles, digging in the mud, or squabbling over dolls.

As children get older—and in some groups, this can be at age two—special schooling oriented toward religious beliefs but also incorporating sensorily stimulating and artistic materials is started. The spontaneity and creativity of the young impulsive child are in some creedal belief systems highly valued; the child is unfettered by most conventions in these orientations, except for a general religious upbringing. In these cases, the roles children will assume as young adults begin to take shape in very early years. Invariably, early orientations toward religious roles follows sex-stereotyped lines.

The Leader-Directed Communal Family

Religious family groups are in a sense leader-directed; however, there are also family groups in which the leader is not a religious, but charismatic figure. Leader-directed families are usually distinguished by their devotion to specified goals and aims that serve as ideals; by explicit group adherence to ways of achieving these ideals. The family's sense of unity comes from respect, admiration and love for the family leader, and a willingness to be part of the community who adopt his philosophy. The authority-orientation of these families is similar to that found in religious follower families, and in fact, some of these groups consider themselves religious, meaning devout, with members as devotees, but their allegiance is to a belief system that is not structured around the concept of God. Instead, tenets of the leader show "The Way," with search for self and for one's role in the social scheme of life often being the focus. This is the reason that these groups are sometimes referred to as psychotherapeutic cults (Singer, 1978).

The group context in a leader group provides a family organization that has social relationships and interactions, a hierarchy for roles within the group, as well as some organized or considered sets of relationships with the outside community. "Someone from the outside world is here" is sometimes heard in one group as a non-group-member visits, but even more casual interactions with outsiders usually have specified goals and constraints.

The development of the personal, but shared, philosophical views encourages the development and practice of cultlike rituals. Practices that can emerge may be polygamous practices in which a few powerful men in the group sire offspring with various women. Or, practices in which parents allow children to be separated from them and placed with group or infant-school caretakers who will see that the child's special powers or "energies" are used to group advantage.

In a group which believes that children and adults are individuals and regardless of age, should be sensitized to their needs for sensuous expression, group activities may involve children or teenagers. Sometimes sexual activities develop naturally in the course of relationships, and then are later rationalized, but as often, a group's philosophical position anticipates and thus fosters these behaviors. Ideology gives significance to behaviors, and to the members ascribing to the ideology. Thus, an information or cognitive base is the strength of the cultist groups (Singer, 1978).

Children who grow up in a leader group are often reared in rather radical ways that again have a stated correspondence with the ideology adults live by. A 24-hour nursery may focus on enhancing cognitive skills, or hedonistic pleasures through overstimulation, or on building children who do not distinguish kin from nonkin parents in the zeal to build for an extended family, rather than two-parent bond. In these, the ideology of the group more or less directs child-rearing philosophy and practice, but these may turn out to be experimental, erratic, and radical. Since there are few tested precursors for child-caretaking arrangements and few adults trained as educators or group day-care workers, it is a challenge for novice caretakers to provide the care and attention that the usual small-family model provides for a child. There are not one but many children to attend to and to relate to. There are also decisions to be made when the needs of children and adults conflict, which can be very often. For the children, the group experience is thought to provide companionship, allies, models for learning, as well as the social competencies that come with having to find ways to live with many other children and various caretakers. Children are usually expected to find their own ways of using the social and cognitive environment. There are examples of strong bonds with parents who direct, encourage, and single out their children for attention. Parents may desire to do this, but if attention is too intense, it is sometimes discouraged as making the child and the adult too dependent on each other. While it is not openly avowed that bonding with parent may diffuse the child's alliance with the leader and the group, that is apparently one of the concerns.

Children usually eat, sleep, toilet, play, are disciplined and taught in the presence of each other, so there is usually a structure about what goes on in regard to children—even in those family groups which strive for casualness, unstructured interactions, and spontaneous interchanges. As with brothers and sisters in one very large biological family, children learn to make their ways with each other, have personal attachments, rivalries, and toy exchanges.

The Family in the Domestic Group

By contrast, the domestic group life is simple, and traditional in a historical sense. Simple houses show a mixture of minimum conveniences and sophisticated books and electronic equipment. The family has usually gathered a group of interested friends, decided to live in proximity to them so they can share companionship, some meals, and some activities, and has also usually demanded at the same time the kind of privacy that can be obtained only in the private dwelling.

The process of building up one's own wherewithal for existence becomes the sum and substance around which family life proceeds. Like the farm family in the 1800s, there is little time or energy left for less mundane, more sophisticated activities. Pleasures include simple respites from hard work, often drudgery, but the greatest gratifications rest with the fact that the family is constantly renewing its vitality and viability by its own hands.

Children have the freedom that has always been provided by farms, busy parents, and an almost exclusive concern for the basics of life. They are around constantly, participate as they are able in parent activities, play in and out of the house, with makeshift toys and spontaneously thought-up games. Their lives are regulated less by their individual needs than by their family's needs—an early-to-rise, early-to-bed household trains children accordingly. Their food and toileting practices and discipline have the same up-front, immediate character. Like their parents, whose own sense of inner discipline may be apparent in their patterns of regularity of work, efficiency, conscientiousness, and determination, so the children's upbringing may go.

Children seek out companions from the intimate circle of family friends residing close by. An occasional playmate may be found in an informal nursery group prior to nursery school, where usually a more middle-class structure prevails. School initiates the combination of home freedom and outside-family structure for the child; both serve usually as fine complements to each other. The parents who have had children always around also enjoy the freedom. Trips to the laundromat, the natural food stores, and the occasional movie are treats—as are candy, Big Macs, toys, and visits from grandparents.

When in an urban setting, the child in a domestic group has a life of a rather informal, relaxed quality with parents and children living in as easy and flexible a way as possible. When parent works away from home during all or part of the day, the child's day is shaped by the caretaking arrangements parents have made: day care, neighborhood nursery group, or babysitter. Parents place minimal demands on themselves, trying to mainly do the things they like to do, seeing the people they like to see, and interacting freely and without ceremony. Parents' demands on children for behavior or conformity are light. Parents see themselves as supportive, meeting minimal needs without pressure, and children adapt accordingly. They relate to parents in a casual way, seeing other adults and children as important persons in their environment. Child-rearing has a casual, spontaneous, sometimes impulsive quality about it—in contrast to the planned, schedules milieu found in many traditional homes. Doctors are seen when necessary, schools used when convenient, friends visited spontaneously.

Some family units share a large home, with parents and child sharing small bedrooms. Others divide rooms more systematically, so like-age and unrelated children sleep together and separate from parents and other adults. Sharing is usually a major philosophic tenet in these arrangements and can be the most planned aspect of the family, and the most conflictful.

Child-caretaking is one area where the concept of sharing leads to freeing mothers for other activities. This can be done with forethought and care and can become a major concern of the group—at least of the women, or it can vary on a daily or weekly basis. Many women have been motivated toward the living-group household because of the opportunity offered to vary traditional roles and permit more personally-gratifying education, social, and vocational experiences.

I shall not take time to describe the lifestyle of the one-parent or unwed couples (Eiduson, 1979c). Obviously these are very close to the two-parent nuclear family in residence and, to some extent, family composition and structure. However, differences seen are often determined by the values these alternatives hold.

Values of Nonconventional Families

The hypothesis under which the project proceeded was that all nonconventional families adhered to the alternative philosophy, whose goals revolved around these few tenets:

1. Humanism, with its opportunities for closeness, intimacy, and significant emotional relationships;
2. A natural–organic perspective which sees man as at one with

the environment, and espouses a "return to the land," and an interest in "natural" foods and drugs;

3. A move away from dependence on technology and invention, and the intellectual perspective that uses only rational and objective sources of knowledge, toward an interest in diverse and personal sources of knowledge, as sensory experience, intuition, astrology, as alternate ways of problem-solving;

4. A self-help philosophy where the individual has more control of his own fate and is less dependent on established societal institutions, as in medicine or education; this is accompanied by

5. An antiauthority thrust, derived from feelings of alienation and distantiation from mainstream values;

6. A withdrawal from materialism, possessiveness, and acquisitiveness as important values in life, and a rejection of the conventional indices of achievement, in favor of achievement for self-fulfillment and creative expression;

7. An encouraging of roles within the family without regard for stereotyped conceptions of sex or age, leading to sex egalitarianism, and an abandonment of age-grading;

8. A desire for immediate gratification, setting of day-to-day goals rather than an orientation toward the future and a reliving of the "here-and-now" in their perspective.

Study of the extent to which identification with these values could be ascertained in anticipatory socialization attitudes and child-rearing behaviors showed that alternatives and traditionals indeed could be distinguished on the basis of identification with these values; and that secondly, there were significant differences among alternatives in the extent to which they affiliated with these basic dimensions (Rochford, 1978).

Of the eight value dimensions measured, three statistically discriminate between traditional and alternative mothers: materialism, sources of knowledge, and attitudes toward conventional authority. Four value dimensions strongly distinguish between traditional and alternative fathers: materialism, a natural–organic perspective, sources of knowledge, and sex-role egalitarianism.

Parents in the four lifestyles showed the following value-orientations:

1. Traditional mothers and fathers express strong commitment to conventional value-orientations. With the exception of achievement,

where single mothers express a somewhat stronger commitment to this orientation than traditional mothers, traditional parents are significantly more committed to conventional perspectives than any of the alternative families.

2. The values expressed by single mothers are more traditional than alternative. Among these women there is a practical concern for "getting ahead" and making a better future for themselves and their child. While strongly valuing achievement and a future-orientation, single mothers are relatively low in their commitment to materialism and humanism.

3. Parents in living groups express an interesting array of value-commitments. A major within-lifestyle division is found between domestic and creedal living groups. Domestic living-group parents are committed to nonconventional value-orientations while creedal parents place an emphasis on both traditional and alternative perspectives. Creedal group mothers and fathers strongly value conventional authority and traditional sex roles, while at the same time rejecting materialism, conventional achievement, and a future-orientation. The religious ideology followed by many of the creedal group parents, especially those adhering to Eastern systems of thought and worship, accounts for this values profile.

4. In general, those values which have been identified as constituting the worldview of the counterculture are expressed by social-contract mothers and fathers, particularly among the committed social-contract parents. There is a rejection of traditional values and a corresponding emphasis on sex egalitarianism, humanism, and a natural–organic perspective.

ANTICIPATORY SOCIALIZATION BEHAVIORS AND ATTITUDES

The extent of identification with the alternative philosophy is of particular interest as we look at parental anticipatory socialization attitudes and behaviors, for one general theme emerges: viz., while on the one hand parents in nonconventional families espouse an alternative perspective, in their anticipatory behaviors they show a striking display of traditional middle-class practices! Are differences in family structure associated with differences in maternal and paternal expectations and aspirations for the coming child? Does the commitment to certain alternative values predict differences in anticipatory socialization behaviors?

Results of questionnaire, interview data, and home observations suggested that parents who live alternatively do want different things for their children. In fact, the process of beginning parenting is different for them. Studies of anticipatory attitudes showed that traditional families were significantly more likely to have planned and anticipated a baby at the time they did. The single mothers were the group most unlikely to have consciously planned the baby, although a baby was not inappropriate with respect to their ideological commitments. About one-third of the single mothers, the oldest, most educated, vocationally competent group, had consciously planned to have the child without continuing the relationship with the father. Mothers in alternative-family lifestyles were also more likely to have had one or more abortions than women in the traditionally married group. In general, even when the pregnancy was not planned, acceptance came soon afterwards (Eiduson & Weisner, 1978).

The alternative-lifestyle parents more often perceived themselves as unhappy as children than the traditional-lifestyle parents. They related this to the feeling that their parents had pushed and directed them too much (Cohen & Eiduson, 1975), and were committed to sparing their children from such pressures. Some tended to look to their own peers and to the natural unfolding of the children's own talents to supply the essential basis for children achieving self-fulfillment. Many were far less likely to want their children to identify with parents or grandparents than were traditional mothers.

Mothers in alternative lifestyles felt far less support from their own parents during pregnancy than did mothers in traditional lifestyles. Not only were maternal grandparents perceived as more uncomfortable about the lifestyle their daughters had espoused, but they were also perceived as feeling less positively about the coming grandchild.

In line with the nonintellectual perspective of the alternative philosophy, there was less concern with traditional kinds of achievement orientation and goals for children among the alternative groups, although achievement orientation may be expressed in other than usual ways. Traditional parents seemed to have more defined goals in terms of education and occupation than did alternatives, yet both incorporated the contemporary interest in fulfilling one's potentials and desires in future achievement.

Some of the values which led alternatives to select their lifestyles had stressed naturalness, an "organic," close-to-environment perspective, and a self-help philosophy. This led us to expect that they would utilize natural childbirth, home deliveries, midwives, and herbalists and that their own interest in natural foods and drugs would preclude their use of more formal pediatric services. Our hypotheses in this regard were not borne out. There were few significant differences among groups in prenatal practices, and even in procedures at birth.

Organized medical services were used by all mothers regardless of lifestyle, at least during the third trimester when they were engaged in the study. There was a significant difference between the traditional and alternative groups in their desires for home delivery, over 40% of alternatives showing an interest in this direction. However, in actual fact, the number of home deliveries was small (20%). Almost every traditional parent and single mother had babies in hospitals. Prenatal care was the order of the day for all mothers, with 98% involved in La Maze or Bradley or a comparable prebirth educational program. Anesthetics proved to be involved significantly less often in the birth process by the alternative mother, however.

Moreover, a rather dramatic reversion to traditional practices was noted in drug and nutritional patterns in all family groups. Studies undertaken during the last trimester showed all groups reporting significant decrease in previous drug use as time for the birth approached. The drug intake of the alternative lifestyle group was reduced more drastically than was that of the traditionally married population, because they had been greater users previously. However the majority of the traditionally married group had been marijuana users, and these parents almost totally abstained from marijuana during pregnancy, a pattern found in both mothers and fathers. In men, the reduction was not as dramatic, but there seemed to be an attempt to support mothers' reduction in intake or to show lack of interest in drug use in the absence of mothers' participation (Eiduson & Project Staff, 1975).

Those trends, of conformity to traditional, middle-class practices, were similar for food intake. In general, all mothers were concerned about appropriate nutrition to ensure the health of the child, and so accordingly reduced unusual or restricted diets or dieting. No significant differences in nutrition during pregnancy were discovered between alternative and traditional married groups, or between the various alternative groups.

BIRTH DATA

It was anticipated that the previous drug and nutritional status of alternative parents and their preference for home deliveries might result in significantly more "at risk" babies in the experimental population. This hypothesis was not confirmed as evident in the birth data (Eiduson, Zimmerman, & Bernstein, 1977).

First, results of the Newborn Neonatal Examination (NNE) (Parmalee & Michaelis, 1971) of the 109 boys and 99 girls indicated that as a total group the children were normal at birth (mean 101.86 ± 21.53, compared to the standardization 100 ± 20), with a range from 65 to 110. Furthermore, no differences attributable to lifestyle were significant: while single mothers' infants were lowest in rank, there was in all only a 7-point difference between the lowest-ranking single mothers' infants and the living groups' infants (100 vs. 107, p = .28). When NNE scores were dichotomized to identify those infants scoring below 80, or "at risk" (one standard deviation below average), 22 or 11% met this criterion. When the children were considered by sex, girls slightly surpassed boys (110 vs. 104), although this did not reach significance (p = .13).

At the time of birth, the mothers in this study were evaluated on the Obstetrical Complications Scale (OCS, adjusted), a measure of the occurrence of any complicating factors in the maternal medical history and the birth process (Parmalee & Littman, 1977). Scores were generally average: mean 111.16 ± 21.38, with a range of scores from 50 to 160, as compared to the standardization mean of 111 ± 11 (Parmalee & Littman, 1977). Here lifestyle differences approached significance, specifically because scores for single mothers were 8 or more points lower than those of the other groups (104 vs. 112, p = .07). Other groups were generally similar to each other. Sex differences approached significance: girls surpassed boys by 6 points (114 vs. 108, p = .06).

When scores were dichotomized to identify those children whose mothers scored "at risk" (below 90), 32 or 15% were located. The average OCS of this group was 75.84 ± 10.17. Only 6 of the 32 or 3% of total population had an OCS and a NNE at risk.

Of the 205 children in this study, only 6 (3%) were possibly premature, using birth weight (equal to or below 2500 grams) as an adequate indication of prematurity. Birth measures of the premature subsample can be compared to the group as a whole: on the OCS (adjusted), the premature infants scored 15 points lower than the total sample (95.83 ± 26.56 vs. 111.16 ± 22.38). On the other hand, the newborn status of these premature infants was average, and similar to that of the total sample (100.33 ± 9.89 vs. 101.86 ± 21.53).

In our general population, 37% of the mothers reported positive attitudes about the birth experience, 39% were neutral or ambivalent, and 24% were negative. Single mothers were slightly more negative than mothers in other groups.

Fathers were present at birth in well over 60% of the cases, excluding the single-mother group. Also, 15% of the single mothers had a male friend present, and 30% had someone else present, usually another woman. Regardless of the status of past relationships, nearly all the new parents contacted their own parents within a few days to inform them of the birth.

INFANCY

It was assumed that, in line with differences in values and attitudes expressed at third trimester, alternatives and traditionals would differ in infancy-caretaking practices. In general, a wide range of early-infant caregiving patterns occurred across all lifestyles. However no extreme or unusual practices relating to feeding, parental health, or caregiving patterns appeared during the first 6 months of life.

Overall, 81% of babies were breastfed. No differences existed between traditionals and alternatives in regard to initiating breastfeeding. By 6 months, however, only one-third of traditional mothers were still breastfeeding, as contrasted with two-thirds of living-group mothers.[1] Solids were introduced much earlier in conventional families; by contrast only 15% of living-group children had solids by 1 year (Weisner & Martin, 1979).

To what extent did the differences in the family styles influence caretaking practices? We had hypothesized that since the number of adults in the home varied significantly by lifestyle, this would in turn influence the number of caretakers available to, and caring for, the child. This proved indeed to be the case. For example, the traditional mother was the sole caretaker in two-thirds of the cases, and was joined by one or two other adults in the remaining one-third; the father was one of these in one-third of the homes. By contrast, only one-third of living-group mothers were sole caretakers, two or more

---

[1] Practices in regard to feeding and some of the other aspects of caretaking were related not only to values in regard to natural–organic preferences, but also to current socioeconomic status. Parents' income showed a wide range, from $3000 a year or poverty level for some unwed couples to $30,000 a year for a few traditionally marrieds. The social-contract group particularly demonstrated the voluntary downward mobility of all those alternatives who protested against scheduled commitments and the Protestant work ethic. Some of this protest may have been a rationalization of their lesser vocational capabilities, for alternatives had less schooling on the average, and less work experience. The importance of the vocational differential among groups is evident 2 years later, when the woman employed in a traditional family is earning approximately 40% more than is the alternative woman. The close to 50% of traditional women who are working contribute somewhat less to the total family income than does the alternative woman, but their competencies make them eligible for higher-level work; administrative and business vocations outweigh the clerical and sales, or semiskilled or unskilled jobs which attract the alternatives.

adults were caretakers in one-third, and three or more persons in the remainder. In 15 cases, 8 or more people were caretakers. Altogether the community or living group has a higher density and a lower space per person. Only 20% of living-group children have their own rooms at 6 months, as contrasted with 66% of the traditionals (Eiduson & Alexander, 1978).

As we look at caretaking activities of parents, it should be noted that traditionally married mothers did not want to be full-time caretakers; alternative parents, surprisingly, did—they saw their parenting role as their main responsibility in regard to the new infant. To a significant degree, a smaller percentage (55%) of traditional mothers expected to be a full-time caretaker for the child, as compared with alternative mothers (71%). Their expectation predicted their behaviors accurately: a smaller percentage (55%) of traditional parents than parents in any alternative group were occupied with housework at the 6-month period, and a greater percentage (over 25%) worked by this time, as compared with only 8% of social contracts, and 19% of single mothers, two of our alternative groups. Traditionals were also employed to a greater extent outside the home than were living-group mothers.

Mother's roles and responsibilities held few surprises. There are many tasks that have to be done when families are new, and have a young child—and by and large mothers are involved in doing them. Supporting these changes is the trend toward sharing of domestic tasks (cleaning, laundry, etc.) by others. Our studies show that one-fourth or less of mothers with a young infant report doing most of the domestic tasks themselves. Except for one-fifth of the group of 50 single mothers, the tasks stereotypically done by women are shared by others. Fathers play an increasing role, but mainly other women are supports.

Traditionally married fathers thought the baby would demand no changes in their regular activities; the social contracts expected their lives would be radically changed by a baby. Living-group men fell in the middle of these two positions.

When daily routines, reports of caretaking arrangements, and distribution of tasks were analyzed, it appeared that fathers did not caretake as much as was their expectation. One reason for this is that economic responsibility for bringing home the "bread" rested mainly with the male. This was not only true in the traditional marrieds, where fathers were almost exclusively sole breadwinners in year 1 of the child's life. It was true also in the social contracts, who were more casual and haphazard in employment patterns, and more prone to pick up seasonal or periodic work. Even living-group fathers were busy with the "real work" of the group—priestly activities or the many auxiliary secular services that make the group viable as an economic or religious unit.

Our data also show that in living groups, men help with children when they are around, and help with other tasks or meal preparation. Social-contract couples also alternate in all activities, though there are few stereotypically female activities that are done by men, *instead* of women.

If alternative parents were committed to reducing the conditioned circumstances that lead to sex-role stereotyping, their own child-rearing behaviors with their children did not reflect this. In daily routines and in interactions, the mother remained the chief nurser, diaperer, or undertook most of the biologically-necessary duties that babies need. Fathers were observed as secondary caretakers in a small percentage of the families, invariably the living groups, but observers found mothers doing noonday meals, even when fathers were home and babies were not bottlefed.

At 18 months, fathers were present in the approximately three-fourths of families with fathers, but they were less focused in on baby, and more focused in on other persons and things: TV, newspaper, dinner, or wife, as other investigators have noted in traditional families (Lamb, 1976).

Further, when observed with the baby, fathers were more involved in physical handling, roughhousing, going for a walk; while mothers taught the babies to play, verbalized, cuddled, and also took children outside (Eiduson, 1978a). A greater proportion of a day found mothers and babies together and interacting with each other, than were fathers and babies. The characteristic most strikingly different for some of the larger alternatives was the frequent presence of other adults who sometimes participated in some aspects of caretaking, or who were as often merely part of the scene. Thus, family activities became associated early with a greater number of relationships and interactions, than in the single- or two-adult unit.

DEVELOPMENT OF CHILDREN

Given the normal distribution of the early neurological data and lack of differences in the cognitive and affective stimulation at home,[2]

[2] Thirty-four measures of social and nonsocial stimulation in the home were accumulated, and subsequently summarized to provide total-stimulation scores. The amount and variability of social and nonsocial stimulation showed no significant differences according to lifestyle. However traditional-married homes provide the highest, and single mothers, the lowest, amount and variety of stimulation. Studies of toys owned by children, another measure of potential cognitive stimulation, again favored the traditional-married child, with social contracts next, and living-group and single-mother children least.

we anticipated that the total population would show a normal distribution so far as intellectual growth in year 1, and that family styles would not result in significant between-group differences.

Bayley Test (8 months). At 8 months, cognitive and motor development of infants was assessed in the home, using the Bayley Scales of Infant Development. The babies were generally normal, with scores closely approximating the standardization sample (MDI = 103.5 ± 15.91; PDI = 105.5 ± 12.62). Differences in Mental Scale scores approached significance as a function of lifestyle (p = .07). Infants of traditional mothers achieved a mean of 108, considerably above the mean of 100 for infants whose mothers were in living groups. Social-contract infants ranked closer to the traditional infants, while babies in single-mother households were closer to the living-group infants. Among the behaviors that seemed important in differentiating living-group infants were items covering the 5- to 7-month period, involving reaching, transferring, and scribbling. On performance items, differences among infants in various lifestyles appraoched significance (p = .07). Social-contract infants seemed to do a bit better than infants in other groups on gross-motor behaviors. On the Bayley test, sex differences were minimal, in line with the literature in this area (Maccoby & Jacklin, 1973). Language items, although few at this age, showed no tendency to favor girls over boys (Eiduson et al., 1977).

Bayley Test (1 year). In readministration of the Bayley at 1 year, a significant relationship was found between the 8-month and 1-year measures—MDI: r = .45, p = .01; PDI: r = .33, p = .01. However neither the mental nor motor scores differentiated children who were living in different lifestyles, for there were fewer than 2 points difference among the groups. The only dimension in which family lifestyle showed a significant difference was in terms of the change of scores from 8 months to 1 year. In general, mental scores increased by 6 points for the 200 babies as a group while performance scores decreased by 7 points; differences were significant at the .01 level. Mental scores increased most for infants in living groups and for children of single mothers, less for social-contract children, and not at all for infants in traditional homes. Differences here are largely attributable to a regression to the mean rather than to inherent differences among groups. The PDI scores decreased slightly for all infants.

Only six children had been identified as "at risk" on both OCS and NNE scores. Bayley scores were apparently not related to such findings: of the six children, at 8 months three were below the median on the MDI and one on the PDI. On the Infant Behavior Record, which is a 10-dimension rating scale reflecting the child's response to the testing session, examiners rated girls higher in goal direction, attention span, and reactivity and general ease of response to the testing; boys were higher in fine coordination.

Attachment behaviors. The Strange Situation Test is a measure of attachment to the parent, exploration, separation reactions, and fear of strangers. The 24-minute test involves separation from the parent, brief isolation, and exposure to a stranger in a free-play situation. This test was given to all children at 1 year and again at 3 years.

Since the literature has hypothesized that the attachment and separation behaviors are influenced by the number of caretakers and extent of exposure to others than mother, we had hypothesized that children from the single-parent and the living-group families would respond differently to separation and reunion with mother than would the two-parent nuclear-traditional, and the social-contract, family.

In general, children in various lifestyles at one year of age did not show significant differences on the Strange Situation Test, supporting the hypothesis that stranger anxiety and separation anxiety are probably developmental phenomena rather than environmentally-determined behaviors at that age period, as Bowlby has hypothesized (Ainsworth, 1969). Our data on locomotion, manipulation of toys, response to stranger and mother, and affective responses to distress are in line with the data provided on smaller samples (Ainsworth, Blehar, Waters, & Wall, 1978).

In our testing, one-year-old children were able to be somewhat differentiated by their mobility in this new sitatuion in which they were close to the mother and exposed to new toys. (p = .08). To the extent that mobility or its absence could relate to the exploration of the environment or attention to toys on the mat, living-group children were most inactive—one-half of these children never left the mat, where they were initially placed. In contrast, over one-half of the social-contract children moved about four or more squares, and were the most active of all groups. The other two samples were more randomly distributed. Children of traditionally-married parents were more apt to hold toys most continuously, while social-contract and single-mother children were less apt to do this.

When the stranger first appeared in the test situation, social-contract and single-mother children seemed most preoccupied with the stranger's presence, looking at her more frequently than the traditionally-married and living-group children. Relatively few children approached the stranger, but the traditionally-married group were least likely to do so. These children were most likely to resist when the stranger approached; living-group children were least wary.

When the test called for the child to be alone with the stranger, children of single mothers were least inhibited in play and moved about freely, as did social-contract children. Crying at being left alone with the stranger was most prominent among living-group children. Children of single mothers cried least; children of social-contract and traditionally-married parents cried about the same. More children from traditional households allowed themselves to be held while separated from the mother; fewer living-group children permitted this way of coping with their distress.

Reunion with the mother after separation is considered a measure of attachment to the mother. Social-contract children were the most complacent, rarely crying or fussing, and the crying or fussing stopped once the mother appeared; only 27% could not be soothed immediately. Children of traditional parents were the reverse: one-half continued to cry or fuss when the mother reappeared, while one-half were either originally calm or quickly comforted.

None of thse data suggest major differences in responses to new situations or persons, or in attachment behaviors among infants who at the trimester lived in family environments differing in size or structure. The parent–child unit remains the "first family unit" of most children in the project, regardless of how much more elaborated or differently organized the more extended family structure is.

This picture of development within the normal range for the total group and each lifestyle is also obtained in the case of physical health, as evaluated in a pediatric examination, in nutritional-status studies, or in reports submitted periodically by outside physicians in regard to the incidence of illnesses incurred by our 200 children.

Minnesota Child Development Inventory (Ireton). We hypothesized that different values around child-caretaking in our family styles and their implementation in child-rearing practices might result in differences in child development, which would emerge as the child matured. Since alternative social-contract and living-group parents were more complacent and even rejecting of middle-class striving for achievement, we anticipated that they might consciously defer from fostering and encouraging growth, and this would be reflected in differences in rates of development between their children and those from traditionally-oriented families, and from the single-mother group that yearned to "look traditional."

Therefore to monitor growth in periods when the child was not seen for study, the Minnesota Child Development Inventory (Ireton & Thwing, 1972), a standardized instrument for using parent information and observations to measure the development of the preschool-age child, was administered. The Child Development Inventory is a systematic means for developmental screening and preliminary identification of children with developmental disorders. It consists of 320 statements describing the behaviors of children in the first 6½ years of life. These statements were selected on the basis of their age-discriminating power which was established in a preliminary study of 887 preschool-age children. The inventory is completed by parent, usually the mother, who endorses those statements which describe the child's behavior. The child's current level of development is measured by eight developmental scales: General Development, Gross Motor, Fine Motor, Expressive Language, Comprehension–Conceptual, Situation Comprehension, Self Help, Personal–Social. Age norms for picturing the child's level of development on each scale are compared to children his own age and children of other ages, and age norms are provided separately for each sex.

On this parent-report measure given at 18 months, the general development index for the total population ($N = 189$) was 101.79 ± 14.06. Gross motor, expressive language, and self-help were rated in the average range by parents. Personal–social behaviors scored high average (119.33 ± 15.5), as did fine-motor behaviors (118.58 ± 85.47). Means of conceptual and situational-comprehension scores fell at the average level.

On this test lifestyle differences were highly significant in the general development score and on the fine motor subtest, both reflecting low single-mother children. Sex differences on self-help and fine-motor subtests favored boys.

This test was repeated at 2 years ($N = 132$) with again a general development score falling in the average range (106.70 ± 16.57). All subtest scores were average for the population, with fine-motor and situational-comprehension subtests high average. Again lifestyle differences in the general index, and on fine-motor and self-help behaviors, reflected low single-mother reports on the children.

During 3-hour time-sampled home observations at the 18-month period, single mothers were found to be significantly more directive of the child's play than were other alternatives. The single mother's child initiated interaction the least. The single mother, like the traditional, was found to seldom ignore her child. Social-contract and living groups were observed to engage in significantly more behaviors that encouraged independence in the child; in the single-mothers group were the largest percentage of children who never or seldom went out of the mother's sight and who followed the mother when she left the room (Jenkins, 1978).

Changes in family patterns. More single mothers (49%) were working outside the home on a full-time basis by 2 years than were any other family group. Single-parent children were being cared for in day care or other caretaking arrangements involving others significantly more frequently than were other children. By 2 years, 9 months, 70% of single parents were working part- or full-time, as were 50% of women in every other group. This employment picture is directly related to financial resources supporting families. Two-parent families with two parents employed have significantly higher incomes than other groups. The single parent has the lowest income on the average. Also because of her limited vocational skills, this parent makes less per hour than other groups.

Let us now turn to another area. At 1 year, significant differences emerge between traditional and alternative parents so far as reported satisfactions with their lifesyles: 75% of traditionals report contentment, as compared to 60% of alternatives, with single mothers the most ambivalent (42%); the desire for marriage and companionship dominates the needs expressed by the single mother (54%), and is echoed to a lesser degree (58%) by women in unmarried relationships. Some of their own unhappiness is correlated with their significantly greater concerns over the child's development and in their characterization of the child at the 18-month period as headstrong, whiny, or stubborn.

With these attitudinal differences in satisfactions with lifestyle, it is not surprising to find changes in lifestyle by the 1-year age period. At this time, 4% of traditional marrieds have divorced, and 13 single mothers are no longer single: 16% are living with a male, 6% have married, and 4% have moved into a group situation. The living groups themselves have experienced significant change: 59% of the project families, originally in a living group, remain in the group; 24% have become a nuclear two-parent family; 7% live as single mothers, and 9% have moved into a nonmarried two-parent relationship.

Of interest is the fact that 27% of the couples in social-contract families are no longer social contracts. However, only 14% have left each other, the others becoming traditionally married to their original partners.

These trends at 1 year are predictive of continuing lifestyle changes. By 18 months, 35% of the total population have changed original lifestyles. Changes continue to occur and significantly more often in the alternative groups than in the traditional families when children become 3 years of age. In general, all changes go in the direction of increasing the number of families who have become traditional marrieds. By 3 years, therefore, 24% of families from the single-parent category, 19% of unwed couples, and 16.9% from living groups have become traditional marrieds.

The living group was the least stable of the four populations so far as lifestyle mobility, but the mobility is significantly greater in domestic living groups than in the creedal.

The patterns of lifestyle mobility in the groups also of course predict mobility in geographical moves, and in change so far as family composition. Thus relationships and interactions for the child are more stable in the traditional unit, and the least stable in the living-group family. These data suggested that attachment patterns of children in the four groups might be different, and encouraged the study of this issue again at 3 years. Alternatives reconcile their moves in the direction of the traditional unit as appropriate now that mainstream society has "incorporated" their once-alternative practices, as, e.g., the loosening of sexual repression, more casual dress, more use of natural–organic foods, alternative classes within public schools. Economic pressures also make alienation from the community less viable. As there is more interaction through work and school with the mainstream community, alternatives perceive the opportunities to work "within the system" as challenging.

Development at 3 years. Infant tests are acknowledged as having poor predictive power for later development or academic performance, even though they may be useful in assessing overall developmental status at a particular time of testing; and, also, tests increase in validity and stability with age of the child. Thus, at three years, children were administered the Stanford–Binet Intelligence; the Peabody Picture Vocabulary Test (PPVT); the Zimmerman Articulation Test; Competing Sets, a distractibility task; and the Barrier Test, a measure of persistence and tolerance for frustration. The Ainsworth Strange Situation Test was repeated, and additionally the Vineland Social Maturity Scale was administered. Fantasy, aggression, and early indices of maturity and ego development were explored through the World Test and the Rorschach Test. Precursory concepts of moral judgment, and of family, were also explored.

Space limits more than a cursory note on 3-year test results. We had hypothesized that on the verbally-loaded Stanford–Binet Test, the children in our four family groups would show differences in intelligence quotients. Since groups differ in the number of adults and in the number of relationships a child encounters in which there is verbal interaction, it was hypothesized that the living-group children might perform better than the single-parent children, and that scores of both two-parent groups might fall in between. These hypotheses were not borne out. The mean IQ for the total sample was 102.9, SD = 14.95, but between groups differences were small, and could not be attributed to groups assigned on the basis of original lifestyle ($p = .80$.)

It was hypothesized too that a number of changes in lifestyle which reflect stability of relationships and the situation at the 1-year, 18-month, or 3-year periods might be more predictive of intelligence level than was original family lifestyle. However, when Binet scores were correlated with these mobility-related variables, differences did not reach statistical significance.

Yet, some significant differences of interest were noted between Binet scores and certain subgroups within the four major lifestyles. For example, the sample of children in creedal groups showed scores 12 points lower (mean) than the equal number of children in domestic living groups, 98.44 ± 18.38 and 110.36 ± 14.83, respectively. This was a first and provocative indication that a focus on more ritualized thinking and behaviors might be showing up in intellectual performance. Of interest, too, were significant differences in scores shown by the different groups of single mothers: nest-builders, 108.25 ± 16.77; adaptors, 97.74 ± 14.82; unweds, 100.3 ± 14.73. These latter data suggest that the motivational-value and anticipatory-socialization differences noted in parents may be influencing performance of the child. Differences in parents' own intellectual potential, a variable of interest, have as yet not been measured, since the project has thought it wise to continue to provide evidence to parents of our primary focus on the child. Testing parents at a terminal phase of the longitudinal work is planned. In the interim, school record data on parents are being obtained wherever possible, and will be an additional index of their abilities.

Of course differences in socialization training are being followed from the periodic questionnaire and interview data. Early child-rearing practices were in general minimal and nonsignificant. However, among groups, ongoing studies of child-rearing in the 2- and 3-year age period suggest that parents discipline differently, with the single parent using restrictive and physical punishment significantly more often than other groups. The discipline practices of our "unwed" mothers appear to be negatively correlated with the IQ scores of their children in preliminary analyses of data.

Of particular interest too are preliminary data suggesting that stresses experienced by the child may put him at risk for cognitive growth, as measured by the Stanford–Binet and Peabody Tests. Stresses have been defined as life-change events occurring in the infancy and preschool periods that have been judged by clinicians as likely to effect the adjustment of the child. They include characteristics of family's physical and psychological environment, interpersonal parent–child events, physical problems in the child, conflict among family members, etc. Our preliminary data suggest that there are significant differences in the number of life-change events to which children in various family groups are exposed during the first 3 years of life. When the nature of the event and its significance for the adjustment of the child is taken into account through weightings provided by clinical judges, stress scores for the entire 3-year period for each child can be obtained, as well as a score for each year of the child's life. It appears from preliminary analyses that the 3-year Stanford–Binet IQ scores are negatively correlated with total stress scores for the total population to a significant extent. This appears to be the case when families are grouped as originally assigned, at the trimester and to some slightly lesser extent as they are assigned on the basis of family styles at the 18-month and 3-year periods.

Supporting this work is the provocative finding that a child who has been flagged as "at risk" at three years on the basis of scores 1 SD or more below the mean on both the Stanford and the Peabody, has the highest total stress score. Incidentally the "flagged" population includes children from each of the four original lifestyles, and in almost equal numbers.

Studies on the relationship between attachment and other socioemotional behaviors to cognitive behaviors, and eight environmental events, are currently in progress. In progress too are studies of 3-year data which attempt to assess task-orientation, ability to tolerate frustration, and persistence—characteristics which will be related to preschool behaviors, as rated by teachers. Almost 80% of all children are in preschool by 4 years, thus making outside validating data of interest.

CONCLUSIONS

The 150 alternative parents whose children we studied were themselves a first body of nonconventional offspring from traditional families. Certainly no one anticipated the extent or the ways they would fall out of phase in their expressed values and attitudes from their own parents. The children in our experimental groups have, therefore, traditional grandparents, nonconventional parents, and now we are looking at the offspring to see their own propensities as they grow from infancy into youngsters.

How nonconventional are children who grow up in unconventional homes with nonconventional parents? Alternative families differ in certain structural features, in value-orientation, and in certain background characteristics from traditional families. Yet none of these differences appears thus far to influence the infant or young child's development in ways that make alternative children stand out from traditional. There are no prominent physical, personality, or cognitive characteristics that distinguish infants who are in alternative families that enable us to readily and consistently differentiate them from traditional-family youngsters. It appears instead that up to this time, the tasks of early development form a powerful agenda so that all children move steadily along, with the modes of socialization in diverse settings exerting little discernible or determining differences in qualities and behaviors measured by tests or observations.

After the first year, the impact of the specific setting and unique socialization seems a little more telling on the child's behaviors and attitudes. However, impact even then is not grossly apparent. Perhaps the absence of distinctive impact on the child of his nonconventional family results from the fact that the adult who has been raised in a Caucasian home of middle-class or stable working-class background shows mores, parenting strategies, and attitudes internalized from own parents when he or she becomes a parent.

It is quite evident from our study that some parents whose beliefs and attitudes seem to be quite nontraditional, who even appear nontraditional in appearance and clothing, and whose lives depart dramatically from the conventional, rear a new child in ways that are remarkably conventional. Newborns seem to call out care that fosters their biological and psychological needs, as the data on diversely organized cross-cultural units have suggested (Whiting & Whiting, 1975).

As the child matures, his perception of family, his experiences and exposures, and particularly his interactions and relationships begin to show some of the kind of variability originally anticipated. There can be a diverse group of regular playmates, some rules and regulations that are unique, some deviations in what his parents do, the persons to whom they relate and who influence events in their daily lives. Yet for most young children this "unconventionality" of their lives comes from its definition by outside others, not themselves. They know the identity of their parents, live like other children whom they see in their surround. They eat, sleep, are disciplined, travel, and play like all children their age with whom they play. Yet in the notions they build up about what will happen to them when they disobey, the regularity of contacts with their own parents and with others who caretake—these are characteristic of the ways in which it appears that alternative children are differing from two-parent nuclears.

Admittedly there is overlap between alternative and traditional values, and in some aspects of lifestyle, but alternatives continue to voice expectations and aspirations for their children that suggest a unique perspective in regard to the children they are raising. Some desire that children maintain a decision-making capacity around their own activities from a very early age. Generally, early independence is highly valued. A greater reliance on peers as models and joint decision-makers than on parents as authority persons is thought wise. Most want children to show more openness and comfort with sexuality, aggression, and emotions in general. They value children who are spontaneous and who also show a refined sensitivity and ability to discriminate between behaviors appropriate to school and other outside involvements and behaviors appropriate to the family. Some alternatives are very conscious and proud of being the kind of marginal individuals in society who are often on the cutting edge of change. They want to have children who will perpetuate this self-perception, and so want their "child of tomorrow" to be different from the middle-class Caucasian child who has been the norm.

Will the nonconventional child, then, show certain trade-offs in skills, competencies, or interests? If parents are turned off intellectually and are interested in the occult, the sensory, in mind-altering experiences, valuing social facilitation and enhanced humanistic potential, perhaps offspring will achieve less in the mainstream sense of success. If group decision-making is the mode by which all problems are aired and resolved, perhaps the middle-class parental push for independence and self-reliance becomes tempered in favor of group activity and action.

Pertinent to the assessment of the extent of nonconventionality of the families, it is also worth reflecting on the flexibility of the family to compromise and change when they find that some values, when applied to child-rearing, are inconsistent with one another. For example, many parents felt very strongly that they wanted close and strong ties with their children early in life, but many parents also felt strongly about egalitarian sex roles, breastfeeding, and working outside the home. Men and women may be able to juggle these effectively, but it is a difficult set of ideals to put into practice with a child on the scene. Thus, we have found repeatedly periods of compromise and shuffling of the hierarchy of values in the face of realities of rearing an infant. We have been wondering if certain styles of accommodating to change may be specifically alternative, and if this will show up in coping strategies adopted by the child.

Today we must remember that nonconventional parenting preferences are interacting with contemporary attitudes and values to shape current relationships and parenting practices. Economic, educational, and occupational factors have supported the emergence of parents' desires to reestablish social and personal ties with the mainstream.

This accommodation must also be viewed, in the context of the pull toward society for all marginal families, as a regression to the mean phenomena. Are nonconventional families, then, really alternative in today's world? Incidence data, and the acceptance of difference and unconventionality that pluralism in family modes has generated, have certainly helped to mitigate the unconventionality that was associated with the alternative family a decade ago. In mainstream society today counterparts of structurally-alternative families are abundant: the one-parent family of divorce is an example; the merging of families into sizable extended families through remarriage or restructured families is another. These structurally comparable but once traditionally married nuclear families seem not to be family units that are similar to the alternatives, however. The roles of diverse motivation, values, and attitudes among family groups keep cropping up as significant in our data and suggest that we can expect that project children will at some later points show the impact of these differences in their personal and family perspectives.

Today there is no definitive answer to the question of whether or not children who grow up in unconventional homes with nonconventional parents will turn out to be unconventional. Perhaps the answer will not be forthcoming for another twenty years, until the youngsters become adults. Admittedly, the child is father of the man—but as we know too well from project parents, transmission of cultural norms does not always occur in convenient and reassuring or predictable ways.

References

Ainsworth, M. D. S. Object relations, dependency, and attachment: A theoretical review of the infant–mother relationship. *Child Development*, 1969, 40, 969–1027.

Ainsworth, M., Blehar, M., Waters, E., & Wall, S. *Patterns of attachment: A psychological study of the strange situation.* Hillsdale, New Jersey: Lawrence Erlbaum Publishers, 1978.

Beit-Hallahmi, B., & Rabin, A. The kibbutz as a social experiment and as a child-rearing lab. *American Psychologist*, 1977, 32, 532–541.

Berger, B. *Child rearing practices of the communal family.* Progress report to the National Institute of Mental Health, Bethesda, Maryland, 1971 (mimeo).

Brim, O. G. Socialization through the life cycle. In O. G. Brim, Jr., & S. Wheeler (Eds.), *Socialization after childhood.* New York: Wiley, 1966.

Cohen, J., & Eiduson, B. T. Changing patterns of child rearing in alternative life styles: Implications for development. In A. Davids (Ed.), *Child personality and psychopathology: Current topics.* New York: Wiley, 1975.

Deutsch, M. *The disadvantaged child.* New York: Basic Books, 1967.

Eiduson, B. T. Looking at children in emergent family styles. *Children Today*, 1974, 4, 2–6.

Eiduson, B. T. *Changing sex roles in alternative family styles.* Paper presented at the meeting of the International Association for Child Psychiatry, Melbourne, Australia, August 1978a. Also in E. Anthony (Ed.), *Changing roles of parents and children (The child in his family,* Vol. 6). New York: Wiley, in press.

Eiduson, B. T. Child development in emergent family styles. *Children Today*, 1978b, 7, 24–31.

Eiduson, B. T. Common problems affecting the mental health of children in nontraditional families. In H. J. Grossman, J. E. Simmons, A. R. Dyer, & H. H. Work (Eds.), *The physician and mental health of the child:* 1. *Assessing development and treating disorders within a family context.* Chicago: American Medical Association, 1979a.

Eiduson, B. T. The commune-reared child. In J. Nospitz (Ed.), *Basic handbook of child psychiatry* (Vol 1). New York: Basic Books, 1979b.

Eiduson, B. T. *Contemporary single mothers.* Paper presented at the meeting of the Society of Research in Child Development, San Francisco, March 1979c.

Eiduson, B. T. Emergent families of the 1970's: Values practices, and impact on children. In D. Reiss ad H. Hoffman (Eds.), *The American family: Dying or developing.* New York: Plenum, 1979d.

Eiduson, B. T., & Alexander, J. The role of children in alternative family styles. In N. D. Feshbach & S. Feshbach (Eds.), *The changing status of childhood: Roles, rights and responsibilities. Journal of Social Issues,* 1978, *34,* 149–167.

Eiduson, B. T., & Project Staff. *Drug-using parents and their children. Part I: Anticipatory socialization behaviors.* (Report to the National Institute of Alcohol and Drug Abuse, Contract #271-75-3033.) Los Angeles: University of California at Los Angeles, Department of Psychiatry, August 1975.

Eiduson, B. T., & Weisner, T. S. Alternative socialization settings for infants and young children. In J. Stevens & M. Mathews (Eds.), *Mother/child, father/child relationships.* Washington, D.C.: National Association for the Education of Young Children, 1978.

Eiduson, B. T., Eiduson, S., & Geller, E. Biochemistry, genetics, and the nature–nurture problem. *American Journal of Psychiatry,* 1962, *119,* 342–350. Also in N. L. Corah & E. N. Gale (Eds.), *The origins of abnormal behavior.* New York: Addison-Wesley, 1971.

Eiduson, B. T., Cohen, J., & Alexander, J. Alternatives in child rearing in the 1970's. *American Journal of Orthopsychiatry,* 1973, *43,* 720–731. Also in J. Clarke (Ed.), *Intimacy, marriage and the family.* New York: Allyn & Bacon, 1975. Also in J. T. Gibson & P. Blumberg (Eds.), *Readings in child psychology.* New York: Addison-Wesley, 1976.

Eiduson, B. T., Zimmerman, I. L., & Bernstein, M. *Single vs. multiple parenting: Implications for infancy.* Paper presented at the meeting of the American Psychological Association, San Francisco, August 1977.

Greenfield, P. M. *What we can learn from cultural variation in child care.* Paper presented at the meeting of the American Association for the Advancement of Science, San Francisco, November 1974.

Herzog, E., & Sudia, C. E. Fatherless homes: A review of research. *Children,* 1968, *15,* 177–182.

Ireton, H. R., & Thwing, E. J. Minnesota child development inventory profile. Minneapolis: Interpretive Scoring Systems, 1972.

Jenkins, J. Interactions of mothers and 18-month old babies in alternative family styles. In J. Alexander (Chair), *Alternative families of the 1970's.* Symposium presented at the meeting of the American Orthopsychiatric Association, San Francisco, April 1978.

Keniston, K. *The uncommitted: Alienated youth in American society* (3rd ed.), New York: Dell, 1965.

Kornfein, M. *Infancy in creedal and non-creedal communities.* Unpublished manuscript, University of California at Los Angeles, 1975 (mimeo).

Kornfein, M., Weisner, T. S., & Martin, J. C. Women into mothers: Experimental family lifestyles. In J. R. Chapman & M. J. Gates (Eds.), *Women into wives: Sage annual of women's policy studies* (Vol. 2). Beverly Hills, California: Sage Publications, 1976.

Lamb, M. (Ed.). *The role of the father in child development.* New York: Wiley, 1976.

Maccoby, E. E., & Jacklin, C. N. Stress, activity, proximity seeking: Sex differences in the year-old child. *Child Development,* 1973, *44,* 34–42.

Parmalee, A. H. & Littman, R. *Obstetrical complications scale.* University of California at Los Angeles, 1977 (mimeo).

Parmalee, A. H., & Michaelis, R. Neurological examination of the newborn. In J. Hellmuth (Ed.), *Exceptional infant.* Vol. 2. *Studies in abnormalities.* New York: Bruner/ Mazel, 1971.

Pederson, F. A. Does research on children reared in father-absent families yield information on father influences? *Family Coordinator,* 1976, *4,* 459–464.

Reissman, F., Cohen, J., & Pearl, A. (Eds.), *Mental health of the poor.* New York: Free Press of Glencoe, 1964.

Rochford, E. B. Values of alternative and traditional contemporary families. In J. Alexander (Chair), *Alternative families of the 1970's.* Symposium presented at the meeting of the American Orthopsychiatric Association, San Francisco, April 1978.

Shields, J. *Monozygotic twins brought up apart and brought up together.* London: Oxford University Press, 1962.

Singer, M. T. Personal communication, 1978.

Skolnick, A. The family revisited: Themes in recent social science research. *Journal of Interdisciplinary History,* 1975, *5,* 703–719.

Spiro, M. E., & Spiro, A. G. *Children of the kibbutz.* Cambridge, Mass.: Harvard University Press, 1975.

Weisner, T. S. & Martin, J. C. *Learning environments for infants: Communes and conventionally married families.* Paper presented at the meeting of the American Anthropological Association, Washington, D.C., November 1976. Also in *Alternative Lifestyles,* 1979, *2,* 201–241.

Whiting, B., & Whiting, J. W. M. *Children of six cultures: A psychocultural analysis.* Cambridge, Mass.: Harvard University Press, 1975.

13

The Common in the Uncommon Child
Comments on the Child's Integrative Capacities and on Intuitive Parenting

Hanuš Papoušek

(General Discussant)

To be at this conference has been like walking through a gallery with a rich collection of pieces of information not only showing how uncommon a child or his environment can be but also proving how valid is what we know about the common child. After all, is it not true in general that the interest in the normal development of children has mainly originated from therapeutic difficulties—medical or psychological—caused by abnormality?

Being used to looking for universal phenomena, biologically significant ones in particular, but for obvious reasons being often unable to analyze them experimentally in children, we are fully aware of the value of the natural experiments documented in the reports of various participants. It is easy to imagine from how many different points of view each reader may appreciate each piece of information. It would be difficult, of course, to include all viewpoints in the comments of one discussant, even if he is given the honor of being a General Discussant.

Hanuš Papoušek • Developmental Psychobiology, Max-Planck Institute for Psychiatry, Kraepelinstrasse 10, D-8000 Munich 40, Federal Republic of Germany. The research in this unit is supported by the German Research Foundation (Pa 208/3), the Stifterverband für die Deutsche Wissenschaft, and the Stiftung Volkswagenwerk (II/35023).

Rather than try to be objective and exhaustive, I will pay more attention to a few personally sympathetic parts of reports and discussion concerning difficulties and suggestions which I share and which are in some way related to my own studies.

In several reports and subsequent discussions, it became evident how difficult it is to find a taxonomy that would help us to describe children's environment, to differentiate common and uncommon environments, or to characterize their crucial structural patterns. These seemingly theoretical problems have relevant practical consequences for all those who consider any engineering of environments for educational or therapeutic purposes. Closely interdependent is the problem of the human adaptation to different environments with its biological and cultural, developmental and evolutionary aspects. To what else should we relate the categorization of children's environments than to the children's adaptive capacities? Their knowledge has increased dramatically as psychology has moved from the concepts of simple responsiveness to the concepts of cognition in the child and admitted an interactional character in the interpretation of the child's environment. Yet another difficult problem has reemerged at the same time and pointed at another gap in knowledge, namely the problem of self-recognition and its developmental roots. It is perhaps the central issue in our speculation on the autonomy of human mind for at least two plausible reasons: self-recognition enables differentiating oneself from one's environment, and it also represents an aspect of the autonomy of self to which we have already found the first methodological pathways.

All three categories of problems I have just mentioned—the structure of the environment, the development of adaptive capacities, and the autonomy of the human mind—have become inevitable to students of the earliest postpartum stages of human development, just as it has become inevitable for students who study those categories of problems in older children or adults to pay attention to the earliest developmental roots of behavior. Therefore I hope it will be legitimate for me to make my comments from the grounds of infancy research. I am going to approach the problems along two avenues of our own studies: the avenue of early integrative capacities in children and the avenue of intuitive parenting.

Avenue One: Early Development of Integrative Processes

Let us suppose that we want to find out what kinds of integrative processes may function in the four-month-old infant. We shall consider a set of processes of increasing complexity such as orienting response, habituation, instrumental learning, and concept formation. For this purpose we shall use a simple laboratory environment, allow the infant to adjust to this environment satisfactorily, and then stimulate her or him with the sound of an electric bell located somewhere in the front of the infant in the sagittal plane.

At first, we shall stimulate at random intervals of, for instance, 1 to 60 seconds, each stimulation lasting 5 seconds. The waking infant will probably respond to most stimulations with some parts of the orienting response: lifted eyebrows, more widely opened eyes, decrease of overt motor activities, a pause in breathing followed by faster breathing, etc. Some of the later stimulations may also elicit smiles or vocal signs of pleasure as if the infant were welcoming someone familiar, although no social interaction will be possible.

Keeping all other conditions constant, we then shall apply the same stimulation at regular 10-second intervals. The first stimuli will probably elicit similar orienting responses again; however, after some 8 to 12 repetitions, orienting responses will decrease or disappear due to habituation. We shall be able to reelicit orienting responses, for instance, if we change the duration of intervals.

In the next sessions under constant conditions, we shall arrange a simple learning situation and stimulate the infant only when she or he happens to turn the head to a certain side, let us say 30 degrees to the left. The infant will probably respond with an orienting response and turn back to the middle from where the sound is coming as usual. However, as more and more head turns are "rewarded" with bell sounds, we shall be able to witness interesting consequences: the orienting response will become more intensive and quite resistant to habituation, and the infant will increase all kinds of movements in an attempt to find out which of them have something to do with the bell until smooth and fast new patterns of head turning develop which we may call "switching-on movements." The infant will very probably carry out more and more of them and show facial and vocal signs of pleasure when being rewarded. Rather than a habituation, we may observe a striking example of addiction or attachment behavior in a nonsocial situation.

Having reached this level of instrumental learning, we shall be able to secretly introduce new and more complex rules for switching on the electric bell. For instance, we shall reward the infant for two consecutive "switching-on head movements" to the left only, or for three or four of them. And the infant may demonstrate the capacity to detect the new rule and to adjust his responses accordingly, carrying out the given number of head movements and then pausing with different signs of obvious pleasure for the time of stimulation. Our rules may be easier or more difficult, and in the four-month-old they may easily reach the efficiency limits of the infant's adaptive capacities, thus creating a problem. The infant's inability to solve such a problem will lead to upset and signs of distress, just as success will be connected with signs of relief and pleasure. Finally, the newly acquired adaptive behavioral patterns will represent observable expressions of simple concepts.

Our own experimental success will be manifold. We shall prove the functionality of the selected set of integrative processes and the preverbal existence of fundamental arithmetic capacity, we shall replicate in abbreviation experiments that opened new ways for cognitive experiments 15 years ago (Papoušek, 1967; Papoušek & Bernstein, 1969), and above all, we shall learn something important about the environmental structure.

All changes of the environmental stimulation in the experiments suggested above concern the temporal and relational structures in an environment standardized in terms of other physical parameters. The structure of the environmental stimulation alone appears to be a powerful agent affecting human behavior. However, the crucial invariants in the structure of stimulation depend on something other than the mere physical properties, namely on the intrinsic invariants resulting from the infant's integrative capacities, for instance, on the degree of familiarity or on the degree of contingency of the stimulation upon the infant's behavior.

Although we may well be able to engineer the structure of stimulation to elicit habituation once and instrumental learning or concept formation another time, the result of such manipulation will still depend on the infant's preceding experience and present capacity to detect contingency or rules of rewarding. This capacity may lead to the expected correct performance in one subject, to "superstitious behavior" in a second subject, and to latent intrinsic results which may become evident only in later observations in a third case.

Obviously, such an explanation of the structure of environment does not make our research easier because it brings up the difficult topic of intervening variables. To ignore them has not made our research easier or more exact, either. On the contrary, ignoring them led to the neglect of invariants the biological significance of which seems to be enormous, although we do not yet understand it sufficiently. Let me mention a few arguments.

First, the ability to detect contingencies seems to have deep biological roots. It must be assumed in all species capable of operant learning. In humans, it was shown to function in the newborn (Papoušek, 1961, 1967) and even in premature infants approximately 10 weeks prepartum (Solkoff & Cotton, 1975).

Second, Mason and Berkson (1975) showed that they could prevent the "irreparable" consequences of early maternal deprivation in rhesus monkeys reported by Harlow and Harlow (1966) if they made the Harlows' surrogate mother mobile and her movements contingent on the infant's behavior.

Third, according to all our observable evidence (Papoušek & Papooušek, 1975), the detection and mastery of contingency seems to be an intrinsic invariant connected with a powerful intrinsic motivation the nature of which is not yet known. Recent advances in the study of neurosecretion allow us to assume that such an invariant might elicit secretion of agents causing pleasant feelings (endorphine?) and rewarding the organism for a successful adaptive–integrative operation.

A better understanding of these phenomena will, we hope, provide more reliable cues for the taxonomy of environment in the future and remove the problems mentioned in the reports by Marci Hanson, Leonard Rosenblum and Edward Plimpton, or Michael Lewis and Stephanie Schaeffer. They may also contribute to our knowledge of species-specific capacities of humans discussed by Gershon Berkson or Leonard Rosenblum and Edward Plimpton. Unfortunately, a lack of comparative studies on cognitive processes in animals compels us to wait with a definite evaluation of their biological role. In our present concepts of the human behavioral regulation (Papoušek & Papoušek, 1978), we view the processes controlling the input and integration of information and organizing adaptive responses as a primary and fundamental responsive system common to all behavioral categories such as feeding, playing, defensive, or sexual behaviors.

We know that the course of learning or problem-solving affects the general behavioral state, i.e., it also changes the subject's responsiveness and motility (Papoušek, 1969). A great deal of motor behavior connected with approach and exploration or avoidance can serve the basic cognitive needs of the organism. An individual variability in motor behavior often interpreted as a temperamental criterion and also included in William Carey's measures of temperament may, therefore, really have a common base interrelated with intellectual parameters.

The interpretation of changes in responsiveness should be careful since similar changes can be caused by different regulatory processes. A decreased responsiveness may result from damages due to nutritional deficiencies in one case, and yet, in another case, may be adaptive if preceding efforts to gain food have led only to repeated frustrations. Thus, the paradoxical responses in malnourished infants and children discussed by Henry Ricciutti might stimulate a more differentiated attention to the fundamental regulatory processes in animal models and malnutrition.

Both in our experimental analyses of integrative processes (Papoušek, 1969) and observations of social interactions in infants (Papoušek & Papoušek, 1975), we have seen avoiding behavior, turning away, interruptions of visual contact, rejection of bodily contact, and also sleeplike stupor with sudden decrease of responsiveness in cases in which the environment, social or nonsocial, was too difficult to cope with. Even the mother was avoided and ignored in observations on repeated detachment if her behavior violated the infant's preceding experience. This is just one of the two directions of coping with problem situations, and an analogy to Schneirla's (1965) concept of approach–withdrawal behavior in animals.

On another developmental level, approach–withdrawal processes may also underlie the behavior of seriously sick or dying children described by Ursula Thunberg. To me, it was fascinating to compare described behaviors of children in so extremely uncommon situations with our speculations on the fundamental behavioral regulation. I can imagine that the alarming signals of an utmost danger for which no adaptive response can be found anymore can first lead to a general agitation and the last attempts to escape or look for help. However, the final intuitive conclusion, "This is the end," may still be the correct integrative operation to be rewarded with a pleasant feeling, now of an utmost intensity as well, and serving as the last natural fuse allowing the man to close his life cycle without pain and without fear of death. If I admit here again that an increased secretion of endorphine could hypothetically be connected with invariants resulting from integrative processes, an utmost response of such a mechanism would immediately explain that the terminal relief and euphoria may also be accompanied by hallucinations as Ursula described.

Gershon Berkson's plea that coping with handicaps should be supported through involvement in rewarding productive activities is certainly justified and valid for child education in general. At the same time, Berkson's plea raises the question of rewards and motivation of the child's activities on which I have already made one speculative comment earlier when pointing out the motivational aspects of integrative processes. When categorizing integrative processes we are repeatedly exposed to the question how to view play and creative activities, their biological roots and motivations. Halbert Robinson approached similar questions in relation to the "happiness" of exceptionally gifted children, and so did Bernice Eiduson from the viewpoint of creative activities in nonconventional families. I do not know any definite truths about these questions; however, we all may help each other by sharing at least our views as long as we cannot share verified discoveries.

In our own concepts of play and creativity (Papoušek & Papoušek,

1978), we see the essence of cognition in the movement from "un-known" to "known," which helps to avoid the Scylla and Charybdis of two unpleasant situations: distress caused by too much novelty and incongruity in the unknown on the one hand, and boredom connected with too little novelty and incongruity on the other. Two strategies and operational levels seem to be involved in the movement from "unknown" to "known" (Figure 1).

One strategy tends to integrate available information about the "unknown" as soon as possible, and results in a rather firmly closed concept. Thus the fear of the "unknown" is reduced; however, the danger of boredom increases. The second strategy tends to reopen seemingly complete concepts, to shed a new light on the "known," to

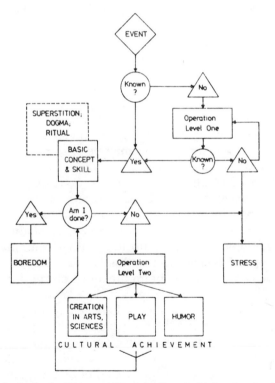

FIG. 1. Flow chart of adaptive operations leading to higher levels of knowledge and protecting against stress from the unknown or from boredom of trivial knowledge. Symbols: O, question; △, answer; ▭, operation; □, outcome. Operation Level One includes learning of basic skills, categories, or rules, and tends to create closed concepts; Operation Level Two tends to reopen concepts, to view events from nontrivial stand-points, and to create and solve new problems.

view it from unusual viewpoints and to experiment with it. Operations on this level are more difficult than the first-level operations; they risk the danger of the "unknown," but open the way for what is the essence of play, creativity, and humor, and what leads to a cultural achievement of a higher order than the basic skills and concepts learned on the first level. A lack of this capacity may be connected with an inclination to stick to superstitions or dogmata in adulthood.

We can imagine that what we have tried to elucidate with a two-level schema represents a much more complex structure in reality. However, it may be advantageous to wait with more sophisticated speculations until more evidence shows how far our fundamental assumptions are justified. One of the important questions is whether the suggested two levels of operations are connected with different forms or degrees of intrinsic motivation, activation of necessary efforts, and intrinsic means of rewards. If someone's observations indicate the existence of such differences, then he may find our model useful for categorizing children's activities, at least roughly.

In several reports, particularly in William Carey's discussion on individual variability, a question emerged to what degree the individual differences can be used as a measure of temperament. This used to be a traditional question asked by people looking for criteria of typological differences and addressed particularly to students of learning abilities like ourselves. Our standpoint (Papoušek, 1977) reflecting the major shifts in modern genetics may be of some help.

The search for unitary typological cues was strongly influenced by the introduction of conditioning into the study of brain functions. Pavlov (1927) himself suggested that genotypes of higher nervous activity would explain differences between the four classical human temperaments. However, he soon became aware of the weakness of any simple typology and added up to 24 other combinations to the original four types in dogs. Later at his laboratories, Krasuskij (1963) found 48 major variants in the brain functions of 116 dogs.

In general, similar typological concepts assume discontinuous processes underlying the differences between typological categories. This thinking brings to mind the essentialist philosophies of Plato and Aristotle and analogous efforts of typologically oriented biologists to detect essential types in the similarity of individuals while variation is disregarded as the imperfect manifestation of an ideal type. As human beings we all probably incline to perceive categorically, and we may do so even when being exposed to continuous phenomena, for instance in color perception or speech perception.

An evolutionist or a developmentalist is usually more interested in the significance than in the mere existence of variability. In biology, the former typological interpretation has been replaced by population concepts (Dobzhansky, 1951; Mayr, 1971) that make the evolutionary advantage of variation in populations evident: a large number of available genetic types within a population increases the survival probability and permits better utilization of environment.

A developmentalist studying ontogenetic changes may tend, as we do, to place an individual in a progression of continuous processes rather than looking for discontinuities underlying typological classification. We should be aware that genetic variation serves to bring about adaptation in whole populations, whereas nongenetic variation adapts individuals. Looking at children in uncommon environments contributes enormously to our understanding of nongenetic adaptation in particular.

Looking at age and individual differences, we have mainly been asking the question *how* development occurs. I hope that the validity of this question will be exemplified in further comments if I now take the second avenue of our research.

AVENUE TWO: INTUITIVE PARENTING

Speaking of the early integrative capacities, I mentioned that operant learning functioned even in the newborn. This is true only if you fulfill several predisposing conditions, such as many repetitions of trials during the optimal waking state. It can be quite difficult to attract the newborn's attention if visual stimulation is to be applied. You quickly realize that similar predisposing conditions will be seldom met in the newborn's everyday environment as long as you consider the nonliving objects. Similarly you will then find as we did that the newborn depends on the adult caretaker just as much for his cognitive needs as for his bodily needs.

For some time we were perplexed about the ways in which the parent might facilitate the newborn's integrative abilities. Human parenting had been neglected so much that the poor list of parental responses left us helpless. However, microanalyses of parental behavior have helped to detect intuitive patterns interpretable as an adjustment to the constraints in the newborn's perception and learning. Without any conscious control the parent modulates the infant's attention, facilitates bodily, visual, and vocal communication, and applies specifically adjusted stimulation with respect to the infant's capacity to process it. The parental behavior thus also becomes contingent, predictable, and supportive in relation to important integrative capacities such as imitation, play, or acquisition of language (Papoušek & Papoušek, 1978).

It is too soon to ask whether this part of parenting is critically important for the infant's cognitive development. However, it becomes obvious that evolution has favored not only early functioning of integrative processes but also an adequate parental care for them, which in the first months may be universal across social and cultural strata. Almost certainly we shall have additional measures for evaluating or reevaluating the role of the child's early experience in the near future. As parents occupy so much of the newborn's first environment, intuitive parenting may also exemplify which engineering of environment has been favored during evolution.

Not very much can yet be said about the universality of parental care for cognitive development across species. Gershon Berkson's and Leonard Rosenblum and Edward Plimpton's observations from primatological research become increasingly interesting from this point of view; however, more systematic research in more mammalian species is necessary to elucidate this area.

Some components of intuitive parenting appear early in ontogeny, for instance, baby talk in 2- to 3-year-old children and instructive mouthing in feeding situations at the end of the first year. The question how early and in what directions children can adjust behavior so as to facilitate communicative or cognitive processes in very young infants is still open. Obviously, it is a relevant question for the interpretation of interactions with siblings and peers analyzed by Michael Lewis and Stephanie Schaeffer.

Our experience that intuitive parenting is relatively resistant to voluntary modification seems to be supported by Bernice Eiduson's observation of shifts from uncommon family patterns back to conventional ones in young people who have become parents.

Rosenblatt's (1975) detailed studies of the regulation of maternal behavior in the rat showed that the role of hormones (estrogen) in activating maternal behavior during pregnancy culminates shortly before parturition but decreases quickly after delivery. Postpartum maternal behavior is subsequently controlled by the psychological interaction with the pups. The period of transition from the physiological basis to the psychological basis of maternal responses represents a labile and vulnerable situation. Prolonged removal of the pups causes waning of maternal behavior to such a degree that by the end of four days mother rats are unresponsive to the pups and let them die.

This vulnerability may be adaptive in that it allows animal mothers to get rid of pups exceeding the number of breast nipples or showing too low vitality. Although we have not enough evidence for implication of a similar vulnerability in human maternity, it is difficult not to think of the rejection of less vital newborns by ancient Spartans. Some of the difficulties in mothers of prematures or of newborns with Down's disease mentioned by Marci Hanson might partly result from an analogous lability.

Several of the reported abnormal circumstances could serve as interesting model situations for further analyses of the determination or importance of intuitive parenting. For instance, it would be worth studying parental behavior in schizophrenic mothers giving their children more frequently away for adoption, as mentioned by Arnold Sameroff and Ronald Seifer, or generally in parents showing antisocial attitudes toward their own children, as described by Michael Lewis and Stephanie Schaeffer.

Kwashiorkor could be another interesting model in which the environmental deficiency influences the mother–infant interaction at the time of weaning, i.e., at the end of the most important period of intuitive parenting. The nutritional deficiency thus appears as a pathophysiological stress, testing the quality of the psychological, intuitive parental care prior to weaning. We should have exciting arguments if the variability of intuitive parenting were shown to be related to the variation in the resistance to kwashiorkor described by Henry Ricciuti.

Our experience with intuitive parenting is still modest, and yet we already see as much variability in it as in all other natural phenomena. As a matter of fact, my own interest in parenting has been motivated by my former clinical experience with parents lacking natural parental responses. In due course it should be said that the lack of intuitive parental behaviors need not be the only cause of inadequate parenting. Intuitive parenting becomes efficient only if tuned and adjusted to every individual child early and frequently during the first year of life. Thus the second major cause of failures in parenting may be a lack of time spent by the parent in a direct dyadic interaction with the infant. This can more easily happen to the father in his typical situation dictated by contemporary traditions in Western society.

In less unfavorable cases, such a failure can be corrected, and the father develops a more rational and less emotional approach to his child when the child starts walking and talking. Otherwise different forms of alienation disturb the father–child interrelations and finally lead to hostile aggressions, exemplified in the paper by Michael Lewis and Stephanie Schaeffer.

In order to conclude my comments with an encouraging example of good parenting I wish to point out the excellent care for both somatic

needs and cognitive growth of all participants provided by the initia-
tors of the conference on the Uncommon Child—Michael Lewis and
Leonard Rosenblum—and all their coworkers.

REFERENCES

Dobzhansky, T. *Genetics and the origin of species* (3rd ed.). New York: Columbia
    University Press, 1951.
Harlow, H.F., & Harlow, M.K. Learning to love. *American Scientist*, 1966, *54*, 244–272.
Krasuskij, V.K. Methods of evaluation of nervous processes in dogs. *Journal of Higher
    Nervous Activity*, 1963, *13*.
Mason, W.A., & Berkson, G. Effects of maternal mobility on the development of rocking
    and other behaviors in the rhesus monkeys: A study with artificial mothers.
    Developmental Psychobiology, 1975, *8*, 197–211.
Mayr, E. *Population, species and evolution.* Cambridge, Mass.: Belknap Press of Harvard
    University Press, 1971.
Papoušek, H. Conditioned head rotation reflexes in infants in the first months of life.
    Acta Paediatrica (Uppsala), 1961, *50*, 565–576.
Papoušek, H. Experimental studies of appetitional behavior in human newborns and
    infants. In H.W. Stevenson, E.H. Hess, & H.L. Rheingold (Eds.), *Early behavior:
    Comparative and developmental approaches.* New York: Wiley, 1967.
Papoušek, H. Individual variability in learned responses in human infants. In R.J.
    Robinson (Ed.), *Brain and early behavior.* London: Academic Press, 1969.
Papoušek, H. Individual differences in adaptive processes of infants. In A. Oliverio
    (Ed.), *Genetics, environment and intelligence.* New York: Academic Press, 1977.
Papoušek, H. & Bernstein, P. The functions of conditioning stimulation in human
    neonates and infants. In A. Ambrose (Ed.), *Stimulation in early infancy.* London:
    Academic Press, 1969.
Papoušek, H., & Papoušek, M. Cognitive aspects of preverbal social interaction between
    human infants and adults. In M. O'Connor (Ed.), *Parent–infant interaction.* Amster-
    dam: Elsevier, 1975.
Papoušek, H., & Papoušek, M. Interdisciplinary parallels in studies of early human
    behavior: From physical to cognitive needs, from attachment to dyadic education.
    International Journal of Behavioral Development, 1978, *1*, 37–49.
Pavlov, I.P. *Conditioned reflexes.* London: Oxford University Press, 1927.
Rosenblatt, J.S. Prepartum and postpartum regulation of maternal behavior in the rat.
    In M. O'Connor (Ed.), *Parent–infant interaction.* Amsterdam: Elsevier, 1975.
Schneirla, T.C. Aspects of stimulation and organization in approach/withdrawal proc-
    esses underlying vertebrate behavioral development. *Advances in the Study of
    Behavior*, 1965, *1*, 1–74.
Solkoff, N., & Cotton, C. Contingency awareness in premature infants. *Perceptual and
    Motor Skills*, 1975, *41*, 709–710.

Author Index

Italic numbers indicate pages where complete reference citations are given

Subject Index